FLASH

FLASH

The Making of
WEEGEE THE FAMOUS

Christopher Bonanos

HENRY HOLT AND COMPANY NEW YORK

Henry Holt and Company
Publishers since 1866
175 Fifth Avenue
New York, New York 10010
www.henryholt.com

Henry Holt ® and 🛡® are registered trademarks of Macmillan Publishing Group, LLC.

All Weegee photographs © International Center of Photography; pages 31, 72, 77: images
courtesy of Daniel Blau, Berlin; page 224: photograph by Bert Brandt and Edward Jerry/
NEA; page 227: photograph by the author; page 260: photograph by Robert Parent;
page 313: courtesy of Matthew Mottel

Library of Congress Cataloging-in-Publication Data

Names: Bonanos, Christopher, author.
Title: Flash : the making of Weegee the Famous / Christopher Bonanos.
Description: First edition. | New York : Henry Holt and Company, 2018. | Includes index.
Identifiers: LCCN 2017041202 (print) | LCCN 2017047815 (ebook) |
  ISBN 9781627793070 (EBook) | ISBN 9781627793063 (hardcover)
Subjects: LCSH: Weegee, 1899–1968. | Photojournalists—United States—Biography.
Classification: LCC TR140.F4 (ebook) | LCC TR140.F4 B66 2018 (print) |
  DDC 770.92 [B] —dc23
LC record available at https://lccn.loc.gov/2017041202

Our books may be purchased in bulk for promotional, educational, or business use. Please
contact your local bookseller or the Macmillan Corporate and Premium Sales Department at
(800) 221-7945, extension 5442, or by e-mail at MacmillanSpecialMarkets@macmillan.com.

First Edition 2018

Designed by Meryl Sussman Levavi

Printed in the United States of America

1   3   5   7   9   10   8   6   4   2

To Ellen and Alexander,
people of New York

Weegee:
I am a reincarnation of Leonardo da Vinci and
Grandma Moses, you might say.

Interviewer:
Well, who do you think you look more like?

Weegee:
Grandma Moses. [*laughs*] . . . No, my name was Arthur.
And, actually, no—I created this guy Weegee, which I have
to live up to.

Interviewer:
You have to live *with*, you mean.

Weegee:
Well—this I find very difficult!

CONTENTS

Introduction   xiii

PART I

OUT OF THE DARK   1

PART II

THE FAMOUS   169

Notes   321

Acknowledgments   365

Index   368

INTRODUCTION

Let's talk about that name first. Or, rather, those three names.

Usher Fellig was a greenhorn, a hungry shtetl child from eastern Europe who spoke no English. When he came through Ellis Island in 1909, at ten years old, he reinvented himself, as so many immigrants do. In his first years in New York, Usher became Arthur, a Lower East Side street kid who was eager to get out of what he called "the lousy tenements," earn a living, impress girls, make a splash. He had turned his name (slightly) less Jewish, and his identity (somewhat) more American, as much as he could make it. As a young man, he was shy, awkward, broke, and unpolished, and at fourteen he became a seventh-grade dropout. He was also smart, ambitious, funny, and (as he and then his fellow New Yorkers and eventually the world discovered) enormously expressive when you put a camera in his hands.

As an adult, he reinvented himself a second time. "In 1925," his friend Peter Martin later wrote, "Arthur Fellig disappeared through a hole in space, and nobody ever heard of him again." In real life, it was a little more gradual than that, but in his place there began to appear a character called Weegee, a persona Arthur Fellig eventually slipped into as easily as he did his ill-maintained, loose-fitting suits. "Weegee the Famous," he signed his name, introducing himself to strangers and talk show hosts as "the world's greatest living photographer." Weegee worked New York City by night and was a man who knew how to take hold of a tough town, snapping pictures of gangsters and movie stars, selling prints to newspapers and magazines and the Museum of Modern Art, consulting on Hollywood movies, jetting off to London or Paris on assignment. In the role of Weegee, Arthur Fellig was able to shed his awkwardness. He was brash, working the angles with cops, talking up his "genius" with interviewers. He could spin off polished wisecracky anecdotes rat-a-tat while delivering four-hour impromptu lectures on the craft of news photography to anyone who'd have him, lingering until the last member of the audience had grown tired of asking questions. He explicitly said, later on, that as a young man "I wanted to go out and make a lot of money, become famous, and meet people."

Both Fellig and Weegee could make a raw first impression. Sixty-two years after meeting him, the actress and playwright Judith Malina remembered that at first "he seemed like a kind of person you didn't want to know." Yet somehow, she explained, soon enough he'd have you charmed. Malina certainly was; she eventually agreed to pose nude for him, and spoke of him warmly, calling him "my good friend Arthur."

Most of us have an image in our heads of the big-city newspaper photographer at midcentury: the squat guy in a rumpled suit and crumpled fedora, carrying a big press camera with a flashgun mounted on its side, a stinky cigar clamped in the corner of his mouth. Central Casting deserves only a little of the credit. Weegee is the man who created that image, and it has outlived his mainstream fame. People who have never heard of Weegee can describe him. He not only took hold of his life and redefined it; the image he created of himself lingers, fifty years after his death, to the point where he has become an archetype as much as a person. "He rather likes to pass himself off as a character," wrote John Lewis, an editor at the newspaper *PM*, where Weegee did some of his best work. "He is, but not exactly the same one." The public-facing persona furthered his career, but it was the one within who framed the shots and pressed the shutter button.

The man himself was real, and as an individual maker of pictures he was both innately talented and profoundly skilled. But we will never quite know if he was merely first among equals. News photography during the early part of Weegee's career was almost always anonymous. When credits did appear, most of the time they attached pictures not to people but to institutional entities: the Associated Press, International News Service, Acme Newspictures. Besides, in the 1930s, virtually no one thought this stuff was art. It was made on demand, for the next day's edition, and if it wasn't quite a disposable commodity, it was pretty close. "Spot news," it was called, and even the work of a good photographer would be filed the next day in the paper's morgue, kept on hand in case the subject reappeared in the news. Unless it depicted something of ageless, recurring interest (the burning *Hindenburg*, say, or Babe Ruth as he put a home run ball in the seats), a picture might not be reprinted for five years or fifty. Most often, it would never be seen again. A lot of news pictures eventually got thrown away.

Even when press photographers were celebrated, they weren't invited to the party. In 1935, *The American Mercury* magazine joined with the book publisher Alfred A. Knopf to publish a big anthology of great news pictures titled *The Breathless Moment*. In its roughly two hundred pages, not one photographer is named, and the introduction doesn't bother to apologize or explain. That's just how it was. Arthur Fellig's work was anonymous, too, until Weegee decided that it shouldn't be.

He became Weegee the Famous because, beyond a doubt, his photography rose to a high level. His best pictures are intensely truthful. Some are painful, others unexpectedly warm, many others funny, touching, memorable. (And, as we shall see, sometimes he would give the truth some extra help.) But we also know Weegee because he was aggressive about letting people know who made those pictures. He was a constant, cheery self-promoter. This set him apart from his more diffident, now-forgotten colleagues. An afternoon spent browsing their work in the New York *Daily News* or the *Los Angeles Examiner* will yield a few photos that hold their own next to Weegee's best. In the newspapers' file drawers, some of the prints will have the photographers' names scribbled on their backs. Others, poignantly, have surnames only ("Petersen" or "Levine" or "McCrory"), with first names forgotten by all but their grandchildren. Many other pictures carry no name at all. Were any of those men—there were virtually no women—consistent enough, reliable enough, aggressive enough to produce deadline art the way Arthur Fellig could? It takes nothing away from his achievements to say that some of them probably were. We'll never know. Weegee the Famous has come to stand for them all.

And that word itself, *Weegee*? It may have been meant to obscure, yet its origins say a great deal about Arthur Fellig. To hear him tell it, he was a photographic clairvoyant, someone who got a mysterious tingle in his elbow when news was about to break and who made his way to the scene just in time. Eventually, someone—in all the retellings, the source varied, from Fellig himself to a friend to a secretary at the photo agency where he worked—said something like "It's as if you have a Ouija board." That fortune-telling gadget was a national craze of the 1920s, and the self-educated Arthur Fellig spelled it the way it sounded: *oui-jee* came out Weegee. Or, as he later wisecracked, "I changed it . . . to make it easier for the fan mail." A variant of this tale refers to the line drawing of a moon face that appears in the corner of the Ouija board itself. Charles Liotta, a photoengraver who worked alongside Arthur Fellig at the start of his career, told people that he had seen an echo of Fellig's doughy, expressive mug in that face and given him the nickname. Perhaps he did.

But there's another story. In his twenties, before he was selling his own pictures, Fellig worked in the darkrooms of the *New York Times*. His particular role on that fast-moving assembly line was to dry off prints before they were pressed onto ferrotype plates for final finishing. Much as reporters would pull a page out of their typewriters and shout, "*Copy!*," whereupon a copyboy would whisk the story off to be typeset, a darkroom printer would announce that a photo was ready to be dried by calling out, "Squeegee!" The young men who responded were called squeegee boys. (Fellig was not the only such apprentice who made good; Frank Cancellare, the photographer whose DEWEY DEFEATS TRUMAN picture everyone has seen, also started out as a squeegee boy.) When Fellig took another job, at the Acme Newspictures agency, he moved up to printing photos himself, and when his colleagues found out that he had until recently been a squeegee boy, they needled him about it. Over time, as he gained their respect and as his technical skills became evident, the mockery flipped into praise. "Squeegee boy" turned into "Mr. Squeegee" and eventually became Weegee. "Like practically everything he ever owned," a friend of his once joked, "the name got worn down."

So: either Arthur Fellig was a near-clairvoyant artisan turned artist with magical powers or he was a schlub in the darkroom, barked at and hazed by his colleagues. If the first story is the true one, he was very, very good at creating a public image. If the second version is true (as indeed it is), that achievement grows even more impressive: he was able to turn a vaguely humiliating nickname into what we now would call a personal brand, one that has endured for nearly a hundred years.

His was a compartmentalized soul. He was sensitive enough to catch extreme delicacy on film but also steely enough to do so when faced with a severed human head or the incinerated victim of a truck fire. He was an uneducated man whose writing displays vigorous, confident wit and flair; a person who was strikingly egalitarian on matters of race while reveling in his misogyny; a great American artist who didn't quite have a grip on what an artist was. He is generally thought of as a photographer of crime and urban mayhem, yet the majority of his working life was spent on other subjects. He was, like most photographers, a voyeur. Maybe more than most.

Among the art establishment, he was respected but also the object of condescension. Too often they called him "a primitive," implying that his skill came without practice or craft. They took pains to point out his relatively crude lighting, his unsubtle extra-high-contrast prints. Most observers thought—and some critics still do—that Weegee made great art only when he wasn't really trying to, and that when he did try later in life the results were a sad joke. (They're not.) But he, in turn, saw things that they didn't. Next to the work of many of his ostensibly more artistic contemporaries, Weegee's is more vivid, more powerful, sui generis. He very early on grasped that the distinction between high culture and low was growing blurry, and he enthusiastically jumped back and forth between those worlds. He realized that pictures of a workaday news event such as a fire are often less interesting than pictures of people reacting to that event, and many of his greatest photographs show the latter. In a lot of ways—his self-referentiality, his acknowledgment of the viewer, his cheerfully held attitude that a news photograph need not be 100 percent factual to be entirely truthful—he was postmodern before we had that word.

Many of us, in various fields of work, create professional façades for ourselves. A messy home life, with troubled kids or even just piled-up dishes in the sink, fades to invisibility if you show up at the office in a suit on Monday morning. A shy person, girded with the journalistic armor of a camera or reporter's notebook, can abruptly become capable of pushing past a police line to ask tough questions. Celebrities reinvent themselves for public view, and we revel in their transformations. Who doesn't enjoy those "Before They Were Famous" photos that gossip magazines occasionally run? We look at them to laugh at the awkward hair and cheesy fashion choices, but also to see whether people destined for extraordinary lives knew it all along. (Did they show their drive, or at least their cheekbones, from the beginning?) Today, one can construct fame out of virtually nothing. On social media, we build representations of our lives that resemble but do not truly reflect our days. "We tell ourselves stories in order to live," Joan Didion so memorably wrote; we also tell everyone else our own stories, and eventually they can become our biographical plotlines, to be debunked, perhaps, only much later.

Arthur Fellig, as Weegee, was in the business of grabbing images that functioned as little one-act plays, both comedy and drama. They were the silver halide equivalent of that six-word novel spuriously attributed to Ernest Hemingway: "For sale: Baby shoes, never worn." Fellig communicated in a visual language that both tabloid-reading subway commuters and arty museum curators grasped right away. You can't say the best narrative he ever fashioned was his own—he made too many great photographs that tell vivid stories about other people—but Weegee himself was certainly the beat he sustained longest. In the archive of his work (preserved by his longtime companion Wilma Wilcox, and today held by the International Center of Photography) there are about nineteen thousand prints. Hundreds of them show Weegee himself, a mix of self-portraits and photographs by unnamed friends and colleagues. He was obsessed with his own public face.

Which makes sense: that image enabled the making of the other images. Weegee was the one who went on talk shows, raced to a burning tenement to beat the competition, got assignments that paid hundreds or even thousands of dollars; Arthur Fellig did not. Was that guy he created immodest? Self-aggrandizing? Pushy? Irritating, sometimes? You bet he was. This was New York, and he was in the newspaper business. Modesty was for *suckers*.

Here's how he did it.

PART I

OUT OF THE DARK

In 1899, the town of Zolochev was not the worst place in the world in which
to be a Jew. Today, it is a good-sized suburb about an hour's drive from
the city of Lviv, in the western part of Ukraine. At the close of the nineteenth century, it was out on the unfashionable eastern end of the
Austro-Hungarian Empire, and Lviv was called Lemberg. Galicia was
the name of the province in which it lay, under the awkward dual control of Vienna and Budapest. It was a crossroads of cultures, and thus of
languages. Most residents spoke Polish because much of Galicia had
once been part of Poland,* but there was German in the streets as well,
and a little Ukrainian, and lots of Yiddish.

Whether for Jews or Gentiles, though, it was not a comfortable or
easy place to live. Galicia was the poorest part of the empire, with frequent famines and epidemics. The industrialization that was improving
life in much of the rest of Europe was not really being pursued here; that
kind of investment was being made, and its profits spent, way to the west.
(Although, within a few years, even Zolochev would have telephone and
telegraph service.) From these eastern territories, most of what the government wanted was a steady flow of wheat and potatoes. Viennese pastry depended upon Galician flour.

The town had roughly ten thousand residents then, about half of them
Jews. If this had been a Russian village, its Jewish residents would have

---

* And would be again: in 1921, after the First World War and a squabble with Russia, the district containing Zolochev was deeded back to Poland. Since then, it has been part of Germany, the Soviet
Union, and, now, Ukraine.

been facing systematic disenfranchisement, attacks, and horrific deaths in the pogroms. In Galicia, by contrast, there was, if not exactly harmony, at least a manageable equilibrium. Quite a few Jews in Zolochev had reached the merchant class, and you could almost tell how successful they were by their language of choice: the more they'd established themselves, the likelier they were to have shed Yiddish for Polish, as they integrated themselves into the local power structure. The town had a Jewish mayor, and it was represented by Jews in the parliament in Vienna. The emperor, Franz Joseph I, had bestowed equal citizenship upon his Jewish subjects, declaring their civil rights "not contingent in the people's religion." In return, the emperor was well liked by the Galician Jewish population, members of which wrote appreciative prayers and songs about him that were printed in their prayer books. There were, roughly speaking, three classes of Jews in town: successful bourgeois business folk, who dressed like city people; the poor but observant, whose dress and religious observance were, in the words of one contemporary, "half-civilized"; and the Hasidim, in their black fur hats.

Berisch and Rivka Felig were somewhere on the lower rungs of the middle group. They lived in House 226, according to public records. By June 1899, they had been married for not quite three years, with a son named Elias, and their second child was on the way. Berisch was literate and had learned Hebrew. He yearned to become a rabbi, although he didn't or couldn't do what it took to become ordained. In his son's memoir, we are told that the family spoke German and Polish, but it is overwhelmingly likely (and records suggest, and the rest of the family agrees) that the household language was Yiddish.

Rivka was also educated, and was a little bit further up the social ladder than her husband because her father owned some property and had his own business, supplying food under contract to the Austrian army. (Berisch worked for his in-laws, in fact.) She came from the large and widespread Imber family. An older relative from Zolochev named Naftali Herz Imber was in the midst of becoming a prominent poet, which suggests that he was well-off enough to do more than grub out a living. One of his poems, half a century later, was set to music and became "Hatikvah," the Israeli national anthem.

Berisch and Rivka's second son was born on June 12, 1899. They named him Usher.* That he would, on another continent, become more famous than his cousin (for making art with a camera, a field that barely existed in 1899 and absolutely did not exist in the worldview of a hungry family in Zolochev) was not foremost in his parents' minds.

When a third son, Feibish, arrived two years later, the pressure to keep the children fed became more intense, and a political shift that took lucrative contracts away from Jews undercut the family business. The local détente was beginning to break down, too: less than a generation later, in 1918, Lviv would be the site of a vicious three-day pogrom. Great numbers of Galicia's citizens were leaving, and even a not-very-ambitious father could see that a better future lay elsewhere. In the twenty years preceding the First World War, three million people emigrated. About a quarter of those went to America.

Berisch went first, alone, in August 1903. That arrangement was not uncommon. The idea was to get a job on the reputedly gold-paved streets of an American city and eventually send some of that treasure home so the family could reunite. Maybe Berisch was just ready to try his luck in a new place; maybe it was because Rivka had found out she was expecting a fourth child, and he simply couldn't support six people on the work he could get. He left on the Hamburg-America Line's steamship *Pretoria*, packed into steerage with twenty-two hundred other people (plus a couple of hundred up above, in first and second class). It was one of the company's newer, faster ships, and the crossing took the typical seven days.

At Ellis Island, he named a cousin, Abraham Zwerling (who listed his address in a tenement at 201 East Seventh Street), as his contact in the New World. (At least, Berisch claimed they were cousins; it was not uncommon for immigrants to concoct a kinship with someone already in America, in the belief that it would ease their admission. There were indeed Zwerlings among the Jews of Zolochev, so Berisch and Abraham were probably related somehow.) Berisch—he quickly became "Bernard," although one document says that he briefly tried on "Barnet" for size—listed his occupation as "laborer," which is telling; he may have been a learned man, but now he would do whatever it took to get by. When he disembarked, he pledged, in accordance with the law, that he had no

* Occasionally spelled "Ascher," "Asher," or "Uscher."

criminal record, was not a polygamist, was not an anarchist. He had four dollars in his pocket.

Even the poorest American city dwellers today would find it almost impossible to imagine the density and intensity of the Lower East Side into which he arrived. In the preceding fifty years, the five boroughs constituting New York City (only recently consolidated into one entity, in 1898) had quintupled their population, to 3.5 million. Most of those new people were not American babies but immigrants flooding in from the Old World. First from Ireland and England, then from northern Europe, and subsequently from Italy and Greece and Russia and Austria-Hungary, came ships packed full of people like Berisch turned Bernard, sometimes a thousand per day. Industrial America absorbed them, to fill factory jobs and build skyscrapers and dig subway tunnels. Because New York was the country's biggest manufacturing center, a lot of these new Americans went no farther than the port city where they'd disembarked.

In 1900, the district known as the Seventeenth Ward, which included that tenement where Abraham Zwerling lived on East Seventh Street, had a population of 130,796, packed into less than half a square mile. The only denser areas were immediately to the south, deeper into the Lower East Side. (Those areas, still pretty crowded, house about a quarter as many residents now as they did then.) A tenement building that today is home to perhaps a dozen people typically held about seventy. Kids slept three and four to a mattress. Some single men did not rent or even share a room; instead, they rented eight hours' worth of a single grimy bed, and two other "tenants," if you can call them that, slept there during the other two shifts. If Berisch had a dime to spare, it was most likely sent home to Zolochev, where Rivka was getting help (probably financial, certainly personal, and absolutely necessary in either case) from her extended family.

Usher knew little of the city where his father was living. When the family was in Europe, he said later, "there was one [American] building that was outstanding. They had pictures of it. That was the Singer Building," at forty-seven stories the tallest skyscraper downtown, brand new in 1908. "That was the only building we knew, and as a matter of fact, nobody believed they really had a building that high."

As a grown man, Arthur Fellig said almost nothing else about this period of his life. He and his siblings always described their origins as

"Austria," which sounded genteel to many Americans, implying schlag and Sacher torte. It also conveyed the lingering national pride that Emperor Franz Joseph's benevolence had instilled. Mostly, though, Galicia amounted to a life and a place that Arthur and his brothers and sisters explicitly chose to leave behind.

In adulthood, Weegee told only one extended story about the old country, and he played it for slapstick and pathos. His father, he said, at one point sent home a packet of a dozen "throwaways," flyers that looked like twenty-dollar bills on one side and carried an ad for a local business on the other. Berisch was probably goofing around (which is what Arthur later suggested), joking as if the throwaways were real cash; he may have been making an honest mistake; he may himself have been conned. In any case, Rivka and her family didn't know what American currency was supposed to look like, and neither did the local bank. She thought that her ship had literally come in, and she booked passage as soon as the counterfeit $240 had been deposited. The family's bags were packed when the bankers came after them and canceled everything. It was a disappointing and embarrassing moment, one that left a mark on Usher Fellig.

In New York, Berisch kept working, eventually with a pushcart, and managed to send actual money sometime later. Rivka and the children were headed to America. It was the summer of 1909. They made their way to Hamburg, where they boarded the *Kaiserin Auguste Victoria*, a slightly nicer vessel than the *Pretoria*. It had, at its launch a few years earlier, briefly been the largest liner in the world, and the well-off passengers in first class experienced luxurious travel. Which is not to say it was especially nice down in fourth class, where the Felligs were: they had paid roughly thirty-five dollars per passenger, which entitled nobody to a cabin. Although conditions in the belly of a steamship had sharply improved in new vessels such as the *Kaiserin Auguste Victoria*—just a few years earlier, many had not provided separate bathing areas for women and men, and the washrooms had had only cold-seawater spigots—this was no vacation cruise. Bunks were lined up barracks style. If you were seasick (and on the Felligs' trip, rough weather made a lot of people seasick), being down there amid the cabbagey kitchen stink and the shared bathrooms only made things worse.

The family was reunited on September 4, when Berisch met them

Non

at the port. Usher Fellig later recalled having his eyes checked at Ellis Island for trachoma, the contagious form of conjunctivitis that was the terror of immigrants not only because it could blind them but also because it could get them sent back to Europe. Everyone in the family passed, and off they went to their new home. That day, spiritually if not officially, Usher Felig became Arthur Fellig.*

The passenger manifest says that he couldn't read or write. When he was presented with a banana at Ellis Island, it was "the most amazing thing," he later recalled. "I'm glad one thing—someone told me to take the skin off." But, he added, "we didn't know any difference. I'd never seen anything like that before." He got an orange, too, and figured out how to peel it on his own.

Berisch had been living in Brooklyn, in a building at 292 Watkins Street. That was smack in the middle of Brownsville, a relatively new tenement neighborhood that had been built up as an alternative to the packed Lower East Side. (Predominantly populated by the poorest of immigrant Jews, it had quickly become a slum of its own. By 1909, it was notorious for street crime, a reputation it still has.) But the family probably needed more space than Berisch had as a single man, and the reunited Felligs soon took another apartment, on the Lower East Side, in a rear tenement at 52 Pitt Street.

That address tells you a lot about the family's financial status. A rear tenement, or "backhouse," was a building in the backyard of another, built to double the owner's income from a small plot of land. Access was usually via the street-facing tenement: to enter the second building, you went in the front door of the first, through a narrow tunnel-like hallway, and out a back door into the yard. The rent in a rear tenement was lower, and so was the quality of life. A backhouse had the unpleasant quality of cutting residents off from the street while offering almost no privacy. The joke popularized by Henny Youngman conveys it:

WOMAN (TO NEIGHBOR): Do you see what's going on in Poland?
NEIGHBOR: I don't see anything. I live in the back.

---

* His mother's name took longer to migrate from Old World to New: through forty years of paperwork, Rivka becomes Rebekah, then Rebecca, and finally Beckie.

The six Felligs occupied two rooms, over a bakery. And although you may imbue that arrangement with a little romance—fresh bread, sweet-smelling pastry—it was terrible. Bakeries on the Lower East Side were notoriously dirty, infested with rats and bugs. In fact, Samuel Goldstein, the baker downstairs from the Felligs, was implicated the next year in a racket wherein he'd been buying rotten eggs from crooked dealers. In the summer, the heat rising from the ovens made life in the building miserable. About the only thing the Felligs' apartment had going for it was a hall toilet rather than the outhouses many tenements still had. Just a few years earlier, both front and rear buildings at 52 Pitt Street had been cited by the city's Tenement House Department for "unsanitary conditions" and "want of repair"—and given the conditions considered acceptable at the time, it had to have been pretty bad. Nor was it an especially happy home. Arthur was still angry at his father over the fake-currency confusion, and the rotten conditions into which they'd arrived surely didn't help. Father and son never really got along again. "You don't look back on this life," Arthur Fellig recalled in his old age. "You want to forget it."

Still, the neighborhood, rough as it was, constituted a support system. This slice of the Lower East Side was full of Galician Jews, speaking Polish and Yiddish. There was a *mikvah*, a ritual bathhouse, across the street. These four blocks of Pitt Street contained nine synagogues and *Landsmanshaften*, the mutual-aid societies that helped old-country Jews hang on in the New World. One synagogue was right next door, at 54 Pitt, its congregation mostly from Krakow. Another, about two blocks away, on Ridge Street, was called Machzikei Hadath Anshei Zlotshov and was populated by immigrants from the very town the Felligs had just left; indeed, its presence may have been why Berisch and Rivka took the apartment they did.

For immigrant children in 1909, there was no English as a Second Language program in the schools. Besides, with kids from Italy, Poland, Hungary, Russia, Germany, and a dozen other Balkan and Baltic countries, such classes would have been a babel of their own. Instead, the greenhorns, as everyone called the newcomers, were tossed in and got more or less the same lessons everyone else did. Most learned, with difficulty, to swim rather than sink.

Arthur was a quick study. Less than eight months after he arrived in America, a census taker listed him as an English speaker, and with the German, Polish, and Yiddish he already knew, he would be able to handle himself in multiple worlds. (He had a great felicity with words and lost himself in books, he said, reading late into the night in his crowded bed.) He was not, however, primed for the tough world he currently occupied. Although he was smart, most of all he was shy.

The standard Lower East Side tale, repeated in so many families, has the patriarch starting with a pushcart and making his way up to a storefront and then maybe a bigger business, and seeing his life grow easier and his children grow up in comfort, climbing society's ladder. It happened this way sometimes, but not for Bernard Fellig. He struggled merely to earn enough for the family, and often came up short. His son tells us that he tried to sell dishes before the High Holidays, when housewives often needed a second set in order to keep kosher. It was heavy, tiring work, especially in bad weather, and Bernard Fellig did not naturally have the hustling, *hondeling* instincts of a great salesman. He could scrape by, but no more.

Or perhaps he couldn't. In March 1910, Bernard was arrested for burglarizing a house in Brownsville, his old neighborhood, after he'd apparently lifted an armload of clothes and jewelry. He was, humiliatingly enough, caught by a thirteen-year-old girl, the daughter of the home owner. She'd glimpsed him during the theft, then spotted him again on the street a few days later and calmly tracked him till she found a cop and had him hauled into the 153rd Precinct. Whether owing to judicial compassion or lack of evidence (or perhaps a case of mistaken identity), the charge was first knocked down from burglary to vagrancy and then dismissed. Although it is nearly impossible to say for sure, as the available records from this era are unindexed, he does not seem to have been arrested again. Still: back in Zolochev, Usher Fellig had been able to build up an image of his father as the family pioneer, off in the United States, forging a better life. Now, after barely six months in America, he was confronted with the fact that his father was not a rabbi or a hero but a poor provider and, perhaps, a petty criminal.

The pushcart came in handy when the family moved from Pitt Street to another tenement, at 384 Cherry Street, way over near the East River. They had three rooms this time, in a fifth-floor walk-up, but they didn't stay long. Within a couple of years, they were in yet another red-brick tenement nearby, at 35 Jackson Street, probably seeking more space as the sixth and seventh children of the family, Jacob and Yetta, arrived. "More space," though, was a relative term: 35 Jackson had nineteen families living on five floors over a saloon. Weekly scrubdowns took place over on Monroe Street, at the public baths. Bernard and Rebekah took on the role of superintendent, cleaning and maintaining the building so they wouldn't have to pay the fifteen-dollar monthly rent.

Their financial struggle was exacerbated by Bernard's piety: he wouldn't work on the Sabbath. This was not an uncommon situation among Lower East Side Jews, usually out of genuine faith but also out of simple weariness. In some other families, the wife ended up handling the pushcart so the husband could linger over the Talmud. Bernard, though, was able to help make ends meet by teaching bar mitzvah lessons to local boys, helped along by an English-language book from which chunks of their speeches could be cribbed. As of 1918, his principal income came from working for a milliner on Wooster Street. Although Weegee later said his father did eventually become a rabbi, what Bernard probably achieved was the role of a *shammes,* a sort of sexton and deputy officiant in the local synagogue.

It's impossible to get into the psychodynamics of the Fellig family at this distance, but here and there, bits and pieces of the story peek out. In his later years, Weegee said almost nothing about his parents and siblings. "I was the black sheep of the family," he sneered after he became famous, adding, "They all live and bask in the reflected glory off me." The Fellig brothers and sisters mostly became successful adults—one was a lawyer, another a nurse, and their descendants have done well in a variety of fields—but they very much went their own ways, and were not especially close with one another. In Weegee's autobiography, he writes about the arrival at Ellis Island of "the five of us—my mother, three brothers, and Weegee," accidentally turning his sister Rachel into a boy. Maybe it's just an editing error, but it's telling that he got his own kid sister wrong. In another life story, he mentions his "five brothers and sisters"; he had six. And while there weren't dramatic feuds or deep resentments, the sense of family was minimal. Liz Cooke, a niece of Weegee's, recalls "no closeness." At her father's funeral, "they brought this person into my room, and said, 'This is your uncle Jack,'" referring to Arthur's younger brother Jacob. In that generation of high-achieving and striving new Americans, some families grew tighter, unifying to march into their new world. Others, like the Felligs, retreated into individual shells. "There was so much shame over being poor, being Jewish, being immigrants," Cooke says. Better to look ahead, even if that meant forgetting.

There was also a divide between the four older children, born in Europe and speaking Yiddish as their first language, and the three younger ones, born in America. The more devout branches of the family eventually de-Americanized the spelling of their surname, going back to Felig. Usher-to-Arthur-to-Weegee is an even more dramatic progression, from an inarguably Jewish name to one that's free of ethnicity. Yet Arthur's cultural Jewishness was never something he rejected, and some of his best photographs are of Jewish New York: street peddlers, garment sellers, bagel makers. His writing is salted with references to hot pastrami and knishes. "A picture is like a blintz," he said later in life. "Eat it while it's hot."

As in so many poor families, the kids soon went to work. Arthur started selling the daily paper, beginning a lifelong relationship with newsprint, but it didn't bring in much: not enough adults on Cherry Street read English, and besides, he later said, "I wasn't a good paper salesman." He soon switched to selling penny candy, making rounds among the teenage girls in the neighborhood's factories, to whom a little sugar provided a brief burst of energy during their grueling days. He stayed in school, at least for a while. In these years, the City of New York required that students stick around through the age of fourteen, and that's what he did. The school principal had seen Arthur's intelligence, and despite pleading with the boy to stay for another couple of years—"the principal of the school was almost heartbroken," Weegee said—Arthur quit halfway through the seventh grade. (This did not make him an outlier. In this era, 84 percent of New York's Russian-Jewish students who'd entered as first-graders dropped out before graduating from high school.) He'd picked up enough general education to get by, including a knack for lively writing. His wits would have to supply the rest.

And shortly before he quit school, Arthur Fellig had an experience, ordinary for most of us, life-changing for him, the very first step toward his creation of Weegee the Famous: a street photographer took his picture.

How often was a street kid likely to have his picture taken around 1913? Photography was not quite in its infancy, but being photographed was hardly an everyday activity for a poor family. Until about twenty-five years earlier, making a picture had effectively required a portable chemistry lab. That had changed with the camera known as the Kodak, which arrived in 1888. George Eastman's invention incorporated two key innovations: a roll of flexible film that was dry and ready to shoot, and lab processing by mail. The early camera came preloaded with one hundred frames, and once you finished them, you sent the whole thing back to Rochester, New York, where the pictures were developed and the camera refilled. "You press the button, we do the rest" was Kodak's slogan, and it brought the price of photography from very high to only moderately so. By the mid-1910s, the basic Vest Pocket Kodak, which folded down to the size of a thick wallet, cost $6, the rough equivalent of $150 today. Picture-taking had become an achievable working-class hobby.

That was for amateurs, though. Most professionals used the setup we still associate with "old-time photographer": a view camera, built of wood with nickeled or brass fittings, equipped with large bellows and a black cloth draped over its back. A street photographer would most likely have been shooting tintypes, so called because they were made not on paper or glass but on thin sheets of metal covered in black lacquer. Some were made to fit in brooches or on buttons. They were produced by itinerant photographers everywhere people gathered: at carnivals, festivals, and the like—and certainly on the streets of the Lower East Side. The operator would typically take your address and deliver a developed image a couple of days later. Magazines of the day ran advertisements for mail-order kits (camera and processing rig, sometimes built into one big boxlike contraption). For twenty-five dollars, you could BE YOUR OWN BOSS! with NO EXPERIENCE NEEDED and MAKE $200 A MONTH. Each photo, the ads explained, would require one or two cents' worth of supplies and would sell for ten times that. Although the era of the five-minute exposure time had passed by 1913, the equipment was still clunky, and it couldn't make action photographs. Everyone had to stand still—as little Arthur Fellig did on the street that day.

Only one childhood picture of Fellig survives, and it may or may not be that one. (He later captioned it "My first portrait," but who knows how casually applied that label was.) It has been cropped for reproduction, perhaps from a group family photo. He's wearing a fur hat and an odd neckerchief, an outfit that would have gotten him teased ("greenhorn!") in an American schoolroom. He looks about ten, so the shot was probably taken around the time the family arrived in America.

What does survive, however, is the impact that street tintype made on the kid. Arthur Fellig was bright; he was curious about the world and about the way things worked. For him, light-sensitive emulsions and a split-second exposure were futuristic technology. And the process itself was intricate and procedural: the fitting together of film holder and camera, the removal of the dark slide before the exposure, the snap of the shutter. Then into the dark: a dunk of the plate into the developing tank and then into sodium hyposulfite, the stuff photographers call "hypo," a slippery alkaline solution that clears the remaining sensitized crystals so the picture can be brought out into daylight. For a young person especially, this is a bewitching thing to watch, and it grabbed hold of Arthur Fellig, hard. As he put it later in life, "Right then, I decided to solve that mystery." And although he certainly had his share of other jobs in his late childhood and early adulthood (before the first glimmers of Weegee the Famous appeared), he spent nearly the entirety of the next five decades trying to make pictures, sell the pictures he'd made, or get into other people's pictures. It is barely an exaggeration to say that, apart from a flirtation with moviemaking much later in life, he never wanted to do anything else.

The teenaged Arthur got himself one of those tintype kits, from a Chicago mail-order house, and set out into the streets to start taking pictures.* The ads for such kits had Horatio Alger overtones, and Arthur could imagine himself as a street photographer working his way up to his own studio, then fame and fortune as a portraitist.

It didn't happen. Despite all the newspaper hawking and candy selling and bootstrap pulling, life on Cherry Street was more complicated than that, and after a short time in the photo hustle, Arthur Fellig quickly decided for himself, he later wrote, that "Horatio Alger was a phoney," and that he was done with "the SCHMO Alger's exploits." He wasn't making a living, and a few months in, he put the tintype kit aside and took a job at a commercial photo studio.

Richard Duckett and Edward M. Adler's business, called Duckett & Adler, was on the skylit top floor of 60 Grand Street, a loft building near West Broadway. (The building still stands, and an ad for the studio painted on an exterior wall is faintly visible.) The company was pretty small: a state inspector around this time found that it had five employees working fifty-four hours a week, which squares with Arthur Fellig's later recollection that his shifts ran from 8:00 a.m. to 6:00 p.m. plus some weekend time. It was 1914, and Arthur wasn't old enough to go to the corner saloon with the other employees at mealtime. He was still living at home, and his mother was still packing his lunch.

The job was about as uncreative as picture-taking could get. Duckett & Adler specialized in product shots for catalogues, so traveling salesmen didn't have to haul around big sample items—things like furniture and chandeliers. They photographed such dull events as a trade-show-style display of New York City municipal initiatives. In Fellig's recollection, the products included shrouds and coffins, too. In order to show the latter in use, "we used to take these black suits, stuff 'em up with newspapers, and they'd photograph them," he later recalled, adding, "I never suspected at one time I'd get the real thing." He didn't call himself an assistant, because he'd already figured out one key to a creative career: just declare that it is your primary job rather than a sideline, and people will eventually believe you. His first appearance in official records after

---

* Weegee doesn't identify the company in Chicago, but another firm, L. Lascelle, on West Forty-Third Street in New York, advertised its twenty-five-dollar kits widely.

he left school is in a New York census of 1915, and under "Occupation" he put down "Photographer."

It was drab work, with a lot of lifting and loading, more like stocking shelves than making great pictures. Still, there was a lot of it, and a young person needs experience. Besides, there was a secondary business at Duckett & Adler, one that was a little more interesting. It involved insurance photography, wherein the owners of burned-out factories needed to document the damage to make an insurance claim. That meant toting a big wooden camera on a heavy tripod to each job site—and guess which junior staffer had to haul the thing around. The camera produced eleven-by-fourteen-inch glass negatives. "They didn't have enlargements back in them days," Weegee later explained. It also required portable indoor lighting, and that was the beginning of one of Arthur Fellig's obsessions: the flash.

It is a little hard to grasp now, when even a disposable nine-dollar camera comes with a built-in strobe, but lighting up an indoor scene in 1914 was difficult. Virtually no electric bulb of the day was strong enough, and the photo film and glass plates of the time were much less sensitive than almost any such material in use today. You had to blast an indoor scene with light to make an image. The product you needed was called flash powder, essentially ground-up magnesium metal with an oxidizer added. Pour a couple spoonfuls of it into a flash lamp (a little trough sitting atop a stick that could be held aloft, literally a flaming torch), add a spark, and the substance would explode in a blinding burst of light. (Kodak marketed cartridges and combustible paper that were a little easier to handle but still made sparks and smoke.) Some photographers used an electric trigger with a battery to set off this tiny bomb. The Duckett & Adler people did it more crudely: "I would put a tube in my mouth," recalled Fellig, "and blow the flash powder onto a rag soaked in [burning] alcohol, which would ignite the powder." The fireball could be a couple of feet across, and it was certainly bright enough to make a picture. It could also set the curtains ablaze. It smoked up the room. Burned hands were common.

Fellig lasted two years in the assistant's job, supplementing his meager pay by selling candy in a burlesque theater at night. He eventually received a promotion from assistant to camera operator, and (just weeks after that, he said) quit in a dispute over money. He'd been receiving barely a living wage up till then—$4.50 per week, creeping up to $7.00—and when he demanded to be paid something like his predecessor's higher salary, the boss refused, whereupon Fellig stormed out. It was his first fight over credit and cash, and not his last.

He also left home for good, and it was not an easy break. "I was restless," he later explained. "It was a difficult and hard decision to make . . . I just had to leave home. I knew there would be trouble with my mother, so I simply packed up and sneaked out." It didn't work: "My mother caught me going down the stairs and let out a heartbreaking scream, 'Usher!' So I went back." Not long thereafter, "making sure everyone was asleep, I left. My baggage was just my curiosity."

He decided to give the tintype game another go, this time with an idea that was quintessentially Weegee—the first moment that hints at the always-looking-for-an-angle character he became. At the time, it was not uncommon for a city street photographer to pose kids on horseback for their portraits. So Arthur Fellig began working for a fellow who had a pony and a view camera, and they started walking the Lower East Side, making pictures of kids and selling their parents the five-by-seven prints. Soon Fellig got his own little horse and began developing the glass-plate negatives in his furnished room. "We called it kidnapping," he said. "We'd find a kid, put him on the pony, take the picture, and then try to peddle it to the kid's mother, five cents a print." He washed the children's faces, too, later saying, "That's how I got pride in my work." An inside photography joke was at the forefront of his mind: he named the pony Hypo.

Maybe it wasn't as harebrained a scheme as it sounds today. Lower East Side streets in the late teens were filled with horse-drawn carts, and it wasn't so difficult to keep an animal in New York City as it might seem today. But as a moneymaker, Hypo was hopeless: he literally ate up all the profits, and when a series of rainy weekends kept the two of them indoors, keeping Hypo fed began to keep Arthur from being fed. He fell behind on the payments, and soon enough, he said, Hypo was repossessed. Fellig then tried posing kids in a toy automobile, an idea that he later offered as "evidence of the changing times." The car didn't require oats and water, but neither did it spark the interest that Hypo had.

Still, this scheme taught Arthur Fellig a lot about the business of making and selling pictures. Hustle worked: get a picture that even a poor family couldn't resist and you'd make a little money. "There wasn't an

East Side home," he later wrote, surely exaggerating, "that did not have one of my pony pictures on the mantelpiece." Broad sentiment or a warm moment that resonated was a more effective sales tool than formality or straight documentation. A gimmick didn't hurt, either.

And, he learned, the print had to have punch. His buyers weren't interested in subtle shadows or gradations of texture and tone. They wanted healthy white teeth and clear, milky skin. Many of those customers were more Mediterranean than Mancunian; the ideal then (and perhaps now) was pink-cheeked and fair-skinned, and Fellig gave an approximation of it to families who were, like him, from the swarthier parts of Europe. He quickly learned to print on "the contrastiest paper I could get in order to give the kids nice white, chalky faces." He never entirely stopped printing that way, and it's not much of an exaggeration to say that this one stylistic choice changed, and came to dominate, and still influences, news photography and thus film noir.

Once Hypo and the toy car were gone, Fellig was at loose ends again. It was, he explained, "impossible to find work." He sought photographic day jobs, picking up the New York *World* at dawn to get to the classifieds first, and by 6:00 a.m. he would be in line for anything that had been advertised. "Usually at about eight o'clock," he later recalled, "there would be a couple hundred other fellows in line and the boss would take everybody's name and address." To fill the idle hours in between those jobs, he bounced around, taking work in the evocatively named Loose-Wiles Biscuit Company and at the Loft candy factory in Queens. He always said he worked as "a hole-puncher at the Life Savers factory," and when someone asked him about the particulars of hole punching, he offered that it "sounds like a gag, but actually I worked one of the machines that really did it." He also bused dishes, briefly and unhappily, in a Horn & Hardart Automat at Broadway and Houston Street.

Although he still gave his address on Cherry Street, in his parents' crowded apartment, he didn't really live there. He was spending most of his nights on benches in Pennsylvania Station, which had, he said, "better sleeping accommodations than the parks and the missions." He'd tried Grand Central Terminal, but the cops there were "too officious." Other times, he'd crash at a Bowery flophouse, a quarter a night. He'd chosen a mangy, rangy street existence—and the freedom, at least theoretically, to pick up a girl now and then—over life with his overbearing parents.

The dollar-a-day-plus-food at the Automat served as his base salary. (Later in life he said, "I think if you dirty up the dishes, you oughta clean 'em up yourself," and claimed to have forced his firing by deliberately dropping a big bin of plates.) He also chased photo work in bits and pieces, a day here and a few hours there. The World War I draft, for which he registered in September 1918, failed to catch him because the Armistice was signed just weeks later. To the draft board, though, he gave his occupation not as factory worker or candy hole puncher or busboy but again as "Photographer."

By that time, he had a regular gig, and although his subjects weren't much more glamorous than the coffins and chandeliers had been, at least the job allowed him to continue taking pictures. The work was at a place called the Seaman Studio, at 25 Broadway, taking passport photos. (Barely any trace of that business survives. In Britain, the Seaman family operated a sprawling chain of similarly named photo studios, run by an array of brothers, and this seems to have been either a New York franchise or, more likely, a business owned by an American trading on that name. Maybe it worked on British visitors, too. Fellig noted that, at this job, the English were the easiest to upsell.) It paid passably, giving him a salary topping out at forty dollars a week, enough to keep him in food, cheap furnished rooms, and, he claimed later, a whorehouse visit each night on the way home. Though that was surely an overstatement, he was certainly settling into an unrefined adulthood.

ID photography, though, was boring, and the Seaman Studio was gone within a few years. Arthur Fellig found himself in the position of a lot of artists-to-be: Do I settle for a straight job, one that means I can (barely) support a family and lead a conventional life? Or do I dump it and keep taking pictures on my own? Although he surely was not thinking about making art, he definitely wanted more out of life, and out of his camera, than making pairs of headshots. "The studios I haunted," he later wrote. "I didn't want a steady job, I wanted to learn all the different fields of photography—portraits, commercial, theatrical, etc."

For a while, he also played the violin (a skill he'd learned from a Little Italy neighbor who gave music lessons on the side) as a silent movie accompanist in a theater on Third Avenue, and tried to take the job seriously, as a future career. That it worked with non-English-speaking immigrant filmgoers was not lost on him, either. "I loved playing on the emotions of the audience as they watched," he later wrote. "I could move them to either happiness or sorrow . . . I suppose that my fiddle-playing was a sub-conscious kind of training for my future in photography." Tear-jerking, it seems, was a knack of his. He occasionally dropped by the violin room at a big music store on Forty-Second Street, where he would carefully try out a five-thousand-dollar instrument, deriving what a small news item about him described as "satisfaction to a soul that craves something finer than his purse allows." His violin teacher was also a bootlegger, and after Fellig finished his shift at the movie theater on Saturday nights, he would go out and help the man make deliveries of illegal gin and beer uptown. "I used my camera case for that," he later said. And what he was begin-ning to see, in the early twenties, was that photographs were being used in an interesting new way, one that might get him out of the grind and into a much livelier career.

Pick up a century-old newspaper today and you'll find many of the design conventions familiar. An old copy of the *New York Times* looks fairly similar to today's *New York Times*—except that, a century ago, the front page often contained not a single picture. When there were photo-graphs in the paper, they were mostly static and decorative: fashion, home decor, portraits. There'd be a story about a socialite, say, and her face and shoulders would appear in an oval, as if on a cameo. Four days after the *Titanic* sank, as the liner *Carpathia* pulled into New York Harbor with hundreds of survivors on board, the front page of the *Times* was made up entirely of type. A couple of pictures of passengers coming down the gangplank, smallish and murky and contributing little to the narra-tive, appeared inside. What was coming to be called "spot news"—vivid pictures of the goings-on of the day before, made at the scene—was absent.

At the *Times*, the only big exceptions were the rotogravure sections, one on Sunday and one called the "Mid-Week Pictorial," nearly a stand-alone magazine that had been added to the paper in 1914 largely to cover the First World War. The *New York Post* of the era looked even more old-fashioned than the *Times*, with almost no news photographs at all. Joseph Pulitzer's New York *World* was using pictures inventively, but many of them were illustrations. There was also some photojournalism going on in Europe, but it was relatively arty, aimed at bourgeois sophis-ticates, and appeared mostly in magazines, not newspapers.

In 1919, Joseph Medill Patterson tossed a bomb into that sea of words with his New York *Daily News*. This was a paper that intended to tell (and sell) its stories visually. At the top of the front page, a little drawing of a camera poked out between the big words DAILY and NEWS, and within weeks of the first issue a subtitle appeared underneath: NEW YORK'S PICTURE NEWSPAPER. Stories were short and punchy, with screaming headlines; photographs were big, active, and dynamic. The *Daily News* was also a physically distinctive product, half the width of a broadsheet paper like the *Times*. "Tabloid," this new magazine-like format was called, and you could read it on a crowded subway car without stretching your arms out. The *News*'s early slogan was "Tell it to Sweeney! The Stuyvesants will understand." The Stuyvesants (as everyone knew in this city where ethnic lines defined so much) were the swells, the good Knickerbocker Dutch families who had settled New Amsterdam, and who probably read the *Times* or (after its two predecessor papers merged in 1924) the *Herald Tribune*. "Sweeney" referred to the archetypal Irish American laborer, going off to work every day with his lunch pail, reading the paper on the IRT subway.

And what Sweeney (or Shapiro or Santangelo or Stavropoulos or, for that matter, Fellig) saw in those pages reflected the world he knew on the Lower East Side or in Hell's Kitchen or Brownsville: schmaltz, pathos, violence, and characters galore. The *Daily News* was not unwilling to hype a story in the interest of drama. It entertained, cajoled, tugged at the heartstrings—and it sold like crazy. Six years after its first issue, it was up to a million copies a day. At its peak, twenty years after that, it was printing 4.7 million every Sunday, a volume no American newspaper has ever matched or ever will again.

In 1924, William Randolph Hearst started up the competing New York *Daily Mirror*, and the two papers spent the following decade trying to outslug one another with scandals, crime, and celebrity news. Raw as they could be, the stories were often pretty well written (especially in the *News*), and neither paper ever really got involved in a race to the bottom. The uncontested winner in that game, at least for a while, was the *Evening Graphic*, a paper founded by Bernarr Macfadden, a bodybuilder turned publisher of physical fitness books and true-romance magazines. Macfadden was a kook (burying boxes of cash for safekeeping, trying to found a religion called "cosmotarianism," hating doctors so thoroughly that two of his children died of treatable illnesses), but he had a great populist ear and had built one of the most successful magazine companies in America. The *Graphic* was a far more lurid paper than anyone had seen before, the TMZ of its day. It not only told stories through pictures but also concocted those pictures, pasting together photos and word balloons, comic-book style, to re-create notorious events. *Time* magazine called the *Graphic* a "daily freak." Its two most prominent columnists, Walter Winchell and Ed Sullivan, soon became household names.

The tabloid wars of the twenties are a subject for another (long, lively) book. Suffice it to say that, one after another, a cascade of nearly unbelievable stories unfurled in these years, as flappers and swells and groundlings and gangsters all indulged in behavior that their Victorian parents found appalling, and the presses rolled. In 1922, there was the Hall-Mills case, in which an Episcopal priest and his mistress were murdered in Somerset, New Jersey, their torn-up love letters arrayed across the corpses. (The trial put the brand-new *Daily Mirror* on the map.) In 1924 came the Leopold and Loeb "thrill killing," the abduction and murder of a young boy by two wealthy Chicago college students. Two years after that, the less bloody story of Frances "Peaches" Heenan and her millionaire husband, Edward "Daddy" Browning, titillated New York. He was fifty-one, and he met her at a sorority mixer when she was fifteen. They married weeks later, and divorced six months after that. Daddy said Peaches was a gold digger; Peaches said Daddy was a pervert; and all three tabloids covered the subsequent alimony trial gleefully. The coverage turned, in part, on a photograph of the couple in Atlantic City, he in a high, hard collar and three-piece suit, she in a bathing suit that revealed her thighs.

The perfect tabloid story, though, came along in 1927. Ruth Snyder, a Queens housewife, was having an affair with (the papers loved to point out this detail) a married corset salesman named Henry Judd Gray. The two conspired to knock off her husband. Gray clubbed him to death with a window-sash weight, and the lovers arranged a fake burglary as a cover-up. The two were caught and tried, amid daily front-page coverage, and both were convicted and received death sentences. Ruth Snyder was to be the first woman executed at Sing Sing in nearly three decades.

Then, as now, picture-taking in the death chamber was not permitted. That did not stop the *Daily News*. Tom Howard, a *Chicago Tribune* photographer who would be unfamiliar to the prison staff, was sent on loan to New York to cover the execution. He strapped a tiny camera to his ankle and loaded it with a single frame of film. At the moment the alternating current surged through Ruth Snyder, Howard raised his pant cuff an inch or so and tripped the shutter with a cable he'd run up through his suit to his hand. The next day, the photograph, its odd low angle adding drama and its smeary blur intimating the spasm of the electrocution, ran on the front page of the *Daily News*, under an enormous boldface headline: DEAD! The caption pointed out the wheeled table, right next to the electric chair, onto which the body of Ruth Snyder was to be placed en route to her seemingly unnecessary autopsy.

The gambit was incredibly tasteless. It was also a great tale of derring-do, with the newspaper photographer portrayed as a brash, anything-to-get-the-story hero. Today, the scheme by which the photo was made is better remembered than the actual Snyder case, and the Hollywood version of the murder, Billy Wilder's *Double Indemnity*, is most famous of all.

People of all classes rolled their eyes at all this seamy stuff. They also consumed the newspapers that reported it, eagerly, avidly, and in great numbers. The tabloids were built for the Sweeneys, but the Stuyvesants were sneaking them into their town houses as well. Barely two years after the *Daily News* got going, well before Ruth Snyder even met her corset salesman, Arthur Fellig saw what was coming. Bored with shooting passport photos, yearning for a faster, sexier life, one that would impress girls and maybe make him famous, he wanted a piece of this business. He quit the Seaman Studio job in 1921 and got a job on a newspaper.

To be sure, he had to start at the bottom, so far down the ladder that he left
that first job out of his autobiography. It was in the darkrooms of the
New York Times, an institution that still didn't go for much on-the-spot
photojournalism but was already well established as the Paper of
Record, the most authoritative in America. (Its new subsidiary Wide
World Photos supplied pictures to many other outlets.) At work every
day on the ninth floor of 229 West Forty-Third Street, just off the paper's
namesake Times Square, Fellig did the menial labor of drying freshly
processed negatives and prints, acting quickly as news broke. That was
where he first became "Squeegee Boy," picking up the first ghost of the
name that would become "Weegee the Famous."

He stayed a few years, gathering proficiency, during which he applied
for a job as a photo printer at the New York *World* that he did not get.
(The interviewer asked him to make some prints on an unfamiliar type
of photo paper, baffling him.) He did a quick turn at an agency called
Keystone and then, around 1924, moved to another darkroom job, at
Acme Newspictures. Acme (which, after a fashion, still exists, having been
folded into United Press, then United Press International, then the
Corbis Images service, and recently a group called Visual China), a photo
agency owned by the Scripps-Howard newspaper chain, had opened the
previous year. The chief was a Texan named Robert Dorman, an early
and swashbuckling pioneer of photojournalism who had followed Pancho Villa during the Mexican Revolution, in part by stealthily hitching
a railcar full of journalists to Villa's troop train. He ran Acme from its

offices at 461 Eighth Avenue, a stolid structure across from Penn Station that was filled with press and publishing companies and called the Printing Crafts Building.

Much like Weegee himself, Acme was trying to get established at the dawn of this new image-driven news business, and one way to do that was to have men with cameras anywhere and everywhere it could. Within a few years, it had bureaus not only in Chicago and Los Angeles but also in Cleveland and other smaller cities. Its job was to anticipate news as well as cover it, putting photographers in the right place at the right time and then getting the film back fast however it could. (Acme even maintained a fleet of homing pigeons that could fly film from Ebbets Field in Brooklyn to the offices in Manhattan on deadline. They only rarely got lost.) Harold Blumenfeld, Acme's editor, spent a large part of his workday reading dozens of newspapers and fishing for subjects and ideas. No photographer got a credit; pictures supplied to the Scripps-Howard newspapers, and to other unaffiliated papers that bought them, were attributed in print simply to "Acme." Of the hundreds, maybe thousands, of photographers who worked for this service, few are known today by name. Staff work was heavily augmented by that of freelances and stringers, many of them far from New York. When a reporter from *Popular Photography* visited the Acme newsroom a few years later, Dorman was in the process of arranging for coverage in Peru and Romania as well as in Brooklyn.

At Acme, Fellig was once again in the darkrooms, and once his fellow gnomes discovered he'd been a squeegee boy at the *Times*, they teased him about it. Here, though, he was doing the printing himself, or at least he was supposed to be. Blumenfeld later recalled that Fellig was almost useless when he first arrived. He'd done contact printing, the simplest way of making a photo from a negative, at the passport house; here, he had to use an enlarger to produce seven-by-nine glossies, and in the beginning he had no idea how this contraption worked, or even how to put a negative into its holder. But his colleagues enjoyed having him in the office—Blumenfeld describes Fellig, in these early years, as "humble and likeable"—and he was quick to catch on. He got twenty-five dollars a week at the start, a low but not poverty-level salary.

He quickly became the best printer in the place, and the "Squeegee Boy" taunts soon gave way to a term of jokey respect: "Mr. Squeegee." In the evenings, as he waited for work to come in, he would while away the time playing his violin. "The scratchings and squealings coming from the darkroom after hours," Blumenfeld remembered, "were proof that music was not his bag." Printing photos was, though. At peak news times, Fellig's darkroom could produce a thousand prints a day. During slack times, when he wasn't torturing his colleagues with the bow, he'd fool around in the way so many technicians have, making joke photos: double- and triple-exposure gags. He never lost that deftness and felicity with an enlarger and printing easel. It is no coincidence that both the night photography on which he made his reputation and the photographic invention he explored in the back half of his career required unusual levels of darkroom skill.

Blumenfeld also later recalled that Fellig was a soft touch. When a colleague with a family really needed money, Fellig would lend him the last couple of dollars out of his pocket and forgo his own bed for a few days. Other times, he'd have a bad run in the end-of-week craps game himself ("I think some of the boys had educated dice") and would have to scrounge up a living. He claimed that he'd bring girls up to the darkroom to impress them, and the news business was glamorous enough—even at this fume-filled, hypo-stained end of it—that maybe this worked for him once in a while.

When he had enough money, he stayed in a ten-dollar-a-month furnished room at a hotel called the Coburg, half a block away on West Thirty-Fourth Street. During the bad stretches, when the landlord padlocked his room for nonpayment, he tried living in the Acme darkroom, quietly coming back in after the staff had left and curling up on a shelf to sleep. Risking a night at Acme was a better bet than sleeping on a bench in Penn Station or outside in Bryant Park, where he'd eventually be awakened by a rap from a cop's nightstick on the sole of his shoe. The photo-engravers at Acme had a stove on which to heat their chemicals, and he'd use it to warm up canned baked beans and make coffee. When his darkroom colleagues arrived early, they'd quietly wake him up, and he'd duck down to the Automat, grab breakfast, and then pretend to arrive at the offices for the day's work. It was one of those men, Charles Liotta, who claimed for the rest of his life to have given Fellig the name "Weegee," after the weird grinning caricature that appears on the upper-left-hand corner of the Ouija board.

At Acme, beating the other services to a story was vital, and the agency's young men turned that competition into gladiatorial sport. Whenever news was breaking in New York, reporters and photographers piled out into the city and made their way to the event in question. Still, getting a cameraman there was only the first step. The film had to be physically brought to the office and then processed, and that took an irreducible amount of time—unless, of course, you did both things at once, in which case any conveyance would do.

"I think my crowning achievement," Fellig later said, "was to develop negatives in the subway. Develop and fix 'em." It was after a World Series game. He'd raced to the train after the pictures were taken, slipped the subway conductor a buck to look the other way, and "locked myself in the motorman's booth. Of course, I had all my bottles with me, developer and hypo, and I started my laboratory work, and by the time we reached downtown, I was all through. And of course the competition could never figure out how I always got the negatives developed first." He used his shirt as a towel to mop up the splattered chemistry.

Sometimes that race did not end in a newsroom. In 1924, AT&T introduced a commercial service called Wirephoto, based on an early form of the fax machine, which allowed a picture to be transmitted over phone lines. Though you wouldn't get a fine-art image at the other end, the shot would be good enough to be publishable as a newspaper halftone. Suddenly, a hot news photo did not have to be airmailed or sent by train; it could go across the country in minutes. (Though not *a* minute; at first, it took an hour to transmit a Wirephoto, when the balky system worked at all. It was an expensive technology, reserved for big events.) Still, the elaborate equipment required to send a Wirephoto was not found in any newsroom. It was only at AT&T's Long Lines building, on Walker Street.

"Whoever got to the telephone company with the glass film on Walker Street," Fellig said, "got on the air first and beat the whole country. Mind you, in them days, there were no planes flying at night or anything like that. So here's what would happen. At a big prizefight, say at the Polo Grounds, I would arrive in an ambulance. And I had the ambulance fitted out as a darkroom . . . As we would arrive, you'd hear a lot of snide remarks: 'Is this for the champ?' and all that business. Anyway, the idea was, I would get the first knockout. A messenger would give it to me. I'd lock myself in the ambulance, develop it, run out on Walker Street, go up to the telephone company, and usually I was there first. And Acme would get a scoop on the country." After the police got wise to the ambulance scheme, Fellig switched to a rigged-up taxicab darkroom, with its backseat windows blacked out.

As valuable as he was to Acme, he wasn't supposed to be sleeping in the office, and eventually he got caught. Early on the morning of September 3, 1925, the USS *Shenandoah*, a dirigible from the U.S. Navy's fleet, broke apart in midair and crashed in the small town of Ava, Ohio. It was 5:30 a.m., and the announcement went out over the United Press wire, hitting New York just after daybreak. Weegee was awakened by the news ticker, and had to choose: *Do I try to do the right thing for the agency and call the boss, saying, "We'd better get to work on this"? Or do I step out and pretend I wasn't here?* "I decided," he said, that "the story is above everything else," and he picked up the phone, called in staff, revved up the stringers in Ohio, and made arrangements for negatives to be whisked to New York by train. (Wirephoto had not made its way to rural Ohio yet.)

Of course, Dorman called him in shortly thereafter and asked him what he had been doing in the office at that hour, and Weegee had to cop to his sleeping arrangement. "Get yourself a room," Dorman told him. It's a fun story, one in which Arthur Fellig turns himself into a small-scale hero. But it also conveys how much he loved the rattle and hum of the business, where news does not stop, certainly not just because the sun goes down and everyone else goes home. Getting on a great story was as important to him as having a bed.

Besides, his managers knew that his single-mindedness had an upside. As is still true at newspapers and magazines, junior researchers and photo editors often get the smaller assignments that crop up between the big ones, and Acme was so ravenous that an ambitious darkroom assistant was useful for the overflow jobs. Fellig was, really, Acme's on-call night man. A local story would break in the very early morning, and an editor at one of the afternoon papers—say, the *New York World-Telegram*, merged into existence in 1931—would get wind of it and call an Acme editor at home. He in turn would call Fellig, who would roll out of bed (or off his shelf), grab his camera, go shoot the assignment, and then come into the office or, if time was short, use the *World-Telegram*'s darkroom. (Afternoon papers, in those days, had a first-edition deadline of around 9:30 in the morning, so that printed newspapers would be on the street at around 1:00 p.m.) It was cheaper and easier to ask a freelance than it was to wake up one of the paper's own photographers, who would have to be paid overtime. Fellig got five dollars per photo, or thereabouts.

"I was scared stiff," he later admitted, when speaking of the first times he went out, but the desire to get the picture outweighed his shyness. He made it a habit to leave the office on his lunch hour and just shoot people in the neighborhood, sometimes on the fly, sometimes asking first. It was painful for him, he said later, when expressing empathy for other young photographers—"I know you're afraid to do it at first"—but he also knew that it was the only way he'd conquer himself. "You have to do it," he explained. "You can't be a nice Nellie and do photography."

He could call himself a professional now, and he did. In July 1925, a syndicated columnist named James W. Dean, who happened to also be the president of Acme, printed a jokey little anecdote about New York life that Fellig had submitted. "Carrying or owning firearms without permit is a grave offense in the state of New York," Dean wrote, "but on the East Side guns are bootlegged as freely as hooch. Artur [sic] Fellig, a photographer, tells me that while he was walking along Third avenue the other night a gorilla approached him and asked him if he needed a gun, saying he would rent him one for a dollar a day." By "gorilla," he meant a tough guy, and readers of the day knew that "Third Avenue" was shorthand for the strip of seedy saloons under the elevated train and the rough customers who frequented them. Most of all, Fellig got called "a photographer" in print by someone other than himself. He and Dean were apparently chatty enough that another (less interesting) anecdote popped up in the column that October, about Fellig's discovery that his photography-supply store was suddenly selling radios.

In September 1927, Fellig was a part of the enormous press undertaking to cover the Jack Dempsey–Gene Tunney championship fight. The bout was in Chicago, and to get photos to New York the next day, Acme "had a special train," he said. "It was parked right around wherever the Dempsey-Tunney fight was. And I was in the train. I was there for twenty-four hours. I was afraid of sabotage from the other syndicates. So as soon as the fight was over, messengers rushed the negatives. I developed and printed 'em, had them in the enlarger. And the *Tribune*, the *Herald Tribune*, had artists—they made the layout. That meant . . . when we reached New York, they had the whole layout on the fight, with all the artwork and everything else." Similarly, when a picture story had to be rushed from Washington, Fellig would rig up a darkroom on an airplane so he'd have prints ready to go by the time he landed in New York.

Because the pictures he was making in the 1920s and early 1930s all went into Acme's river of output without his name attached, we'll never know what most of them were. Hundreds of Weegee's photographs are out there, in newspaper morgues and in the form of microfilmed half-tones, unlikely ever to be identified. The earliest photo that can plausibly be identified as his accompanies a pretty square story, a roundup of forgotten World War I heroes, and it shows a man named Michael Sacina, then working in a barbershop.

But the next photo that's definitively his is a little odder and some-what mysterious. It's a portrait of a beauty contestant wearing a sash read-ing MISS AMERICA 1931. She's just standing there, slightly awkward, not posing in any particularly interesting way; Fellig had his camera on a tripod, so he wasn't moving, either. (We know the photo is his work because a colleague also snapped a portrait of Fellig making the picture.) She appears in a white swimsuit and a tiara, and she's smiling.

So what's the mystery? For one thing, there was no Miss America crowned in 1931. The pageant skipped a few years owing to the Depres-sion. Moreover, the young woman is African American, and the Miss America contest was whites-only until nearly forty years later. It turns out that this benign image conceals not a pleasant event but a crime. There was indeed a beauty contest held that year, at the end of August, called the Miss Colored America pageant. Thirty-one contestants, including this young woman—her name was Billy Bow, and she had come up from Key West to compete—convened at the Savoy Ballroom in Harlem. This was apparently a warm-up, perhaps a qualifying event, for a bigger contest at another Harlem venue, the Rockland Palace, a week later. But that event was postponed, and ultimately never held: it turns out that the whole thing had been a scam conducted by a rogue police officer, who'd scheduled the event, collected entry fees, sold tickets, and found sponsors and then skedaddled with the cash. He was arrested a few weeks later.

Even without the underlayment of criminal activity, this photo is sur-prisingly reflective of much of the next thirty-five years of Weegee's life and career. He is shooting a cheesecake picture, something he did often

The first known picture of Weegee at work: photographing a contestant in the Miss Colored America pageant in the summer of 1931.

and enthusiastically. He's mugging for the camera, and maybe leering, two habits for which he would be widely known. He needs a haircut, and his suit is a disaster, dirty and worn and not just rumpled but crumpled. His pockets are bulging, probably with camera accessories. Nearly every subsequent story of an encounter with him would begin with an affectionate retelling of his slovenliness, and it's already on full display here.

In that picture, and in this early part of his career, Fellig was using a German-made camera called an ICA Trix, bought on time for five dollars a week, he said. In the early thirties, though, as he began to sell his pictures, he moved up to the instrument with which he would be indelibly identified: a camera called the Speed Graphic. The vast majority of newsmen used one. That little press camera pictured in the *Daily News* logo was modeled on it. Manufactured by a company called Graflex, in

Rochester, New York, it was tough as anything, built mostly from machined aluminum and steel, with a boxy leather-wrapped wooden shell into which the lens and bellows folded. Open or closed, it could survive a drop onto pavement or a bump from the sharp elbow of a rival photographer. Other manufacturers, notably one called Burke & James, made similar models—the generic term was *press camera*—but from the 1920s into the 1960s, the Speed Graphic dominated American newspaper work. It was as ubiquitous in its time as Canon and Nikon digital cameras are today.

A Speed Graphic, in its basic form, did not take rolls of film. Rather, it was loaded one shot a time, with individual four-by-five-inch glass plates or (later) film sheets in metal or wooden holders. Once you pressed the shutter, you had to close up that holder with a sheet-metal slide, pull the holder from the camera, and replace it with a fresh one. This clumsy and slow arrangement, though, was balanced by great flexibility when it came to actually taking a picture. The camera had two shutters, making possible different kinds of effects; it could be used with many different lenses, and they could be tilted and adjusted to correct for optical oddities (or, occasionally, to produce them). You could do a lot with a Speed Graphic, and professionals learned to overcome its limitations, deftly slipping film holders in and out fast, like casino dealers shuffling decks.

The Speed Graphic was also big and obvious, which was not necessarily a bad thing. As Weegee later counseled new photographers, it was useful to carry equipment that signaled "press." Walk up to a crime scene with a little amateur camera and you'd look like a tourist. Walk up with a Speed Graphic, he explained, and "the cops will assume that you belong on the scene and will let you get behind police lines," whether you carried a press card or not. It was a marker of professional respectability (if there was such a thing when it came to newspapermen). Many years later, Weegee's first book proclaimed the Speed Graphic "his love"—although, when the money was right, he'd cheat on it with other photo gear. He got his first Speed Graphic secondhand.

In early 1929, a writer named Herbert Corey spent a night watching Fellig at work out in the city. Corey was a well-established newspaperman of the previous generation, an Ohioan who'd gone to New York to write and then became a success covering the First World War in

Europe. Now he had returned and was writing a hayseed-in-the-big-city column and selling it back to papers in Middle America. The column was advertised as a "feature of throbbing scenes and up-to-the-minute events from the 'sidewalks of New York,'" and Corey, the ads said, was known for his "inimitable brilliancy of word pictures." Some papers called the column "About New York's Days and Nights"; others, "Manhattan Days and Nights"; and Corey was sometimes called "the Anecdote Man."

Well, Arthur Fellig was an anecdote-manufacturing machine, and he showed Corey a good time, at a "gabfest" (an actual event, more or less a speechifying contest) and a few illegal bars. Weegee was in print, under his pseudonym, at last.

> Weegee is a newspaper photographer. It might be urged that newspaper photographers must be slightly cracked or they would not follow such a furious occupation, but that might only be the venom of one who is associated with a rival line. In any case, the things that happened might have been experienced by any one else. Most of them anyhow.
>
> Weegee took his camera and rambled down to the recent gabfest . . . when he got into conversation with a slender, blonde, pretty woman. After a time Weegee said:
> "My throat aches, I'm so thirsty."
> "Me, too," said the pretty woman.
>
> They went on a round of speakeasies. This, however, was no low drinking tour, but an enjoyable course in higher philosophy in which drink figured only as a motor forcer. The pretty woman knew more speakeasies than Weegee did. Now and then the doors did not open, or a suspicious eye told them through a peep-hole to go away, but as a rule they were admitted and furnished with restoratives.

The two talk a bit about philosophy, or at least what passes for it. She gets drunk and slips under the table; he splashes some water on her face to revive her. She reveals that she's a recent widow and goes off on a digression about communication with the dead. And then:

In the next speakeasy, as they discussed philosophy, a horrid cry was heard. A young girl had attempted suicide by drinking iodine.

Weegee[,] who is familiar with casualty through his occupation, called the nearest hospital, and in his capacity as a newspaper photographer rode in the ambulance, and the pretty woman pursued in a taxicab.

In the receiving ward of the hospital first aid was being given the girl when Weegee waked to a recognition of his duty.

"She might have been somebody important," he explained, "and so I took a flashlight."

By which he means not the one you'd carry in a blackout but a flash-powder photographer's lamp, the kind he'd learned to use at Duckett & Adler, the kind that routinely burned his hands.

Nothing annoys hospital authorities more than to have a flashlight go bang just as they are resuscitating a dying woman. They seized Weegee by the neck.

They had to let him go, however, because his flashlight had set fire to the receiving ward. Weegee explains that flashlights are unreliable that way. You never can tell just what they're going to do. While the interns and the policeman were extinguishing the flames he slipped the plate-holder out of his camera and slipped another in. The Fire Demon—Upper case F and D—having been baffled, the officials returned to Weegee's neck.

"Listen," said he, "I know now I done wrong. I should not have banged away with that flash in a hospital. Just to show you my heart is right, I'll smash that plate." So he smashed a plate.

The other plate, when developed at the office, showed a lovely dying girl, an infuriated intern, some nurses and a policeman who seemed mostly eyeballs.

It was now daylight and the pretty lady took Weegee to his office in her taxicab and went on home. Nothing has been heard from her since. Not even philosophically.

I ask you. Could a nutty sequence like that happen anywhere except in New York?

You could argue over the answer to that last question. You could also say, pretty assuredly, that all this could not have happened in one night, and that whatever did occur has been embellished. Yet although it's likely an embroidered composite of many evenings, one thing is unmistakable. Even when he had been chasing a girl all night, Fellig, having become Weegee, couldn't resist a good story and a potential payday. He pretended to destroy his negative, to get the hospital staff off his back; then he spirited the good one off to Acme and sold it. And then, most typical of all, he became the smart-aleck hero of a story about himself that he planted in the press. There are forty years' worth of tales about Weegee's nights that follow this one, and just about every one follows some version of that template.

Except that few of them include the "flashlight," which was becoming obsolete. In 1925, a German named Paul Vierkötter patented the first flashbulb: a hollow glass ball containing bits of magnesium metal that would flare brightly when hooked up to a battery. About five years later, General Electric started selling improved flashbulbs in the United States under the name Sashalite. They were expensive and bulky, as big as today's standard light bulbs, and they could be used only once. But they also removed the clumsiness and risk of flash powder from the photojournalist's life. No more measuring out low-grade explosives that could set a hospital emergency room on fire. Night pictures could be made fast, and the photographer could then move on to the next thing. Arthur Fellig, a man who worked late and saw photojournalists on the job, knew this was significant. More than thirty years later, he recalled seeing the first GE bulbs come through Acme's office, and described the moment almost with reverence, as if he'd seen the future.

By the early thirties, Brownsville, Brooklyn, was the home base of one of the century's most effective crime organizations. It had been started about a decade earlier, on the Lower East Side, by a couple of *shtarkers* named Meyer Lansky and Benjamin (Bugsy) Siegel, who shook down shopkeepers for protection money. Soon their reach and ambition grew, and in 1929 they struck a deal with other similar racketeers—Al Capone, in Chicago, and Charles (Lucky) Luciano, in New York, were probably the most famous of them—to form a network. In the press, it became known as the National Crime Syndicate, an umbrella organization that adjudicated turf wars among its component groups. The Syndicate was mostly a bootlegging outfit, at least until the end of Prohibition in 1933, but it also got into gambling, loan-sharking, and prostitution. Those tough businesses required enforcement, and a newspaperman named Harry Feeney gave that enforcement arm its own name, owing to its formal structure and hierarchy: Murder Incorporated. Its hit men killed often and efficiently, and its bosses became tabloid celebrities.

There was (and is) a perverse romance to this world, and Weegee, who knew its neighborhoods and behaviors well, gleefully glommed on to it. "They used to have a garage in Brooklyn—they used to practice on targets," he recalled later in life. The gang's recruiters, he added, "used to go around looking for nice clean-cut junior-executive types." When Weegee had weekend plans, he said, "I sent back word to the 'boys' to go easy on the shootings . . . on weekends unless such were absolutely necessary." Occasionally he'd imply that he was briefed on the location of killings before they happened. Eventually, he said, the cops and crooks started calling him "the official photographer for Murder Incorporated."

Of course, there was no such job, and gangsters took no such direction. Especially when they're arrested, criminals don't actually want their business aired in the papers, no matter how sharply they dress, and they certainly don't book a newspaper photographer to be there. Fellig was simply riding the coattails of their fame. Still, he did encounter these guys regularly—occasionally the high-level criminals, more often the foot soldiers—and over the next decade he photographed a lot of them, sometimes when they were dead, more often when they were under arrest. "When there isn't much doing," he said, "I take a walk with my camera, and just follow a guy with a pearl-gray hat." He hoped, he said, to catch a murderer in the act. "As long as they're gonna do it anyway." Did it ever happen? "Not a murder, no . . . But I have great hopes." (Never fulfilled.)

The *News* and the *Mirror*, especially, covered this scene with enthusiasm, their business only somewhat dented by the Depression. In the early thirties, nearly a quarter of the *Daily News*'s editorial space was devoted to crime, a sizable portion of that being organized crime. The paper's writers and deskmen were establishing the hard-boiled lingo that we still associate with this time and place—terms such as *gun moll, gang slaying,* and *triggerman.* (Hollywood picked it all up, too, beginning in 1931 with the Edward G. Robinson hit *Little Caesar* and its famous line "Mother of mercy, is this the end of Rico?") The *News*'s coverage in June 1930 of Jake Lingle, a Chicago crime reporter who had been shot by a member of Al Capone's gang, depended heavily on a photo that could easily be mistaken for one of Weegee's better pictures. It shows Lingle facedown in a pedestrian tunnel near the Randolph Street train station, and it appeared in the *News* for five days in a row. Lingle's story got even juicier after the public learned that he had been on the take, augmenting his three-thousand-dollar annual newspaper salary with nearly sixty thousand dollars a year from Capone and acting as middleman between the underworld boss and the Chicago police commissioner.

When asked about a particular gangster, Weegee was known to joke that he and the man in question had "a shooting acquaintance." (Bullets and pictures both.) That kind of familiarity extended to Dutch Schultz, who was the man to cover in New York. Schultz, whose birth name was

Arthur Flegenheimer, was one of the principal figures in Murder Inc., although he eventually fell out of favor with his partners for too aggressively campaigning to have Thomas Dewey, Manhattan's district attorney, bumped off. Schultz was notably brutal, and (atypically) a slobby dresser. "Looked like an awful dope, dead or alive," Weegee recalled after the gangster's inevitable end.

In June 1931, Schultz was picked up just inside an entrance to Central Park for gun possession and assault, after a confrontation with two policemen outside the Fifth Avenue apartment where he was staying. Weegee made it uptown to the East 104th Street station house as Schultz was brought in for booking and found the gangster there begging for something to calm his nerves. "He asked me for an aspirin, so I gave him two," Weegee said, and he offered Schultz a smoke as well. A picture (likely but not definitively by Weegee) of Schultz as he's questioned by detectives appeared in the next day's *Post*, and other photographs from the arraignment went to the AP. "From then on," Weegee said, "we were friends." Maybe "friends" was pushing it, but even a passing familiarity with a high-profile criminal would have been a valuable thing for a news photographer. All Fellig needed, the next time Schultz came through a police station, was a moment when the gangster recognized him and paused without covering his face with his coat. A loose, hey-good-to-see-you-again acquaintanceship would provide that.

Weegee was also around to make a portrait when the police brought in Vincent Coll that October. "Mad Dog" Coll had been a Schultz deputy, a kidnapper and hit man known for his great wardrobe and particular viciousness. In 1930 he broke with Schultz, forming his own gang. Over the next year, the two groups burst into open warfare. Coll was arrested in late 1931 for a kidnapping, and Weegee caught him at the police station, faultlessly dapper down to his Art Deco belt buckle, as he awaited booking. Coll got off that charge, but a year later he was dead, after Schultz's guys put fifteen rounds in him as he made a call from a phone booth at the back of a candy store on West Twenty-Third Street. Weegee didn't get there fast enough to photograph the corpse, but he did, soon afterward, make a spooky picture of an unnamed observer peering at the location. You can just make out the bullet holes in the folded door of the booth. *If I can't get the moment*, Weegee must have reasoned, *I can at least get the atmosphere.* "Where Coll was bumped off in a phone booth," he wrote in the margin of one print.

He was already straining to outdo his colleagues, even when he wasn't supposed to. The day the George Washington Bridge opened in October 1931, Fellig was there as a messenger, to run the freshly shot negatives back to the darkroom. Standing around the bridge with little to do, chafing at his joyless role, he had the idea of getting up to the top of the towers, which, oddly enough, no other photographer had arranged to do. "I go up to where it looked like there might be an entrance," he said. "There was a worker man there. I says, 'How can I walk up?' He says, 'We have an elevator.' I says, 'Do you mind taking me up?' He says you have to have permission. I says, 'Where do you get permission?' 'Department of Plans and Structures, tomorrow.' I says, 'Listen, bud, I have a deadline to meet.' I gave him what looked like a big roll of bills—three one-dollar bills. And he took me up in the elevator. I made the shot, looking towards Jersey, one to New York." The picture ended up on the front page of the *Herald Tribune*, showing up the rest of Acme's people. "I submitted a bill to Acme. Three bucks, [plus] a torn overcoat—I'd ripped my overcoat a little bit. Good chance for me to get a new coat." Acme paid it.

Fellig's reputation within the agency was good enough that, in the summer of 1932, he got himself an out-of-town assignment. The summer Olympic Games were coming to Los Angeles, only the second time they'd been held in the United States. Acme's West Coast bureau in this era was essentially the home studio of George Watson, a member of what would eventually become a four-generation family of photographer-cinematographer-actors. The Watsons, collectively, made pictures of just about everything of note in twentieth-century Los Angeles, from Charlie Chaplin to the Northridge earthquake, becoming prominent enough to receive, sixty-seven years later, a star on the Hollywood Walk of Fame. Just before the Olympics, George Watson had been covering the murder trial of Winnie Ruth Judd, who had arrived in L.A.'s Union Station with a trunk that was soon discovered to contain a corpse.

Watson's photo lab needed extra hands for the Games, and Fellig, experienced enough to jump in without any extra training, was the guy Acme sent out. Seeing it as an opportunity to get a look at a little bit of Middle America, Fellig told Harold Blumenfeld that he wanted to go by bus, a slower route than the train, one that would let him meet people. He'd never had money to travel, unless you count the steerage trip from Zolochev or those back-and-forth darkroom runs to Chicago and Washington. A solo business trip, even on a Greyhound, must have seemed glamorous to him. Especially to Hollywood: since his days playing the violin in silent-film theaters, Fellig had been a voracious moviegoer, and now he was headed to the source.

The Watsons were a busy crew, with their own interests in crime photography: lineups, court cases, everyday police station stuff. Even if Weegee wasn't out shooting the Judd murder trial, he saw up close how the job was done. Yet he felt a certain level of anxiety in Los Angeles, perhaps because he was so far from his usual milieu. His first night in town, something—he never said what it was—rattled him, and he spent the rest of the trip with a mild case of paranoia, switching to a different hotel each day. And he ran up against the same frustrations he'd had in New York. "My job was to stay in the darkroom from beginning to end," he later recalled in an interview. "So if I wanted to see the Olympic Games, during lunch hour I'd go to the movie theater and see it on the newsreel." At least, the interviewer noted, you were getting the pictures of all the athletes. "Oh, yeah," Weegee replied acidly. "Jumping in the water, and jumping over hurdles. And I was jumping the prints into the developer, hypo, and water."

He may have had his grumbles, but there exist several gag photographs of Fellig from that trip, and they show a man having a good time. In one, he's in George Watson's office, standing over the Acme Teletype. He's wearing a hat and a uniform jacket with an Olympics logo badge reading MESSENGER. The jacket is borrowed and too small, not nearly buttoning across his belly, and he's cinched it with a wide belt, giving the whole scene a goofy costume-party vibe, capped off with a smirk on his face. You can imagine Fellig, a moment later, giving a joke salute and clicking his heels like a military attaché, then rolling his eyes like Groucho Marx. A cigar dangling from his mouth adds to the irreverence. In another picture, he and Watson are clowning around, Fellig posing as Watson pretends to beat him up. And in a third, staff members are arrayed around the office, most holding cameras, one posed with a bandage around his head, a couple pretending to doze off—and Arthur Fellig, standing in the back, in a suit and tie, is blowing into a trumpet, playing reveille, waking

A playful composite of photos from the 1932 summer Olympic Games in Los Angeles.

the troops exhausted by the relentless Olympics coverage. A souvenir program from the Games is stuffed into the horn's music rack.

The most telling artifact of Fellig's Los Angeles trip, though, is a print he almost surely made himself. He took that first "messenger" photo and put it in an oval vignette at the center of a sheet of photo paper, surrounded by floating images of American athletes at the Games, as well as an American flag and a striped banner with the Olympic rings at top. "Weegee Acme & America are always first," he wrote across the bottom corner, in ink.

Already, he was comfortably at play in the darkroom, putting six images on one sheet of paper, their borders softened, the way one might print a group of bridesmaids. In this screwball assemblage, he was also puffing himself up, equating his errand-running and assignment-cadging with the elite performance of Ivan Fuqua, whose team had just broken the world record in the 400-meter relay. It's the kind of tableau a schoolkid with big dreams would make. Arthur Fellig was an immature thirty-three, still a striver, still more Arthur than Weegee. In costume, though, he was already acting a part, if a subservient one. And Weegee, Acme, and America were first in his mind. In that order.

That same summer, in New York before and after the Games, he also found himself at least one eccentric outlet: weekend visits to a nudist colony. It was not quite as outlandish an activity as it may sound. Spending your time unclothed was enjoying a little vogue in sophisticated circles in the early thirties; *Nachtkultur*, some called it, because it was an import from northern Europe. The idea was that fresh air, exercise, vitamins, and a lack of sexual shame were the way to live life to its fullest. Believers were evangelistic about it, including Bernarr Macfadden, the man who'd started the *Evening Graphic*, and who was now producing a bunch of nudism-friendly magazines devoted to bodybuilding and physical culture. Fellig, a shy, sexually frustrated young man, was surely drawn to this world for the healthy-looking naked girls as well as its air of sophistication. In 1932, he joined a group that weekended at a nudist camp in New Jersey, just over the George Washington Bridge. (Most likely it was Sky Farm, established that year in Basking Ridge, a successful early nudist resort that is still in operation.) He was, he said, the group's official photographer and also its photography teacher, coaching the hobbyists at the camp. In the cold months, the group convened in the city, renting a gym with a swimming pool in the basement of a theater at 2561 Broadway, on the corner of Ninety-Sixth Street. That continued until a raid shut down those sessions in the spring of 1934.

He was, it was clear, growing weary of the Acme job. Blumenfeld later explained that Fellig was taking enough of those little side assignments that he was beginning to cut into the Acme photographers' work, and "he often outshot them on routine and planned stories." His willingness to work late-night and early-morning hours created envy when those photos got good play. "Professional photographers from newspapers and wire services," Blumenfeld said, "resented him." Fellig was making a passable living, enough to feed himself (and, he said, drop by the local whorehouses regularly; "a successful day would be one white girl and one black girl"), and was beginning to be known to photo editors beyond the Acme offices. Although he was still shy, he had the innate hustle for which he'd be known later on, and his introversion did not mean a lack of intensity.

In fact, that solitary quality positioned him especially well for the night-crawling aspects of the job. Nicholas Pileggi, the legendary mob reporter who got to know Weegee some years later while working for the Associated Press, explains it this way: "Reporters worked an eight-hour day, and you got in at 4:00 and worked till midnight, and by 11:30 you were packing it in. All the other photographers at the time were not freelance—all were working for newspapers. They had regular scheduled work hours, two days off a week; sometimes they had vacations with their wives. He, Weegee, didn't have to deal with any of that."

The Depression was continuing, too, and although the tabloid press was hardly in trouble, it had receded somewhat from its twenties strength. The *Evening Graphic* went out of business in 1932, hammered by libel suits and further hurt by the loss of its major asset, the columnist Walter Winchell, to Hearst. The *Daily Mirror*, even with Winchell and the two hundred thousand readers he was said to have brought over, had also seen its circulation dip. Most of the papers did not have night photographers out in the streets, and Arthur Fellig smelled an entrepreneurial opportunity. He couldn't get a permanent role at Acme, but he was selling enough pictures that he thought he could make a living. "Success with his night-prowling photos," Blumenfeld said, "overtook his darkroom duties, and there was an amicable parting of his employment . . . He devoted all of his time to free lancing." Just as he had at Duckett & Adler, and again at the passport studio, Fellig had made the bold choice: rather than work a straight job and accept some ease in his life, he was going to do what he wanted and grab for the brass ring. Around the end of 1934, he quit Acme, and he never really had a straight job again. "I had to have two straight whiskeys—Seagram's—before I could tell the boss," he said.

It was a gamble, and he was not guaranteed a living. "I took my little camera," he said, recalling this time, "and I started hanging around police headquarters, at the Teletype desk, and took pictures. I had no business there, because you're supposed to have a police or press card." What he did have was the Speed Graphic, and little more. "I did it for two years, on my nerve." Simply carrying a press camera allowed him to accompany the herd of staff photographers through a police line without looking like a rube. He had his wits, and news sense cultivated over the past decade that told him what Acme and the newspapers wanted. And most of all he was always, always there.

"There" was usually the block-long police headquarters building at 240 Centre Street in Lower Manhattan. It had been built in 1909, and looked a little like one of the Parisian *hôtels* of the Haussmann era, with a big green copper dome on top, seventy-five jail cells below, and hundreds of cops within. A small support system of businesses clustered around it, catering to police, reporters, lawyers, and anyone else doing work there. Moran's, a luncheonette on the corner, cashed paychecks and sold coffee. Across the way, on Grand Street, a slightly dandied-up saloon called the Headquarters Tavern (LUNCH ALL DAY) kept officers in good pork chops and whiskey, though it probably wasn't all that hard to find a bottle at someone's desk. There's a story, likely apocryphal, that the Headquarters Tavern and the police headquarters were linked by a tunnel to ease the wobbly trip back from the bar.*

The rear entrance of 240 Centre Street—"the hole," down a flight of stairs, where the wagons pulled up and the accused were hustled to their cells—faced a one-block through street called Centre Market Place. The rest of the buildings on the street were much less impressive than the police station, really just a row of tenements on the fringe of Little Italy. The storefront at No. 7 contained a business called George F. Herold, a dealer in guns and police equipment, whose founder had been an NYPD retiree. No. 6 had until recently been a poolroom but now contained stores run by two more police suppliers, Frank Lava and J. K. Carmichael. (Lava himself lived down the block.) No. 2 had Isaac Davidoff, known as Dave the Tailor, who specialized in cops' uniforms. He later moved to a shop at No. 5, the building where John Jovino, yet another gun dealer, had the storefront and basement. Jovino, *The New Yorker* reported, outfitted "about three-quarters of the city police force, selling them all sorts of accessories, from shoes to whistles; and he has no objection to selling the more harmless items to civilians." Several rooms

---

* Onieal's, the restaurant in the old Headquarters Tavern building, prints the story on its website and cites a cellar vault that extends a few feet under the sidewalk and could be a bricked-up tunnel. It is one of those tales that is too good to check.

in this block of buildings were leased by newspapers, serving as field offices where police reporters could make phone calls, type stories, eat, drink, and kill time playing cards or shooting craps. A lot of the job involved doing that, as they waited around for something to happen.

Around the start of 1935, Arthur Fellig turned himself into a solo news operation based out of 5 Centre Market Place. It was less an apartment than a sort of half room on the stair landing over Jovino's shop, although Weegee grandly called it "my studio." It cost him seventeen dollars a month, and it was a dump. The bathroom was out in the hallway, and its one window let in barely any light. Aside from his coat and a camera case, both of which sat wherever they had been dropped, the furnishings amounted to an iron cot with a thin mattress and, next to it, a single chair that looked like a street find or maybe a castoff from a police captain's office. For his first couple of years in the apartment, a cardboard carton of Westinghouse flashbulbs functioned as a nightstand, with nothing on it but an alarm clock; a small, plain radio; and an ashtray. (Later on, he got himself a beat-up side table and a desk.) The floor was covered in linoleum tile and was not especially clean. The door soon gained a painted plaque: ARTHUR FELLIG, PHOTOGRAPHER. Underneath, a pasted-on typewritten addendum read: CRIME STUDIOS / MURDERS ETC. On the bookshelf, the titles included *Live Alone and Like It* and *The Sex Life of the Unmarried Adult*.

He made only one gesture toward decor: soon after he moved in, he began tacking up newspaper clippings and other ephemera on the wall over the bed. Most were pages from the papers where he'd sold photos. A front-page picture that got two columns in the *World-Telegram*, another that had been played big on the back page of the *Daily Mirror*, a day when he had nearly the entire front page of the *Post*—these were trophies, like taxidermied heads on a hunter's wall.

Apart from the camera gear, the table radio was the one thing in the room that exhibited any spending power at all, and it was there for work as well as pleasure. Flashbulbs were not the only new technology (or furniture) on which the news photographer was coming to depend. A few years earlier, the NYPD had begun using radio signals to broadcast to its cars. Anyone with an ordinary receiver at home could tune in and hear the calls at WDKX, at 1684 on the AM dial. By the time Fellig moved to Centre Market Place, the police broadcasts had switched over to

WPEG, at a shortwave frequency of 122.5 meters; it was perhaps slightly less public, since one needed a fancier radio to listen in, but shortwave sets were fairly commonplace at the time.

That station was always on when Fellig was in his studio, and especially overnight. He also got himself permission, somehow, to install a bell connected to fire department headquarters, one that would ring with every single alarm. By day, he catnapped through the gunshots as cops took practice on the firing range in Jovino's basement. Sometimes he'd head downstairs to one of the adjunct newsrooms down the block, or hover over the Teletype, watching for a good story to come in. At night, he'd listen to the radio's crackle, waking and dozing, smoking one of the twenty cigars he went through daily, mostly just waiting. Most people thought he slept in his clothes, because his suits looked so rumpled on the job, but he said he usually stripped down to his underwear. If a good murder or a robbery came over the air, or that fire bell went off, he could be on the sidewalk in thirty seconds. If it didn't, he trafficked in tips from the other reporters in the building. He installed no telephone.

At the very beginning of this period of his life, he'd cadge rides from other reporters or make his way to the scene by subway, but he soon got himself some driving lessons and practiced during the downtime between murders, killing time in the *Journal-American* offices or at the police station "practicing my shifting with a broomstick." Eventually, he bought an aging Model A Ford from a kid in the neighborhood—never mind that he didn't quite have his license yet. He hired a teenager named Louis D'Amico Jr., whose family lived in the apartment upstairs from his, to drive him around and give him lessons. Once he got his learner's permit, he could speed to crime scenes if he had a reporter with a driver's license along. On the weekends, led by a tip from a "sex-mad letter carrier" he knew from Acme, he began dropping by brothels more frequently, particularly one uptown in the West Seventies, run by a woman named May. Until he got past the learner's-permit stage, he had to bring his teenage driver along to the whorehouses. "The trick was, seeing I was boss, to get there first. No wet decks for me," he said, using an expression analogous to "sloppy seconds." His voyeurism, one of the forces that compelled him to make photographs in the first place, was already in full bloom at this time, and May was ready to indulge it. "Speaking my language, she had holes cut in the wall," Weegee recalled later in life, "and the two of us would watch my chauffeur in action."

At least once in the winter of 1935, he made his way out to Flemington, New Jersey, where the trial of Bruno Richard Hauptmann, the accused kidnapper of Charles Lindbergh Jr., was unspooling. As good a story as it was, Fellig was unlikely to have gotten much out of the trip. Flemington was blanketed with reporters and press photographers. The *World-Telegram*, just to take one example, had an entire news bureau set up in a rooming house near the Hunterdon County Courthouse. Everyone in the scrum was chasing the same few photographs: Lindbergh and his wife, the few pieces of evidence on view, Hauptmann himself. Sammy Schulman, an ace from Acme's rival International News Service, was there, getting good pictures of the aviator. Fellig had no competitive advantage, and his photos, if he sold any, were just part of the pack.

Fellig's purported Ouija board abilities did not require much in the way of magic. His knack was more proletarian: he lived to chase photos, and he put himself on call, all the time. "I went," he later said, "and made a job for myself." He also got to know the night. The waves of activity, he discovered, could be counted upon and grew familiar to him. "Most fires happen around one or two in the morning," he explained. "Five o'clock is the jumping time—people are out of liquor and the gin mills are closed. Their resistance is low, and if they're going to do it, that's when they do it." New Year's Eve always brought the first-baby-of-the-year photo opportunity at the hospitals, but it came with a catch: "It usually would be illegitimate, so that would kill the story. Before I went out on it, the cops had to prove [the parents] were married and still loved each other."

His predictive abilities were about paying attention and being there, no more. Nonetheless, the story of his special mystique had begun to take hold among his newspaper colleagues, even if it was beginning to grate on some of them. In January 1936, a reporter from the *Brooklyn Eagle* recounted the following story in print.

"CLUBS" ONLY PICKS, DUD ALARM SHOWS

Arthur Fellig, free lance photographer called "Weegee," because he is always expecting something to happen, was prowling around in the snow at Manhattan Police Headquarters, early today and saw two suspicious-looking men lurking in the rear doorway. The men were holding what looked to be baseball bats in their hands.

Recalling the recent robbery of the gunsmith shop of George F. Herold . . . across the street from headquarters, Fellig put in an alarm. In a few minutes two radio cars and the squad car from the Elizabeth St. station, five blocks away, rolled up . . . The two suspicious-looking chaps turned out to be WPA workers with pickaxes to break up the ice and snow, who were just taking a rest and trying to get warm.

This little anecdote took up three column inches on page 9. It's basically a slapstick scene, and Weegee is the goofball at its center. It also mentions him by name, right up top, positing him as a man who's always on high alert, fine-tuned to what's going on in the neighborhood and beyond, in close touch with police affairs. He'd already become a public character, and the other reporters at police headquarters were starting to take notice.

The fifty dollars a week Arthur Fellig had been making at Acme was hard
to match as a freelance in Depression-era New York, but he did manage to
sell enough photos into the anonymous stream to keep from sleeping in
Bryant Park. There was a demand, and he was a hardworking supplier.
In 1935, there were nine dailies with news holes to fill, as well as the
agencies that supplied the national press, each with different editors and
inclinations. Any one of those could find itself in need of a photograph
from a breaking news event, even if it was in a rough neighborhood.
"Others wouldn't walk the streets at night," Acme editor Harold Blumenfeld recalled many years later. Weegee would, and he had that little slice
of the market almost to himself.

The three Manhattan morning broadsheets were not his best market. The *New York Times* was not above running a major crime story or
a picture of a big fire, and Fellig no doubt knew people there from his
squeegee-boy years, but, then as now, the paper was restrained in layout, prim about bloodshed, more interested in Berlin than in Benson-
hurst. Even a decade into the photojournalism era, the *Times* ran very
few spot-news pictures, and frequently hit the streets with an all-text
front page. The *Herald Tribune* was comparable in worldview but center-
right in viewpoint, often better written, more creative, and more grace-
fully laid out than the *Times*, and even more patrician. (Fellig loved to
talk about the time he went out on a *Herald Tribune* assignment for
Acme without putting on a tie, after which he and his boss got a repri-
mand.) The third of those papers, William Randolph Hearst's *American*,

was far brasher, displaying open disdain for President Roosevelt and a decent appetite for scandal and gore. The Hearst empire, though, was big enough to have its own photo operation, via its subsidiary International News Service. All three papers bought Fellig's stuff from time to time, but they didn't provide him a living.

He did somewhat better business with the two morning tabloids. By the mid-thirties, the *Daily News* had become the biggest paper in America, thick with ads, printing 1.65 million copies on weekdays and twice that on Sundays. It did buy pictures from Fellig now and then, when its night photographers hadn't been able to get to a particular event—and, because it had a large news hole to fill and used so many photographs, that happened somewhat regularly. The same was true of Hearst's *Daily Mirror*, even broader and louder, with at least as much crime and celebrity coverage. (Typical headline: KIDNAP KILLER LINKED WITH 6 MURDERS.) The *Mirror* also had Winchell, whose purview had spilled outward from his Broadway gossip beat into national politics, carrying him onto the radio airwaves every Sunday evening. He was the best-known, most powerful columnist alive, conversing regularly with President Roosevelt and members of the cabinet, and if you crossed Winchell, you could expect slashing revenge in the two thousand newspapers that ran his column. Winchell also worked nights, mostly among the swells at the Stork Club but also in the saloons of Broadway, and (according to Weegee, anyway) the two men were friendly, crossing paths from time to time.

The dailies that published in the afternoon, though—they were Fellig's steadiest buyers, at least at the beginning. There were four of them in the mid-thirties, all broadsheets, all thinner than their morning competitors and therefore less heavily staffed. Besides, for a man who worked the overnight shift by choice, they were ideal: their editors would be making news decisions as Fellig finished up the night's work at around 7:00 a.m. If Fellig showed up just then and said *Hey, I got that murder on Tenth Avenue*, the photo desk would certainly take a look. He could also get a tip, now and then, from the morning papers themselves. The city edition of the *Daily News* printed overnight and hit the street at perhaps 4:00 or 5:00 a.m., whereas the early editions of the afternoon papers wouldn't lock up till a few hours later, at 9:00 or 10:00. (In these days, most large newspapers ran several editions a day, updating their print run every hour or so to catch breaking-news updates and, especially, late sports scores.) The gap between the arrival of the morning papers and the dead-line for the evening ones provided a window of opportunity.

The *New York Evening Journal*, the third Hearst paper in town, was a noisy, lower-middlebrow broadsheet with eccentricities such as its "Ama-teur Page," for which readers could send in their own cartoons or arti-cles. (You will not be surprised to learn that it got a lot of funny stories about their dogs.) Like Acme, the *Evening Journal* had a carrier-pigeon team that flew film back to the office on tight deadlines. And despite its in-house resources, certain aspects of the *Evening Journal* were great for Weegee's mien. Its editors definitely liked a good murderess, for one thing, and a crusade for traffic safety that carried through all the Hearst papers manifested itself in gruesome photographs of smashed-up cars, under such headlines as THIS MIGHT HAVE HAPPENED TO YOU. In 1937, just as Wee-gee was getting into the thick of his freelance career, the *Evening Journal* merged with the *American*, and the resulting *New York Journal-American* marched on, gradually becoming, as its later correspondent Jimmy Breslin put it, "a paper where, believe me, ya couldn't even believe the weather report." Before and after the merger, the Hearst empire supplied the paper fairly well with photographs, diminishing its need for freelance help, but Weegee had good relationships with its photo editors, and he'd regularly sell work to and get assignments from them.

The New York *Sun* was a stuffy Republican newspaper with a weirdly large section devoted to antiques collecting, and it was grappling with an illustrious past and a shakier future. (In 1897, it had been the paper that printed the famous "Yes, Virginia, there is a Santa Claus" editorial, and in the teens it had been home to the great columnist Don Marquis and his uncapitalized alter ego, archy the cockroach.) The *Sun* in Wee-gee's time printed some metro news, but it was no showcase for photog-raphy. Once you got through the blah shots of socialites disembarking from ocean liners, there were often only two or three spot-news photos, most of them small, in the paper. A significant number of those were Fellig's, because the paper didn't have a night photographer in the streets.

The *New York World-Telegram* was looser and funnier than the *Sun*, with bolder headlines. Thinner than most of the other papers in town, it put up a good fight: foreign news on the front page many days, more or less centrist politics (though it tipped farther rightward as the years went on), a decent little business section in the back, and bigger and better photographs, on the whole, than most of the other broadsheets ran. The paper, owned by Scripps-Howard, was best known in the mid-thirties for the strident far-right columnist Westbrook Pegler and his droll liberal counterpart Heywood Broun, plus its exhaustive, exclusive coverage of the Dionne quintuplets, who for a while appeared in the paper nearly every day. The *Telly*, as the *World-Telegram* was sometimes called, was also building a reputation for stylish feature writing, and went so far as to splash its star writers' names on the sides of its delivery trucks and even in its headlines. (*The New Yorker* periodically hired away the best of those writers, most prominently the brilliant A. J. Liebling and Joseph Mitchell.) It was probably the snappiest of the smaller papers in town, and Weegee sold his work there often in the mid-thirties.

He didn't have a home port, but if anywhere served as one in these very early days of his freelance work, it was the *New York Post*. This *Post*, mind you, was not the loud-and-proud tabloid, known for headlines such as HEADLESS BODY IN TOPLESS BAR, that the paper became under Rupert Murdoch in the 1970s. Owned by J. David Stern and then Dorothy Schiff, it was a left-leaning, moderately intellectual broadsheet that had its own prominent Broadway columnist, a less pugnacious competitor to Walter Winchell named Leonard Lyons. Apart from the *Times*, the *Post* was the only New York broadsheet not hostile to the New Deal, and it covered unions and strikes with nuance rather than a wrinkled nose. (Jewish bylines were commonplace at the *Post*, and that was not true everywhere.) The two underdog broadsheets carried on a long-running feud, nicely summarized by an anecdote Winchell published: "The *Post* called the *Sun* 'a yellow dog.' The *Sun* replied: '. . . The attitude of the *Sun* will continue to be that of any dog toward any post.'"

About the only thing Stern's *Post* had in common with today's is that it was lousy at making money. It had the smallest print run of the afternoon dailies, although it had recently clawed its way up from a near-death five-figure daily circulation to about 250,000. Like the *Sun*, it had no night photographer on staff, and thus depended on photo agencies plus whatever Fellig brought in each morning. As he put it, "The city editors are glad to see the free lance man come in with the goods along about 7 a.m. in time for the first edition." Fellig was likewise dependent on the *Post's* largesse, because he often used its darkroom at the end of a night's work if he didn't have time to go back to Centre Market Place. There he would produce "the Weegee service," the night's batch of work, making a quick dozen prints of each picture. He continued to shoot on glass negatives for a few years after film became the standard, because the plates could be carried in their holders while still wet, saving him a few minutes. Symbiotically, the paper got first crack at his take.

That was where you'd find him at dawn most days. As the sun came up, he'd head to the *Post*'s darkroom and photo desk on West Street, down near the southern tip of Manhattan Island. Then he'd head to the *Sun*, on Chambers Street, and then over a few blocks to the *World-Telegram*. The route then led to Midtown and the wire and syndication outfits: the Associated Press, Wide World, International News Service, and then Acme—for whose editors, Fellig said, he held back a few good frames out of goodwill owing to their long relationship. Acme was probably providing more of his income than he let on, because it always needed everything. Its "commercial division," aimed at trade journals and the like, always bought his car-wreck shots, two for five dollars.

As for the morning papers, Acme by this time also had space in the new Daily News Building on East Forty-Second Street, so he could hit both offices with one elevator ride, and the *Daily Mirror* was just three blocks away. "I would casually mention to Manny Elkins," the *Mirror*'s picture editor, "that I had just sold a set of pictures to the *News*. Then the *Mirror*, too, had to have it, because they were in fierce competition." Occasionally the *Times* or the *Trib* might buy something. Finally, if the night had not been too exhausting, he'd take in an 8:30 a.m. movie on Forty-Second Street. "I take off my shoes and first thing I know I'm asleep."

He had a loose working agreement with those four syndication services that they'd avoid distributing his photos in New York, because his income depended on his selling directly to the local editors. A couple of other local outlets occasionally picked up a photo from him, too, such as the *Jewish Daily Forward* (published in Yiddish for two hundred thousand readers, an unimaginable circulation today) and the Communist *Daily Worker*.

"One good murder a night, with a fire and a holdup thrown in" was his nightly goal, and he occasionally made it. More often, once he got going, it was every third day or so. But in that freelance freshman year, he sold comparatively little, and even less that can be identified. He surely published pictures over the next twelve months, but he must have been draining his savings to survive. He spent a lot of time "dry shooting": practicing, with no film in the Speed Graphic, growing so familiar with its works that he would later be able to act on instinct, quickly, when a real news moment presented itself.

Only two pictures from 1935 can be attributed to Fellig, and they are likely but not positively his. One is pretty ordinary. It ran in the *Daily News* and was taken on Centre Market Place in January, after a mass arrest brought 166 people to police headquarters for a day of lineups and the block was choked with police vehicles. The other one, though, was a big score. It involved Dutch Schultz again, and he needed a lot more than aspirin this time. On October 23, 1935, Schultz had been shot in the bathroom of a restaurant in Newark where he was having dinner. The hit men bolted from the restaurant; Schultz staggered back to his table and collapsed face-first into his dinner plate, then was rushed to Newark City Hospital, where he lay dying. Weegee was among the pack of journalists who followed him there. Back at the restaurant, a *Daily News* staff man, who'd been too late to get a photo of Schultz slumped at his table, had a plainclothes police detective re-create the pose and photographed *him*. At least it was Schultz's blood on the tablecloth.

The assassins had prepared their bullets in advance, letting them rust before loading their guns to heighten the risk of infection. In this pre-antibiotics era, it worked. Schultz became delirious and lay in his hospital room muttering incoherently, as police stenographers took down his words, hoping for information that would be useful later on. What the papers really wanted, of course, was photos of the man himself.

As Schultz lingered, Weegee put on a doctor's white coat, slipped into Schultz's hospital room, and made, he said, "beautiful candid shots of him, paying special attention to the bullet holes in his chest." A photo fitting that description (uncredited, not even to Acme) ran on the front page of the next day's *Post*, under the headline SCHULTZ IN DEATH DELIRIUM; RAVES AGAINST SICILIAN MOB; RACKET OVERLORD FIGHTS FOR HIS LIFE. A variant image from the same set went out over the AP wire. (At least one other photographer, the *Newark Evening News*'s Ervin Hess, also finagled his way in and made a similar picture. The *Post* and AP versions are probably Weegee's.) Weegee called it his "scoop of scoops." A few hours after the evening papers landed on newsstands, Schultz was dead.

Weegee's bed was in his room on Centre Market Place, but a lot of his time was logged in the police headquarters building. (He also was a frequent presence at the station houses on West Forty-Seventh and East Fifty-First Streets, which together handled a lot of Midtown crime. Each had its own reporters' shack nearby.) Today, this simply isn't done: a reporter cannot hang around the squad rooms, mixing with police officers all night long. At the time, though, the atmosphere was more casual, the rules more porous. A reporter could hover over the same Teletype in the lobby that told cops what was happening in the rest of the city. And that's what Weegee started to do: hang around, mostly seated by the main entrance on what was known as the "mourner's bench." "Most of your job," he said, "is just sitting around waiting for some baby doll to toss a knife into her daddy or for some second-story men to lift an emerald necklace from the madam's dressing table while she takes her nightly exercises. Sitting around police headquarters waiting for a news break is three-quarters of your job."

He'd do small favors for police officers, keep them company, chat with them, maybe pick up coffee or donuts once in a while. "If they wanted a quiet little snooze," he noted, "they'd use my studio." In return, he could occasionally cadge a ride to a crime scene or, just as important, a ride back. Sometimes that ride would be on the back step of a police wagon, with Weegee gripping the handle next to the door the way a sanitation worker will hang off the back of a garbage truck. "He snaps Moriarity's baby at the christening, takes pictures of the force on their outings and picnics," explained one contemporary. "If they have a photograph they are fond of, he makes them up extra prints." Cops weren't supposed to smoke at crime scenes, and Weegee would warn them to drop their cigarettes before he shot, so they wouldn't get in trouble.

Whether because he called in all those small favors or just because he kept at it, he was working somewhat steadily by early 1936. A building that burned down in February gave him a good portrait of a fire truck covered in icicles, and another of firemen similarly encrusted in ice. The *World-Telegram* bought both and ran the fire-truck picture on its front page. A dramatic water-main break in Queens a week later shut down the subways and, in the process, brought Fellig a rare moment in the *New York Times*, which wouldn't print his bloodier pictures. The *Post* and the *Sun* bought it, too. A few days later, when the city's building services union went on strike, leaving apartment houses unstaffed, Weegee's pictures of picketing elevator operators and other staff sold to the *Post* and the *Sun*; pictures of city workers who had volunteered to be on call for emergencies got him into the *Times* again, and another photo that appears to be his went to the *World-Telegram*.

He was, effectively, taking on a role as Acme's night police-beat reporter, and he kept an eye on more systematic crime. "They called me their underworld contact," he later explained. "In other words, if a story happened, I would call up [Acme] and say, 'Look, a guy's been bumped off,' and I would tell them I'd cover it. I usually did. If it didn't sound interesting to me, I would say, 'Look, there it is—I'm not covering it.' You know, I had done my job," filling them in. More often, though, he was shooting less exciting stuff, effectively as a stringer. Acme's early-morning editor E. Stuart Fergusson later recalled that he saw Weegee "practically every night."

Most of these (the dramatic Schultz photos aside) were workaday photographs, just slices of the day's news, but some were differentiated from the others of the day: a little better at telling a story, a little more eye-catching, a little more evocative. That photo of the firemen covered in ice was inventive and strong—hardly a picture nobody had ever made before, but definitely one that nobody had made that night. More important to Weegee, for now, was that his expenses were so small even occasional sales were enough to keep him housed and fed. At his usual five bucks a photo, each brought in about a week's rent for the studio on Centre Market Place. One good night's work could cover the month's shelter and a few meals. He was a big-game hunter, shooting to eat, and the hunting-trophy tear sheets proliferated over his bed. Murderers on their perp walks, overlapped with burning tenements and car wrecks, were interspersed with girlie photos that had been either bought or shot on the sly or printed as Weegee's own souvenirs from the nudist camp. In the first eighteen months of his freelance life, not a single photograph on those walls had been published with his name attached.

Sometimes he couldn't catch a break. From April through July of 1936, he seems to have sold almost nothing. (He did make one good photo of a holdup gang's young female lookout as she left the police station on bail, smiling cheerily. It ran in the *Journal* for a couple of editions and then disappeared before the final.) Weegee later wrote that a photo editor told him his murder pictures were all alike, that the papers were bored with his shtick, that the trade in dead-gangster photos was itself dying. He also griped that amateur photographers with Brownies were stealing his thunder, running up to news events and making pictures before even he could. That was indeed happening now and then—in June 1936, for example, the *Mirror* went big with a car-crash photo taken by an amateur who happened to be on the scene and caught an image of the driver bleeding on the ground. (Caption: "What makes this attractive is that it is a spot news picture.") There was even a young adult novel around this time, Robert Van Gelder's *Smash Picture!*, about a cub photographer who'd made it onto a newspaper just that way. Really, though, Weegee was probably just going through a dry spell. The front pages that season were constant blares about the Spanish Civil War and the Olympic Games in Berlin, pushing local news to the back and usurping picture space.

By midsummer, Weegee was nearly broke. He even considered hocking his Speed Graphic, which would have kneecapped his ability to make a living. One late July day, when he dropped by Acme to sell a couple of auto-wreck photos for a lowball price, he ran into Robert Dorman, who offered him a chance to go back to his darkroom job. Fellig was desperate enough to consider it. Really, what he needed was a lucky break—and then, abruptly, he caught one, or rather he created one for himself. As the summer of 1936 reached its height, he not only got out of his slump but also made a series of pictures that would constitute both his commercial breakthrough and his first great moments as a photographic artist.

Friday, July 31, was not one of those sweltering city nights when the murder rate is said to spike. The temperature didn't even get out of the seventies. That did not matter in the MacKnight household, across the harbor from Lower Manhattan, on Avenue A in Bayonne, New Jersey. Around 6:00 p.m., Edgar MacKnight came home from work to discover his wife, Helen, hacked to death. She had, it quickly became apparent, died at the hands of their seventeen-year-old daughter, Gladys, and her eighteen-year-old boyfriend, Donald Wightman. It was fabulous tabloid material, for quite a few reasons. The families were well-to-do: Edgar was an executive at a cable manufacturing company, and Donald's father ran the local yacht club. Gladys was a member of that newly named species known as a "teen-ager," and she was described in the news reports as sullen, tomboyish, athletic, and reliably combative with her old-fashioned mother. Donald looked squeaky-clean and collegiate. In Weegee's great description, "he could have made the all-American axe team." As for Helen, she'd had a nervous breakdown a few years earlier. She and Edgar had disapproved of their daughter's relationship with Donald, and a few minutes after he arrived for their tennis date that evening, Helen got into a quarrel with Gladys about dinner. (Gladys claimed later on that her mother had caught her and Donald in the kitchen, necking.) Depending on whom you believed at the subsequent trial, either Gladys or Donald had grabbed a hatchet from atop the refrigerator and killed Mrs. MacKnight with six blows. The young couple jumped into a car and fled a few minutes later, then came back and turned themselves in around 10:00 p.m. When she was arrested, Gladys displayed a certain press awareness. "Will I get the papers?" she asked her jailer. "May I see reporters in my cell?"

It had happened early enough to make the Saturday-morning New York editions. The *Times*, in a move that was a little unusual for such a seamy case, put the story on its front page, though the murder was subordinated to international news. The *Daily News* just squeezed it into its final: GIRL, 17, AND BOY KILL HER MOTHER was the big black headline on the back page, confusingly appearing over a photo from a celebrity divorce trial that was playing out just then. (The headline didn't bother with the customary "alleged," but the story inside the paper is hedged.) A good story—but, significantly, the arrest had happened late in the evening, and the story had likely been phoned in to the *News*'s city desk from Bayonne. There were no photographs.

Weegee got hold of the city edition of the *News* at 3:00 a.m. and immediately called the *Post*, saying he'd go after the story on spec. Being an afternoon paper, the *Post* wouldn't be locking up its own first edition for another five or six hours, so the desk editors said yes and assigned a twenty-four-year-old reporter named Leo Katcher to meet Fellig and head out to New Jersey. The two men already knew each other. Katcher drove because Weegee had been too broke to gas up his car.

They got to the police station in Bayonne around five, an hour before the sun came up, and found not a single reporter on the scene. They'd all been there earlier, but the warden had declared "no more pictures tonight," and the men from the press had left with, Weegee said, "a gentlemen's agreement" that they'd all come back the following morning around eight or nine, so nobody would get scooped. But he hadn't been there at the time, and "Me and Leo Katcher didn't know about the agreement." But Katcher, who had grown up in Bayonne and worked at the *Bayonne Evening News*, did know the warden. Quickly he persuaded him to bring the couple up to be photographed, and Fellig shrewdly told Gladys to make herself up, to look her best. "Smile," he told her. She bared her teeth, saying, "Haven't enough of those things been taken yet?" Then she relented and posed, grimacing, with Wightman and on her own. Weegee kept shooting, and when he finished up, Gladys sent him off with "Okay, Toots. I'll be seeing you."

The police captain, standing nearby, called her the "freshest, boldest girl I ever saw." Donald Wightman was more reserved, but he, too, sat for portraits, looking crestfallen. Weegee used up every glass-plate negative he had brought in his camera bag. As she headed back down to her cell, Gladys whispered to him out of the side of her mouth, "How do I photograph?"

Pretty well, it turned out. Within an hour or so, reporter and photographer were back through the Holland Tunnel and in the *Post*'s building on West Street, Katcher typing up his copy, Weegee in the darkroom. That afternoon, the *Post* had it: a full-length photo of Gladys (in tennis skirt and sneakers) on its front page, Katcher's snappy jailhouse interview with the couple on page 2, and a montage of pictures of Gladys and Donald on page 3. "*Post* Photo," read the credits beneath them, but it was the freelance Weegee who got paid that morning. The caption writer did his damnedest to turn the pictures into a hard-boiled drama.

> Nice kids, the townsfolk in Bayonne always thought. Gladys MacKnight was a bit of a tomboy, sometimes a bit sullen and quick-tempered, but she came from one of the first families of Bayonne . . . Donald Wightman was well liked, a bit of an athlete—in short, a promising boy. Who would have dreamed, as these two youngsters tennised and motored about town, that today they would both be in jail, charged with the horrible ax-murder of Gladys's mother? One quick flash of temper, one moment of yielding to weakness, and now they face long terms in prison, if not the electric chair. Study these faces. Do you see any clue to such a quirk in their characters?

Gladys MacKnight and Donald Wightman: just two
all-American New Jersey teenagers who had murdered
Gladys's mother with a hatchet.

The next year, at the couple's trial, a prosecutor held up a newspaper image from that day, showing a defiant, smirking Gladys. The lawyer asked the jury, "Does this look like a girl suffering from shock . . . ? I think not. Nor do I think you do."

Weegee's competitive advantage evaporated by midday: the rest of the pack caught up when the couple was brought out in the morning to be arraigned, and the final editions of several papers had photos not dissimilar to Weegee's. But Acme and the Associated Press had each bought his take. The *Herald Tribune*, usually prim about murder stories, ran an Acme photo (his). So did the *Daily Mirror*. The *World-Telegram* bought and used a couple as well. Altogether, Weegee said, he pulled in seventy-five dollars for that one job: enough to gas up the car, pay the rent, stock up on film and flashbulbs, and sustain himself for a couple of weeks. (The equivalent, in 2018, would be about thirteen hundred dollars.) The city editor of the *Post* paid him in cash, on the spot. Leo Katcher earned some of the credit as well: just a couple of years later, he himself was promoted to city editor of the *Post*, then published a couple of well-regarded books, and eventually went out to California to write screenplays, successfully.

Whether it was because photo editors had noticed Weegee's hustle and story sense on short notice, or merely because he kept chasing, Fellig was back in the paper within days—this time literally. Early in the morning on August 5, the police Teletype led him into Brooklyn, to a weedy vacant lot where Court Street meets the Gowanus Canal, next door to a sailcloth company and a lumberyard. A worker from the latter had spotted an old steamer trunk sitting unattended, tied up with clothesline. Untying the rope and opening it, the man found a corpse bound at the wrists and ankles, and he called the police. The man in the trunk was—or had been—William Hessler, a small-timer in what was left of the Dutch Schultz organization. He had a couple of arrests (kidnapping, attempted extortion) on his record but no convictions, and was known for shaking down the local madams for cash. He'd been stabbed forty-eight times in the chest with an ice pick, then trussed up and put in the trunk while still alive, probably about fifteen hours earlier.

The local police captain theorized that it had been not a typical gangland revenge murder but a hurried, spontaneous act. Too many details indicated a lack of professionalism and planning: identifying labels hadn't been removed from the victim's clothing, for example, and few mobsters would've been so careless. Most likely, Hessler had gotten into a fight over a card game nearby in Brooklyn's Little Italy, and some fed-up enemies, already irritated by his encroachment on their whorehouse turf, had taken the opportunity to get rid of him. His body was, that morning, identified by his fingerprints. He had one nickel in his pocket. It was mob custom to leave victims with "carfare," and also to have every man present inflict a few of the wounds, in order to make everyone guilty and reduce the chances that someone would squeal.

Fellig rushed over the bridge to Brooklyn, getting there early enough to make his pictures before the body was removed from the trunk (and before it started to rain, messing up the tableau). One thing he knew, though, was that such a gory picture would be difficult to sell, so he shot two versions of the scene. One showed the opened trunk, Hessler's curled hand and foot just barely visible. The second shot was made later, at the Seventy-Sixth Precinct, showing the trunk standing on end after the body had been removed. A police photographer made an evidence photo at roughly the same spot, showing the trussed-up dead man on the floor of the police station.

William Hessler, however, is not the only human presence in the photos. Arthur Fellig himself is also there. Both times, he had propped his camera on a tripod, stepped around in front of the lens, peered at the trunk as if he were a bystander, and fired the shutter with a cable release concealed in his hand. His presence turns a very grim photograph into one that's almost a cartoon, his raised eyebrows conveying a *Hmmm? What's this?* Each was a better and more salable photo for having an observer in the frame. "Editors demand people in pictures" is how a fellow reporter described Fellig's maneuvering. No doubt he snickered at the chance to get himself into the paper, too.

Few editors today would tolerate a freelance who inserted his own face into a spot-news photo, but on that morning in 1936, nobody noticed or cared. The *World-Telegram* bought the photo of him standing next to the closed-up trunk. The *Post* used the one with the lid open, referring to Weegee in its caption as "a curious passerby." No paper put it on page one—it was awfully gory, and anyway, news of the war in Spain again dominated that day—but they each gave it good play inside.

The *Post*'s editors, however, decided that their readers couldn't tolerate the sight of Hessler's corpse, and either they or Weegee removed the body from view, painting it out with stippled black and white to mimic the lining of the trunk's interior. (Such retouching was fairly common in newspaper work, although usually the alterations were simpler: a whited-out background to silhouette a single figure or a few lines sharpened with ink so they wouldn't blur out in the paper's coarse halftones.) The *Post* had, oddly, ended up running a photo of the photographer while eliminating his subject.

The Hessler portrait was a juicy one, but barely twenty-four hours later Weegee outdid himself. On August 6, he made the first of his

When the New York Post *ran this picture, its editors found the corpse too gory and retouched it out. They left in Weegee, who is the man peering into the trunk.*

canonical photographs—the ones that established his reputation, the set of photos that he later in life called "the Forty Famous Pictures." And this time, a case of mistaken identity helped him do it.

Dominick Didato had been, like William Hessler, a low-level organized-crime foot soldier. He wasn't anymore, because on the night of August 6, he ended up dead on a sidewalk. He'd been eating dinner at a place on Elizabeth Street called the Sciacca Restaurant, and a few minutes later he was lying just in front of the doorway, two grand in his pocket, four .38-caliber bullets in his flesh, the murder weapon a foot from his hip, his straw hat flipped over on the bloody pavement. One small difference between this rubout and any other was the victim's name: there had been *another* Dominick Didato in the Luciano organization, this Dominick's cousin, and that man had been a much bigger deal until his own murder in 1933. It was the fifth murder of the month that had stemmed from a small-scale turf war between Luciano and what was left of Dutch Schultz's gang.

The small-time Didato, the one who had died on this night, had fallen to the sidewalk just three blocks from Weegee's apartment, which means the photographer was able to get there just after the police did. The body had not been covered; the tableau was untouched except for a battery-operated light that a policeman had set down to illuminate the scene. Weegee got off three exposures. One was made from inside the restaurant doorway, framing the corpse, showing it over the tilework threshold. (This picture was the goriest one.) A second was what newsmen called a "ten-foot shot": a portrait from the near middle distance, showing the body and a few uniformed policemen and bystanders standing around, eyeing it.

Best of all, though, was the close-up. Weegee crouched down low and photographed Didato as if the dead man had turned away, his face barely visible, his body lying on the diagonal, his hat in the foreground. He looked far less bloody from that angle, and his pale summer suit was barely marked. You could almost believe Didato was just a passed-out drunk, except for the small bloodstain by his back pocket and the gun dropped next to him. As Weegee said of his best murder photographs, "I gave them all my love and care, made 'em look like they were just taking a little rest."

The *Daily News* ran the gory one. The *Post* went with the group shot and put it on the front page, above the fold, under the great headline IT'S BAD LUCK TO CHISEL IN ON LUCKY. Its editors had probably mixed up the two Didatos, or at least chose to elide the distinction. (The *Journal*'s editors really screwed up, going all in on the mistaken identity with a banner headline in its early edition, after which they wised up and heavily revised the story for the final.) Strangely, the great low-angle photo—the best of Weegee's three pictures, the one that today appears on book jackets and in museum shows—sat unrecognized at the time, and was published only much later.

In one week, three front-page stories, plus whatever small-time fires and car crashes he got in between those: he was out of his slump. At the

A classic from 1936, shot on the sidewalk in front of 90 Elizabeth Street in Little Italy. "I made the stiff look real cozy, as if he were taking a short nap."

photo desk of the *World-Telegram*, at least, the editors appeared to take notice. Twice in the next two weeks, they bought pictures from him and credited them not to the usual "Acme" or "*World-Telegram* Staff" but instead to "Arthur Fellig Photo."

The next few weeks after Didato's murder were busy. On August 8, Fellig had another picture run big in the *Post*, this time under the morbid-twice-over headline BURGLAR SUSPECT SHOT TO DEATH AS HE CLIMBS CEMETERY FENCE. Two days after that, a section of the old Fulton Fish Market building, on a pier by the Brooklyn Bridge, collapsed into the East River just after midnight. Weegee's pictures, likely made with multiple flashbulbs to light up the whole length of the pier, caught the early editions of the *Sun* and the *Post*.

The night of August 21 brought a twofer. At a tenement fire late in the evening on Cherry Street, just a few doors away from the Felligs' old home, an African American family with five small children had rushed to the street. One of the kids was overcome by smoke and had to be hauled out by firemen. Weegee caught the other four children, together under a blanket, lined up sad-eyed and looking straight ahead, a poignant and powerful image. Despite its photographic strength, that picture ran way inside the *World-Telegram*, probably minimized by the editors because the family was black and because nobody had died.

The night's other event played big, though. At around 4:00 a.m., a drunken cop crashed his car into a horse-drawn truck, knocking its driver off the approach trestle of the Williamsburg Bridge. The man, named Charles Schlanger, fell nearly one hundred feet to Delancey Street below and was killed. Weegee dutifully made the long shot of the ramp, to which the *Post* makeup men added the customary dotted line showing the plunge. (Somewhat surprisingly, the next morning's *Herald Tribune* shook off its usual hauteur and did the same.) The photo everyone wanted, though, was the portrait of the drunken policeman, who was named William Glendening. In court, Glendening had tried to cover his face, until the magistrate ordered him to reveal himself: "You're ashamed of yourself now, but you weren't ashamed this morning." Weegee, along with five other photographers, got the cop's picture as he was arraigned that morning.

Those scrums of newspapermen, all going for more or less the same "ten-foot shot," really did work the way they appear to in old movies, jostling at each other's elbows. "The unpardonable crime," Weegee once explained, "is for one news photographer to get in front of the other one. Suppose let's say somebody had eight feet, or closer—six feet. You cover up the other one, you'd be marked lousy. So that means, usually, all cameras are set at ten feet. You make sure you don't get in the way." It sometimes led to a sameness among the "exclusives," which weren't especially exclusive.

Even though Weegee had the advantage of working late at night, and thus dealt with fewer of these crowds of press, the habits and customs of his colleagues definitely made their way into his work, especially early on. He very quickly learned how to set that ten-foot focus on his camera by feel or with a pocket flashlight. That plus a prefigured lens aperture (f/16, usually) and the same shutter speed, flashbulb, and film every time essentially took the camera out of the equation. Unlike sunlight, the angle and intensity of a flashbulb's illumination never changed. If you were at the right distance with those standardized settings, you'd always get a crisply publishable photo, and you could shoot by instinct without pausing to work out the details. (It was just the right distance to frame a sidewalk corpse or a fireman toting a stretcher.) Fellig also relied heavily on a second set of rote settings, for a six-foot shot, that was better for faces. The great majority of Weegee's photos conform to those two templates.

What he'd begun to see, though, was that he could set himself apart by looking for emotion rather than just getting the facts of the moment. "When I watched the other photographers on stories," he later wrote, "I saw they used the camera like a machine and that they thought like machines. My idea was to make the camera human. I was dealing with people at their most tragic moments—fires, murders, etc.—and all this I tried to show in my pictures." Surely, he's selling his colleagues short, for there were plenty who understood this as well. Still, it is true that many of them did their work somewhat routinely, and, increasingly, Weegee did not.

It's often said that Weegee was a master of the technical aspects of news photography, but that's not entirely correct, at least in these early days. What he had done was narrow down a particular slice of repeatable photographic technique and rehearse it relentlessly, mostly so he could work really fast and rely on muscle memory. "With concentration on six and ten feet, and a lot of practice, one can guess these two distances," he wrote. "Don't try to guess-focus the markings in the scale . . . no one can do that . . . just practice six and ten feet, but do your practicing at home or your leisure," he recommended. "You won't have time on a story." The nights of dry shooting, fiddling with his camera as he sat around waiting for a stabbing, were starting to pay off.

He had a lot of those nights mostly to himself, making pictures as the stories came. A brawl took the life of a Greenwich Village café owner, and Fellig caught the anguished wife in tears; that one sold to nearly every paper in town. The same was true at a particularly dramatic shootout on the Upper West Side, where one hundred of J. Edgar Hoover's men descended on a building, firing machine guns and throwing gas bombs, to drive out a bank robber and kidnapper named Harry Brunette. The suspect was taken unhurt, though his wife was winged by a bullet to the leg; photogenically, one of the gas bombs ignited curtains in the building, so the fire department came roaring in to join the cops and the G-men. The *Post* put a big grouping of Weegee's photographs on the front page, running the story as the off-lead (right under a completely erroneous banner headline announcing that the Chinese general Chiang Kai-shek had been executed in a coup).

There were less violent stories in his purview as well. In September, two sweet-looking little girls in pinafores, saved from a shipwreck, appeared on the front page of the *World-Telegram*. In November, he headed to Times Square on Election Night and managed to get a perch atop the Hotel Astor's marquee as FDR's election announcement ran across the news ticker; the resulting photo, filled edge to edge with a sea of people watching the returns, ran across six columns in the *Post*. Perhaps oddest of all, one afternoon in November, Weegee was out in Brooklyn covering a routine fire story when two fishermen towed a fifty-ton whale into Sheeps-

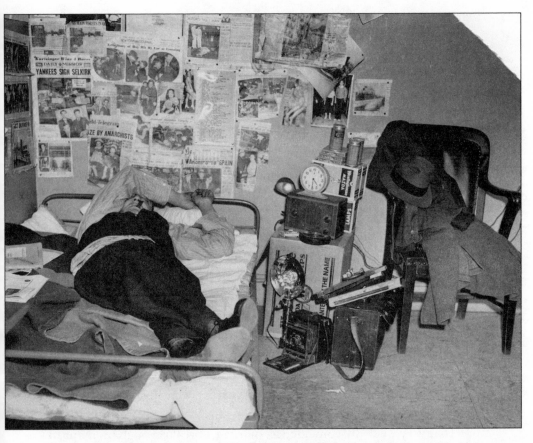

Weegee in his room at 5 Centre Market Place, 1937. The clock says 4:30: Is it a.m. or p.m.?

head Bay. (Having found it dead, they hoped to auction its bones and blubber. The NYPD wouldn't let them stay.) He happened to be close enough to get there before the carcass was towed back out to sea. At one of the newspaper offices a few hours later, "the guys said they had seen me at the fire, and were . . . wondering how could I get a picture of a whale," he later recalled, laughing.

As his list of sales grew, the tear sheets from many of these stories began to cover Fellig's entire wall at 5 Centre Market Place. Sometimes, he would scribble "by Fellig" in ink across the margins, next to the agency credits printed on the page. Even though nobody else would see it, he was staking his silent claim.

With increasing frequency, one or another of these items, even if it seemed on the surface to be local and small-time, would take off nationally on the strength of Weegee's pictures and the stories they told.

During an extended national sailors' strike in late 1936, the Seamen's Church Institute, a century-old Episcopal charity organization with headquarters on South Street, was a place where merchant marines could get a cheap bed for the night. But it did cost something to stay there, and on the evening of November 27, a group of strikers applied to stay the night on credit. One, named Owen Savage, was turned down, and he began to make a fuss. The cops were called; Weegee arrived moments after they did and made a compelling series of photos as Savage was hauled down the stairs and out of the building.

Savage continued to protest, and Weegee kept shooting, his final frame showing Savage slammed to the sidewalk. The connection to the national strike meant that papers picked up the photos from as far away as Iowa, and the *World-Telegram*, back home, ran not one photo but four. The *Daily News* put one of them on its front page, under the headline NO DOUGH—NO SLEEP. The story contained the essence of good spot-news photography, conveying a story vividly and almost wordlessly; it was also something the broadsheets would not (and probably could not, technologically speaking) have run a dozen years earlier, when pictures were used mostly decoratively.

That very week, by coincidence, marked a breakthrough moment in photojournalism. For a couple of years, Henry Luce's Time Inc. had been preparing to launch what it called its "show-book of the world," a sibling to *Time* built around photography. (*Time*, in those days, was known less for pictures and more for its weirdly turned-around and condensed lingo, known as Timestyle, in which movie fans were "cinemaddicts" watching "cinemactors" and people got things done "in time's nick.") There was no weekly picture magazine in the United States, although the French *Vu* and the German *Berliner Illustrirte Zeitung* were cousins to what Luce had in mind. The void was abruptly filled with the first issue of Luce's *Life*. Put on sale on November 19 and dated four days later, it sold out on many newsstands within hours. Almost immediately the run was a million copies per issue, twice the size of any other weekly magazine's, straining the presses' capacity and exhausting the supply of the slick paper on which the magazine was printed. It turned out that people really wanted to look at the rest of America and the world beyond.

Anyone who wanted to get famous as a photojournalist would have wanted to work for *Life*, and Weegee certainly did. Time Inc.'s offices were in the Chrysler Building, less than two blocks from the *Daily News* and almost as close to the *Daily Mirror.* Weegee simply added them to his rounds. He would, he said, "go up to *Life* magazine and leave my pictures on the desk in the early morning hours." And although *Life* didn't call right away, every night brought a story that the magazine's editors would have seen in the New York papers. A power failure at Newark Airport allowed Weegee to make great pictures of an ultramodern facility operating by kerosene lanterns, and he also got another good fire photo into the *Sun* just two days before Christmas.

The new year, 1937, started off with a bigger month even than his breakthrough August. After one of the first big arrests of the year, an accused murderess named Anna Sheehan glowered for the camera appealingly under her hat brim. (She'd stabbed her husband to death during an argument at a New Year's Eve party. Every paper wanted that one.) A few days after the Sheehan arrest, as Weegee sat around the police station on a quiet Saturday, a cop told him there'd been a hit-and-run just a couple of blocks away. Weegee grabbed his camera and bolted, stopping by the reporters' shack to alert everyone, and perhaps sixty seconds later he was on Lafayette Street, where a seventy-year-old man named Frank Tapedino lay on the pavement, holding a handkerchief to his head as he was given first aid. As Weegee made pictures of the scene, he heard a scream from a window nearby, and a moment later he found himself face-to-face with Tapedino's sobbing daughter. His portrait of her anguish, paired with a set of images of her father looking dazed, was sensational, and when it appeared in the *World-Telegram* the following afternoon, the accompanying copy poured on the drama: DRIVER, HERE ARE THE PAIN AND SORROW AND FRIGHT THAT YOU HAVE CAUSED, the headline read. The captions also addressed the vanished motorist: "Sir, this is the wailing daughter of Frank Tapedino . . . Look now at your bewildered, suffering victim . . . How do you feel about the sufferings you brought?" And then, underneath, in unusually large type: "These pictures, which capture the excitement and horror of an automobile accident, were made by Arthur Fellig, free lance photographer, who arrived on the scene a few seconds after the accident."

The prominence of the credit suggests that Fellig knew he had an unusual story on his hands, and that he'd given the set of photos to the *World-Telegram* on the condition that his name be put on them. But it

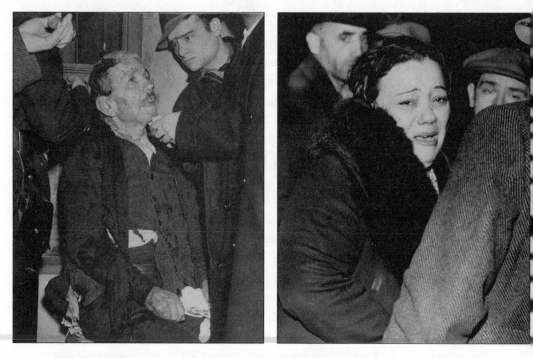

Frank Tapedino, seen perhaps one minute after he was hit by a car on Lafayette Street in January 1937, and his sobbing daughter.

was hardly a *Telly* exclusive. The *Post* ran two of the pictures on its front page; the *Journal*, with its obsessive coverage of traffic safety, ran them big inside. Papers all over the country, from Burlington, North Carolina; to Hope, Arkansas; to Ogden, Utah, ran the story, sometimes on the front page, communicating outrage with headlines such as PICTURE RECORD OF GRIEF RISES TO HAUNT FLEEING MOTORIST. (Some of them took pains to turn it into a local story. At the end of the captions, the *Xenia Daily Gazette*, serving Greene County, Ohio, tacked on the sentence "Similar scenes—even more tragic ones—attend every hit and run accident in Greene County.") Altogether, Weegee pulled in one hundred dollars for that set of photos, a couple of weeks' wages.

There were still more. That same week, a holdup at Barney Pressman's discount clothing store on Seventh Avenue—today, it's called Barneys, having long since ditched its apostrophe and its bargains—turned into a shooting. Over the next few days, the cops pulled in four of the five stickup men, and Weegee managed to get unique photos of the first three. One of them, named Lawrence Mullen, usually called La La but sometimes known as Mugsy, was barely tall enough to see over the desk at his booking; Weegee got behind the counter and shot straight at him, emphasizing La La's stature as well as the facial bruises he'd received in a fight with his partners.

Night after night, Fellig's instincts for getting a salable picture grew better. After a particularly seamy bathtub murder in Queens in mid-January, a dry-cleaning tag left at the scene led police to a young man named Major Green; Weegee was the one who got down into the cells and made his portrait through the bars. (Green was tried, convicted, and executed within a few months of his arrest.) A particularly nasty car wreck led to a trio of pictures played prominently in the *News*.

As did the arrest of a pretty, tough young woman named Nellie Gutowski, alias Norma Parker, alias Jean Williams, alias Jean Johnson, alias Jean Carroll, and always described in headlines as the "Broadway gun-girl." Weegee photographed her not once but twice, first after she was picked up for knifing a female acquaintance, then three months later, after she was caught for sticking up a series of restaurants with a cap pistol. Weegee puffed up his involvement in the latter case over the years, spinning a yarn in which he'd remembered his earlier photo of her and passed it to the cops, leading to Gutowski's eventual identification and arrest. In fact, he had not been the amateur detective, and she was caught by much more conventional means. The DA's case file reveals the truth: that she'd been grabbed and disarmed by one of the restaurant's workers, who plunked her into a phone booth till the cops arrived.

After a counterfeiting bust, Fellig's picture of all the equipment and fake cash made the back page of the *Mirror*. A Murder Inc. rubout in a parked sedan on Fourteenth Street practically captioned itself, because the hit men had scratched the words ICE WAGON (slang for "hearse") into the car's paint. For years thereafter, he told increasingly embroidered stories about that photo, too. "I sent back word to the boys that it's very difficult to photograph black limousines on a rainy night with flashbulbs," he said. "I says: 'Next job you have, when you go out to steal a car, get a gray Cadillac. And watch the interior decor. Everything had to be in good taste. If it gets too confusing, then it's no good.'" Mobsters, photo

Nellie Gutowski, aka Norma Parker, aka the "Broadway gun-girl,"
arrested for knifing an acquaintance in late 1936.

gear, and a hint that Weegee could do what no other reporter could—it
was a story that had everything.

Those are all pretty straight photos: the gun-girl's face is expressive,
but fundamentally it's just a picture of a woman being led to or from police
headquarters. Over the next year or two, Weegee's photos show the first
signs of moving beyond those basic get-it-and-sell-it instincts, hewing
slightly less tightly to newspaper conventions. (As the historian Luc Sante
has astutely noted, as long as a press photographer got the story into his
frame and minimized any distractions, he was free to do whatever else
he wanted.) He had learned to "slant pictures," as one observer put it.
"For instance, when a cop kills a criminal, Weeg makes a gory shot of the
corpse for the tabloids and a dignified shot of the cop for the others." Yet

although Weegee continued to take pictures of the dead body, the burning building, the wrecked car, the accused arsonist, he began—perhaps because he'd had such success with the Seamen's Church Institute and Lafayette Street hit-and-run stories, perhaps just because his instinct for a powerful picture was improving—to turn his camera around. There was much more material, he found, to be mined in the faces of the onlookers, those who survived, as in the places left behind by those who did not. He'd done that with those four kids on Cherry Street, and he would begin doing it more frequently as time went on. In an interview three years later, he explained it pithily.

> We'll assume that a horse-drawn wagon is going over the Williamsburg Bridge. A car hits it and the driver is tossed into the water and gets killed. The other photographers will take a picture of the bridge and then have an artist draw a diagram showing how the guy fell into the water. What I do is go and see what happened to the poor old horse.

He wasn't making this scenario up. In January 1937, that very event had occurred (the eighth such crash in eight years, highlighting a safety problem on the bridge), and Weegee's photographs of it had run in the *Herald Tribune* and the *Post*. The car that hit the wagon had been a taxicab; both papers did indeed run pictures of the bridge ramp with the falling wagon driver's path (indicated, once again, with a dotted line, the same as in the Glendening wreck of a few months earlier). And the horse in Weegee's portrait had its head turned, the *Post*'s caption noting that the animal was "looking back as if in astonishment."

Photo editors (and horses) weren't the only ones beginning to spot Fellig's hustle. One night in 1936, a subway running on the Third Avenue elevated line in Manhattan crashed into a slow-moving work train and derailed near Seventy-Third Street. The subway cars were old, made of wood rather than steel, and they had splintered and telescoped upon impact. One hung precariously off the trestle, threatening to fall onto the street below. As police and fire squads made their way there, so did the mayor, Fiorello La Guardia. (He showed up at a lot of emergencies. La Guardia was a well-known fire buff, and his driver sped him to every big blaze, siren wailing.) So did Weegee, who'd seen the news on the police Teletype. "I was up there by cab in about twelve minutes," he said. But he still didn't have press credentials, being a newish freelance, and was barred from the scene by police.

Just as he had when Dutch Schultz lay dying, he resorted to a slap-dash disguise. He folded up his Speed Graphic and stuck it under his jacket—in this era, no matter how hot it was, even the most slovenly member of the press didn't go out to work in shirtsleeves—and fell in among the men who were digging people out of the wreckage. He grabbed a shovel and made his way up the stairs to the train tracks. As soon as he pulled out his camera, it became obvious why he was there, but the mayor himself waved off the cops. "Let that guy snap the wreck," La Guardia said. "It happened, didn't it?" And Weegee later joked to a reporter, "I give you one guess who I'm going to vote for when the next mayoralty election rolls around."

He wasn't the only photographer there, but he got strong images of the injured being carried off on blankets and stretchers, and the *World-Telegram* played them big the next day (with credit, again, to "Arthur Fellig Photo"). The best of them was a good portrait of a concerned-looking La Guardia overseeing the rescue in a pale summer suit. They were two of a kind, Fiorello and Fellig: stumpy, jowly, feisty, voluble men who'd spent their childhoods far from New York but who had soaked up a fundamental understanding of how their city worked. Weegee later claimed that he'd been a builder of the La Guardia legend: "I helped to make the 'Little Flower' famous. He was very helpful and cooperative. Say there was a two-alarm fire—I'd grab a baby, stick it in his lap, and say, 'Fiorello, do something, coo at it, make faces,' and he would, and I'd get a good picture out of a bad fire."

Fellig was also getting more aggressive and persuasive with people, busting through his earlier shyness. In January 1937, a band of jewel thieves was hauled in after a series of burglaries in Washington. One member of the group, to whom jewels had been shipped in New York, was a woman named Agnes Olson Johnson. Weegee knew that pictures of female criminals were a better sell, being less ordinary and potentially more titillating. A woman jewel thief was even more interesting, with hints of feminine wiles and hotel room shenanigans. "Especially on a Sunday," he later explained. "The papers are very hungry for pictures on

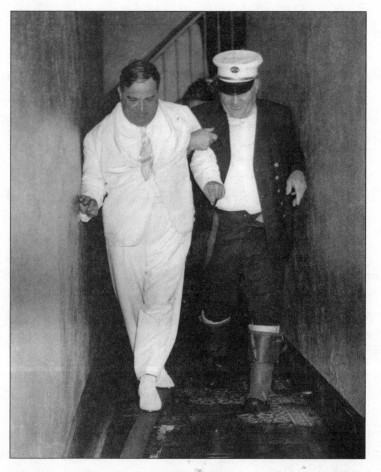

Mayor Fiorello La Guardia, a fire buff who raced to every big blaze, often found himself before Weegee's lens. This one was on July 26, 1939.

a Sunday for Monday." Seeking a payoff, he made his way down to meet Johnson, who put her hands over her face as he raised his camera. "Why should I let you?" she asked him.

Covered faces are a wearying cliché in this kind of photography. Standing at the sergeant's desk, sitting in a jail cell, being marched in from a police car—in all these situations, suspects look like convicts. Their instincts, and their lawyers, tell them to obscure their faces, usually with a handkerchief or a coat collar or (more often then than now) with a hat brim pulled down low. "Editors don't like it," Weegee explained. "They'd say, *Don't give me any excuses. Gimme a picture so our readers can see.*" The celebrity criminals, Weegee once noted, didn't much mind having their photographs taken—Dutch Schultz, say, or Jack "Legs" Diamond, or Martin "Buggsy" Goldstein—but the less seasoned criminals did. "The only ones that tried to cover up," he said of the gangsters, "were the young punks who really saw too many movies. . . . I would say, 'Listen, you punk! Wait till you get a reputation.'" Usually, though, he did better with gentler methods, often in the form of a pack of cigarettes slipped to the weary crook. (He carried extras for just such a situation.)

The non–organized crime figures routinely hid behind their hats, too. On the back of a picture Weegee made of a murder suspect named Robert Redwing, the man's fedora clapped over his face, is an irritable-sounding note: "Big Chief Redwing," Weegee wrote, "who was imported from Washington D.C. by the N.Y. Daily News & Who posed for exclusive pictures for them (no doubt for a nice consideration) covered up for the common photographers from the other papers." The claim checks out: the newspaper pictures that show Redwing's face carry a *Daily News* syndication credit.

Because photo editors would rarely buy pictures of hats rather than faces, it was often Weegee's job (and his colleagues') to sweet-talk a subject into posing. The cigarettes helped. Sometimes he'd flat-out sneak a picture, as he had in the emergency room that night in 1929. Another time, he left his camera sitting on a table pointed at the suspect, announced conspicuously that he was headed out to get some food, and snapped the shutter from twenty-five feet away, using a remote release he'd hidden in his pocket. Still other times, it was just a matter of persuasion. He'd done it that night in Bayonne, with Gladys MacKnight, and here, with Agnes Olson Johnson, he did it again. "Look, lady, save your energy," he recalled saying to Johnson. "Do you want your picture to appear in the papers—a rogues'-gallery picture, with your number underneath it? Or would you let me make a nice home portrait study of you, using nice soft lighting like Rembrandt would have done? Talking and arguing with her, I convinced her that that was the only logical thing for her to do."

The idea that a Weegee portrait was somehow kinder than a police mug shot seems implausible, almost hilarious. The flashgun clamped to his Speed Graphic was anything but gentle, and did not remotely provide the soft sidelong lighting that a Dutch master would have rendered. Besides, he was conning her about the rogues' gallery shots. "They wouldn't give out [those photos] anyway," he later explained to an interviewer. "Only

[for] criminals with records do the cops give out a rogues'-gallery picture, and they usually take the number off." It didn't matter: she bought his line, he got his picture, and Miss Johnson and her two cronies were on the front page of the *Post* the next day—"a clean sweep," an exclusive all around. "By arguing with people," he said, "you can get them to uncover. People are reasonable. Even jewel thieves."

As in any news career, there were busy days and quiet ones. A walk through one lively workweek in April 1937, though, may give a sense of Weegee's nightlife in this hardworking period of his career. In five days, he had at least nine individual photographs appear in the New York newspapers, and because the pictures also sold to the syndicates, they were published all over America. He didn't get to every one of those news events first, but he was competitive every night.

Monday morning, April 19, began with a hammer murder. Or, more accurately, the arrest of a hammer murderer: the police picked up a man named Mischa Ross, a theatrical booking agent and musician who'd smashed the skull of his ex-girlfriend the previous day in a Times Square rehearsal room. She was a Juilliard-trained violinist, twenty-five years old, and performed as "Tania Leelova" and "Tania Lubova" but was named Julia Nussenbaum. Ross had secreted her dying body behind a curtain at the back of the hall, and after the arrest, one photographer—it may have been Weegee; the pictures are uncredited—managed to get a frankly nauseating picture of her blood seeping out from under the drapery.

Ross was caught by the police around 2:00 a.m. on Monday. No reporter was able to get a good picture of him that night, so Weegee did the next best thing: he found one. This was (and is) a common workaround for news producers: Ben Hecht, the Chicago newspaperman who went on to cowrite *The Front Page*, got his start this way, as a so-called picture chaser, talking his way into widows' apartments to "borrow" a portrait off the mantelpiece. Since Nussenbaum and Ross were musicians, they both had headshots, and Weegee managed to get copies of them to Acme, the *Sun*, the *World-Telegram*, the *Post*, the *Daily News*, and the Hearst papers that morning. (Ironically enough, given that Weegee had so much trouble securing credit for his actual work, the *Sun* published these two pictures over the words "Fellig Photos," which they only sort of were.) Unless he was responsible for the blood-under-the-curtain photo that Acme circulated, Weegee appears to have been beaten on this particular news story: the *Daily News*'s night man, whoever he was, managed to photograph Nussenbaum's body being carried out under a blanket.

Early that same morning, though, a smaller story gave Weegee somewhat better photos, and these (unlike the headshots) were his own. For several weeks, George Preston, a portly little sad sack of a night watchman, had been getting drunk and setting fires in his neighborhood in the Bronx. On this night, he'd been on East Nineteenth Street in Manhattan and tried the same thing in a couple of tenement hallways. This time, though, a tenant saw him running from a building, chased him a couple of blocks, grabbed him, and handed him over to a cop, who took him to the Thirteenth Precinct. There, Weegee was able to catch Preston for a portrait, in which he looked a little cross-eyed and shifty, playing to type. Preston then took police and press along on a little arsonist's tour, as the "firebug" (in the newspaper parlance of the time) returned to the two tenements and tried to explain how he'd attempted to set the fires, one of which had been kindled in an unoccupied baby carriage.

Tuesday night brought about the beginning of the week's biggest local story, one involving a unique New York celebrity. His name was probably George Baker, or maybe it was Frederick Devoe, but everyone knew him as Father Divine, the diminutive Harlem evangelist who claimed to be the Messiah. (He wouldn't give his age, which was about sixty, saying he'd been born in "the time of Abraham." His large flock of followers, really a cult, believed him immortal, and in fact he lived into his nineties.) Father Divine preached a gospel of civil rights, peace, celibacy, and teetotaling from a mission on 115th Street that he called "Heaven." On this night, earthly cares intruded. Around 2:00 a.m., during a banquet, a process server tried to serve a warrant on the minister. Parishioners defended him, and an altercation broke out. A man named Harry Green, who'd accompanied the messenger, was stabbed. Joseph Denove, a reporter for the *Evening Journal*, happened to be in the room and left to call in the alarm. Despite being beaten up by a group of Divine's followers who didn't want the police involved, Denove managed to get away, bleeding from the face, and found a patrolman. By the time the cops got to the scene, Green was still bleeding on the floor, Father Divine himself had vanished, and Denove had called the report in to his office.

The *Journal* had no night photographer on duty and got the rush assignment to Weegee. (How the editors reached him fast is a mystery, given that he had no phone; they probably called the *Journal*'s police reporter and asked him to bang on Weegee's door.) Fellig was in a cab up to 115th Street immediately, and stepped out, in his words, "to find a mob of black people—quiet, sullen, terrible." The anger that the *Evening Journal* reporter had faced certainly extended to photographers. "You can't take God's picture!" they shouted at him. "Get out of Harlem, white boy, before we slice you up." He eyeballed the parishioners, some of whom were wielding not only knives but bats and rocks, and hesitated before raising his camera. Only when he spotted another reporter he knew— another man from the *Journal*, John Weisberger, whom Weegee knew to carry a gun—did he make two quick pictures, "shaking like the well-known leaf," then bolt in a fellow reporter's car. (He wasn't exaggerating much: in one of the *Journal*'s photographs, members of the crowd are glaring pretty hard.) "An assignment is an assignment," he later said, "but a neck is a neck." Weegee did manage to settle his nerves and catch one more story before he kicked off for the night. At 6:00 a.m., an out-of-control truck at Eighty-Fifth and Broadway jumped a curb and smashed into a dress shop, then knocked over a fire hydrant, then took out a light pole, and finally smashed into a haberdashery, flipping over and spilling several tons of cargo on the sidewalk. It made for a dramatic photo, a genuinely unsettling one, and added to the night's tally of unrest.

The next night, Wednesday, was a quiet one, and Fellig appears to have shot and sold nothing. Thursday made up for it, though. Early that morning, the gangster Martin "Buggsy" Goldstein, a hit man and co-leader of Murder Incorporated, was picked up and brought through police headquarters to appear in a lineup. Goldstein and a deputy, the impressively named Seymour Magoon, had been caught in an investigation of a labor racket to fix contracts for the painting of city schools. That made for a pretty straightforwardly salable photo: Buggsy leaving the lineup, sneering good-naturedly at his "official photographer."

It was only a prelude for the next twenty-four hours' activity, however, because late on Thursday night, Father Divine himself was located by police up in Milford, Connecticut. Arrested at about 2:00 a.m. on Friday, he was brought down to Manhattan for questioning within hours, and his followers gathered outside in a growing crowd. Weegee was all over the story, taking pictures of the minister himself at the police desk, of the crowd outside as Divine was led to criminal court to be arraigned, and finally as Father Divine was released on bail and departed for the 115th Street Heaven in his immense Rolls-Royce as parishioners chanted and cheered. The most dramatic pictures from Weegee's set, which, via Acme, appeared in papers all over the country, showed Father Divine escorted in and out of court by a pair of tall, sharply dressed African American plainclothesmen. ("Colored detectives," the *Herald Tribune* noted, inevitably.) The officers' height emphasized the minister's lack thereof, doubly so when Weegee caught them on a staircase.

Many photographers would have knocked off after an evening like that, but Weegee had one more in him. The next person through the lineup after Father Divine was a pretty, well-dressed woman named Helen Harper, who'd been quietly embezzling from the lumber company where she worked. She'd been caught passing bad checks, and had turned out to have stolen fifty thousand dollars and plowed it into a company her husband was trying to start; Weegee got her into a couple of the papers the next day. Why hadn't he gone home and gone to bed? "Girls," he explained, "usually make a sure-fire sale."

When *Life* made its debut the previous November, its editors had proceeded from the idea that most of each week's magazine would be filled with pictures from Acme, Wide World, and the other photo services. That turned out to be an optimistic view. The editors soon found that most wire-service photos were relatively static and square, good enough to accompany a written story but unable to tell that story on their own. The magazine needed to seek out different talent and hired a photo editor, Wilson Hicks, from the Associated Press, to do that. He almost certainly knew Weegee's work; after all, Weegee had been stopping by the AP every morning for years, not to mention making his morning drops of photos at *Life* itself.

Just as (and perhaps because) Hicks arrived at the magazine, Fellig got his first assignment from *Life*. It was to be a night-in-the-life-of-police-headquarters story, one where he was to show an accused criminal's trip through the building: how he was booked, where he was fingerprinted, and so forth. (*Life* often sent its photographers tight scripts specifying sets of preconceived pictures for a given spread, constraining their work to a sometimes frustrating degree.) This particular story, more or less what we'd now call a police procedural, held easy appeal to readers far from New York, who had seen their share of gangster movies and were curious about the real thing. The enormous appetite for stories about urban crime had not abated with the end of Prohibition. In the public mind, crusading reporters could be nearly as powerful as the gangsters themselves, whereas the photographer was perceived as the lowliest bottom feeder: "the catfish of the newsroom," as one later observer put it.

The *Life* editors were, apparently, a little surprised when Fellig turned in his story. Yes, the photos did indeed show a suspect's walk through the system, but in the dozen or so pictures (the perp walk in handcuffs, the trip through booking, posing for a mug shot, standing and scowling behind bars), Weegee had persuaded his police friends to let *him* pose as the suspect in every frame. He'd either gotten a friend to press the shutter button or used a cable to trip it from a distance.

They may have been unexpected, but they were entertaining pictures, and *Life*'s editors evidently just decided to rethink the editorial framework around them. The reimagined story ran in the magazine's "Speaking of Pictures . . ." section of April 12, 1937. Weegee had, by either accident or cleverness or instinct, managed to score a public-relations coup by making the whole thing about him, spinning "how Police Headquarters works every night" into "how Arthur Fellig, police photographer, works every night." Only a couple of the posed photos appeared, showing Weegee hovering over the police Teletype and cadging a ride on a police wagon. The rest were news photographs he'd sold since beginning his freelance career. The Hessler trunk-murder photo appeared, both in its original form and with the *Post*'s retouching. (*Life*, seemingly more Middle American than the *Post*, was paradoxically freer to be ghoulish.) So did shots of Major Green in his jail cell, the collapsed Fulton Fish Market, the dead nightclub owner's weeping wife, and a particularly nasty car crash.

Readers also saw Weegee feigning sleep fully dressed beneath his wall of tear sheets, and learned that he was "a swarthy, pleasant, uncultured man [who] loves his work and even likes the people he photographs. He thinks murderers are 'very nice people' because they rarely give a cameraman trouble." He also contributed one very aggressive composite gag photo of himself. In it, he stands mugging and bug-eyed with a cigar, while a picture of a pretty young woman floats, comic book style, in a thought bubble over his shoulder—as he holds a pistol to his temple. "Fellig's dream girl is just one of his jokes," wrote *Life*. "He faked this picture to burlesque his bachelor existence. Fellig has no home, no wife, no family, doesn't seem to want any." For a man who wanted to be regarded as the greatest,

For Life magazine, Weegee illustrated the post-arrest walk-through: booking, fingerprinting, mug shots, and being taken to a cell—using himself as the model.

hustling-est police-beat photographer in town, one whom editors could count upon at any hour to run out and shoot, the story was a little masterpiece of self-promotion.

They kept buying, and he kept working. A new law closed the burlesque halls that May; Weegee showed up at Minsky's, the most famous of them, and at another on Irving Place, to take photos of the cops and the showgirls. When he got a good car-crash picture, even if it didn't make the papers, he could sell it to Acme and also sometimes, he said, to the driver's insurance investigators.

In August, a tenement collapse on Staten Island that killed most of the building's occupants got him lots of play. Acme bought his take, and

Life went with his best photo from the day, which showed one of the few survivors as she was dug out of the debris. Several newspapers also ran that one, including the *Herald Tribune*—although Weegee probably hadn't worn a tie to the building collapse—and it is evident why they did. All their staff photographers' pictures were made later and show the wrecked building as police and firemen and gawkers milled around it, long after the rescue activities had dispersed. Only Weegee got there fast enough to record the frantic activities of the rescuers and the faces of the rescued. The other photos are still lifes. His are busy, messy, active pictures, and they bring heat.

August 8, 1937, became the busiest and most lucrative night he'd ever had. Well, *two* nights, because the rush of work began on August 7, which had been a relatively quiet Saturday afternoon until the police arrested one of their own, a mounted policeman named Arthur Chalmers, who was said to have killed a young Frenchwoman named Irma Louise Pradier. The *News* had already reported that they were after Chalmers, and "about four o'clock [that] Saturday afternoon," Weegee said, "I noticed a couple cars pulling away. In them I recognized cops from the photo studio and fingerprint department. I knew something was up." Word came back about an hour later that Chalmers had been nabbed and was being held at a precinct house uptown. Weegee stayed put, expecting that the accused would eventually be brought down to headquarters and that he'd have a better chance at an exclusive photo there. It happened exactly that way, late that evening, and Weegee caught Chalmers as the police commissioner, Lewis Valentine, watched the questioning, giving him a highly salable photo. "His intense feeling plainly apparent from the scowl on his face, Police Commissioner Lewis Valentine looks on . . ." went the Acme caption.

That, however, had been just the start of Weegee's evening. He didn't even have time to process the Chalmers film before he got word, minutes later, of a second killer. "A friendly cop gave me a tip," he said, "that a fellow named [Lawrence] Marks, who was under suspicion for raping and murdering an 8-year-old girl, was about to be arrested in Brooklyn." Once again, he knew this was a big enough case that the suspect would end up downtown, and once again his knowledge of the system paid off; it also meant that he knew he had an hour or so to duck into the darkroom and develop the Chalmers pictures. And then, that very same night, a young guy named Terry Roberts had shot a man, then committed a robbery. "Something told me this would be a good story," Fellig said. "I rushed up to 95th Street, where Roberts was being held. Before I got there the wounded man had died. Roberts was a murderer! And so I had three murders in less than thirty-six hours. . . . On Monday morning, when all three killers appeared, Marks was crying. Terry was unconcerned. Chalmers was broken-up." And Weegee had $150 in his pocket for a weekend's work. "Three murders in 36 hours," he said. "Boy, was business good!"

Increasingly, he tried not to settle for the familiar picture that he might have produced a year or two earlier. When two Dutch Schultz deputies named Frankie Ahearn and Marty Powell were arrested—the day after Nellie Gutowski was, in fact—he couldn't sweet-talk them the way he had his lady jewel thief, Agnes Olson Johnson. The *Daily Mirror*, to take one example, settled for a picture of the two men shot through a police car's window, with their faces snugged down into their coat collars. Weegee, though, caught them in the back of the police wagon, sitting toe to toe. Literally so, because whether by luck, cropping, or forethought, he gave up on showing their faces and instead photographed their feet.

Their feet? Yes, because their feet perfectly conveyed their relationship. "Factory Frankie" had been an insider. He'd been close enough to Dutch Schultz that, as Schultz lay delirious and dying in Newark Hospital, he muttered his name. ("Henny, Henny; Frankie! You didn't meet him; you didn't even meet me.") Powell, by contrast, was a footnote in the story, a guy who worked on the docks and in the organization. The print Weegee made, showing both men from the waist down, manages to convey all that, mostly from the quality and condition of their tailoring and cobbling. Ahearn's pressed suit ("a symphony in brown," the *Post* said that afternoon) and polished shoes made a visible storytelling contrast with Powell's dungarees and scuffed, creased oxfords.

With photos like this, he was beginning to bust out of the standardized forms that news photographers had been settling on for a generation, turning in pictures that were less familiar and thus more vigorous and intense. He could also, occasionally, get away from the murder-and-fire beat entirely while still making a salable photo, and those pictures, looked at in retrospect, already show an interest in themes he'd revisit again and again.

"Factory Frankie" Ahearn and his associate Marty Powell, seen from the waist down, on February 17, 1937.

Take sleep, for example. Over and over throughout his career, Weegee photographed people as they slept, beautifully cataloguing their expressions, their positions, their environs. Partly he did so out of convenience and propinquity: he was working at night, when he was awake and most people weren't. Also, a man who could still be shy and awkward no doubt found it easy to photograph people who wouldn't turn away. But also, consider his usual material: unconscious victims of smoke inhalation, passengers flung from car crashes, freshly murdered gangsters. Weegee often remarked that he took pains to make the dead look like they were just taking a little nap; it was probably a relief for him to photograph people who were, in fact, taking a little nap.

It was a theme he returned to constantly. He made sleeping portraits of Omero Catan and George Horn, each of them waiting overnight in his car in order to be the first man to drive through the new Lincoln Tunnel, one at each end of the tube. He did the same for two other guys camping out in line at the Polo Grounds for bleacher-seat tickets to the World Series, their coats wrapped around them against the late September chill, newspapers under their heads. (And another young man, similarly posed, a year later at Yankee Stadium, though he woke up and smiled at the camera just as the photo was snapped.) Fellig also snapped a brace of young women, clerks at a Fourteenth Street Woolworth's, on strike for better wages and asleep on cots in the store. All of them posed, inadvertently, for Weegee's lens.

Or was it inadvertent? After all, it's easy enough to feign sleep, and if a photographer offers to get your picture in the paper if you do, it's not hard to say yes: you don't have to try to smile. Consider those photos of Omero Catan and George Horn, for example. The men are dozing, one lying across the bench seat of his car, the other curled over his steering wheel. They are both covered in blankets. But in order for the photo to be made so that we can see them clearly, the car doors are wide open . . . in the middle of December . . . in the middle of the night. These stolen moments are, when you start looking closely, almost surely bogus.

Now, this doesn't rise to the level of full-on journalistic malpractice. A great many news photos get at least a little bit of help, after a fashion. A photographer sees a subject doing something, and says, "Hang on, let me get that," thereby interrupting the flow of the moment. (This is even truer in documentaries, where scenes of everyday life are often highly constructed, then shot and reshot and edited and re-edited, to convey just how *vérité* the *cinéma* is.) Even without that pause, the subject is often aware of being photographed, and adjusts his or her behavior slightly. It is largely a question of the reader's expectations of truth, and if Weegee was not breaking any unspoken rules, he was certainly edging up to their limits. That he was doing it in order to improve the storytelling in his pictures perhaps mitigates the rule-breaking. After all, Omero Catan was indeed sleeping in his car that night. Is it a lie to wake him up and then ask him to pose with his eyes closed?

Weegee's fellow photographers talked about this, particularly as he grew more famous, and especially as he began to add an extra dimension to his photographs: the internal caption. Starting with a couple of

great photographs in 1939 and continuing throughout his career, Weegee steadily made pictures that contained their own punch lines, wherein
people posed under signs or posters or graffiti that provided commentary. Some shots were poignant; most, though, were mordant and funny.
It wasn't a new idea—think of that Margaret Bourke-White portrait of
a disaster-relief breadline under a billboard reading WORLD'S HIGHEST
STANDARD OF LIVING. But it was an idea that Weegee executed with as
much wit and relish as anyone, and one he returned to again and again.
Making every one of these pictures required a lucky coincidence of event
and action. Weegee was a man who was known to make his own luck.

The mailbox photo was the one his friends wondered about, with
equal parts admiration and suspicion. It was a murder picture like so many
others: a corpse on the sidewalk at the corner of Elizabeth and Bleecker
Streets, sprawled and half-covered with sheets of torn paper displaying
a smear of blood. Behind the dead man, whose name was Lewis Sandano,
a cop stands taking notes. In the foreground, a mailbox is bolted to a lamppost; it bears a small sign that reads MAIL EARLY FOR DELIVERY BEFORE
CHRISTMAS. The juxtaposition of holiday cheer and a dead body was irresistible, a Charles Addams *New Yorker* cartoon with a gut punch of
realism.

Was it a setup? "His friends all said he moved that body," one friend
recalled after Weegee's death. "He wouldn't admit it." Weegee himself
insisted otherwise, even when an aggressive radio interviewer named Long
John Nebel grilled him about that very picture.

> LONG JOHN NEBEL: Why don't you be honest and tell what you've
> done? . . . Did you ever move a body?
> WEEGEE: No.
> L.J.N.: Did you ever claim that you moved a body from one place to
> another to make a better picture?
> W.: No.

And then, after Nebel challenges him further:

> W.: . . . I *moved* a body?
> L.J.N.: . . . What did you do? Did you move a wreck?
> W.: Yes. I'll tell you how—

Weegee's friends suspected that he moved the body to juxtapose it with the sign on the mailbox, but the evidence leans toward its being an honest photo. Made on December 19, 1940.

L.J.N.: No. Did you move the wreck to make a better picture?

W.: . . . One time, driving by, I think it was Second Avenue in the Forties, I see an automobile wrapped around a narrow pillar. I knew right away the *News* and *Mirror* would be there, because it was right around [their newsrooms]. . . . While I'm mulling over the scene, a towing truck drives by. And I says to this driver, "You want to do me a favor? I'll pay you a little. Let's move this wreck from Second Avenue to Third Avenue." And we moved it, and I took my picture. And I laughed to myself: When the other photographers arrive on the scene . . . there will be no wreck!

In another interview, he offered more detail: the car had hit a pillar of the Second Avenue elevated train at Forty-Eighth Street and was relocated to the Third Avenue el at Forty-Sixth.

Three things are striking about this story. One, he hired a guy to rearrange a car crash purely to gain himself a little competitive advantage, which is itself a staggering thing to do. Two, he copped to it in a public forum, multiple times. And three, while admitting to this misbehavior, he insisted that the mailbox photo was honest work.

The probable answer lies in the picture. It's awkwardly framed, with Sandano's corpse several paces behind the mailbox. There's also a highlight of glare on the glossy paint of the box itself, because it's too close to the flashbulb. The dead man is positioned a little too deep into the background; it's not even obvious at first glance that he's there. Frankly, if Weegee had set this up, he probably would have staged it better. Only the cop looks posed, and that would've been easy enough to arrange. The evidence, skimpy as it may be, falls in Weegee's favor.

Certainly, some Weegee photographs received their share of help, sometimes from tow trucks, other times from other kinds of advance preparation. But looking at hundreds of Weegee's photographs reveals a different kind of truth: nearly all of them were made in situations that were comparatively fleeting, and it would have been impossible to set up those situations to any meaningful degree. The few that were fabricated, or at least "helped," got an outsize share of attention, aided by Weegee's reputation for showboating. It may also have been a matter of degree. Tampering with evidence by dragging a murder victim down the street, or hauling a crashed car a full block for a photo op, clearly crosses the line. But how about minor adjustments of a scene? A fedora moved to improve the composition slightly, say? In Weegee's time and place, that was a venial sin, not a mortal one.

There's also the fact—and it is a fact—that, as Weegee began to get written about himself in the press, other newsmen began to feel envious. He'd already had problems like that at Acme, when, as a darkroom man, he'd occasionally outshone the staff photographers. Later on, he fraternized with the newspapermen at the police shack, but he was, in the end, also competing with them. "Every newspaper has staff photographers," Weegee explained, "and how they hate the average free lance picture shooter. The boys on the payroll regard free lancers as thieves, stealing the bread out of their mouths. You've got to make these guys like you, or you can't get anywhere."

Mind you, they did look out for one another. "You work with them all the time," Weegee once explained, and that meant more than keeping out of one other's sight lines. "Supposing somebody misses a picture," he once explained. "A guy will give him a print. I've done it many times." He also stayed out of their way, particularly by working those odd hours, when the other guys were mostly asleep. Still, nobody let his guard down. There were little professional feuds, some of them small pranks, some of them rising to more malicious levels. Weegee would come home to nasty notes stuck on his door: COCKROACH CAFÉ, one read. His grandiose claims of prescience left reporters rolling their eyes. "Predictions!" one snorted when asked about Weegee. "He says, 'Boys, I feel a fire coming tonight,' and if there's one anywhere in the whole city he claims he knew it all along." Good as he was with an anecdote, Weegee was not capable of the quick riposte, the snappy comeback. Ida Wyman, a photographer and printer who got to know Weegee a few years later when she came to work at Acme, saw that he was still being hazed when he dropped by the office. "He didn't have any good rebuttals," she recalled. "He just built up his persona in response." It didn't help that he would begin phone calls with "This is the fabulous Weegee talking," or that he described himself to at least one reporter as "modest and assuming."

Weegee's friend Louis Stettner saw a rival try to exact revenge one night in 1938. They were covering the Westminster Kennel Club Dog Show at Madison Square Garden—hardly a high-pressure news event—and Weegee set his camera down and walked away for a moment. When he returned, he found that "someone had apparently closed his back focal-plane shutter while he had been working with his front Compur flash synchronization." In layman's terms, another photographer had sabotaged his Speed Graphic. Had he not noticed, his evening's photographs would have come out solid black.

Stettner says Weegee was never quite the same from then on. "After that he thought of every photograph he managed to get published with his credit line as another victory against the mysterious 'them.' 'Them' came to mean almost all professional photographers who had not passed the most rigid test of friendship . . . [From then on] he never completely trusted or mistrusted any fellow professional."

Weegee took precautions thereafter, to an almost paranoid degree. Around this time, he began having his suits made by a police tailor (probably his neighbor Isaac Davidoff) to his particular specifications, roomy to the point of bagginess. "They were famous for not touching his body," a friend once said. In addition, though, Weegee had zippers sewn into all his pockets, and added a couple of inside secret compartments as well. Henceforth, nobody would be able to "borrow" a flashbulb or a cigarette from him, and nothing would fall out, or be caused to fall out, if he dozed off on a bench somewhere. He would let his guard down only with amateur photographers, Stettner noted. "In their presence he usually relaxed, and held forth . . . sharing a genuine love of the medium with those unpoisoned by jealous competition."

There were a lot more of those amateurs than there had been just a few years earlier, and in 1937 they'd gained a how-to magazine: *Popular Photography*, aimed at the serious hobbyist as well as the pro. That December, just eight issues into its existence, it ran a big feature about none other than Arthur Fellig. "Free-Lance Cameraman" was the title, and this time, there was no posing in jail cells or handcuffs: the piece was a detailed, immersive, well-rendered portrait of Weegee and his work habits by a woman named Rosa Reilly. Nine of his photographs, from Father Divine to a flophouse fire on the Bowery, accompanied the story, as did a second self-portrait, in front of his trophy wall of clippings. The writer pointed out the police radio on the bedside table, and the alarm clock reading 1:35. (Was it a.m. or p.m.? Impossible to say.) Whereas in the *Life* story he'd made vague reference to his predictive abilities, here he flat-out claimed to be psychic, heading to murder scenes because "my elbow itches." He honed and told the story about the great payoff on the three-murder night. In one caption he was labeled "Weegee Fellig," which was not quite right but peculiarly accurate. One man was, at this moment, becoming the other.

By early 1938, he had found a heady nightly routine, one that gave him a steady income and set him apart. Despite that boast of "one good murder a night, with a fire and a holdup thrown in," he was in fact a little choosier, seeking grabbier stories and exclusives that he could sell everywhere instead of just following the pack. "The ex-darkroom man of 1935," his friend Louis Stettner wrote, "was very different from the Weegee of 1939, who had spent a thousand and one nights experiencing and getting to know New York intimately." His pictures were often unique and more confident, and so was his news sense. "During the night," Weegee explained, relating the way in which he stood apart from his staff colleagues, "[the editors] send them out on a lot of wild goose chases. In the morning, they'd have a big assignment schedule. They'd send them out 40 times during the night. They got no pictures, but they kept the guy on the run. I worked it different. I usually used to pick about three stories during the week." Those were the big payoffs, and the rest was infill, taken as it came. Anything to avoid having a paper use a staff photo instead of buying his. "The easiest kind of a job to cover was a murder, because the stiff would be laying on the ground—he couldn't get up and walk away and get temperamental," he later said. "And he would be good for at least two hours. . . . At fires, you had to work very fast."

There were extra checks coming in, too. *Life* had begun buying his pictures semi-steadily, a few a year, generally running them in its weekly spot-news roundup, "*Life* on the American Newsfront." It's hard to plot out exactly where he made most of his money, but a sizable portion of his income was from sales to the photo agencies, especially to Acme and the AP: they seem to have bought (for distribution nationally) almost all the photos he was selling to the local New York newspapers, and they often went for extra frames and variant shots that the papers couldn't use. With multiple outlets and repeat sales, he was making, he said, "a very large living." And it's true, at least by the standards of the blue-collar Depression world he knew: he was taking in about five to ten dollars per photo, about four thousand dollars per year all told, or about three times the average American household's earnings, making him fairly well-off. His father died that year, and his mother lived with and was supported by two of her sons in Brooklyn, so he had no family expenses whatsoever. Put that together with his zero-amenities single life, and he had money to spend.

Enough, in fact, that he could dump his secondhand car and get something nice. (Though he had replaced his first old Ford by then: he once said he "used up five cars" in his years covering spot news.) What he bought himself was a 1938 Chevrolet "business coupe," a model ideally suited to his particular needs. It had no backseat, but it did have an immense trunk, more than five feet deep, with a high, domed lid. The Chevy cost him about $650, and he was proud of it—what could be more a sign that the boy from Zolochev had become a success in America than a fast, shiny automobile? He spent his share of time just cruising around, trying to pick up women. "Not having the time to live a so-called normal life . . . I gave that all up for my work. So how was I going to meet girls? My brand new shiny maroon-colored Chevy coupe . . . opened a new life for me," he said. "Maybe it wasn't nice, but neither were most of the stories I covered." And he was having fun. "Riding around with me gave them and me a thrill."

At least a few times, he said, he was fleeced by those young female hitchhikers. (One agreed to go with him to a movie, then slipped out of the theater and got a refund for the ticket he'd bought her.) But, really, he treated the Chevy mostly as a mobile office. The lip of the trunk served as a worktable and desk, and the cargo space was packed with photographic plates and film, flashbulbs, a spare camera, extra shoelaces, maps, flashlights, a stash of cash, another stash of cigars, and a pair of high rubber boots that he called his "fire shoes." (His "murder shoes," not so waterproof, were upstairs in his studio, next to the bed.) Though it

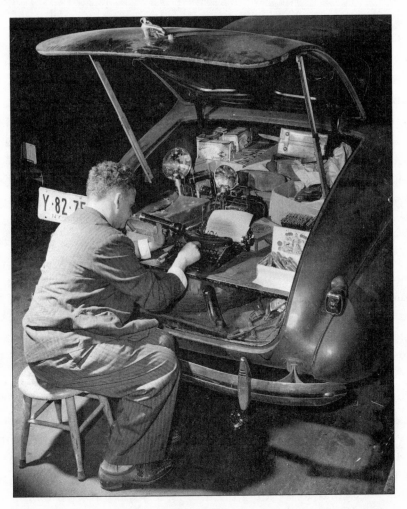

Typing captions on the run. The trunk contains cigars, extra cameras, a change of shoes, and a whole lot of photo gear—but not, as is often believed, a portable darkroom setup.

may have been an exaggeration, he claimed to carry a bunch of disguises in the car, such as that doctor's coat he'd worn to sneak into Dutch Schultz's hospital room. Very soon, the interior was littered with old newspapers and discarded film boxes. He added a typewriter to the trunk, and one photo shows him with a stool pulled up to the bumper, typing captions on the fly.

The car grew to be a big part of the Weegee legend, so much so that accounts of his life almost always say that he had a makeshift darkroom in its trunk. It's a vivid idea, suggesting that his work was urgent and speedy enough that he needed to conjure his images at the scene, but it's not so.

Weegee claimed many things about his work habits over the years, but he never mentioned processing pictures in his car. Photographs of the trunk reveal no tanks, no trays, no bottles of developer or hypo. Almost surely, people folded together his anecdotes about feats of photo-lab prowess at Acme (those stories about creating ad hoc darkrooms in the subway motorman's cab, in the ambulance, aboard the chartered train) with images of his Chevy crammed full of gear. The resultant tall tale got incorporated into the lore of the news business. For once, Weegee wasn't the one doing the mythmaking.

But shortly after he got the new car, he did gain one other tool that was all his own. For a few years, Walter Winchell had been accorded a singular privilege: a permit for a police radio mounted in his car, so he could chase stories all night long. That required sanction from the NYPD, and by the late thirties a few other reporters had radio receivers as well. Weegee, after he bought the new Chevy, managed to get a radio permit as well—the only one, at the time, held by a civilian with a camera. The license cost him twenty-five dollars per year; the Bosch radio itself was eighty bucks.

It's not recorded how or why he was able to get that permission when no other photographer was. Weegee said simply, "I made application and I got one," and later on offered, "I knew the boys." It seems likely to have been a situation where all that favor-currying (the coffee runs, the extra prints and weekend wedding pictures he'd made for cops) had made him a familiar local character, and then he just kept asking till he got approval. The radio-equipped car was the most valuable tool he had, after the camera itself. Now he could cruise from story to story, instead of constantly returning to headquarters to check the paper feed spitting out of the Teletype machine. It also meant that he was no slower out of the gate than the cops themselves. Weegee could arrive on the scene as they did, or perhaps even a moment before. Given that he'd promulgated the idea that he was the Edgar Cayce of crime photos, this provided the means to approach that ideal. He could now surf the city all night, changing direction in midocean if a better story came up than the one he was chasing. He was operating a mobile crime photojournalism unit, one with a tremendous competitive advantage.

He also made a seventy-five-cent investment that paid off big. Around 1937, he bought a rubber stamp and began using it to mark the back of every photo he sold. CREDIT LINE MUST READ / PHOTO BY A. FELLIG, this first version of the stamp read, and in small type it added that the picture had been sold for a single use only. The credit rule was honored in fits and starts. The *Daily News* and *Daily Mirror* ignored it, but most of the other papers began to obey the instructions on the stamp, fitfully and irregularly. A few times a month in the *Post*, the *Sun*, and the *World-Telegram*, and once in a while in the other papers, his photos would appear with a variant of the language on his stamp: "Fellig Photo," "Photo by Fellig," "Felig Foto." Then his name might disappear again for a while, under the cloak of Acme or the Associated Press.

Possibly because of Weegee's nudging, possibly because times were changing, several of the papers began crediting their own photographers as well, making their work traceable and visible today. The *Post*, for example, brought on a highly productive general-assignment man named Barney Stein, who stayed for decades. It also regularly ran pictures by an up-and-coming freelance named Irving Haberman, who was working a lot of the same angles at Brooklyn's police headquarters that Weegee had staked out in Manhattan. Haberman and Weegee, in fact, had a loose agreement to stay off each other's turf, which benefited Weegee in particular because, he said, he was always getting lost when he went to Brooklyn. (Haberman, from a business standpoint, had gone one better than Weegee: he'd started his own syndication bureau, called News-photos Inc., out of an office on Flatbush Avenue.) The *World-Telegram* got a lot of work out of a young man named Alan Fisher, who did his share of crime-scene time as well. These aggressive younger guys, in fact, seem to have cut into Weegee's business. As 1938 progressed into 1939, his presence in the *Post* and the *Telly* fell off noticeably. The photos of his that they did run often arrived through the agencies, especially the AP, rather than directly from him.

He'd also gotten into a fight with the *Post*. He never said publicly who he'd squared off against, but it was probably Paul Sann, the paper's night city editor. It was, once again, a battle over money and credit—Stettner later said it was because an editor had cut a photo of two crooks in half, running them separately, and the dispute was over whether Weegee should be paid for one picture or two—and it ended with an ultimatum. "Even if you're right, you're wrong," the editor told Weegee, and Weegee wrote him an angry letter telling him off in return. Although he sold a few of his pictures to the *Post* in the couple of years after that, the cozy relationship he had had with the paper was broken, and he stopped using the *Post*'s darkroom in the early morning, switching to the one at the Associated Press.

Still, he was more than making a living, and his four basic classes of photos (crashes, crime scenes, arrests, and fires) continued to be bread-and-butter work for him. There were auto wrecks all the time, although he seems to have become pickier about those, going for only the crunchiest ones in which the twisted metal is sometimes barely recognizable as a car. And, of course, he made lots of six-foot shots at police headquarters, some of people who wanted to be seen, others of those who shied away from the lens. Maxine Tursen, a Queens stenographer booked for fencing stolen cars, averted her eyes. So did Waxey Gordon, a prominent Prohibition beer baron who'd moved on to selling dope, as he headed into court. But Blanche Simms, a Harlem woman who'd stabbed a fireman after a sexual encounter (possibly a paid one), leveled her gaze at Weegee's camera as she was brought in. So did Fritz Kuhn, head of the German American Bund and America's foremost Nazi, arrested for forgery and larceny, who looked up from the booking desk just in time to face the flash. Each shot was a moment of human intensity in the face of stress. They were evocative, strong, punchy portraits. Yet there is, admittedly, a slight sameness to many of those head-and-torso shots made in a hurry. The surroundings and essential nature of the photos were limiting.

Out in the streets, though, he had more options, and his photos were more varied and often more interesting. Some were just odd situations to begin with, such as the time a yearling steer got loose from a First Avenue slaughterhouse and went galumphing down Madison Avenue one December day in 1938. Weegee managed to get there fast enough to photograph the unique scene as New York City cops tied it up on the sidewalk. Others were just awful little crimes. After downing eighteen beers, a guy named Robert Joyce got into a barroom fight over the Brooklyn Dodgers, then shot two Giants fans dead, and Weegee got Joyce's goggle-eyed remorse and confusion as he sat with a cop. Still others were deeper, more penetrating slices of urban life, and in the fall of 1939, he launched into the prime of his career, making a series of his most memorable pictures in just a few weeks. Several fires and murders from that season are

On this night in July 1938, Robert Joyce (at left) downed eighteen beers at a Brook-lyn bar, got in an argument over the Brooklyn Dodgers, and then shot and killed two men.

some of *the* Weegee news photographs, standouts among standouts, each extraordinary in its own way.

The fire pictures, being of everyday families and heroic firemen rather than gangsters and small-time crooks, are, if anything, more ago-nizing than the murders. The instincts Weegee had been honing, impel-ling him to turn the camera on the observers rather than the primary event, were beginning to produce results. "Editors told me," he explained in one interview, "that a fire picture had to show more than the burning building and that there was more to be photographed at a murder than the dead body. Human interest and the humorous touch was what they wanted. That was my cue. So, at fires, the last thing I did from then on was to photograph the burning building. I always watch out now for the human element—people being rescued, or watching the fire." Later in life, he went further, saying that he himself had straightened the bosses out: "The dopey editors—if there's a fire, they say, 'Where's the burning building?' I says, 'Look, they all look alike! . . . Here's the people *affected* by the burning building. Well, some understood it and some didn't."

There are hundreds of fire pictures, too many to list. Old ladies and young children being carried down ladders. A middle-aged couple, the man clutching his one good suit jacket and his wife's dress on a hanger (caption: "I don't know their names . . . but I did hear someone call him 'Pincus'"). Weary firemen, as they're being treated for smoke inhalation; smiling firemen, relieved as they pause for a cup of coffee at the end of a shift. More than once, as a house of worship burned, Weegee snapped the "rescue" of a plaster angel or a Torah, adding a schmaltzy note about its magic ability to survive. Those heart-tugging images were counterbalanced by the grimmest ones: canvas-wrapped bodies, sometimes brought out one at a time, sometimes lined up in groups. And, once, an incinerated truck driver, still in position at the wheel, recognizably human in form but not in detail. "I cry sometimes," Weegee explained to an interviewer, "but, I don't know . . . I think it's my job to record these things, like the police, the firemen, the ambulance drivers, and so forth."

The one that, according to Weegee, got to him most deeply was made at a tenement house on Bartlett Street in Brooklyn. A shoddy building in a fringe neighborhood had caught fire early in the morning of December 14, 1939. A pair of residents, a seven-year-old boy and his mother, had died, overcome by smoke as they tugged at a window, trying to get it open. (Many months later, the *Times* soberly reported that the landlord had skimped on fireproofing and had pleaded guilty to manslaughter.) Weegee was not the only photographer there: Irving Haberman got good photos that day that went to the *Post* and the *Sun*.

Weegee, though, got the great one. The *Mirror* ran it big the next morning, and it went around the world the next day on the wires. A woman with a black shawl thrown over her head like a hood stands, looking up, devastated, keening and sobbing as she learns that her sister and her young nephew are dead. Her young daughter stands next to her, her face also contorted with sobs. In other views of the two women, they are being led off by police and firemen, the older woman having just identified the bodies. In Weegee's telling, a fireman had just come downstairs and told the chief, "Boss, this is a roast." (Meaning that there were corpses to retrieve.) For whatever reason of positioning or luck, Haberman didn't quite catch the full degree of anguish in the women's faces and poses that

Henrietta Torres and her daughter Ada had just escaped their burning tenement on Bartlett Street in Brooklyn one December night in 1939. Ada's sister, Ramonia, and her young son, Edward, had not.

Weegee did. That photograph, even more than the set of hit-and-run pictures he'd made a couple of years earlier, seems to have run in nearly every paper in America that subscribed to Acme's service, often printed under the word ANGUISH. Weegee himself gave it a title that was uncharacteristically solemn: "I Cried When I Took This Picture." It's a believable claim. He was a man who played up his hardened nature, but he was not without sensitivity or soul, and he knew those firetrap tenements well. "The horrors that he saw as a news photographer," his friend Louis Stettner wrote, "could have crushed him; instead, they made him all the stronger." Weegee expressed pride a few years later after the FDNY used this particular photograph in a Fire Prevention Week campaign—and also cynicism, saying, "a lot of good it did for the young mother and the baby."

The burning buildings may have been more agonizing, but the murders were the pictures that were making him famous. Maybe it's the simple binary quality of life and death; maybe it's his technical felicity with "Rembrandt lighting," with angles and shadow play and gleaming streets slicked with rain (or is that blood?). But mostly it's that a lot of the murder pictures, implausibly, are more fun. Particularly when the dead men are gangsters, and thus presumably had it coming, their final portraits inspire a certain coal-black gallows humor in many of us. We can enjoy them, chuckling with our hands covering our mouths, as we keep our distance. Every newsroom has reporters and editors who make mordant, unpublishable wisecracks during tragedies; Weegee figured out how to get that tone into the newspaper itself, and bring readers in on the joke. What else can you say about (just to choose one) a tableau, recorded under the elevated train one night, in which a severed human head sits next to a cake box, roughly the same size, on the sidewalk? The scene includes a police photographer at work, his upper body covered by his camera's black cloth, so the total visible head count in the group comes out even. Weegee later explained that a cop had picked up the cake box from a local bakery in order to carry the head back to the police station, where he arrived with the box in one hand and his coffee in the other. It is the darkest of dark humor, a real-life version of *The Godfather*'s "Leave the gun. Take the cannoli."

Or (to choose another) see the photo he made one warm evening in September 1939, during the Feast of San Gennaro in Little Italy. During the big annual street fair, gunfire had broken out, and a racketeer named Joseph "Little Joe" La Cava ended up shot dead. The picture of him sprawled on Mulberry Street was memorable, but when he landed neatly below the neon sign for a scungilli parlor called O Sole Mio! (named for the Italian folk song whose title translates to "My Sunshine"), that was priceless.

A murder paired with a sign, in fact, was becoming a Weegee signature. On the night of December 9, 1939, he found himself on a corner of Tenth Avenue in Hell's Kitchen, as the police dealt with a run-of-the-mill rubout: David "the Beetle" Beadle, a midlevel operator on the docks nearby. He was also a loan shark with one robbery conviction who, it was rumored, had gotten away with a triple murder in Brooklyn a few years back. He'd recently been caught up in a battle for control of some longshoremen's jobs, and that night, as he exited a bar called the Spot, the Beetle took several bullets to the head, and fell to the curb, bleeding in the gutter. As usual, Weegee got there fast enough to photograph the corpse, though he did not have the exclusive: at least one other newsman (probably from the *Daily News*) made a picture of Weegee standing along-side the cops, sizing up the scene. But again, Weegee's version is the clas-sic because, like the mailbox photograph, it is self-captioning. (He had asked a cop, just outside the frame, to hold up an extension flash to make sure the sign was lit and readable.) To be put "on the spot," in the par-lance of the day, was to be the subject of a hit; add to that the fact that this was a spot-news photograph, and the sign over the barroom door reading THE SPOT carried a triple meaning. At least once, Weegee called this scene "my favorite murder."

The onlookers, though, whether at a murder or a fire, were even better material than a good internal caption, akin to the one Weegee found on the night of November 16, 1939. Around dusk, a small-time hood named Angelo Greco stepped out of the soda fountain and café he ran at 10 Prince Street. He was out on bail; a cop later described his field, presum-ably bookmaking, as one "where money is made more easily than by handling a shovel." Two customers were inside the café. As Greco lit a cigarette, four shots were fired. Two struck him in the head, and he was dead moments after he hit the ground. The shooter, or shooters, vanished.

Given that it was only a few blocks from police headquarters, the cops would've shown up fast, but there wasn't much for them to go on. One of the two customers had bolted the moment the shots were fired. The other had stuck around to finish his drink, but he claimed that he hadn't seen what happened. Next door, at 12 Prince, Pauline Cosenza and her nine children (ages seven through twenty-five) watched from the windows of their twenty-eight-dollar-a-month apartment. When the call came over the radio, at around 9:00 p.m., Weegee had just rolled out of bed and into his Chevy, planning to, as he put it, "take a nice little ride and work up an appetite."

What caught his attention when he stepped out of his car was not the body in a doorway but the surrounding human drama, especially the tenement families upstairs. From every single window, three or four heads were poking out, including the Cosenza kids and all their neighbors. He knew that they saw it like a cops-and-robbers movie, or maybe a lowbrow

The bar's sign was a double joke here. To be "put on the spot" was to be the victim of a hit, and "spot news" was the kind of grab-and-go photography Weegee practiced.

A rubout in the doorway of a soda shop at 10 Prince Street, every window filled with observers, on the night of November 16, 1939.

opera. One of the other papers' men made the customary ten-foot shot, as did the police evidence photographer, and so did Weegee. But he also stepped back—"about a hundred feet," he said—and set off a blinding burst of flash powder, the same stuff he'd used to photograph coffins at Duckett & Adler twenty years before. It was a tool he deployed infrequently these days, but in quantity it could throw more light than a flashbulb, and it was still useful when he had to illuminate half a city block in one blast.

Weegee titled the picture "Balcony Seats at a Murder," and the next day, it ran in the *Post*. Then he sold it to *Life*, where, the following week, it ran along with another photo he'd shot, a still life of the drawers in the city morgue. He kept a copy of the check stub he got from Time Inc., which read, "TWO MURDERS . . . $35.00." For years afterward, he joked that the "Balcony Seats" victim had been taken out with five gunshots and the other had been killed with two, saying, "*Life* pays $5 a bullet." (In fact, the magazine was just paying its standard rate, probably twenty-five dollars for a full page, ten dollars for a partial.) A few months later, the photograph won him a national award: third prize in *Editor & Publisher*'s annual photo contest. The certificate went on the wall over his bed, the twenty-five-dollar award went into his bank account, and a small gold medal—"with a real genuine diamond," he told people—went into his pocket. (He should've won: the photos that came in first and second are a lot duller.) For quite a while afterward, when other newspapermen knocked him or teased him, Weegee's response was "Let's see *your* medal." It was, he said, the photograph that established his national reputation.

The cops never found out who killed Angelo Greco, and those men milling around in the photo have long since joined him in the great beyond. But Vito Cosenza, who was upstairs at 12 Prince Street, was seven years old then, and he's eighty-five now, living in New Jersey. He doesn't remember much about that night; he was young, it was very long ago, and his siblings are gone, so there's nobody to ask. But he sure does remember being in *Life*. "There's a little face on the third floor, looking out," he says. "That's me."

"I keep to myself, belong to no group," Weegee once wrote, and it was true that he remained an odd-shaped peg that fit in few holes. Despite his eagerness to talk about taking pictures, he never joined the New York Press Photographers Association, as nearly all his colleagues did. (The NYPPA's annual dues were six bucks, and staff photographers were able to charge them to their employers. For a freelance, the fee was probably just enough to make him ask, "Why bother? What's in it for me?") Nonetheless, in the early forties, he did sidle his way into the fringes of one club, perhaps because it was so thoroughly devoted to the nuts and bolts and art and craft of photography.

The Workers Film and Photo League had gotten its start in New York around 1930, an outpost of a leftist photographers' and film-makers' association in Berlin. In 1936, the American group split in two, and the half devoted to nonmoving pictures renamed itself the Photo League and rented a floor at 31 East Twenty-First Street. There, one flight up from an upholstery shop, it became one of the very few places in the United States focusing on documentary photography—distinct from press photography because it was concerned with recording everyday life more than particular events—and especially documentary photography as art. (Alfred Stieglitz's gallery An American Place was another, but Stieglitz, aging and ailing, put on very few exhibitions.) The young Museum of Modern Art had only just begun paying serious attention to camera work, creating a dedicated department for photographs in 1940.

The Photo League's main force was a big, intense fellow named Sid

Grossman. He edited its journal, served as director, and coached and taught (and often harangued) younger photographers to make their pictures more honest and substantial. Serious photography was a small town at the time, and he got a lot of help from people who are now known as great talents of their generation: Berenice Abbott, Ralph Steiner, Walter Rosenblum, Aaron Siskind, W. Eugene Smith. Two giants of the era, Morris Engel and Ruth Orkin, met and later married after Orkin went to hear Engel speak at the League. Lewis Hine, a generation older than they, is famous today largely because Abbott and her Photo League colleagues rediscovered him in his final years—when he was forgotten, frail, and broke—and championed his work. Up-and-comers such as Arthur Leipzig took classes at the League. And the place also had its share of dilettantes and hangers-on, people who, as Leipzig later recalled, "just liked being there. Sometimes there'd be a speaker who'd come in and talk, and we enjoyed that. Other times there was a lot of garbage."

When Weegee started dropping by the gallery on Twenty-First Street, at first he would just sit in the back and listen to the other photographers talk. (His shyness could still manifest itself, apparently.) Given the extroverted stances some of them exhibited, there was plenty to hear. The group's worldview was colored by the members' politics, which were generally socialist leaning toward Communist. Many of the League's members, such as Leipzig and Rosenblum, were the children of working-class or middle-class Jews from Brooklyn and the Lower East Side. (Rosenblum had grown up a block or so from the Felligs' rear tenement, and indeed one of his largest bodies of work was a series called *Pitt Street*.) Nearly all strived for their work to inspire social reforms, but instead of going to the Dust Bowl to send pictures back to *Life*, most of the men and women of the Photo League did it at home, among the first-generation Americans they knew. Grossman made notable pictures of the labor movement. Others photographed streetscapes, tenement life, poor and working-class kids, and scenes from Jewish and Italian and African American ghettos. The League's front room on Twenty-First Street was a gallery where shows of this work could be hung and lectures delivered, with darkrooms built down the side, where the photographers could process their work. It was a contentious but congenial clubhouse for energetic people whose hands smelled like hypo. An annual membership cost $3.50 in 1939, plus an extra $1.50 if you wanted to use the darkrooms, though the fees were known to go uncollected and forgiven.

A significant part of the League's life, though, was not professional or political but social. There were regular competitions, such as the Crazy Camera Ball, for which members were asked to dress as the subject of a famous photograph, and a contest called the Photo Hunt, in which participants were given a topic to go capture on short notice, inventively. And, indeed, Weegee attended the Crazy Camera Ball in April 1941; he also entered a photo in the Photo Hunt and placed second, winning himself a new Kalart flashgun. (The picture showed one of his portly colleagues, camera in hand, shot dramatically from below, with the man's belly in the foreground. Regrettably, nobody seems to have recorded what the assigned topic of the night was, or whether Weegee came in costume.) At the League, the more established photographers were known to advise and coach the younger ones, of which there were many. Walter Rosenblum once noted that "if I was working in the darkroom and had a problem . . . there was usually an older member in the room who would be glad to set me straight." Leipzig said that Weegee was sometimes one of those older members: "He'd often walk into the darkroom, see me working, and he would discuss it with me—he was interested in what I was doing."

Although photography was a generally male business, there were significant numbers of women at the League, which surely drew Weegee there as much as the photo talk did. One of them, Erika Stone, who met him there, recalls that "he was after me—he was after everyone! I had to fend him off." Others told the same story.

One woman who was there, Wilma Wilcox, was quite different from most of the others. She'd been born not in a New York tenement but in Hartland Township, South Dakota (population: 746). In her thirties, she'd earned a master's degree in sociology from the University of Pennsylvania and was alternating seasons between Iowa and New York, holding down a job in the Midwest and doing further graduate studies for a few months at a time at Columbia University's New York School of Social Work. (The school was, at the time, a block from the Photo League's clubhouse.) She found herself stressed and unhappy, and a psychologist who evaluated her offered some advice, telling her (as she recalled it), "If you have an artistic ability and didn't use it, you got an emotional reaction."

She'd recently bought a camera, she said, and "the examiner raised the question about my continuing with photography . . . commenting that I would have to do the darkroom work. And so, as the result of that, I began looking for a place to get instruction in photography. It resulted in my going to the Photo League."

She signed up for classes and took to the darkrooms, and as the evenings progressed, she fell in with Weegee. She didn't know who he was at first: "During the course of the class, the instructor would stop and say, 'Weegee's just come in.' Didn't mean a thing to me!" And, anyway, he kept his distance at first. "He would come in every evening, and the instructor would say . . . 'Come on up and join us.' But he never would." Instead, he'd wait for the class to break up and then hold forth to a smaller, very young group of acolytes who would gather around him on a semicircle of chairs, some of them still wearing their wet darkroom aprons. He'd talk and talk, dropping cigar ashes as he went. Often three or four of the young crew would head down to the street afterward, so he could show them the Chevy parked out front. George Gilbert, a Photo League member, recalled "the delight of the small audience that formed beneath the street light to view the Master's Office." Then, Gilbert said, "He would drive away, leaving behind an unbelieving group who envied the independence and the casual way of life that they imagined for this friendly man."

Weegee and Wilcox had only a passing acquaintance in the beginning—"We'd have coffee together, he would stay for a little while, and then he would disappear because he had to get on his beat for the newspapers"—but an attraction between them formed. The first time she came by his apartment, she was shocked to see that he stored his photographs not in files but tossed into a pork barrel. He stopped by her Greenwich Village apartment now and then, but he didn't linger. "I'd come over more often," he told her after one visit, "but you need to get rid of all these pots and pans." It was a cryptic brush-off that Wilcox said she never entirely understood, but it was in character for him. Weegee was as undomesticated (and undomesticatable) a man as could be imagined, and he had zero desire to be fettered to the ordinary pleasures of "a good-looking wife, a hot dinner, a husky kid," as he'd joked in that *Popular Photography* profile. Besides, a conventional dating relationship was probably beyond him, given his hours and his dishabille. He was a solo operator by nature, and he seemed to want an impossible combination, someone who would provide companionship when he needed it but also let him be by himself much of the time. Wilcox, with her mix of social-worker patience and prairie sturdiness, was able to ride out this erratic affection, and let him do just that. She also spent those long periods in the Midwest, which perhaps allowed him to feel less pinned down.

Starting in mid-1941, Weegee became a dues-paying member of the Photo League, but he never quite became an insider. "He never was very close to them," Wilcox later explained. "He was a loner—he knew them, they knew him, but he was different. They knew that he kept to himself." Unlike most of the group, he was not (explicitly) devoted to social-justice commentary; he was shooting to sell as well as to inform. The Photo League's members tended to intellectualize their work. And even though his photographs consistently reflected many of the League's activist ideals, he was (perhaps owing to his lack of formal education, perhaps to his streetwise cynicism) suspicious, even dismissive, of those who claimed they were doing something for the greater good. "Messages?" he once told his friend Peter Martin. "I have no time for messages in my pictures. That's for Western Union and the Salvation Army. I take a picture of a dozen sleeping slum kids curled up on a fire escape on a hot summer night. Maybe I like the crazy situation, or the way they look like a litter of new puppies crammed together like that, or maybe it just fits with a series of sleeping people I'm doing. But twelve out of thirteen people looked at the picture and told me I'd really got a message in that one, and that it had social overtones."

The social aspect of the Photo League led to networking as well as flirtation, of course. In the spring of 1940, the talk of the New York press world was a new newspaper that was meant to overturn just about every conventional approach to the business. Ralph McAllister Ingersoll, the strong-willed and patrician editor who had helped launch Henry Luce's *Fortune* and *Life*, had been thinking for a couple of decades about everything that was wrong with the press and how he might start anew. He had, the previous year, taken an open-ended leave from his role as general manager of Time Inc. to get his idea going, and his connections had helped him raise a great deal of start-up capital. One of the biggest investors was Marshall Field III, the department store heir, and the rest of the list included a lot of household names: Wrigley, Whitney, Schuster, Gimbel. There was so much interest that Ingersoll said he ended up turning down a million dollars' worth of investments, a move he would regret later.

Ingersoll saw an underserved readership: New Yorkers who wanted a leftist newspaper that was smart about international and domestic affairs (like the *Times*) but that also embraced powerful photography (like the tabloids and *Life* and its competitor *Look*) and sharp, voicey writing, especially opinion writing (as in the *Herald Tribune* but from the opposite side of the aisle). The general idea was to do a tabloid for the highest common denominator rather than the lowest, and Ingersoll thought he could peel off "the most intelligent million of the three million who now read the *Daily News* and the *Daily Mirror*." His prospectus, widely quoted and reprinted multiple times in the paper itself, put forth the memorable line "We are against people who push other people around, just for the fun of pushing, whether they flourish in this country or abroad."

It was to be a liberal but not radical paper, pro-Roosevelt, pro-union, pro–New Deal, and anti-anti-Semitic. From the beginning, it was loudly critical of fascism and especially the Nazis. It was supposed to be not just factually solid and journalistically sound but emotionally engaging. It was to be readable, more like a magazine than a newspaper, eschewing the clutter and chaos of most tabloids' pages. It would have no ads, and to make up the difference, it would cost a nickel at the newsstand instead of the other papers' two or three cents. It was, Ingersoll said, to be "written in words and pictures . . . written in English—as distinct from journalese." It would take "an interest in the stage on which news is played. In *PM*, the murder will not be committed at 2614 Amsterdam Ave., but 'in a six-story red brick tenement on upper Amsterdam Ave. (No. 2614), the ground floor of which is shared by a German delicatessen and a Polish newsdealer.'" Most of all, "Over half *PM*'s space will be filled with pictures—because *PM* will use pictures not simply to illustrate stories, but to tell them. Thus, the tabloids notwithstanding, *PM* is actually the first picture paper under the sun." An innovative process involving heated ink and chilled paper made those pictures look sharper and more nuanced in *PM* than they did elsewhere and gave them more visual power. As George Lyon, Ingersoll's managing editor, put it, *PM*'s photos were supposed to "make customers reach for a nickel."

The prepublication hype was immense. In *The New Yorker*, Wolcott Gibbs called its charter subscription drive "one of the most vehement pro-

motion campaigns since Lydia Pinkham's Vegetable Compound," referring to a ubiquitously advertised patent medicine. *PM*'s circulation
manager told Gibbs that "We offered 'em everything except a twenty-
dollar bill with each copy." But it did look like a genuinely promising paper,
and Ingersoll was apparently deluged with employment applications from
idealistic young reporters. Weegee, by contrast, didn't chase a job; instead,
he said, he waited for them to come to him. The photo editor hired to
help launch *PM* was William McCleery, who had worked at the AP
and at *Life*, and thus was sure to have known Weegee's work and growing reputation. And what McCleery and Ingersoll had to offer him was
significant: instead of suppressing its contributors' styles and credits in
favor of an institutional voice, *PM* was going to go the opposite way and
try to showcase the individual personality of everyone who worked there.
(As one reader recalled, "They'd climb right up on your lap and muss
your hair.") Not only would photos carry their makers' names; there
would be substantial captions that would sometimes make an attempt,
in the manner of that "six-story red brick tenement" from the prospectus,
to show how the news had been gathered and made. If you did great
stuff for *PM*, everyone would know *you* had done it.

That was the way to get him. Weegee had spent half a decade arguing with "the dopey editors" over credit, and the route to his heart was a
promise of personal recognition. Still, he was such a relentless nonconformist that he couldn't make himself into a staff photographer, so he
made a deal with *PM* that was mutually beneficial: he would bring them
his work first, on no fixed schedule, and they'd put him on a retainer of
seventy-five dollars per week. That was upper-middle-class money for a
single man in 1940, nearly as much as he'd been making as a freelance.
(Ben Hecht, who earned way more knocking out movie scripts than Weegee ever would, also got seventy-five dollars a week from *PM* for a column,
which he wrote principally for the prestige and the platform.) For the
first time in his freelance life, Weegee would have a guaranteed steady
income, and a good one at that. He would also be able to keep selling his
work to Acme and the other syndication services and to any magazines
that came calling. *PM* would merely get first crack at his take.

There may have been another reason he finally accepted a semi-
exclusive deal: the murder rate was falling. Prohibition, ended in December 1933, was receding into the past, and although New York was still a

mobbed-up town, the organized crime that had developed in the twenties and early thirties was simply less of an everyday presence than it had been. Ordinary urban mayhem—disorganized crime, if you like—was on the wane as well. The widespread coverage of gangs and gangsters in the tabloids had actually had an effect on public opinion. Politicians began to call for more law enforcement. The FBI got more agents and a bigger budget. In 1933, the final year without beer, the per capita murder rate was 9.7 killings per thousand people. By 1940, it was 6.2, the lowest it had been in twenty-five years. In Chicago, the homicide rate fell by half.

That year, *Life* ran a big story titled "Murder Inc.: Justice Overtakes the Largest and Most Cruel Gang of Killers in U.S. History." It included a large photo, credited only to the New York *Daily News*, of a gangster named Irving "Puggy" Feinstein whose burned corpse had been found the previous year in a vacant lot in Brooklyn. Though it carried no name, it was a Weegee special. Just as he had at the Hessler trunk murder, Weegee stood over Puggy's partially uncovered body and pointed at it as he made his picture, again putting himself into the action. One of Puggy's killers, Martin "Buggsy" Goldstein, had already made a couple of stops before Weegee's camera himself, including one during that very busy week in 1937, in between Julia Nussenbaum's murder and Father Divine's arrest. Murder Inc. may not really have had an official photographer, but its unofficial one had done a pretty good job of documenting the group's latter days.

At *PM*, Weegee was, for the first time, top dog, one of two established talents on the team, the other being the already legendary Margaret Bourke-White. Brilliant and glamorous, and paid triple what Weegee was getting, she still didn't last in the job. She was far too obsessive and perfectionistic an artist to deal with newspaper work. She'd be sent out to document some corner of Hell's Kitchen or Brownsville, and would come back with hundreds of not-yet-processed negatives an hour before her press deadline. She washed out and went back to magazines within the year.

Once she left, Weegee became the ace of the photo department, with a talented bunch around him. Irving Haberman came on staff, as did the *World-Telegram*'s Alan Fisher. Morris Engel, who was all of twenty-two, and Arthur Leipzig, who was even younger, started as freelance contributors and were soon hired. In classic newspaper-photographer fashion, the others tended to admire Weegee's pictures while grousing that they could do just as well, and maybe better, themselves. "I liked what he did—I didn't like his attitude. His attitude was Weegee-only, and that turned me off," Leipzig recalled seven decades later. He did admit, however, that Weegee "had a sense of timing and what he could do." What did he do best? "Dead people." Fisher thought even less of Weegee, calling him "close to a fraud."

It may have irritated his colleagues, but Weegee's rough-edged garrulousness got him places. On one of his first days at the *PM* offices, possibly even before he signed on, he was cracking wise to a colleague about something he'd seen, and Ingersoll overheard him. The editor recognized Weegee's voice for what it was—funny, distinctive, New Yorky, exactly what he wanted in his paper—and as Weegee later told the story, "He insisted every time I took a picture, that I write a story with it. So to get out of that, I said, 'Look, Mr. Ingersoll. I can't spell.' He says, 'I can get plenty of guys that can spell. I can't get guys that can write like you.'" Ingersoll had also hired the great crime novelist Dashiell Hammett because he liked his hard-boiled voice on the page; why not get his counterpart with a camera? Weegee didn't file a story with every single picture, but he did it often enough to become what amounted to an irregular columnist. "At first I was scared," he admitted, "but I sat down to a typewriter and finally found words for what I had seen and felt. That's all there was to it."

Ingersoll got one of those quasi-columns into print before *PM* was even officially a publication. For three days ahead of the paper's launch, he produced full-scale test issues of *PM*, numbered "Volume 0." In the third of them, dated Monday, June 17, 1940, Weegee delivered a spread that set the tone for his work there and, arguably, for the publication itself.

The previous afternoon had been a warm Sunday in June, meaning that the beach at Coney Island was filled with New Yorkers getting a few hours' relief from their stuffy apartments. Newspapers routinely ran a photo of the busy beach, and Weegee "figured that, being hot, I might as well go to Coney Island and get the first crowd picture of the season. Being a free-lance photographer, I knew I could sell a few here and there . . . I jumped into my little Chevvy, bought from the profits of crime pictures, and was on my way." He claimed to have picked up a girl hitchhiker on the way who showed him a shortcut around the traffic.

What he saw was not merely busy. "The crowds at Coney were enormous . . . I started walking on the beach, getting sand in my shoes, stockings, and underwear. I reached a lifeguard lookout station . . . I climbed out . . . Just the spot to get an elevation shot from." (Those strings of sentences and fragments joined by ellipses, by the way, are in direct imitation of Walter Winchell's rat-a-tat column and radio delivery. It's a device Weegee used in most of his writing, to give it news-ticker forward motion.) He wanted a full-frame image of the crowd, packed edge to edge with people.

It wasn't a completely fresh idea, mind you: newspapers ran some version of a crowded-beach picture every summer. The *Sun* had printed one almost exactly a year earlier, produced not by a photojournalist but by a local chamber of commerce affiliate called the Coney Island News Bureau. The Hearst papers had sent photographers in airplanes to record the beach covered in sunburnt humanity. But that didn't mean it wasn't a salable image every year, and Weegee was out to make a better one, or at least an interesting fugal variation on the same old theme.

Although he said that he clambered up on a lifeguard's chair, the landmarks visible in the pictures suggest that he was standing on the inland end of Steeplechase Pier. Either way, that put him about twenty feet above the sand, enough to get a good view of the dense crowd. He faced northeast, down the beach and angled toward the boardwalk, and then began screaming and hooting like a madman. Hundreds of people peered at him, squinted, waved. He tipped his camera so that the horizon line ran corner to corner, giving him the largest possible swath of the crowd on his negative, and made two quick photographs. When he cropped down the image in the darkroom that evening, he was able to cover the photo paper almost completely with waving, sweaty bodies. Only a couple of small lakes of space revealed the sand beneath them. McCleery must have been delighted, because he not only gave this photograph the two-page centerfold of the new paper; a column of type down the left side brought Arthur Fellig out of the anonymous Acme shadows for good.

"Weegee, whose real name is Arthur Fellig, took this picture at four in the afternoon," it began. "The temperature was 78 degrees. The Coney Island Chamber of Commerce guessed there were 700,000 people. Nobody really knows. Herewith is Weegee's own story of how he took this picture." And that was followed by four digressive, spirited paragraphs in which Weegee recounted his day: the drive to Coney Island, the female hitchhiker he picked up, the shortcut she showed him to avoid Prospect Park traffic, the size of the crowd as compared to that of the world's fair out in Queens, the cute redhead whose phone number he'd collected on the beach, even the f-stop and shutter speed and type of film he'd used. "After looking over the crowd," his account wound up, "I think they ought to move the World's Fair to Coney Island . . . I can get a Kosher pastrami sandwich at Coney Island . . . Show me where you can get it at the Fair. And there are millions like me."

Indeed: the man had, even before *PM* was officially open for business, found his audience and his conduit to it. His photo-gearhead interests, his unique voice, his shticky sense of humor, his view of proletarian New York, his photographic ambitions, even (in the form of that pastrami sandwich) his Lower East Side Jewishness—all of it fit into *PM*'s editorial ethos. He even got another Coney picture into the same issue of the paper, showing a few kids waiting anxiously with policemen at the station where parents could collect lost children. Since the test issue of *PM* hadn't really been circulated, he resold the crowd photo to the Sunday *New York Times*'s rotogravure section, getting his name in the paper of record for the first time. The *Times* being the *Times*, it credited "Arthur Fellig" rather than "Weegee."

In *PM*'s first month, Weegee's pictures appeared in the paper eight times, none of them quite as big as the Coney Island double-truck (that is, facing pages), but all with some presence on the page, and all with engaging, lively captions. The paper itself was a half success, its strengths and weaknesses alike bound up in Ingersoll's arrogance toward his competitors. Readers had expected a transformative media experience from *PM*, and what they got instead was an inconsistent and often late-to-the-story but pretty good newspaper whose reach, editorial and otherwise, exceeded its grasp. (In just one of many gaffes, the circulation department accidentally lost the entire list of paid-up charter subscribers, and those readers never got their papers.) Yet although the writing and editing were uneven, Weegee, Haberman, Fisher, and their colleagues hit their targets a very high percentage of the time. Almost every edition contained at least a couple of great photographs. For the very first Sunday paper, Weegee had gone to Manhattan Beach and (somehow) managed to persuade three swimsuit-clad cuties to pose wearing rubber masks of

Hitler, Mussolini, and Stalin. ("Maybe this comely pyramid is spoiled by the faces," wrote reporter Charles Michie in the story underneath. "Made of molded latex and hand-painted, [the masks are] selling like hot cakes at a dozen novelty stores. The Hitler false face, at $1.75 to $3, is most popular.") In the paper's early days, Weegee covered a bombing at the world's fair and a lightning strike at a department store on 125th Street.

He also published a picture that's a little masterpiece of wiseacre editorial commentary. Joseph Elsberry McWilliams was a candidate for Congress in 1940, from the district in Manhattan that included Yorkville, a working- and middle-class German American neighborhood on the East Side. He ran his independent campaign under the banner of the American Destiny Party, but he was fundamentally an America Firster in the vein of Henry Ford and Charles Lindbergh. Winchell called him "Joe McNazi." Born in dirt-poor rural Oklahoma, McWilliams had adopted as his symbol a horse-drawn Conestoga wagon, in which he rode around New York City as he campaigned.

On Thursday, July 4, 1940, when a speech McWilliams was giving crossed into unvarnished anti-Semitism, things turned violent. The candidate ended up arrested for disorderly conduct, paying a minor fine, and was back in his wagon, making more speeches, by Sunday. That's when Weegee caught up with him and managed to place himself at the side of the horse, photographing McWilliams upward from his feet. And what readers saw in the paper the next day was a masterly pairing of headline and subject. MCWILLIAMS, FASCIST CANDIDATE, FACES HIS FUTURE UNDISCOURAGED, it read. What does he face, in the foreground of the photo? The back end of his ride. Not every reader figured it out, but the joke was pretty plain: *Joe McWilliams is a horse's ass.* Weegee may not have been an overtly political artist, but as a proud Jew he was more than happy to give the business to a Nazi, and here he did it with a gag worthy of Mel Brooks.

Unless you count that picture as an editorial, the closest Weegee ever came to explicit activism was probably a set of photographs he made that same month, in July 1940. He (or perhaps an observant policeman or editor) had begun to notice a striking number of car crashes on the Henry Hudson Parkway, the elevated highway along the western edge of Manhattan, right by the Seventy-Second Street on-ramp. Over the preced-

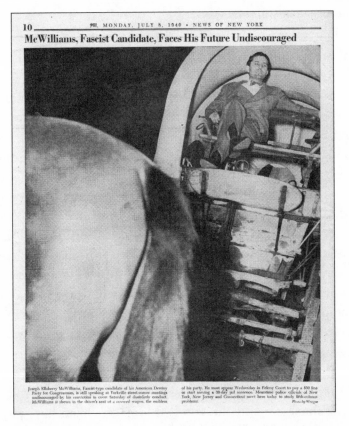

McWilliams, Fascist Candidate, Faces His Future Undiscouraged

Joseph Ellsberry McWilliams, Fascist-type candidate of his American Destiny Party for Congressman, is still speaking at Yorkville street-corner meetings undiscouraged by his conviction in court Saturday of disorderly conduct. McWilliams is shown in the driver's seat of a covered wagon, the emblem of his party. He must appear Wednesday in Felony Court to pay a $50 fine or start serving a 30-day jail sentence. Meantime police officials of New York, New Jersey and Connecticut meet here today to study fifth-column problems.

Photo by Weegee

Joe McWilliams, an openly fascist candidate for Congress in 1940, rode around in a Conestoga wagon to flaunt his view of Americanness.

ing year, he had collected a horrifying set of photographs of twisted cars, over and over, every one at the same spot. In fifteen months, ten cars had crashed, four people had been killed, and nineteen had been hurt. This was classic outrage reporting, a small-bore version of what the radical investigative journalist I. F. Stone did, but instead of gleaning facts and figures from public records Weegee did it with a camera and patience. (He wasn't always so patient. Weegee once delivered a similar story to the *Post* as well, and for that one, he had come up with eleven wreck photos on the streets, then padded out the total to a baker's dozen by visiting an auto junkyard.)

This time, at least, it worked. The city undertook a traffic study, and a few months later guardrails went up and the curb was rebuilt. *PM* took credit for it, reproducing its page from the previous summer with a new photo of the reconstructed intersection. It was a small victory, but Weegee was proud of the result. "This work," he later wrote proudly, "I consider my memorial."

Whereupon he went and shot the Coney Island picture again.

Why not? The test issue of *PM* hadn't been widely or officially circulated, and the photo imperfectly showed the sheer density of the crowd: it revealed a few bare patches of sand. So he went back, now that it was July, when the beach was likely to be even hotter and more crowded.

The second version ran on July 22, 1940, and this time it was impeccable. *PM*'s treatment was the same, with a better headline, one that read like a news ticker: YESTERDAY AT CONEY ISLAND . . . TEMPERATURE 89 . . . THEY CAME EARLY, STAYED LATE. The editorial note on top mimicked the previous one; this time, the chamber of commerce estimate put the crowd at a million. (And, again, "Nobody really knows.")

Weegee's July caption was a tighter, funnier rewrite of the one from the June test issue. He recounted parking difficulties again, and noted that he'd arrived early to take pictures of couples who refused to give their names ("It's just me and the wife"). He hadn't been happy with the results, he said, and had gone back to Manhattan; then he returned to make the crowd photo, and again stopped by the lost-children shack under the Boardwalk, which, he reports, had seen 150 kids that day. This time the girl hitchhiker was someone he picked up on the way back to Manhattan. And instead of just telling us he got a pastrami sandwich, he offers a stomach-roiling food diary of the afternoon: "While I was at Coney I had two Kosher frankfurters and two beers at a Jewish delicatessen on the Boardwalk. Later on for a chaser I had five more beers, a malted milk, two root beers, three Coca-Colas, and two glasses of buttermilk. And five cigars, at 19 cents." That final paragraph was picked up, without the photo, in at least half a dozen other papers around the country as a witty little news item all on its own.

As for this second version of the photo it, too, was better. He had raised his eyeline just enough to catch Coney's tallest ride, the Wonder Wheel, in the background, anchoring his photo with a familiar piece of the cityscape. (Doubly so today, because the Wonder Wheel, opened in 1920, is still operating.) He had done his hooting and hollering well enough that everyone in the crowd, it seems, is looking straight at the

On a hot weekend in July 1940, the head count on the beach at Coney Island approached one million.

lens. And he'd once again turned the job around in no time, ready for the next morning. It was a strong enough image that the *New York Times* bought and ran it in the Sunday paper yet again, this time using a slight variant of the *PM* photo, made a moment earlier or later. That same weekend, an unnamed *Daily News* photographer (perhaps it was Weegee, but more likely a staff man, ripping him off) shot a front-page picture from the same spot with the same framing. The dramatic crowd photo was great documentary populist photography, the kind of thing the Photo League folks aspired to and, apparently, something newspapers liked so much that they didn't mind being the second or third to publish it. It was the story of a city and its people.

Except his chronicle of that eighty-nine-degree day may have been more fanciful than Weegee let on. One of the people who appears front and center in that photo is a three-year-old girl named Katherine Kolea, now Katherine Costa. She was there with her father, James Patrick Kolea, and her cousin on a visit from Philadelphia. And she and her brothers and cousins are pretty sure—not *absolutely* sure, mind you, but pretty sure—that their trip to Coney Island happened the weekend her brother Phil was born. Mr. Kolea, an old-world Albanian, had two daughters at the time, was desperate for a boy, and hoped somehow that leaving town might turn his luck. He took his kids up to New York and went to the beach. And they made the trip not on July 21, the day before the picture was taken, but two weeks earlier, over the Fourth of July long weekend. James Kolea got his wish when his first son, Phil, was born on July 5.

In other words, if the Koleas' collective memory is accurate, Weegee made the picture at his leisure on a reasonably warm afternoon (the high on July 5, 1940, was eighty degrees) that was sure to be crowded because it fell across the holiday. Then he banked it, waiting for a scorcher, and offered it to his editor as fresh material when it was two weeks old, with a concocted travelogue about his day. That might not be a firing offense, but it's certainly a cheat. (The hitchhiker, the unnamed couples; were they made up, too? How about the lost kids? The buttermilk? At least the parking headache was true, because it's always true.) It is worth noting that he didn't fake anything about the image itself: he certainly didn't, as rumor had it, beef up the density of the crowd by double-exposing. It's the backstory that's piped, and the backstory was less about the picture than about Weegee himself—more of his mythmaking.

Still, you have to ask: If the date was falsified, is that photo a lie? It shows us a hot and incredibly crowded day at Coney Island in July 1940, and it does indeed tell the story of such a day, very well. Does it matter that the day he described and the day he photographed may have been a couple of weeks apart? Yes, it does. Was the Fourth of July weekend busier than all the others? Yes, it was. Does the fudging affect the truth of the moment he captured? A little. It is, regardless of the date underneath, a great picture of a real moment. Just, perhaps, not *that* real moment.

Hard-news events, of course, could not really be manipulated in that way, and much of Weegee's work continued to be straight-up spot-news photography. On May 10, he'd even had a close call with real injury on the job. At 12:25 that morning, a water main under Seventh Avenue broke, filling the street with mud and drawing Weegee uptown to shoot it. Half an hour after the event, by which time the other photographers had done their work and left, a gas main exploded, blowing a twenty-five-foot hole in the street and spewing steam and mud onto passersby, including Weegee. One woman was badly burned and ended up in the hospital. Weegee escaped without severe injuries, and made the exclusive pictures of the night's event, showing a fourteen-story geyser erupting into the Manhattan sky.

As 1940 rolled on, he published in *PM* once every three days or so, and he kept up a slightly diminished freelance presence elsewhere. The *Journal-American*, for example, ran an action shot of a fireman rescuing an apartment dweller on July 20, less than a month after *PM* had launched. Weegee lobbed a story into the trade journal *Editor & Publisher* about that one, claiming proudly that it was the first time he'd made it to a fire in time to photograph the rescue. (It wasn't; he'd published at least one such picture before. Why not just say, "Yes, folks, I've done it again"? Because he knew that a milestone makes better copy.) As usual, though, he gave the reporter lots of chatter and color. "Fellig says that his big problem when shooting so fast," reported *Editor & Publisher*, "is to get rid of the used [flash]bulbs. With so many firemen and policemen about they can't be thrown aside indiscriminately, and so he just says 'Here' to some passerby and hands him a hot bulb. He naively adds that they all seem so surprised. . . . Fellig's procedure is ingenious to say the least, and might be adopted by any photographer who isn't particular about what happens to him."

He was, it was evident, working all the time and enjoying his success. *PM*'s idea of a good picture was broader than the tabloids', and not every frame he shot had to sell itself quite so hard as it had when he'd been living without a retainer. That meant he could mix the car crashes and fires with bits of urban life, the stuff generally categorized under the hoary catchall term "human interest." When several photographers contributed to yet another hot-weather story later that summer, about men with jobs made unbearable by the heat, he offered a joking self-portrait: Weegee in his undershorts as he stood in a basin of cold water in the darkroom. The editors ran it, too.

His news sense meant that his standards for originality in these feature pictures were high. Even in the realm of newspaper staples, such as funny animal photos, he avoided the ordinary. A photo of a litter of kittens born in a restaurant on Rivington Street would probably not have made any New York paper even on the slowest of July news days. But when the cat in what the caption writer described as "Mike Guerrera's Oriental restaurant at No. 56 (Scungilli, Capozzelle, steaks and chops)" was spotted nursing five kittens and two puppies, that was weird enough to perk up the editor's ears. And when the inventive photographer dropped those seven furballs into seven of the restaurant's lined-up water glasses, that caught the photo desk's funny bone. It took up four columns in *PM*. The *Sun*, which had a weakness for cute-animal items, went so far as to give the backstory a few column inches (under the headline 2 DOGS FOUND IN CAT LITTER; OWNERS BAFFLED BUT BELIEVE WHAT THEY SEE; THE DOCTORS ARE SURPRISED). Weegee had a certain amount of scorn for this kind of picture—"mental masturbating," he called it—but five bucks was five bucks.

Similarly, when a tenement house burned down on West Thirtieth Street, he made his usual photos but also caught two pets that had been rescued from the flames by their owner. *PM*'s caption used the occasion to tweak him about his knack for heightening reality: "Weegee, who never fakes a picture, found two refugees in an 11th Avenue coffee pot around

Inflating the balloons for the Macy's Thanksgiving Day Parade: when Weegee photographed him, even Santa Claus looked a little like one of those corpses laid out on the sidewalk.

the corner. They are identified as Pick and Pat, twin pets of Theresa Nastroserio, 11."

Come November, he applied the same kind of creative eye to a scene that's now cliché but was quite inventive then: the inflation of the giant balloons for the Macy's Thanksgiving Day Parade. Among several great images he made that day, a helium-filled Santa Claus, pinned down by ropes and canvas on West 106th Street, took up a full page in the paper that holiday morning. Santa, his eyes open and black and a little unsettling, looks faintly like one of the guys Weegee usually photo-graphed dead on the street in Little Italy.

This is not to say he didn't keep his hand in on his old subjects. A car ended up in the river at 3:30 one July morning, having careered off the edge of Battery Place, and the shot of the derrick hauling up the wreck and its dead driver went into *PM*. A burning house one night in Long Island City, an early-morning raid on an illegal moonshining operation on the West Side, a barge rammed and half-sunk by a British freighter in the East River—all inspired him to hop in the Chevy and get there. In the case of an actress in a horrible domestic dispute—she'd been set afire by her husband—he even played picture chaser once again, supply-ing her headshot to *PM*. On another night, he was nosing around a crime scene with a flashlight and found a scattering of teeth that had been shot out of a man's mouth. He turned them over to the police.

What was noticeably less present in *PM* was the dead bodies. Their absence may have stemmed less from the paper's desire to go high-brow than from the markedly diminished homicide rate. The Prohibition-into-the-Depression boom in crime was simply over, and the public infatuation with pinstriped gangsters who machine-gunned one another was on the wane. Maybe it was the FBI's attempt to deglamorize crimi-nal behavior; maybe it was the increasing sense, as a mass murderer took over Germany and then Czechoslovakia and Poland and France, that kill-ing people wasn't so much fun. The result, though, was that weeks would go by without a corpse on the pages of *PM*, and even the tabloids' dead-guy coverage (not only Weegee's but everyone's) slackened. Most of the deaths Fellig covered for *PM* were gruesome but less premeditated: fires, car crashes, the occasional suicide. That suspicion-inducing photo of the corpse under the MAIL EARLY FOR DELIVERY BEFORE CHRISTMAS plac-ard was the only shooting victim he documented for *PM* in all of 1940, and it was not a gangland hit. The dead man, Lewis Sandano, had been a small-time thief shot by police when he reached into his pocket for—they thought—a gun. There was no gun.

In fact, Weegee not only was beginning to pull away from the low-down murder beat but was also starting to find subjects at the other end of society, the part sometimes called Society. In December 1940, he made his way to the opening night at the Metropolitan Opera, then in its old house on West Thirty-Ninth Street, near Broadway. It was probably at the behest of *PM*'s photo editors—they had dispatched two other photographers there that night—and he was, he admitted, out of place. Wearing his regular clothes among the crowd in evening dress, he said, "I felt like an Italian in Greek territory . . . Without a high hat, the cops showed you the street. They gave me dirty looks but I was saved by my press card." Alan Fisher was shooting the glamorous ladies in dresses and jewels, and he knew who was who; Weegee, by contrast, just wandered around looking for something unexpected and interesting, and he got it. As the crowd broke up after the performance, four men stood at the curb waiting for their drivers. He photographed them—but from behind, as a strip of top hats and collars. It was a witty solution, one that came off just right for *PM*, as a tweak to the starchy nature of the event. It definitely was a picture that would have "told it to Sweeney," that imagined archetypal reader of the *Daily News*. But here, in *PM*, it also told it to Sweeney's striving kid, who had gone to City College and gotten his degree. Steiner and Ingersoll put it on the front page, cropped to its essence: four hats and shoulders, their satiny sheen popping them off the night-sky background, in a narrow strip, with a long line of type underneath: "The Opera Opened Last Night. Weegee made this picture. He tells how on page 2." It was not the last great photo he'd make at the Met.

He had one more great story before the end of the year, one that only someone with his specially tuned sense of the cops' daily activity could have made. The NYPD had figured out that a very swank rented town house on East Sixty-Eighth Street, just off Fifth Avenue, was home to a dressy gambling operation run by George Herrick, an associate of the late gangster Arnold Rothstein. They planned a late-Sunday-night raid, and Weegee, who said he'd initially thought he might take the evening off and get some sleep, delivered an account in *PM* the next day under yet another "Weegee's Own Story" headline. "I was awakened by the rumble of moving cars. I learned that Police Inspector Mike Murphy was on a raid . . . I know that Mike don't go after cheap crap games," it began. Most likely, Fellig had been tipped off by one of the cops that something big was going down.

He arrived at the house just as the low-key raid commenced and flashed his press card to get past the plainclothesman at the door. "Inside," he wrote, "I was surprised . . . The place looked like Anna Swift's on 70th Street." (Swift, owner of a fancy West Side "massage parlor" that

Weegee later claimed to have patronized, had recently been raided and jailed for operating a house of prostitution. He'd photographed those arrests, too.) "The same beautiful furnishings . . . it looked like intermission. Beautiful gals in ermine and minks." He went on to detail a scene in which the *News* and *Herald Tribune* reporters had commandeered a roulette table and started playing, and the buffet table had been picked clean by the cops.

PM turned Weegee's pictures and captions into what editors call a tick-tock, a procession of words and images detailing exactly how the raid went down. The police cars pull up. A uniformed policeman breaks the glass in the front door so he can turn the inside knob and enter. We see the house's luxe furnishings, and the dice and roulette tables, and the police, and a few expensively dressed patrons and servants. On the back page of the paper, one of those patrons, a woman with her white fur pulled over her face, is being ushered out by the police.

It was a fabulous catch for Weegee, doubly so for a Monday paper, and it filled three of *PM*'s thirty-two pages. The raid had happened just early enough to catch the final editions of the morning dailies, and the *Mirror* put one of Weegee's pictures on the front page. By the time the afternoon papers locked up, he had had his chance to make rounds and sold pictures there as well. "When my flash bulb went off," he said, "one gal, wrapped from head to foot in ermine, swore at me. Such bad Park Avenue manners." She had good reason to be cursing if she was from one of those families that was inclined to stay out of the press, because, a few days later, the photo appeared as *Life*'s "Picture of the Week," as a full page captioned "Gambling lady scuttles anonymously from New York 'joint' following police raid." Two days later, Weegee spent Christmas Eve covering lost men in the missions of the Bowery and the Lower East Side, and came home to a gift waiting on his doorstep of tea and lychee nuts from his Chinese laundryman. He'd seen people wearing both furs and rags over the course of forty-eight hours, and it was pretty clear where his sympathies lay.

He had—despite his lone-wolf instincts, and despite taunts like that COCKROACH CAFÉ sign someone had pinned to his door—fallen into the camaraderie of police reporters. When the *Times*'s John J. Gordon retired in January 1941, after thirty-four years on the job, Weegee photographed his good-bye dinner and wrote a warm send-off for *PM* ("Words and Pictures by Weegee, a Police Reporter Himself"). He couldn't resist taking a poke at the man's employer: "On the right is Frederick T. Birchall, *Times* editorial writer and life-long friend of Gordon. I've often wondered what a *Times* editorial writer looks like. Personally, I prefer Winchell. The *Times* editorials are all double talk to me."

Gordon and his fellow police reporters and photographers had, in fact, become his literal neighbors. A few months earlier, a group of them had raised funds to buy and rebuild 4 Centre Market Place, creating a modern press center right next door to Jovino's gun shop, one with decent lighting and clean tile showers. More than fifty reporters used it, and although it was formally named the Headquarters Press Building, it became known as the Shack. Color-coded lights on the façade could summon any given news organization's people from headquarters (or the Headquarters Tavern) in a hurry. The building had a direct line to the NYPD's public relations office and housed a stock of reference material, such as phone books, that the reporters could share.

The Shack had its share of oddballs—and, Weegee told one writer, "I hate half of those guys." One reporter was a dog fancier, another a brooding depressive who regularly locked himself in his office. Most, though, were just working stiffs. "They could easily have been cops," recalls Nicholas Pileggi, who worked there a few years later. "A lot of the papers and photographers and reporters were more detective than they were press. They were all streetwise. And they had wonderful rapport with the cops." Despite the pranks and the sniping, there was a certain foxhole camaraderie among the newsmen, and they at least respected Weegee's work: a print of "Balcony Seats at a Murder" hung on the wall of the Shack for years.

The day after Gordon's retirement photos appeared in the paper, there was a shoot-out on Fifth Avenue, right in front of the B. Altman & Co. department store, and Weegee, for once, was not there to catch it. Two brothers, William and Anthony Esposito, had held up a local businessman who put up some resistance and paid for it with his life. The thieves fled, running through Altman's with guns drawn, and just after they exited through the other end of the building, a policeman shot William, who fell to the sidewalk. Before he passed out, he returned fire, hitting the cop, a cabdriver, and a bank security guard who tried to intervene. As for Anthony, he ducked into a nearby Woolworth's, where a crowd of angry female shoppers began beating him up until six policemen stepped in. The police commissioner, Lewis Valentine, called the Espositos "two mad dogs," and "Mad Dog Killers" became headline shorthand for the brothers. It'd been nearly a decade since Vincent "Mad Dog" Coll had been bumped off in that phone booth, so there was room for a couple of new rabid nicknames.

This detailed blow-by-blow account exists partly because a man named Max Peter Haas was there. He worked for a photo agency called European Picture Service, directly across the street on the sixth floor of the Empire State Building. As the shooting began, he grabbed his camera and got downstairs and documented the action as it happened. It was as compelling a set of pictures as Weegee's series on the car crash a couple of years earlier, and it was played around the world. It was also a group of photographs Weegee could not have made, because Haas was using a newish weapon in the journalist's arsenal, one that was not yet very popular among American newsmen: a Leica 35-millimeter camera. Instead of inserting single film sheets in holders, ten or twenty seconds apart, he could click-advance-click-advance and get off a dozen exposures in half a minute, using an instrument that was small enough to carry in a coat pocket. A few years earlier, most professionals had scoffed at what was called a "miniature camera," but by 1940 Henri Cartier-Bresson, Helen Levitt, and others were giving it legitimacy. (Many of the Photo League crew, including Levitt, were early advocates for the 35-millimeter format.) Users of the new format even had their own magazine, *Minicam Photography*. It highlighted the difference between a photojournalist-artist and a press photographer—one was embedded into the action and shot along with it, cinematically, whereas the other was outside, framing it for just a couple of discrete shots. Uncharacteristically, Weegee had been slow to adopt new methods to keep up.

Weegee got his own crack at Anthony Esposito inside police headquarters, two days after the attack in front of B. Altman, and the picture he made is, in its own way, a classic. It doesn't show action; it doesn't show the crime. But Weegee found the heat in the event anyway, catching the Mad Dog's swollen and bandaged face, his glare, his sneer. The portrait is atmospheric, weirdly and quietly intense, composed, almost intimate. ("For the first time since Bruno Richard Hauptmann," the caption read, "police today permitted photographers in the line-up room at headquarters . . . The

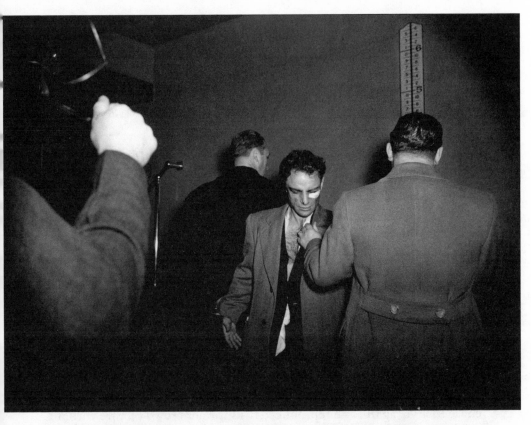

Anthony "Mad Dog" Esposito had been arrested, and clearly roughed up, after a shoot-out on Fifth Avenue in front of B. Altman & Co. Weegee caught up with him at the police station on January 16, 1941.

angry gunman ducked after Weegee took the above.") The police have turned to obscure their faces. Weegee explained that, atypically, they didn't want to be in the picture. Because the cops are facing away from the lens, their dark clothes recede, and your eye goes right to Mad Dog's bashed-in features. A year later, after a failed attempt to assert an insanity defense, the two Esposito brothers got the chair.

The weekly guaranteed salary did nothing to slacken Weegee's hustle. In 1941, well over one hundred stories with his pictures appeared in *PM*. Nobody else on the paper, even the excellent Irving Haberman, was doing spot news with more verve or relish. A chef who was stabbed in a restaurant on Stanton Street after four customers got angry about being served warm beer? Weegee made photos of the victim's Great Dane, Rocco, standing guard over his master's corpse. In January, he revisited Steeplechase Pier yet again, and reproduced his summer crowd picture without a single soul on the beach. (The two images ran side by side, of course.)

He also filed his first out-of-town story to the paper. In early 1941, Weegee went to Washington, D.C., for the weekend, seemingly without any particular aim. The report he filed, called "A N.Y. Police Reporter's Impressions of Washington," ran in *PM* on March 2, and he found comedy in much of the trip. The bus ride down there took ten hours, with endless rest stops, driver changes, and a pause at a Photomatic booth, where he had his picture taken. ("I got the photo in about two minutes. This was the first time I have received a mechanical insult.") Once he disembarked, he wandered through the capital, dealing with its absurd blue laws. He couldn't get a drink unless he sat down; it was illegal to change tables unless a waiter moved his drink; whiskey became available at midnight on Sunday, then was prohibited again at 2:00 a.m.

But he was most struck by the drawls and the slow pace, and Washington's essential southernness created one moment when the humor evaporated from Weegee's account. When he stopped in to see a movie, he discovered that the theater had a wall down the middle where an aisle might normally be. He photographed it, matter-of-factly explaining that "This is a Washington movie house before the show began. The partition keeps the colored and white people apart." He wound up trying to chat with a cop, as he might have at home, and it didn't go well. "I found the cops who are appointed by political pull walk around with chips on their shoulders and do not give you polite answers . . . Everybody seems to need a shot in the arm in Washington. I am glad to get back to New York."

In his familiar milieu the next week, he returned to his high-energy night rounds. He got to one of those increasingly rare gangland rubouts in Little Italy on April 17, and again made a picture that showed both the corpse and the eagerly attentive crowd. He managed to arrive at the scene of a car wreck on Second Avenue not only just as the police cars pulled up, perhaps three minutes after the actual crash, but also in enough time to make his way to the roof of a nearby building so he could take in the whole scene from several floors up. Another ninety-degree day that summer? He caught not only a sleeper in Central Park but also a squirrel gathering nuts next to him. (Caption: "Hoarding for winter on one of the hottest days of the year . . .") And another hot night on the Upper West Side delivered one of his great joke signboard photos. "After riding around two years, I made my drunk picture," he explained. "A guy on Amsterdam Avenue, one Sunday morning around 5 o'clock, he was sleeping under a canopy of an undertaking parlor. That, to me, is a picture!" (The address on the awning was perfect, too: 711, a craps game winner.) He made two variations, one with a passerby giving the sleeper a quizzical look, and titled it, inevitably, "Dead Drunk." That passerby was one of the key elements of the best Weegee photos: the New York observer, observed.

That was an approach *PM* liked as much as Weegee did, especially given the paper's instinct to teach (and sometimes lecture, and occasionally hector) its readers. In February 1941, Weegee photographed a murder victim on the street, and he also made a portrait of seven or eight citizens watching the scene intently. *PM* ran the latter picture, large, with the caption "This is a New York sidewalk audience. Study their faces. Then turn the page to see what they are looking at." An arrow then pointed to the right, and once you followed the instructions, you were rewarded with a (smaller) picture of the body, toes up on Mott Street, a cop standing over it. The news of the dead was subordinated to the reaction of the living.

Maybe it was simply because warm weather brought people outdoors and into view, but Weegee's most evocative city-life pictures do often seem to be the summer ones. The first hot day of 1941 supplied another classic, a picture that encapsulates tenement life like no other. Weegee didn't exactly give it a formal title, but nearly everyone refers to it as "the kids on the fire escape," and it's one that even the highest-brow folks at the Photo League could admire.

It was not his first time making a picture like this. "When I became a free lance photographer," he wrote in a letter to the great photographer Edward Steichen, "I used to go looking for HOT WEATHER pictures. I'd ride through the east side streets looking up at the fire escapes. When I saw bed sheets I would stop the car & walk right in. There are no locks on the doors of the houses." One building, on Attorney Street between Delancey and Rivington Streets, "was my favorite fire escape . . . it made a good elevation . . . I'd go there every year and find a new family." He had indeed caught a very similar scene the previous year, with three boys, and that one ran in the *Daily News*. (Another strikingly similar picture, unattributed, ran on the front page of the *New York Evening Journal* after one hot June night five years earlier. The vantage point is nearly the same, and so is the masonry around the tenement window. Can't say it's his, but it's a good bet.)

As the 1941 version ran in *PM*, it shows a family's four children huddled on their blankets, the oldest of them laughing out loud rather than sleeping. (The caption is mangled, putting the scene at the intersection of "Irving and Rivington," two streets that never meet.) But the alternate version is the classic that's in museum collections and coffee table books, and it passes from evocative to almost otherworldly. It is framed a little wider than the others, and shows the four children foot to foot with four others, meaning that the narrow fire escape slept eight that night. A ninth child peers from inside the apartment, curious about the sleepers, a flashlight in his hand. Weegee said he'd left a couple of bucks with the kids' father, telling him to get them some ice cream the next day. It's also a picture that *PM* couldn't have run, because of the girl in

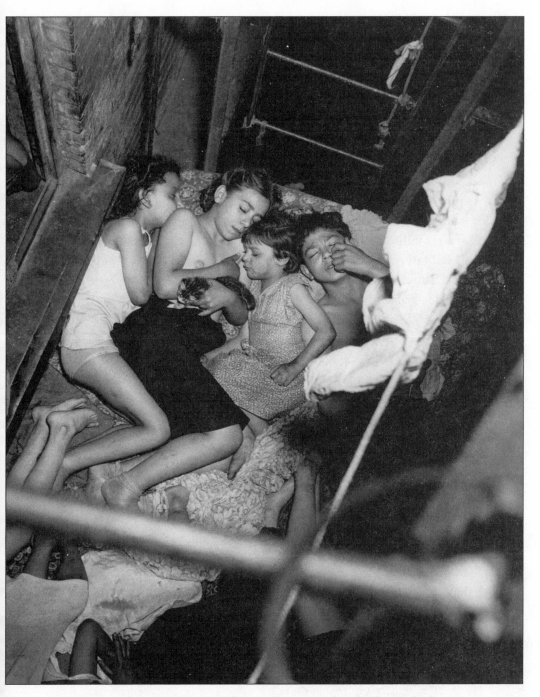

A classic Lower East Side summer scene of kids sleeping on the fire escape—and, most likely, one that's posed.

the center, who seems to be about twelve or thirteen. The top of her dress has slipped down slightly; her nipple is visible, and she is just old enough for that to make the image inappropriate to publish. Curled in her arm, as she sleeps, is a tiny kitten. Once you see it, the young woman becomes a kid again, one who is crammed in among her brothers and sisters yet makes room for a furry little animal, despite the heat.

Were they feigning sleep, or were they really caught unaware? In the two frames Weegee made that night, one shows the children sleeping and the other shows them laughing. If the pictures were shot in that order, it's plausible that the flash awakened everyone. If not, well, then it's posed. If you had to guess, you'd probably choose the latter scenario.

Especially after you hear from someone who was there. Louis Liotta (himself later a star photographer on the *Post*, and the son of the man who claimed to have stuck the nickname "Weegee" on Weegee in the *Times* darkrooms twenty years earlier) had begun assisting Arthur Fellig around 1940, after a few years' apprenticeship at Acme. "With Weegee I didn't get paid," Liotta explained in an interview with the writer Joyce Wadler nearly fifty years later. "I went with him to learn. He did a lot of thinking before he made a picture. He made two or three shots, but he made sure every shot counted." And Liotta himself knew that this picture was a setup. "That famous hot-weather picture with kids sleeping on the fire escape?" he said.

> He made that picture two, three days before. Like if he heard on the weather report it was gonna be real hot on a Thursday, Tuesday night he'd set up the picture. His mind was always workin'. He'd get four or five kids, stick them out on the fire escape, have their mother put them in little flimsy underwear or their shorts, with the mattress or pillow or blankets. Maybe slip the mother a few bucks. Set it up? Sure he set it up. Just look at the pictures, see how well they were framed. And he got away with it for 40 years. Because they thought it was legit . . . I thought that was very enlightening, that a guy could make a picture that could get through these so-called picture editors' hands without them ever knowing it. He made it look authentic. They *were* authentic—he just helped them a little bit.

Eight decades ago, this modest image of tenement life, whether strictly journalistic or not, read differently from the way it does today. We have all heard so many memories of immigrant existence that the idea of families sleeping on the fire escape has been romanticized, or at least imbued with a certain coziness: "a simpler time," if you like. The underfurnished yet still claustrophobic Lower East Side apartments in these pictures can now often look wholesome rather than miserable. Even the sleeping drunk under the undertaker's awning can seem almost quaint. But these images, when they were new, were not nostalgic; they were alarming. Those children on the fire escape were at risk of being bitten by rats. Their clothes and faces were dirty. What these pictures conveyed to well-off folks uptown was not alfresco life or a breezy night under the stars but desperation, the need to escape stifling heat and crowding and bedbugs. Weegee, like the more overtly class-conscious strivers from the Photo League, was simply showing readers the city he knew. "Later," he once said, "people seeing those pictures would wonder how I knew about such things. How did I know about them? Hell! That's the way I slept." He knew that those kids would have to scramble indoors if it started to rain, and that there would be bloodsucking vermin to deal with once they did.

He was, in other words, realizing that he was a messenger from the indecorous parts of the city to its nicer ones. This was nothing new, mind you. Reporters have been going into the slums and coming back with stories for centuries. Before Weegee was born, the reformer Jacob Riis published *How the Other Half Lives*, showing the appalling conditions in the tenements and sweatshops in the 1880s. What was new here, though, was that the hardened, distinct layering of society was beginning to crack. A generation earlier, a society dame would never have been seen going to something as tawdry as a Hollywood movie, let alone a barroom. For many people, though, especially those who'd come of age in the twenties, the rigid rules had begun to bend and break. A few years earlier, the heiress Ellin Mackay had eloped with Irving Berlin, formerly Israel Beilin, a Russian-Jewish immigrant reared on Cherry Street. (After a grace period that was anything but gracious, their relationship was finally accepted by Society.) Now Eleanor Roosevelt, a onetime debutante whose conscience had driven her to work in Lower East Side settlement houses, was speaking the language of social justice from the White House. In media, the *Graphic*, making its way into Park Avenue apartments a decade earlier, had been only the beginning. Educated people now kept up on the plotlines of the Sunday funnies, unashamedly. *The New Yorker* was running so many stories about fringe characters that its editor Harold Ross had begun to classify features as "high life" and "low life," and paid more for the former. The distinction soon became impossible to make, as writers such as Joseph Mitchell began to turn in articles that had one foot in each world. Ross ultimately ended up paying Mitchell a bonus for one story he called "a humorous high-life low-life," his top-dollar category. What Mitchell was describing at the typewriter Weegee was often printing in the darkroom, and "the humorous high-life low-life" is not a bad encapsulation of the latter's photographic career.

You can see him straddling the gap in the issue of *PM* that came out on April 28, 1941. On page 13, Weegee had a picture of Murder Inc. associate Sidney "Shimmy" Salles, lying in a pool of blood on a downtown sidewalk as dozens of people gawk. Turn three pages, and Weegee is playing the fish out of water as he covers the Cinderella Ball, a black-tie party at the Waldorf-Astoria. It was clearly a sly let's-see-what-he-does-with-this-one assignment on the part of the photo desk, and on the page, it came complete with wisecracks. ("Champagne was $16 a bottle. Myself, I like beer with a rye chaser.")

There was one particular address in New York where this high-low melding was on full display, every night. In 1934, a man named Sammy Fuchs had taken over a saloon at 267 Bowery, near Houston Street. After a few years of serving the clientele that the local flophouses provided, Sammy was surprised by an atypical customer, titled and British and wearing an actual monocle. He told Fuchs that he'd begun coming in because he liked the grungy atmosphere—he was, as the previous generation had begun to call it, "slumming." Sammy (few people used his last name) saw an opportunity, got himself a cabaret license, and replaced his jukebox with a few singers and dancers from the dying vaudeville circuit. The bar got a new neon sign, reading SAMMY'S BOWERY FOLLIES OF THE GAY '90s. The plump women who performed there wore a previous generation's costume, with feathered picture hats and sparkly outfits, as they worked the floor, belting out old tunes, mingling with the crowd. The word *retro* didn't exist yet, but Sammy had figured out that easy-to-swallow nostalgia was an angle worth working.

The customers were drawn from two pools, local funk and uptown chic. Skid Row alcoholics would drift through, some trying to smuggle in bottles of cheap booze (which were gently removed from their coat pockets at the door). Sammy called these folks "the escapists," and he was a benevolent neighborhood guardian, sometimes nudging them back out the door with a gentle "don't drink till your day off." He gave food to the hungriest and most hopeless, slipped them a few bucks here and there, and acted as go-between to help them reconnect with their estranged families. His big personality and generosity got him a nickname, the Mayor of the Bowery, and the saloon itself began to be known as the Stork Club of the Bowery. Actual Stork Club patrons began to drop by, too, to mix with or ogle the drunks, performers, and eccentric-looking downtowners, including a feisty guy, four feet tall, who was (inevitably) known as Shorty. One regular patron declared herself Queen of the Bowery, although most everyone at Sammy's knew her as Tugboat Ethel.

There was nothing more high-life-low-life than the scene at Sammy's Bowery Follies, and even though (or perhaps because) it was half-concocted rather than entirely authentic, uptown folks and tourists ate it up. So did journalists and writers—Damon Runyon called it "the Bowery in a minor key," and Winchell and his rivals, such as Earl Wilson, mentioned it frequently. Tour buses began to unload at Sammy's. The place even got its own radio show, broadcast two nights a week from WBYN in Newark. Celebrities and debutantes and even the debutantes' parents began to head there, after the opera or the theater or whatever they did on their evenings out.

So did Weegee, who lived just a few blocks away and recognized a great social contrast when he saw one. He also knew and liked Sammy, who, like him, understood that the crossroads of high and low was an entertaining place to be. So Weegee made Sammy's a regular spot on his nightly rounds, and apart from police headquarters and large venues like Madison Square Garden, it probably appears in more of his photographs than any other single location does.

His slow move from crime into slice-of-life photography was by no means absolute, but his approach to the former was definitely changing. In October 1941, Weegee headed out to Brooklyn to photograph a small-time murder at the corner of North Sixth and Roebling Streets. "Pupils were leaving P.S. 143, in the Williamsburg section of Brooklyn, at 3:15

A high-water mark in Weegee's career as a spot-news artist: the observers at a street-corner killing in Williamsburg, Brooklyn, in October 1941. He called it "Their First Murder," and among the children and adults can be seen nearly the entire range of human emotion: anguish, fear, curiosity, glee.

yesterday when Peter Mancuso, 22, described by police as a small-time gambler, pulled up in a 1931 Ford at a traffic light a block from the school," read the text block accompanying the photos the next day. (The words probably came from Don Hollenbeck, *PM*'s chief caption writer and later a CBS newscaster.) "Up to the car stepped a waiting gunman, who fired twice and escaped through the throng of children. Mancuso, shot through the head and heart, struggled to the board and collapsed dead on the pavement. Above are some of the spectators. The older woman is Mancuso's aunt, who lives in the neighborhood, and the boy tugging at the hair of the girl in front of him is her son, hurrying away from her."

He delivered two pictures. One is more or less conventional, at least for him: it shows the body mostly shrouded in newspapers, flanked by the detective, the doctor, and the priest giving last rites. Good, but familiar. The other, though, shows instead about a dozen schoolchildren and two women who collectively display nearly the entire range of human emotion. The aunt is distraught, sobbing. The kids in the back are leery. Others push forward, curious. At least one is grinning maniacally, perhaps at the gory violence of the scene, most likely because he's excited by the prospect of being in the newspaper. Another boy is aggressively pushing a girl's head aside as she uneasily side-eyes the body. Most strikingly, Weegee is not at a remove but right in their faces, his feet most likely planted between them and the victim. *PM* had the good sense to put that picture up top, and it was one of those moments when Weegee's approach to the news perfectly chimed with the paper's. It was a deeply mordant expression of city life. So was the title Weegee later gave it: "Their First Murder."

Never mind that it had too much flash and washed out the faces in the fore-ground: "Their First Murder" was the kind of picture whose power even the Photo League's most craftsmanlike members could not deny. Over the preceding couple of months, they had begun to acknowledge Weegee's talent. On July 25, 1941, he gave his first of many lectures at the clubhouse on East Twenty-First Street, about his days and nights covering the cops. He usually showed up for these talks armed with photographs mounted on big poster boards, and he would spin yarns about the stories behind them, talk about photographic technique, and hold forth for as long as the audience would listen. At least once, he used a pistol (presumably unloaded) as a pointer, which must have unnerved his audience. One talk that he gave at the City College of New York that year lasted till 1:00 a.m., and (an attendee said) it could've continued except that Weegee excused himself to get out on his nightly rounds.

"The Genius of the Camera," he had taken to calling himself—except that in his Lower East Side honk, "genius" came out slightly wrong, and he misspelled it as well. When a writer named Joseph Mackey visited Weegee's apartment to profile him for a magazine called *Who* in 1941, Mackey openly teased him.

> "I have a psychic nose for news," says Weegee. "I'm the Genuis of the Camera." (Note that he doesn't *quite* say genius.) "He's a screwball," say the merry men of the press . . . On the walls are some of his front-page pictures; also one of Weegee, inscribed

THE GENUIS OF THE CAMERA. Asked who inscribed it, he says: "Me. I have no false pride. . . ."

He gets—and ignores—requests for a letter of advice about breaking into his line. "If I did answer them," he says, "I'd say there are easier ways to earn a living. Sometimes it's hard for even me, and I'm a genuis." Almost a genius, in other words.

Whether a genius or genuis, he was enough of a presence at the League that, a month later, the group gave him an exhibition in its gallery space. Weegee knew he was going to be judged by a sophisticated group of his peers, and he admitted to one reporter, shortly before opening night, that he was "more scared than when guns are blazing and axes flying." Yet he was visibly giddy while he was hanging the show. As he should have been: a man who'd striven for acceptance and respect from his ostensible betters, not to mention a decent living from the world, was seeing it happen. His connections allowed him to publicize the exhibit enthusiastically. "Arthur 'Weegee' Fellig, for 20 years a free lance photographer operating out of police headquarters, is holding his first one-man show," wrote the *Post*. "The prints show many spectacular scenes of riots, wrecks, murder victims, fire rescues, suicides and other violent phases of picture reporting in New York." *PM* plugged it, too. Weegee chose a title for the exhibition that was straight out of a pulp novel: *Murder Is My Business*. The show opened on August 13 for a three-week run.

By today's standards, the presentation was amateurish. The prints were merely pasted to large panels, with no matting or protection, and they began to peel off their backings and curl up within days. Weegee chose thematic groupings (one board for fires, another for car wrecks) and labeled them with dime-store cutout letters that were glued up crookedly and, in a couple of cases, backward. One panel was devoted to Weegee's own self-presentation, with a picture of his press card, a recent magazine interview, and a few photos of himself at work. He even included a copy of the "TWO MURDERS . . . $35.00" check stub from Time Inc., hanging it right next to a picture of a facedown body, and labeled the pair of images "C.O.D." and "D.O.A." Cutout photos of revolvers flanked his name. Weegee himself daubed on streaks of what looks like red nail polish at the barrel of each gun, in imitation of either bloodshed or a muzzle flash. At the end of the row, a panel displayed a blank vignette like an empty jewelry-store window, reading THIS SPACE RESERVED FOR THE LATEST MURDERS. One picture in the show, of a young man lying dead on a tenement rooftop next to a graffito reading ROYALS, was almost that fresh. It had been made less than twenty-four hours before the opening.

The presentation may have looked a little cheap, but that was easy enough to overlook. The power of the show was undeniable. On one board, titled FACES, Weegee had assembled sixteen of his six-foot shots into a tableau: the sobbing daughter at the hit-and-run, the relieved fireman drinking his coffee, a picture of the playwright Alador Laszlo in agony just as he learned his stepdaughter had committed suicide, plus one of Weegee himself behind bars, from the *Life* story in which he'd posed as a criminal. He also included an image of a homeless man peering at the luxury goods in the windows of the lobby haberdasher at the Ritz-Carlton, a picture that he later admitted setting up. He'd seen the fellow a couple of blocks away on Park Avenue, and had given him a quarter and a pack of cigarettes to come over and pose.

Another grouping, called THREE OF A KIND, put the Joe McWilliams horse's-ass picture together with a booking photo of the Nazi Fritz Kuhn and an unsettling six-foot shot of a little person who might have been recognizable to viewers from the news. Jerry Austin was a former vaude-villian, a character actor who'd been arrested a few months earlier for rape as part of what the papers called a "midget vice ring." On the FIRES panel, Weegee displayed "I Cried When I Took This Picture" with an additional curiosity-stoking caption headed FAKE. (The label was itself a fakeout. The fine print explained that a few newspapers had accidentally run the photo over a story about an event in Helsinki, and misidentified the women as Finns.) Weegee probably didn't realize it, but he'd described the entirely honest picture of the sobbing women as a fake and the faked picture of the homeless man at the Ritz as the real thing.

There were no gags or stagings on one panel, though, and it was arguably the best array in the show. The events on view hadn't even hap-pened as of the show's opening night. On the morning of August 17, four days after Weegee's exhibition opened, a steamship chartered by a large African American chapter of the Odd Fellows Lodge had been sched-uled to go up the Hudson River for a picnic. At the dock, an argument over possibly counterfeit tickets escalated, and the result was an angry stampede. Forty people were hurt, and three women were trampled to death. It took police two hours to quell the riot. Amazingly, the trip was not canceled, and Weegee's pictures show the ship headed out onto the river with 1,250 passengers aboard, leaving behind three draped bodies surrounded by police and a pier covered in crushed picnic baskets and other debris. Again, Weegee caught the sobs and the twisted faces of those reacting to the sickening scene. He must've considered the event big enough, and the pictures good enough, to add it to his exhibition on the fly, in mid-run.

What is notable about that set of photographs today, though, is not just the horrible news event. It's that Weegee in Harlem was much like Weegee in the Lower East Side. He may have been an outsider, one who was more at home amid his neighborhood's white-ethnic divides, where Italians stayed on their side of the Bowery and Jews stayed on theirs and other, even more marginalized groups took the leftover bits of carved-up territory where they could. But these pictures do not have the quality of ethnology. There's almost none of that "Here's how those people live" overtone, as there sometimes is in photos made by white people to show other white people the troubles of nonwhite people. (The Photo League, over several years, was assembling a large series titled *Harlem Document* that, although its good intentions were evident, perhaps overemphasized the neighborhood's beat-down aspects.) Time after time, the black folks in Weegee's photos are just city people, living their lives, alternately joyful and put-upon, facing down the tough time every other underclass has. Maybe tougher. In the awful aftermath of the excursion-boat deaths, they are simply reacting rather than standing in as racial archetypes. In Weegee's professed indifference to social-activism photography, he had turned out to be great at it.

Murder Is My Business did good business itself. In the League's newsletter, *Photo Notes*, an unnamed writer—probably the editor, Cora Alsberg—exulted over it. "New York at night is cruel, brutal, human, and humorous. Come ready to be shocked." Weegee himself crowed a bit to her, no doubt intending to tweak the artier members of the League. "When you see a picture, you've just got time to take it," he said. "There's no time to worry about exposure meters, filters and all of that bunk . . . If people laugh in the background of [a] murder shot, well—that's life. Many photographers live in a dream world of beautiful backgrounds. It wouldn't hurt them to get a taste of reality to wake them up. Anyone who looks for life can find it. And they don't need to photograph ashcans. The average camera fan reminds me of polyanna [sic], a lolly pop in one hand, and a camera in the other."

The show was attention-getting enough that, instead of taking it down on September 6, as planned, the League allowed Weegee to revamp and reopen it for another three weeks. This time, it had twice as many pictures and slightly more professional mountings. DUE TO INCREASE IN MURDERS, the sign at the entrance read, THE PHOTO LEAGUE PRESENTS / 2ND EDITION / "MURDER IS MY BUSINESS" / BY WEEGEE. Even the *Times* put a little item in the paper about it this time.

Friends and strangers alike offered praise for the show in the guest-book. "It's terrific!! A must for everyone studying or practicing photography," wrote Herbert Krim, a sometime *New Yorker* contributor. Sally Pepper, who later became the picture editor at *PM*, called it "gruesome but superb." Other visitors threw around the words *genius* and *wonderful*. About the only criticism Weegee got was for eliminating a dishy blonde murderer during the extension of the show, to which he wrote, in response, "boo hoo." Weegee's friend and fellow Photo League regular Louis Stettner was more prophetic, writing:

> These photographs are ample proof that if anyone knows New
> York it is Weegee. And knowing New York City, the heart of
> the whole industrial system, is something. I suggest that he should
> write a book illustrated with his photographs.

Inevitably, Weegee took pictures of the exhibition itself, and of the visitors. As usual, he was watching the watchers—only now they were gawking at his work. And if his productivity for *PM* dropped off a little while the show was up, that was a very brief break. In October, he had photos in the paper ten times.

The lectures he was giving raised his profile further, and he discovered that he liked holding forth for an audience. By the end of the year, he'd placed an item in the *New York Post* photography column written by John Adam Knight, looking to build up his public speaking career. "Arthur (Weegee) Fellig, famous freelance news photographer," he wrote, "is available for a limited number of engagements on Friday nights only, to talk on 'Murder Is My Assignment,' [*sic*] illustrated with some of his magnificent pictures of night violence in New York. Camera club program secretaries should communicate with Weegee at 5 Center Market Pl. There is no charge for this lecture by one of the most successful news cameramen in the trade, but the clubs whose invitations will be accepted must be able to accommodate the large audiences sure to be attracted."

He was beginning to be famous, and at some point around 1941, he made that status part of his very name. He had already replaced the PHOTO BY A. FELLIG rubber stamp he'd bought to assert his byline, back around 1937, with a newer stamp reading CREDIT PHOTO BY WEEGEE. But now came a new one, and it read CREDIT PHOTO BY WEEGEE THE FAMOUS. It was almost comical in its hubris, like something a kid would write.

In quick succession, he also lined up three more substantial stories about himself, all of them glamorizing his high-low life. One, in the *Esquire* spin-off *Coronet*, included an impressive twenty-four pages of pictures with Weegee's captions. Another, in a magazine called *Good Photography*, was akin to his lectures, a sort of how-to manual called "So You Want to Be a Free-lance!" It was written in the first person, with an editor's note reading, "Weegee recently bought himself a typewriter to help express himself even more graphically and poetically than he does with the camera. This friendly message to the amateur is one of his first excursions into the field of free-lance WRITING. He does a tidy job." And he did, laying out his increasingly familiar origin story: up from the Acme darkroom, secondhand Speed Graphic, police-band radio next to the bed, TWO MURDERS . . . $35.00, all of it. A large portion of the story is pure practical business advice: how to approach photo agencies when you're starting out, which rights you retain when selling to newspapers. He also let on what his real "psychic" power was: watching and waiting. "At a department store fire," he wrote, "I spotted a lot of dummies in the front window and figured a shot of a fireman 'rescuing' a dummy would make a funny picture. And sure enough, one of the firemen did exactly what I thought he would."

That photograph is just one early example from an entire body of eccentric work. Weegee made funny mannequin pictures at least fifty times in his career. He shot dummies as they lay in the shattered display windows of shops that had been burgled; he included their blank-eyed stares among those of sidewalk gawkers staring at a burning

Mannequins appear in Weegee's photos constantly, for both their uncanny dead stare and their ability to turn even the most somber scene a little bit antic.

building; he used them as observers over the shoulders of people at work; he included them in self-portraits. Once, while covering a fire in 1941, he actually pulled a fur coat–wearing mannequin out of a window display and posed it among the sidewalk spectators. "I didn't think a little air would do her any harm," he told his editors.*

---

* Their glassy eyes turned up often enough in his photographs, in fact, that it's been speculated that he

He may, when he started on this kick, simply have been responding to praise. His boss Ralph Ingersoll, at the very start of *PM*, had seen a photo Weegee brought in from a flooded store that "showed the proprietor submerged to his waist in muddy water, embracing a wax dummy who seemed to resemble the Duchess of Windsor," wrote Wolcott Gibbs in a profile of Ingersoll. "For some reason, Ingersoll was bewitched by this odd scene and insisted that it had to be printed immediately. 'It's wonderful!' he said. 'It's got everything!'"

It's not all that difficult to see why Weegee was, at least superficially, drawn to these figures. The store-window dummy adds a frisson to many unsexy photos. The mannequins, after all, are often unclothed, and you couldn't very well put a naked girl in the paper in 1940, but you could show a little T and A if she was made out of plaster. There was a *tee-hee* sexuality to many of these pictures, doubly so if the fellow pulling her out of the wreckage was embracing her in a curiously human manner. It provided a rescue without agony, a victim without pain or death, an eye-catching and laugh-provoking moment at a tragedy. And if it was not quite unique, it was out of the ordinary enough that editors would almost always go for it.

Repetition like that, too, was becoming a Weegee hallmark. If you got a great picture, like the Coney Island crowd or the fire-escape kids, you could do it again the next year, and the next, and the next. There were so very many newsprint pages to fill, after all, and your second or third try was probably better than your first. There are perhaps half a dozen Weegee devices—the edge-to-edge crowd photo, the firemen dripping with ice in winter, the sleepers of all kinds, and all those mannequins—that were deep wells from which he drew frequently and successfully. He made the Coney Island throng-on-the-sand picture at least six times over four years, every one a little different and memorable.

There was plenty of room for variation within those tropes. A few weeks after that winter trip to Coney Island, the one where he'd photographed the empty beach, he made a visit to the Eden Musée, a wax museum near the boardwalk. There he shot pictures of its exhibits, closed to the public but under preparation for the spring season, and it

---

kept a dummy in his car, to be hauled out and inserted into any picture where it was needed. That, at least, is unlikely to be true; the mannequins differ from picture to picture, and none show up in pictures of the crowded car trunk.

A truly creepy tableau of a notorious 1920s murder, rendered in wax at Coney Island's Eden Musée. It's the off-season, which explains the dust covers on the heads.

was a uniquely eerie sight. President Roosevelt stood (yes, stood, albeit with a cane) staring ahead as a woman dusted him off with a brush. Weegee spotted a couple of seated waxworks on the sidewalk, airing out. Most unsettling of all, he photographed a diorama of the Ruth Snyder murder—the very one that had made the *Daily News* a force and that, very indirectly, had led to his own crime-photography career—under its off-season wraps. Both the murderers stand silent, Snyder in her nightgown, Henry Gray with the window-sash weight in hand, ready to smash Albert Snyder's head in as he lies in bed. The wax killers, though, have their heads shrouded in big flared paper hoods, to keep them clean through the winter. They look vaguely like French nuns; they also could be taken for Klansmen. Because Weegee's flash causes the scene to taper off to darkness at the edges, and because he's using a lens that doesn't quite cover the entire frame, vignetting the image, it almost seems that we're peering through a peephole. Where many of his actual murder pictures can be almost placid ("takin' a little nap"), this tableau is anything but. The waxworks fakery looks more ominous than the real thing.

It wasn't exactly Ouija-board psychic of him, but a week and a half before Pearl Harbor, Weegee published a picture that foretold the next four years. It had, once again, been opening night at the Metropolitan Opera, one year after his evening there produced that *PM* front page showing four men in their top hats. That was surely on his mind when he paused near the Met's cloakroom on November 24, 1941, and saw that the rows and rows of silken black opera hats were punctuated by the brownish twill of servicemen's uniform caps. "There was a showing of gold braid and a generous turnout of plain khaki," noted the caption below Weegee's picture the next morning. "The fancy-peaked cap above is a captain's, the other just a lieutenant's."

On Sunday, December 7, the paper included a grim little local scene by Weegee, one in which three men had shot a policeman to death in front of a funeral parlor in Midtown. (In a dark echo of Weegee's drunk-at-the-undertaker's photo, the cop had fallen dead in front of a funeral chapel, under a sign reading DELIVERY ENTRANCE.) The paper hit newsstands just as radios began to break into their regular programming to deliver the news from Hawaii. It was war, and by the time the sun went down that night, the news business had shifted gears. Gangster shoot-'em-ups, already fading from the news pages, abruptly became footnotes to a global story.

Although Weegee would continue making pictures of street-level crashes and crimes after December 7, 1941, he would, for the first time, frequently produce photographs that explicitly made reference to the news beyond New York City's borders. (Before Pearl Harbor, he had only occa-sionally intimated that there was a larger world, through some pictures of immigrant life and a few outliers like the Coney Island girls in their rubber masks.) His first *PM* photograph after Pearl Harbor, on Decem-ber 10, showed schoolchildren gathered in the street and staring at the sky during their inaugural air-raid drill. One of them pointed a revolver aloft. "The alarm found most New Yorkers calm," *PM* wrote, "but left them puzzled as to what it was all about. . . . Whatever the cause, we needed the practice."

He adapted quickly. His work for *PM* in early 1942 began to tell local stories through the framework of the larger one. A news item about some-thing as small as a parking ticket was tied to gasoline rationing. He made the fascist sympathizer Joe McWilliams look foolish again, catching him in an awkward pose atop his covered wagon. A photo of the Headquar-ters Press Building on Centre Market Place showed a banner with eight stars outside, one for each of the reporters serving in the army or navy. (This is not to say that every story was turned to face overseas: just a few days before that picture ran in *PM*, the paper went big with a Weegee portrait of Irma Twiss Epstein, a Bronx nanny turned baby murderer.) When a fight about the war broke out between sailors and longshore-men in a Park Row bar, he got there before the ambulances carted off the two men who, stabbed and bleeding, lay in the gutter. When men over forty-five years of age were first called to register for possible con-scription, he photographed the clerks and the graying citizens standing in line. Car-wreck photos could become war pictures, too: in mid-1942, he photographed a collision between a patrol wagon and a jeep full of soldiers. Even one of those litter-of-puppies photos could have an angle. In August 1942, Weegee posed seven pups that had been born in a Little Italy storefront, once again tucking each one into a glass for maximum adorableness—but this time, the wineglasses were arranged in a V for "Victory." *PM* frequently ran his slice-of-wartime-life pictures of laid-up cars (no tires, no gas), of servicemen out on the town, of window signs announcing shortages of rationed goods—and, sometimes, of more aggres-sive activities. There's a photograph from October 1942 in which we see a group of Lower East Side kids (middle class rather than scruffs, by the look of their clothes) dangling a crude homemade dummy from a street sign at the corner of Elizabeth and Broome. YOUNG EAST SIDERS HANG

JAP IN EFFIGY TO ADVERTISE THEIR SCRAP HUNT, the headline read, with a caption clarifying what's going on. "The boy highest up is biting the Jap's ear—'Commando tactics,' he explained." In another photo that probably seemed funny back then but is downright alarming today, a six-year-old named Joseph Luparelli holds up a huge protest sign reading, DOWN WITH THE JAPS / THE RATS. He's at a rally, and he's wearing his grown-up brother's army uniform hat and jacket.* The young women Weegee had photographed a year earlier, wearing rubber masks of Hitler and Mussolini, had become almost quaint.

Remember, too, that this was in the middle of Little Italy. All these children of Italian immigrants would, in some parts of America, be considered the enemy within. In New York, they were (mostly, and correctly) seen as American citizens and patriots, and Weegee regularly photographed activities in the neighborhood that affirmed that patriotism: banners hung for the young men serving overseas, rubber and scrap metal drives, and finally, in September 1943, the cheering in the streets when Italy fell to the Allies. There are similar photos from Chinatown, where Chinese Americans were likewise eager to affirm their American identities and to ally themselves against the hated Japanese.

Despite a few limitations, Weegee's nightly rounds were barely affected. He put eyelid-like hoods on the headlights of his Chevy, conforming to the War Department's dimout regulations. He could still get his work done; he had, at various times, X-level and C-level gasoline rations, the ones issued only to people whose fuel consumption was deemed necessary to the war effort. To forestall dirty looks, he affixed placards to the car reading NOT A SUNDAY DRIVER / THIS CAR BEING USED FOR BUSINESS AND NOT FOR PLEASURE. Mostly, though, the war just added texture to the kinds of photos he had already been making. A war rally in Times Square got him a full page in PM. A blackout drill there allowed him to photograph the weirdly empty streets.

It also allowed him to deploy a brand-new tool. Infrared photog-

---

* One of the most notorious mob figures of the 1970s, also named Joseph Luparelli, was born in Little Italy at about the same time as the boy in Weegee's photograph. This other Luparelli grew up to be a hit man, was contracted to kill the Mafia boss Crazy Joe Gallo, and became an FBI informant. Owing to the fact that he's gone into the witness-protection program, it's difficult to say whether the two Josephs are the same person. There's only one Luparelli family in the neighborhood in the 1940 census, and it includes a son, Aurelio, who did indeed serve in uniform during the war—but Joseph's name is missing from the listing.

raphy had begun to gain popularity in the mid-1930s, after Kodak and other manufacturers introduced new films that could pick up wavelengths of light that do not register on the human retina. If you used infrared-wavelength flashbulbs with this kind of film, you could take a flash photo in which the burst of light was invisible. A photographer could make pictures in total darkness, and the subject would never know it had happened unless he heard the click of the shutter and the clink of the bulb, by which time the work was done. It was a great medium for a voyeur who worked by night.

Weegee first used it for publication on the last night of April 1942, during a wartime blackout drill. He'd been shooting people on the streets, mostly GIs and girls, plus a party taking place behind drawn curtains. Under the new regulations, it would have been irresponsible and possibly illegal to fire off a flashbulb in the streets. Instead, he photographed a stopped streetcar with infrared film and flash, its patrons sitting glumly in their seats. He also made his way into a darkened theater, where he caught an air-raid warden standing in the aisle, watching the moviegoers as they watched their movie. (Weegee, and *PM*'s readers, constituted the third layer of watchers.) Infrared, despite seeming a little sneaky, was suddenly patriotic.

It was also weird, because infrared film makes unconventional pictures. Kodak's film did not have what's called an anti-halation layer, which stops the scattering of light within the plastic negative sheet. Its absence causes a curious halo to appear around the people being photographed on IR film: they appear to glow. The film fails to register much blue light, so the sky is always dark, even in the daytime. Infrared flashes also penetrate the skin slightly, giving people a strange liquid look that renders faces simultaneously sharp and soft-focus. Men photographed with infrared almost always appear to have a five o'clock shadow, even if they're freshly shaven. And, most of all, the eyes—their pupils dilated, because they're in the dark—become solid black dots, like a shark's eyes. The effect is otherworldly, and it is doubly eerie when the pictures are from a darkened theater, which is already a space meant to transport us away from our regular lives.

Weegee, who loved a technical tour de force with a hint of magic, returned to IR film again and again. "Made with invisible light" was his pet phrase. In the next several years, he made repeated visits to movie theaters and opera houses and arenas, and in their darkened aisles he photographed all sorts of private behavior being carried out in public. He regularly caught adults and kids as they picked their noses. Others nibbled absently on snacks as they stared straight ahead. We see a few adults in near rapture, captured by what's onstage or on-screen, but more often they look bored, or they're sleeping. There are random bits of intimacy: in one, a middle-aged man has removed his shoes and tucked them under his theater seat. And, most memorably, we see couples with their hands on one another: touching, necking, groping. One young woman has practically shoved her boyfriend down into his seat, aggressively leaning into their open-mouthed kiss.

Many of those couples are enthusiastic, but some of the embraces aren't warm at all. In some, the woman is pushing the man away; in one, she's clearly trying to ignore him and watch the movie. And in another image, the grapple is not sexy but disturbing. The woman's date, a sailor, has his arm extended fully around her shoulders and neck, his hand lowered onto her breast. She leans back hard in her seat, her hands clenched, her body stiff. She's clearly unhappy about letting him have his way, and would no doubt look terrified if we could see her face, but his big head blocks our view. Behind her, another man has become aware of their clinch, just visible to him in the light spill from the screen, and he is scowling into the near-darkness. Once again, we are watching the watchers as they are watched, in a moment of violation, and there is almost assuredly nothing posed about this scene.

Nor is there about another infrared portrait he made one night in the early forties at Coney Island. Weegee was nominally there to photograph people sleeping on the sand, which was not uncommon on very hot days. Really, though, he was looking for amorous couples on their blankets. He did indeed catch a couple with his invisible light. But he also caught another, less settled picture: a single young woman, sitting up high on an unmanned lifeguard chair, with a thousand-yard stare. She seems to be biting her fingernails and looks ill at ease. Weegee made the shot and moved on, but he remained haunted by her for the rest of his life, far more than by most of the dead bookies and gangsters he photographed. Wilma Wilcox recalled much later that "it always bothered him . . . because he was afraid that she was a suicide prospect, and that possibly he should have talked to her to find out what was wrong and whether or not he could

Weegee used "invisible light"—infrared film and bulbs—to photograph movie audiences eating, sleeping, and making out. This one's from 1953, and shows his friends Al and Joan Levin.

help." The black eyes that the IR film renders do nothing to make the image any less unnerving. "It's a very forceful picture," Wilcox said, "expressing what could happen to any of us."

As is one of the two sets of pictures that cemented Weegee's reputation for spooky news clairvoyance, made in December 1942. In fact, it was a fluke. He'd taken a picture of a drunk sitting on a cold Bowery sidewalk outside Sammy's, the kind of photograph he'd made any number of times. This time, though, the man—his name was Frank Birskowsky—then stood up, wobbled down the sidewalk, stepped off the curb, and was immediately hit by a taxi. It was like the scene with Frank Tapedino, the hit-and-run victim Weegee had photographed on Lafayette Street a few years earlier, but instead of arriving a minute after the man was hit, this time he'd been there a minute before. That it happened around Christmas made the scene that much more maudlin, and never mind that Birskowsky, despite appearances, turned out to be not all that badly hurt. The point, especially in Weegee's retelling of the story, was that the camera had been there before the story was, giving him the holy grail of news photography: before-and-after real-time coverage, including shots of a priest arriving to administer last rites. When you've been adopting the name of a predictive fortune-telling game for a decade, such a moment only goes to enhance your own mythmaking. He was proud enough of the reputation he was constructing that he had the reflector of one of his flashguns gold-plated.

Audiences provided him fodder over and over in these years, and nowhere was that truer than at the circus. When the Ringling Bros. show made its usual trips to Madison Square Garden, he took dozens of pictures of audience members, shooting mostly children but adults, too, often using infrared film. (Mayor La Guardia turns up among them.) Backstage, he photographed members of the troupe, catching them in candid moments behind the performers' artifice. In one beautifully lit shot, he caught a giraffe that had bent over to peer at its trainer, who was sleeping on a cot next to the animal's stall. In another, a clown, aging and weary-looking, sags in a foldable sling chair, its canvas filthy with years of greasepaint. It was one in a long series of clown photographs, many of which are pairings showing the men of the circus with and without their trademark makeup. His twinned portraits of the most famous of them all, Ringling's Emmett Kelly, made it into *PM*. Another, of the Clyde Beatty Circus's "dwarf clown" Jimmy Armstrong, shows the small man's muscular frame, his proportions emphasized by the intense white makeup on his face.

The problem with taking pictures of an audience is a practical one: only from the stage is the angle any good. Threading one's way through the crowd limits a photographer to a few people sitting on the aisle, and basically makes the front row off-limits. It was conspicuous to make audience photographs unless he was working in the dark, doubly so when he came trundling down the aisle with that enormous Speed Graphic. In Weegee's words, "the minute they see the camera, they 'FREEZE' up on you."

In July 1943, he took care of that in a way no other press photographer would think to. Ringling Bros.' "Spangles" circus, a second troupe that toured separately from the main Ringling show, was at the Garden, and he'd made good pictures of audience members there a couple of weeks earlier. This time, he arranged to shoot the crowd not from the aisles but from the viewpoint of a performer. For two nights, Weegee would become a clown with a camera.

Before the show, one of the troupe's veterans, Roy Barrett, was assigned to make Weegee up, and first he covered his face in Crisco. ("I felt very hammy," Weegee joked.) Then came layers of makeup and a white costume with decorated collar, cuffs, and cap. He skipped the big floppy shoes, incongruously wearing his own battered oxfords instead. Whereupon, fully costumed, Weegee stepped into the spotlight and made his pictures from the center ring and the track surrounding it.

In print, the story was a two-pager, again taking that slightly pedagogical tone that *PM* favored. On the left, it was headlined WEEGEE, AS CLOWN, COVERS THE CIRCUS FROM INSIDE . . . There, readers saw the man at work, galumphing around the ring with his (very unclownish) camera in hand. In one photo, he's checking out a sturdy young female tumbler, her skirt flipped up as she stands on her hands. "I must admit I was suffering from stage fright," he wrote. "The Garden management in honor of the occasion of my first appearance followed me with a spotlight." He got laughs; when he made his way to the rail and raised the Speed Graphic to the audience, they expected it to be a prop camera, and that they'd be squirted with water. Instead, they just got the usual burst of light. The pictures of Weegee are, obviously, not by Weegee; he said only that "one of my students" took them.

On the facing page, the headline continued: . . . THESE ARE PICTURES HE TOOK OF THE CROWD. There are lots of smiles, a couple of astonished faces, and, at the bottom right, a fellow journalist. Robert Coleman, the drama critic of the *Journal-American*, had come to check out Weegee at work, and he was clearly amused by what he saw. "He told me I gave a 'finished performance,'" Weegee reported afterward. "I just wonder what he meant."

If in the past Weegee had coaxed people into the frame, or sidled into it himself, or concocted a scene, this dive into the middle of the story was something comparatively new for him. A generation later, George Plimpton headed onto the field with the Detroit Lions or went a couple of rounds with Archie Moore and got a lot of attention for reinventing

For two nights in July 1943, Weegee dressed up to join the Ringling Bros. circus clowns in the center ring.

what is known as "participatory journalism." Weegee was doing something quite similar twenty years earlier, with camera instead of notebook. In print, his part of the experience, the backstory, takes up as much space on the pages as the portraits he made. Weegee, while doing the job, was also beginning to perform the role of press photographer full-time.

He was also cultivating a knack for encountering people who were famous or about to become famous or going to be famous later on. A bit like the Woody Allen character Leonard Zelig, who is so desperate for approval that he transforms himself based on his surroundings and ends up incorporated into a series of epic historical moments, Weegee just kept finding himself next to celebrities. It didn't happen the night he was costumed as a clown, but that same summer at the circus, on the last night of its run at the Garden, a pair of special guests arrived. The Duke of Windsor, only a few years removed from his abdication from the British throne and his marriage to an American divorcée, was in New York. He and the former Mrs. Simpson sat in the front row. Weegee was no paparazzo, but he knew perfectly well that the duke and duchess were some of the most talked-about people in the world, and that the odd setting would make his pictures irresistible to editors. He also noticed that the duke was smoking a cigar, which gave Weegee an extra idea.

At first he hung back, waiting for his moment. He knew that one circus clown's act involved tossing a ball to an audience member, so he guessed that one would be heading the duke's way, and when that inevitable moment arrived he was ready to go. From there he began popping off flashbulbs, making pictures of the laughing couple until the duke himself asked Weegee to lay off, explaining that the flashes were making it impossible for him to enjoy himself. Weegee, who may have been willing to sneak a photo of a covered-up gangster, was not about to do that with royalty, and he backed down. He was rewarded, at the end of the evening, with a unique moment: the duke called him over to thank him and shook his hand. (A colleague caught the moment, which ended up in *PM*.) "I then packed up," Weegee told his bosses, "and went to a nearby Automat for a cup of coffee." The onetime shtetl boy who'd slept on park benches had shaken hands with a king, at the king's behest, and had smiled and taken it in stride.

As for that cigar? Weegee had known all along where his picture was going to go: he sold it immediately to the Cigar Institute, a trade group that liked pictures of famous people smoking stogies. Even more entertainingly, the image then won first prize in the institute's annual photo contest. *PM* ran a delighted item about that, saying, "Our Weegee has come through again." Weegee later added a spurious detail in the retelling, saying that the prize had included a lifetime supply of cigars. It hadn't, but the real award of fifty dollars wasn't bad, either.

That was a somewhat silly honor, but the next one was anything but. It came from the Museum of Modern Art, where photographs had become increasingly important to the institutional mission. A young art historian named Beaumont Newhall, initially hired to run the museum's library, had curated a show devoted to the history of photography as the medium neared its centennial. Newhall's accompanying book, titled *Photography 1839–1937*, was something new, recounting that history as not only a technological progression but also an artistic one. (Revised a few years later, it became a standard text and is still in print.) A couple of other ambitious shows followed, and in 1940 the museum had made Newhall the curator of its new department of photography. His wife, Nancy Newhall, was a similarly forward-looking art historian and critic, an acolyte of Alfred Stieglitz, one who as early as 1940 was writing about, among other things, the artistic possibilities of television.

By 1943, Beaumont Newhall was in the navy, and Nancy was filling in for him as MoMA's photography curator. The summer exhibit she planned was called *Action Photography*. The years since the introduction of the flashbulb, and the development of the electronic strobe by MIT engineer Harold Edgerton, had occasioned vast numbers of photographs that tried to freeze movement as never before. You didn't have to be in bright sun to catch a dancer in mid-leap or a bird in flight; the gear was now mass-produced and readily available to anyone who could afford it (and could lift it: one of Eastman Kodak's early strobe setups weighed fifty-nine pounds).

The one-room exhibition opened on August 18 and stayed up for a month. (Museum shows had shorter runs back then.) It was wide-ranging, with an emphasis on scientific photographs, including Edgerton's, and a section devoted to Barbara Morgan's portraits of Martha Graham frozen in mid-spin. But one wall was given over to journalistic work, centering on the famous picture of the burning *Hindenburg*. The museum bought and included in the mix not one Weegee photograph but four, including "I Cried When I Took This Picture" and "Their First Murder."

There were people who said the Weegee shots didn't belong there. The *Times* ran a rather stuffy but positive review of the show, not-

ing that the news photographs were "for the most part sensational, falling within the 'horror' classification." (Admittedly, all four images involved
some kind of physical agony or worse.) The *Herald Tribune* was grumpier, noting that the news photographs on view, including Weegee's, were
not strictly speaking about action or new technology, and that they "might
as well have been made with a box camera." Nonetheless, the reviews
didn't hold down enthusiasm for the show, which went on to tour museums around the country, going as far as Seattle.

The Newhalls and their MoMA circle, following the leads of Stieglitz and also Ansel Adams, were among the few people in the world arguing for news photography to be represented in museums as art, as much
for its aesthetics as for its basic content. That put Weegee in a whole new
contextual universe. The Brooklyn kids at their first murder and the
Torres women learning of their relatives' fiery death, pictures that despite
their power would have a couple of years earlier been considered nearly
disposable, were appearing at the same institution that Picasso had asked
to safeguard his masterpiece *Guernica*.

A few months later, the prestigious photography magazine *U.S. Camera* celebrated "Their First Murder" by printing it as large as it possibly
could, across two big pages, along with a brief but dazzled editorial appreciation.

> As murders go, this is not an unusual story. What is unusual—
> even astonishing—is that all of this is caught in a picture that
> portrays the scene so much more effectively than words. How
> did the photographer happen to be there? Who was he? How
> did he get such a whale of a shot?
>
> When you mention the photographer's name, the answers are
> matter of course. Arthur Feelig [sic] (Weegee) scores another
> scoop . . . This very picture is a hit of the Museum of Modern
> Art's Action Photography Show. One over-enthusiastic Museum
> official calls it the greatest newsphoto of the last ten years. Even
> so, it is a great picture, one that really deserves the overworked
> phrase, "great." Weegee knew that a shot of the "body" would
> not merit a bonus for the staff news boys would be there to cover
> it. Therefore he turned his camera on the spectators—with this
> result.

At the bottom of the page, *U.S. Camera* also reproduced Weegee's CREDIT PHOTO BY WEEGEE THE FAMOUS rubber stamp, with the commentary, "Not the least admirable of Weegee's charms is his sign. Weegee believes it. So does practically every editor who uses pictures."

Weegee was delighted at his acceptance into the elite circle of photography, excitedly telling a friend at the Photo League that he'd also just sold pictures to *Look* and *The Saturday Evening Post*. "He says he's turned over a new leaf—no more murders (unless very special)," she noted in the club's newsletter. Weegee didn't use the word *art*—not yet. What he was most proud of was having busted out of anonymity. "I'm getting famous!" he told her. The words on the rubber stamp were coming true.

PART II

THE FAMOUS

No more murders? Surprisingly enough, and despite his reputation, it was nearly true. There were still dead bodies at fires, dead bodies at car wrecks, but no new Weegee photo of someone who'd been deliberately killed appeared in *PM* after the end of 1942, and very few went to Acme or the local papers on "the Weegee service." By the time *Action Photography* had opened at the Museum of Modern Art, murder was no longer really his business. Though he talked as tough as ever about his nightly beat, he was gravitating toward those slightly softer subjects that nonetheless revealed the lives of underclass New Yorkers as vigorously as the corpses had.

Although he later said he'd photographed a thousand murders, and occasionally upped the claim to five thousand, the real count is nowhere near that. (He sometimes included a caveat: "I don't waste my genius on most of them.") Count them all up, and that reputation rests on a few dozen murder victims and a few dozen murderers. Beyond that, the newspapers of that era ran a smattering of uncredited dead bodies, perhaps a few per month, some of which are likely his. Even if every one of those pictures were Weegee's—which simply cannot be true; the *Daily News*'s night men weren't just playing cards while Weegee ran around working— his total almost surely would not crack two hundred. That's still a lot more dead bodies than most people will probably see, but it's nothing like five thousand. "When there was nothing major—murder, fire, things like that—he would work on human-interest stories," his friend and colleague Sid Kaplan explains. "Because the thing about *PM* . . . they've gotta fill up the page."

And often there was indeed nothing major going on. In 1940, the Brooklyn prosecutor Burton Turkus had finally broken the back of Murder Incorporated by getting the mobster Abe "Kid Twist" Reles to turn state's evidence, and in the early forties he sent seven of the group's leaders to the electric chair. When *Popular Photography* interviewed Weegee in 1944 (calling him "the famous New York news photographer whose specialty is crime and fire picture-taking"), he told the reporter that "there is hardly any crime now, and the cops and detectives don't like it. And besides, when they do make an arrest, the story and pictures don't get into the papers; too much war news! My free lance photographic business has taken a nose dive. Gone are the days of auto crashes, fires and gang killings. The different gangs seem to have signed an armistice for the duration. When I recently dropped into a police station house with my camera, the police sergeant was so glad to see me he gave me a cigar." Wilma Wilcox recalled that he was frustrated—"provoked," as she put it—because he was having trouble maintaining his customary pace. "When he got a picture that turned out to be just what he wanted," she recalled, "he would telephone me, even in my office, and say, 'Oh, I got one!'"

There was, at least, plenty of alternative material for him downtown. The wartime photos of Little Italy proliferated, as did the portraits of life during shortages and restrictions: butcher shops with no meat, shoe stores mobbed with customers on the last day before a particular rationing coupon expired. Another of his hot-weather pictures, in June 1943, was made at a public pool on the Lower East Side (on Pitt Street, in fact), and showed the water packed almost as full of bodies as the Coney Island sand had been. A whiskey shortage got him a big photo in *Life* that fall, and just a few days before that one, he made a photograph for the ages: maybe the greatest humorous high-life-low-life picture ever made, certainly the one for which Weegee is most remembered, the one that eventually became known as "The Critic."

It was November 22, 1943, and he was again at the Metropolitan Opera's opening night, the company's sixtieth anniversary. It was Weegee's fourth year covering the opening for *PM*, beginning with that row of top hats in 1940. (This was, incidentally, still at the Met's old opera house on Thirty-Ninth Street, an outdated, frumpy brick heap of a building that gave little hint of the great auditorium and acoustics within. The move to Lincoln Center was more than two decades away.) In 1942, he'd happened upon a great scene just outside the doors of the Met. It had occurred at the end of the evening rather than the red-carpet beginning, and it showed a distinctly New York interaction, as a box-seat operagoer in white tie and tails paused next to a shabby standing-room-only patron with a foot-long beard. The well-dressed man turned out to be a British diplomat with the irresistible name of Bertram Cecil Eskell. "How are you, my good fellow?" he asked his fellow music lover, whose name went unrecorded. Weegee got a lot of mileage out of juxtapositions like this one—they happened all the time at Sammy's—and *PM* did, too, running the photo at a full page, headlining it WEEGEE BRINGS BACK A "DIFFERENT" PICTURE OF OPERA'S OPENING NIGHT.

It evidently stuck in Weegee's mind that, if you put a down-and-outer next to a natty operagoer, the contrast made a highly entertaining photograph, one that *PM* would go for. Now, a year later, he was faced with the prospect of one-upping himself. Just as he'd repeated the fire-escape sleepers every year, and the Coney crowds, why not try for another hit?

Of course, he could not count on seeing a near-homeless figure at the stuffiest society event of the year, but Weegee knew how to take care of that, even if it involved some maneuvers that the Photo League might not have approved of. Late in the afternoon, he headed to Sammy's with Louis Liotta, where they knew they could get help from a female pal of Weegee's. (Her name is lost to history, but the photojournalist Sam Vandivert later said he knew her, and that she was someone Weegee was dating. She's definitely not Wilma Wilcox; she's not Frances Avery, another friend and occasional assistant in this era. Nor does she appear to be Tugboat Ethel, the Sammy's regular and Queen of the Bowery.) Whoever she was, Weegee and Liotta poured cheap wine into her, and at around dusk they got her into Weegee's Chevy and headed up to Thirty-Ninth Street.

On the opening-night program was Mussorgsky's *Boris Godunov*, chosen to celebrate American-Soviet cooperation on the European fronts. This was supposed to be an austere wartime evening, but you had to squint to see the cutbacks. The fall weather was just cool enough that plenty of mink had come out of storage. ("There was the same old smell of camphor hovering over the fancy furs," wrote one reporter.) Still, there were fewer limousines than usual, owing to gasoline and tire shortages, and quite a few people in full evening dress had made their way there by public transportation. The *Times* fashion writer noted that "one matron dazzled the crowd surrounding the doors with her array of diamond bracelets from wrist to elbow. With emerald earrings and a diamond and emerald necklace, her bugle-beaded white chiffon provided a perfect setting."

That could only have been Marie Muller Kavanaugh, customarily referred to in print as Mrs. George Washington Kavanaugh. Unlike many *Social Register* folks, she was not Old New York; she had grown up well-off but not rich, in Virginia. She married into money not once but twice, first to a brewery heir, then to Mr. Kavanaugh, a textile magnate. And she loved everything about being rich: the living quarters (at one point she bought the town house next to hers, to ensure that it didn't fall into the wrong hands), the fashion (she wore orchids to every big event), even the appearances in the press. She was, according to her great-granddaughter Alexandra Warner Nash, "the original person who was famous for being famous." When her picture appeared on the society pages, she would send the photographer a bottle of champagne if she felt he'd made her look good. Her friends occasionally referred to her as "Tiffany's front window." Photographs of her over the years at the opera reveal at least three different diamond tiaras. The diamond earrings she wore on this night weighed twenty carats each.

Weegee probably didn't know her name. ("I didn't know Society," he once joked. "I'd never arrested them before.") But he didn't have to, given that she presented herself as a giant pouf of snowy pelts and precious stones. She was literally a sparkly object, clearly worth photographing, and as she arrived that night, a bit before 8:00 p.m., he was ready.

The standing-room-only line, on which people had been waiting since 4:30 a.m., snaked down Thirty-Ninth Street. The rest of the newspaper photographers, making red-carpet pictures, were a few steps up from street level, in the Met's Thirty-Ninth Street foyer, near the entrance that Society folks used because it had a porte cochere for their drivers. Weegee's competitors offered their customary ribbing—perhaps a little more barbed than usual. A reporter brushed him off when Weegee asked who one of the socialites was, responding that he should find out for himself or "go back to your corpses." Weegee's response, he explained to a friend later, was "being a nonconformist, I said to myself *fuck that nonsense.*" He went back out into the chill.

Anyway, he had a scene to set. His downtown female friend, unsteady from the amount of wine she'd consumed, tottered outside the entrance, Liotta propping her up down by the curb. Weegee stood a few steps away on the sidewalk, his camera set up for a fifteen-foot shot. Mrs. Kavanaugh (no subway for her) exited her chauffeured car. She often came to the opera with her daughter Leonora, but tonight she was with her friend Elizabeth Wharton Drexel. A Philadelphian from the Drexel banking family, she'd outlived two husbands and was now on her third, an Irish peer named John Beresford, Fifth Baron Decies. That marriage had made her Lady Decies (pronounced "DEE-shees," though people tended to turn it into "DEE-sees"). She lived in Paris most of the time, and had published a dishy semi-memoir about the absurdities of high society in the Gilded Age. She was the sort of person who, when she'd disembarked at the New York piers one day in 1940, expressed dismay to a newspaper reporter that she hadn't been able to buy the fur coat she wanted in Paris because Hermann Goering had snapped it up for his wife. She made a splendid companion for Mrs. Kavanaugh, and even more fodder for the men with cameras.

From his place on the sidewalk, Weegee signaled Liotta, who released the disheveled woman and gave her a little nudge into the frame. Judging by the photograph, she is reeling, barely able to stand. If there was one thing Weegee knew from the scrum of photographers at police headquarters every morning, it was how to make a few shots very quickly, swapping in film plates and bulbs as fast as he could. *Flash:* he caught Mrs. Kavanaugh and Lady Decies as the third woman observed them. *Flash*, again, a moment later, as the two ladies turned, passed him, and stepped into the lobby, facing half a dozen other photographers with the same tight smiles. Liotta later said there were three or four bulbs set off, almost too fast for him to parse. That was it. No different from shooting on Centre Market Place, any day of the week at 9:00 a.m., as the night's suspects were marched in.

Then Weegee went on to finish the evening's work. Pictures of audience members, rich and poor (separately), rounded out the story. He shot a group of operagoers in the cheaper seats, using infrared film, and although they weren't necking, he did find something in their open-mouthed stares. These were the people who'd come in their business clothes, who were there for the music rather than to be seen. Mrs. Kavanaugh spent the intermission at Sherry's, the café behind the box seats. There she explained to a *PM* reporter that, despite the wartime mood, she was wearing her usual complement of jewels "to keep up morale."

Although Weegee had staged the sidewalk encounter, he couldn't have known quite how perfectly the tableau would square up on film. The two ladies in fur are almost pure white, nearly blown out by his flash. Mrs. Kavanaugh's smile is taut and paper-thin, the essence of fatuousness; Lady Decies looks quizzical, perhaps a little sour, her mouth pursed. They both face the camera square on. The drunken woman, by contrast, is caught in perfect ninety-degree profile, giving her features a sharpness against the nearly black background. Because her clothes are darker, she doesn't pick up the flash as the bejeweled ladies do. Her coat reads dishwater gray, her hair lank, her scowl dark, her eyes rolling. She seems shorter, too. Weegee wanted a contrast; he got more than he could have asked for.

Whenever Weegee told the story of that night later on, he left out the wine, the setup, the assistant, and the planted observer. He'd just thought he was making a picture of Mrs. Kavanaugh and Lady Decies, he always said, claiming that he "could almost smell the smugness." He never saw the disheveled woman, he said, until he was in the darkroom. A few years later, writing about it, he flatly stated, "This is an unposed shot"; in another account: "that was really honest." None of these statements is true. But he certainly may have been surprised at just how entertaining a scene he'd built, and cropped it down to show just the trio. (In the uncropped negative, the ladies occupy only about a third of the frame, next to a line of people waiting for admission.) The next morning, he brought the photo to *PM*.

They didn't want it. In retrospect, it seems impossible that McCleery and his colleagues wouldn't recognize one of the great photographs of the twentieth century when it landed on their desks. But *PM* was steeped in war coverage just then and aspired to an occasionally pointy-headed good citizenship. After months of blackouts and scrap drives, the editors flinched at the sight of Mrs. Kavanaugh's diamonds. Rather than seeing a chance to make a statement at her expense, they simply rejected the

Opening night at the Metropolitan Opera, 1943: one of the most famous images of the twentieth century, and the one that cemented Weegee's reputation. Forty-odd years later, Weegee's assistant came clean, admitting that he and Weegee had gotten the disheveled woman drunk beforehand, then planted her at the scene.

photo. (It was a move that Weegee, using a favorite word, described to an acquaintance as "dopey.") The news of the evening was made by another picture that is nearly forgotten today. Grace Doherty, the widow of an oil magnate, had thumbed her nose at a *Daily News* photographer named Walter Engels and ended up on the front page the next morning. That dominated the opening-night coverage, along with the news that a horse named Silver, onstage in *Boris Godunov*, had turned his behind to the audience during a tenor's aria and then trotted offstage. The *Times* critic archly said that Silver's pirouette had been the best performance of the night.

    Life's editors liked Weegee's photograph more than *PM*'s had and ran his picture of the three ladies the next week, in its issue of December 6. Even there, though, it was buried: it ran at perhaps an eighth of a page in size, in a row of pictures along the bottom of a spread, with a dry-wit text block reading, "The fashionable people were laden with jewels. Most bejeweled were Mrs. George W. Kavanaugh and Lady Decies whose entry was viewed with distaste by spectator." It was paired with another portrait, of the standing-room operagoers—"The plain people," *Life* called them, the rest of the caption making it clear that they were preferable to the rich folk down in the boxes.

Although this clearly was a great picture among many that Weegee made, it was not deemed exceptional right away. That is probably inevitable: there's no way for an artist to predict which of his or her works becomes *the one*. But it did have one thing that is necessary in popular art: it could arrest the eye and evoke a reaction.

One of the eyes it caught and held belonged to Nancy Newhall, who in early 1944 was selecting photographs for another exhibition at the Museum of Modern Art. This time, though, it wasn't a little show like *Action Photography* had been. It was an extravaganza called *Art in Progress*, marking the Modern's fifteenth anniversary. For the first time, every department in the museum would be showing simultaneously, blurring boundaries among media.

Photography appeared on the first floor, and the installation was more refined than it had been a year earlier: large black boards with lots of space around the photographs and the artists' names discreetly displayed along the top edge. The pictures had been grouped and sequenced with care. Given the tiny size of the American art photography community just then, the show could include a little from almost everybody, and it did: fifteen prints by Ansel Adams, three by Berenice Abbott, handfuls by Helen Levitt, Edward Weston, Alfred Stieglitz, and many others. Lisette Model, a German expat friend of Weegee's who had a similar knack for making rich portraits around the fringes of society, was represented, too. Weegee himself had five prints in the exhibition: two shootings, one fire, one circus performer, and the one that MoMA not quite correctly called "Opening Night at the Opera, N.Y.C. 1944."

The show was up for four months, starting in May. Very quickly, it became obvious that something magical was happening in front of that Weegee photograph. People laughed, pointed, reacted. A week into the run, either *PM*'s editors picked up on it or, more likely, Weegee himself told them, and on June 2, the paper tacitly acknowledged its blown call the previous November. This time, it ran the photo at large size, saying:

The big picture at lower right is the center of attraction in Weegee's section of the Art in Progress photo exhibition now on view at the Museum of Modern Art. It shows Mrs. George Washington Kavanaugh and Lady Decies outside the Metropolitan Opera House—and the eloquent facial reaction of another woman. The other pictures on this page were snapped by Weegee as visitors to the photo exhibition looked at his pictures . . . Four out of his five exhibits have appeared in *PM*. The opera shot got the most laughs, Weegee reports.

It surely had, and Weegee's voyeurdom had gone into a dizzying, recursive closed loop: he was photographing the observers who were looking at his photograph of a woman he'd posed as an observer, who was looking at a pair of dowagers who had been, in turn, looking directly at him. In the painting galleries at MoMA, visitors could see work by the Cubists that aimed to represent multiple points of view in one flat plane. Down on the first floor, it was happening in real time, using not the traditional tools of fine art but a Speed Graphic wielded on deadline.

Weegee called it the photograph that changed his life. A decade later, he claimed that he'd sold ten thousand dollars' worth of prints and was still getting requests for it. "With this picture," he said, "I MATURED as a photographer and HUMAN BEING."

Mrs. Kavanaugh, for her part, seems not to have minded any of the portrait's tone. She didn't stop posing at the opera, and Weegee and she chatted amiably at the next year's opening. She kept on her flibbertigibbet ways for the rest of her very long life and, if anything, grew more famous for being famous. *Life* magazine photographed her at home; when she lost a five-thousand-dollar bracelet a couple of years later at the Met, the search and recovery made the magazine, too. Weegee later said that she'd told him she found the photograph "too divine." Today, there is, according to her great-granddaughter Alexandra Warner, "an *enormous* amount of family lore about that picture." Warner herself, while in boarding school, was once in an English class where students were assigned to write about their reactions to a photograph, and you can guess which one the teacher unknowingly chose.

Even more extraordinary was the story that Mrs. Kavanaugh's grandson Charles Warner told. He'd been in the army in early 1944, fighting at Anzio, when a blizzard of enemy propaganda leaflets was dropped by plane over his squad. One of them read YANKEE—YOU DIE FOR THIS? and displayed that picture. (Warner did not reveal to his fellow GIs at that moment that the photo was of his own grandmother.) It sounds like a suspiciously great coincidence, and one of Warner's old friends later offered that the leaflet had merely been picked up by a friend in Germany rather than fluttered down upon Warner's own head. (Even that may be a stretching of the truth: no such flyer has ever surfaced.) Still, it's only appropriate that a photo that was set up to look authentic inspired a war story that was too great not to tell and was itself stretching the truth.

As for Lady Decies, she buried her baron husband just weeks after that November evening, and she herself died the following June. Weegee found himself moved by her passing. As Wilma Wilcox later explained, "He felt that this picture had done so much for him . . . enough so that he went to the funeral at St. Patrick's Cathedral, wondering how he might pay tribute." He sat toward the back, she recalled, "trying to figure out what picture he could take that would be an honor to her. And to him, too!" As the casket was brought down to the side exit of St. Patrick's, he followed, watching. Then, as the pallbearers—he believed them to be paid, rather than friends or family—began making their way down the steps, a quintessential Weegee moment presented itself. Across Fifty-First Street, there was a burger joint, its awning reading HAMBURG HEAVEN. A little careful positioning, and he had it: Lady Decies, at her final moment on earth, pointed directly toward the word *heaven*. On the prints he made, he combined two similar negatives and retouched the awning to sharpen up the letters. One more darkroom tweak to throw reality into extra-high relief.

And what did the unnamed third woman, the one upon whom "The Critic" depends, have to say about it? Weegee later wrote that she'd sent him a note after seeing the picture in print. "She wanted to trade pictures with me. If I gave her a copy of this photograph she would give me one of her etchings." He went by her place with a print and asked her what she thought. "I kinda like it," he said she told him. "But my friends are kinda critical."

The mystery scruff of "The Critic" was not the only woman Weegee was going around with in late 1943. By then, Wilma Wilcox was back in his life. She had left New York two years earlier, getting a job with Iowa's Department of Social Welfare, and was living a back-and-forth life, returning to Columbia's School of Social Work from February to May 1943, then going back to Iowa. There, she had a defining moment. "I had returned to my home," she explained later, "and was back on the job of driving all over the rural county, helping children with their problems. I went down to an adjoining city on business, and had trouble with my car. So I took it to a garage, and went to the library to wait. I happen to be a great magazine reader, so I looked around for a magazine, and found a *Saturday Evening Post*." It turned out to contain a big spread devoted to Weegee, written by his friend Earl Wilson. "And as I read it, I realized the extent of our attraction for each other."

Wilcox, then and there, told herself that she was going to settle in New York. It was difficult for her, she said. "To decide to stay there, to get a position there, and to become a New Yorker—who ever heard of doing such a thing in my particular group?" She re-enrolled at Columbia in June 1943, stayed for the next year, and landed her second master's degree.

Was she there for love? She was indirect, nearly opaque, when she talked about what Weegee and she had. "It was based around the relationship that had developed as I saw him at different times, as I was going back and forth, in this educational pursuit." The move, she said, "was stimulated also by the fact that I realized there was an attraction between the two of us. So that New York was more personal than impersonal." They made an extremely odd couple, the prim-looking Quaker social worker and the kibitzing Jewish newsman. "We stopped traffic sometimes," she admitted with a chuckle, when someone asked her about that. "Especially when I was carrying the tripod."

Weegee had begun selling to *Look* that summer, beginning with a photo essay devoted to women wearing pants, still a sufficiently uncommon topic as to be newsworthy. Acme was buying his daily take. *PM* was still running about three Weegee stories per week, one world-class picture after another: a Lower East Side couple, the Di Maggios, awaiting news of their kidnapped son, and then the block packed with celebrants when he got home safe; two antic young women, grinning despite the fact that they'd just been recaptured after escaping from prison (they were picked up while watching a movie called *The Youngest Profession*); the pensive faces of New Yorkers as they watched a Times Square news flash about the fall of Mussolini, and the extremely unsober response on the streets of Little Italy when the Allies poured onto the Italian mainland and an armistice was signed.

More than once in these years, he found himself photographing men who dressed as women. Homosexuality and sodomy were crimes in New York, although the laws were enforced only in fits and starts, and the police, because of custom or bribery, ignored certain bars and clubs. Periodically, though, those bars were raided, and men in drag were hauled in under a law that explicitly prohibited cross-dressing. (A "three-piece rule" applied: if you were wearing three pieces of clothing that were traditional to your sex, you were okay. This allowed women in trousers, just barely, to go out on the street.) In 1938, Weegee had photographed a robbery-turned-raid at the Howdy Revue, a lesbian bar on West Third Street. Beginning around 1939 and continuing into the forties, he caught on film the aftermath of gay-bar raids several times, at Centre Street and also downtown, at a precinct house on Whitehall Street. In the most memorable of these pictures, an undated portrait from around 1940, a young guy steps out of the police wagon, not ashamed to be arrested but delighted to be getting his picture in the paper. He's wearing a fur jacket and nylons and has lifted his skirt a bit to flash his slim and shaven legs, and it is undoubtedly one of the most cheerful arrest pictures ever made. Weegee may have intended to portray him as just another New York freak, and certainly the *Mirror* would have, but he's so winning a character that it's hard to see anything but charm there.

Another drag portrait, from November 1943—made just three days after "The Critic"—is less chipper. This one's not from a raid; the uneasy man being arrested wears a floral-print dress and has his teeth clenched. The flash reveals his stubble. A headline writer, giving the picture a title that Weegee himself later used, referred to him as "Myrtle from Myrtle Avenue." In real life, he was a mugger named Donald Gill, a man who'd cross-dressed in order to sneak up on his potential victims. He'd been caught when he chatted up the male half of a Brooklyn couple, then (in the words of a *Post* reporter) "began punching him in a very competent and unladylike manner." He turned out to be a newly discharged soldier with a rap sheet for burglary and larceny. Why was he in drag? "Well, you know," he told the *Post*, "it was Thanksgiving, so I decided to masquerade as a woman."

These pictures, admittedly, are aligned with (if not entirely part of) the long, grim tradition of covering gay people as pervs and kooks. They aren't profoundly sympathetic, although the smiling gent in the back of the police wagon does seem delighted to be there. But there is another set of cross-dressing photos made by Weegee that is extraordinary, and prefigures the openness of the future. (They're also undated but seem to have been made a few years after these.) In that series, we see a man in late middle age—he's identified as Vivian—in a spartan furnished room. He is first in street clothes, then disrobes. Weegee shows us his suitcase, filled with women's clothes and, prominently displayed, a brassiere and a pair of falsies. Over the course of about six photos, we see the man's transformation take place, and by the end he appears fully in drag. In the final image, we see his partner, a toothless and very old person of indeterminate gender. They're holding hands.

Weegee may have been (a little) more accepting than most people of his generation when it came to this kind of thing. On the subject of race, his sympathy and egalitarianism are more visible. One of his best portraits from Harlem shows a man in his formal Sunday best on Easter

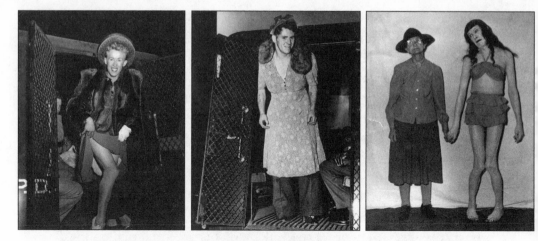

Three cross-dressing New Yorkers, three views of the world: delighted and public, uneasy and grimacing, and almost painfully private.

morning. The man turned out to be a haberdasher who liked to dress, and Weegee laid nothing more upon him than that. But a larger story about race in America was beginning to insert itself into the news ever more insistently, and thus into his consciousness. Despite his general indifference to activism, Weegee had seen enough as a poor Galician Jew to recognize discrimination when it came along. (That photo of the Washington, D.C., movie theater, with its Jim Crow partition, was his kind of statement.) Twice in the second half of 1943 he found himself covering the front lines of New York's early skirmishes in the civil rights movement.

The first story broke on the night of August 1, when an argument between a Harlem woman and a policeman escalated and an African American soldier named Robert Bandy tried to intervene, grabbing the cop's nightstick and knocking him over the head with it. The policeman then shot at Bandy, nicking him and sending him briefly to the hospital. Rumors spread that he had been killed, and over the course of the night, frustration among black New Yorkers—fed up over their continued second-class treatment even as their young men served overseas—erupted. By dawn, five people had been killed by police, about four hundred others had been hurt, about five hundred had been arrested, and more than forty-five hundred store windows had been smashed.

Weegee's photos that first night were good—he caught the NAACP's president, Walter White, in deep conversation with police chief Lewis Valentine, and also spotted Mayor La Guardia at a police station, directing efforts to manage the situation—but he was one among many. (*PM*'s Dan Keleher made some of the best action pictures of the night.) Weegee's most evocative photographs instead show 125th Street just after daybreak, after quiet descended and people began to clean up. Acting on his instinct for great internal captioning, he took photo after photo of broken windows and busted-up storefronts, many with signs hurriedly attached reading, EVERYTHING O.K./BUSINESS GOING ON AS USUAL and DRUG STORE OPEN. The most poignant one read THIS WAS A DRESS STORE. REMEMBER?

A few weeks later, another, smaller racial skirmish erupted on West 166th Street, between Edgecombe and Amsterdam Avenues. It was in Washington Heights, an area that was racially mixed but emphatically not blended. The block to the south, on 165th Street, was filled with African American residents. The one to the north, on 167th, was all-white. West 166th was the literal color line: two buildings had just begun to accept black tenants. An African American family, Bernice and Alphonso Lythcott and their two small children, had moved into the first floor of one of those buildings, at 453 West 166th Street. (Alphonso worked as the superintendent, and the family had just moved from the Carolinas. The last white tenants had just left the building, which had several unoccupied apartments.) Down the block, the other black-occupied building bore new graffiti reading THE NIGERS STINK [*sic*]. The police were aware of the trouble and had kept an eye on the block.

On the night of October 16, when the patrols were off, the Lythcotts' window was broken by thrown rocks, in a rank act of intimidation. The family hadn't even unpacked yet. Weegee got it all, for a page in *PM*: the graffiti, the Lythcott family amid their crated-up possessions as three-year-old Alphonso Jr. held the rocks that had smashed their windows, and Bernice Lythcott, no more than twenty-three, standing with her son Leonard in her arms, looking through the broken pane in her front door. Her skin appears fair enough in the photo that her granddaughter Monique Trinkleback says that young members of her family have asked, "Grandma was a white lady?" But she wasn't, and Mrs. Lythcott and her darker-skinned husband faced the same evils, even far from the Jim Crow South.

In 1943, Bernice Lythcott and her one-year-old son Leonard were among the first black tenants on a formerly all-white Washington Heights block. Their front-door window had been shattered by racists with rocks, and graffiti on the building read THE NIGERS STINK.

In the photograph, her gaze is even; Leonard has his eyes wide, and his hand to his mouth, as if stunned. It is a more traditional news picture than Weegee is known for making, and it's technically better than most of them, too, with relatively subtle highlights and careful framing that didn't require cropping. It's a great, penetrating image of a hard American moment, a portrait that holds its own next to Dorothea Lange's migrant woman or Walker Evans's Alabama sharecropper.

His ability to get the most out of his gold-plated flashgun gave Wee-

gee another great moment a few weeks later, this time at a fire. On the
night of December 18, an alarm call led him down under the entrance
ramp for the Manhattan end of the Brooklyn Bridge, to an industrial
building at Dover and Water Streets. There, clouds of smoke and spume
enveloped a seven-story building that housed a spice factory and also
Ameko, the American Kitchen Products Company, a manufacturer of
bouillon cubes. It was, once again, the signage on the building that Weegee found irresistible, because Ameko's instant-soup slogan was painted
on the building's façade, and it read SIMPLY ADD BOILING WATER. It probably took a few tries to get the combination of wind, smoke, hoses, spray,
and flash just right, but if he took other pictures of the scene, he discarded
them. The survivor is a technical tour de force, one of the most adeptly
made photos he ever published. The smoke mixes with the firemen's spray,
and both pick up the light of Weegee's flashbulb—or rather three flashbulbs set off at once, which is what it took to illuminate this huge scene—
as well as the fire department's floodlights, creating white teakettle steam,
translucent and beautiful and frozen in place. The rising plumes feather
in around the sign, vignetting and highlighting the joke. They also happen to obscure the Ameko name up above, eliminating any distracting
words. (They do not, however, cover up a billboard on the roof advertising Hygrade Frankfurters, which often leads viewers of the photo to
think that the boiling water is for hot dogs rather than soup.) It is a
beautiful photo, in its way—and although the fire shut down traffic on
the Brooklyn Bridge for a while, nobody seems to have been hurt, so it's
not a tragic one, either. The picture was published as far away as the *San
Francisco Chronicle*, clearly on its strength as a pure photograph, because
why else would San Franciscans care about a two-bit Manhattan fire?

Weegee didn't really see its beauty beyond the joke, maybe because
he'd made so many pictures of burning buildings in his life. Wilma Wilcox
once remarked to him that it was a remarkable image even without the
slogan, and he sneered. "He was disgusted," Wilma recalled, "and said
'What's the point of the picture if it didn't have the sign on it?' Both she
and he were right, but Weegee's reaction reveals how dismissive he was
of arty photographic subtlety. The point, he often said in interviews, was
impact. "Get punch into your pictures" was his preferred explanation.

That's how the editors of the magazine *U.S. Camera* had recently
headlined a profile of Weegee: PUNCH IN PICTURES. It ran under Weegee's

The factory made bouillon cubes; the sign made its own caption. This perfect mix of billboard and blaze occurred on Water Street, next to the Brooklyn Bridge, on December 18, 1943.

byline, and told a few stories of his resourcefulness, including one gem. He'd encountered a murderer—later interviews reveal that it was Patricia Ryan, a woman who'd killed her policeman husband—who had, like most, hid her face on her way in and out of police headquarters. Only when she got to the police wagon did she uncover, whereupon she was immediately caught on film by Weegee, who had quietly crept into the van and was huddled there with his camera shutter cocked and his flash-bulb loaded. "That's a dirty trick," she snarled at him, and he agreed. Then he headed off to the photo desks to pull in a month's rent in one night.

All the while, he was keeping up his visibility. Earl Wilson, the *New York Post* columnist who'd written that *Saturday Evening Post* feature on Weegee, started a radio show in August 1943 and brought him on as a guest. Weegee also taught another round of classes at the Photo League, starting in late July. But not everyone there approved of his self-promotional style, and his disdain for their artsiness and their corresponding disdain for his earthiness could cause fractures. In early 1944, he scrawled an angry letter on a *Look* tear sheet. "To the Boys & Girls of the Photo League (White Collar Branch): Do you teach how to take photos like this, that sell for fantastic sums of money? If so, who is teaching there, half baked or otherwise? What is the purpose of the Photo League?" He signed it not only with his name, twice, but also with his WEEGEE THE FAMOUS stamp, and mordantly added, in a blank space under the photos, where the credit would go, "This Space for Rent."

He was on solid ground, too, because the pictures on that *Look* page were another small tour de force. They'd been made during Frank Sinatra's concert at the Paramount, where young women were invariably described as "swooning." Although Weegee made a few pictures of Sinatra himself that night, he had kept an eye on the crowd—watching the watchers, as always—and spotted one young woman, maybe sixteen years old, who seemed especially entranced. His predictive powers in this one case were real, and he caught her in seven perfect frames: enraptured, crying, dreamy, and finally almost passed out in what *Look* sniffily called "erotic ecstasy."

Commercial success aside, he obviously craved institutional acceptance, whether from the League or from *Look* or from the museums, and at least once the pursuit came with a warning light. That was the day in the spring of 1944 when he met Alfred Stieglitz.

Then eighty years old, Stieglitz was considered the greatest photographic artist alive, though he hadn't taken pictures in a decade. He was the man who, as much as any single person can be credited with doing so, had pulled the genre out of the territory of mechanical documentation and into the realm of fine art. At this stage of his life, he was frail, with a bad heart, and had nearly withdrawn from public life. His gallery, An American Place, showed very little work and took in very little money, and he had taken to sleeping in its back room on a daybed. He was a titan and a village elder and a forgotten man, all at once.

Weegee later said that he'd bumped into his idol on the street one day, but in fact he had sought Stieglitz out. "Something I'd said sent Weegee to see him," wrote Nancy Newhall to her husband in April 1944, "and Stieglitz was tickled." Newhall saw a weird echo between the courtly old European aristocrat and the mouthy press photographer. "Weegee appeals to St[ieglitz] as he does to me. He's a 'collector's piece'—naive, with a macabre humor, bombastic, ridiculous, there's reality there, imagination, an unsentimental & very genuine sympathy for people, And ambition to be a really great photographer." Mostly, though, they talked about women. "Weegee's love life, as one might expect, has been promiscuous & unsatisfactory. He got the essential point of most of Stieglitz's stories, but missed the overtones, & would come back with a remark that convulsed Stieglitz and me." Afterward, she told Weegee how many women had pursued Stieglitz in his younger days, and Weegee "groaned with envy."

Weegee left that part out when he wrote the story as a *PM* feature the next day. What he did set down, however, was vivid and memorable: a scene where he had visited a giant and seen a ghost. When Weegee introduced himself, he said, Stieglitz "stared at me as if I had waked him from a dream . . . I apologized for the intrusion and told him that for a long time I had wanted to meet him. He became gracious and invited me to come up to his studio." Weegee noted that the gallery, one of the two or three most important places in the history of photography, had "a smell of disinfectant like in a sick room." They talked about business, and Stieglitz told him the phone "never rings . . . I have been deserted." He told Weegee that he thought himself a failure, that artists he'd supported were making money and had left him behind. Stieglitz expressed disdain for Kodak's famous slogan "You press the button, we do the rest," saying that a photograph required thought and effort, that it captured "a certain fleeting fraction of a second; and that once that passed, that fraction of time was dead and could never be brought back to life again." Stieglitz admitted that his gallery's finances were failing, that he might be evicted, that he hadn't made a photograph of his own in years. During their meeting, an angina attack caused him to double over in pain. "I waited till he recovered," Weegee wrote, "then left quietly . . . wondering if that elusive fame I was after was worth while."

Of course, he made Stieglitz's portrait, using not Stieglitz's subtle natural light but his own customary hard flash, throwing a deep black shadow against the gallery's wall. Newhall saw the picture the next day and didn't think Weegee had captured the master. "He'd gotten something of Stieglitz's tragedy & loneliness—but not the beauty, the fire, the passion, the indomitable fighter," she wrote. "I told him so, and he said he'd suspected it & would try again." There's something to what she says, but she was underestimating that picture. It's an image that gets at Weegee's own great fear, of slipping away forgotten, as much as it gets at its ostensible subject.

In the summer of 1944, Weegee had a small show up at the Metro Photo Shop on Fourth Avenue, perhaps the first of many such small-scale retail exhibitions he did over the years. By then, he was well enough known that *Popular Photography* could make reference, without explanation, to another photographer who was rushing to cover "a regular Weegee-type fire." Everyone who was reading that magazine knew who Weegee was: the guy who could get there first, Speed Graphic in hand. And it surely helped, that summer, when he made the most eyebrow-raising of his so-called psychic pictures, the one that he used above all to justify his moniker.

A couple of years earlier, when Weegee had photographed that Bowery resident who was about to be hit by a car, the reasoning behind the "before" image was easy to understand: Weegee was looking for poignant lost-soul pictures during Christmas week. But early on the morning of July 5, 1944, he seems to have surprised even himself. Two beat cops had given him a lift to Chinatown, and he found himself at the corner of Mott and Pell Streets at 2:00 a.m. He'd just said hello to Shavey Lee, a local

A visit with Alfred Stieglitz, the grand old man of art photography, left Weegee unnerved: What happens when you outlive your fame?

political character loosely known as "the mayor of Chinatown" who had an office in the corner building, when he made a picture of the two policemen as they did nothing in particular. The cops were puzzled: one shouted, "Why waste the film on us?"

Five minutes later, the street caved in. A water main had broken and, as the pavement above it buckled, a gas main also broke, starting a fire. The lamppost next to the cops fell into the open hole as flames leaped up around it. Six hundred people were evacuated from the neighborhood, both for their immediate safety and because there was a concern that the buildings nearby would later collapse. The street was closed for months thereafter as repairs were made.

Does it even need to be said who got the best photos of the event? Weegee had the good sense to duplicate his previous pose, documenting the same corner from the same angle five minutes after the first picture, before heading for safer ground. To *PM*, with its didactic way of presenting photojournalism, this was just about perfect. WEEGEE KNEW SOMETHING WAS BREWING—AND IT WAS!, the headline read. It produced a story he told for the rest of his life, with a variety of ostensibly psychic explanations along the lines of "It had been too quiet" or "My elbow itched." His actual method of divination was simple to describe but exhausting to execute. If you were always on duty, with your eyes always open, eventually something would happen right before them. In the grind lay the makings of greatness.

In the guest book at *Murder Is My Business* in 1941, Louis Stettner had written that Weegee ought to collect his photos into a book. By the time of his second Museum of Modern Art moment, in 1944, others were suggesting the same thing, although Weegee continued to profess an aw-shucks attitude about the larger resonance of his work. "I was just like Grandma Moses," he wrote, "going along taking pictures in my primitive way." He gave a talk titled "Realism in Photography" at MoMA on April 5, a few weeks before the exhibition opened. "After the lecture," he later explained, "a lot of people came over to tell me that I should have a book"—including, he said, one literary agent.

Yet that talk at MoMA had actually been more contentious than he let on. He'd been on a double bill with another news photographer, named Herb Giles, and when they met before the speech, Weegee pulled him aside, asking him, "There's one thing: Let's not pick on each other or anything like that." Giles went first and spoke about his willingness to help a scene along when reality didn't quite conform to his deadline needs, just as Weegee had with the opera ladies and the fire-escape kids. He recalled a day when he'd needed a picture of a survivor of an oil-tanker rescue on the New Jersey shore, and had paid a young guy ten bucks to grease up and dive into the Atlantic. Weegee followed Giles onstage and played to the room instead of honoring the bargain he'd struck. "That guy is such a faker!" he said, gesturing to Giles. Then he delivered his lecture and took questions—whereupon the distinguished photographer Paul Strand, already a legend, stood up and asked a pointed question:

"Weegee, do you ever do any staging?" *No,* Weegee replied piously, *never.* "But Weegee," Strand continued, "did you ever, on one of those world-famous bodies of yours under the El, take the man's fedora and put it on his chest?" Weegee turned his head away and went silent. He couldn't wisecrack his way out of that.

Even Giles admitted that Weegee had delivered a good and interesting talk that night, though, and perhaps there were indeed a few people there who suggested that he ought to have a book of his work. Besides, he had time on his hands. "Things got quiet," he explained. "There were no fires or murders. I couldn't understand that with so many millions of people . . . it didn't look normal . . . but it did give me a chance to look over the pictures I had been accumulating. . . . They seemed to form a pattern."

The dummy volume that Weegee soon put together was, effectively, a survey of his ten-year freelance career, with photos thematically grouped. Some of those themes were obvious, such as the fires and murders and car wrecks, and each got its own chapter. So did other subjects, though, those he'd been driven to by his own interests rather than by pure news value: Coney Island, Harlem, the Bowery, spectators at all sorts of events—and the Metropolitan Opera, where his four years' worth of opening-night photographs were combined in a loose continuum that suggested a single evening. Several thousand words' worth of captions and introductory copy tied the photographs together, as did a warm, enthusiastic introduction by *PM*'s William McCleery. "Persons looking on Weegee's incredible photographs for the first time," McCleery wrote, "find it hard to believe that one ordinary earth-bound human being could have been present at so many climactic moments in the city's life. The simplest explanation of the phenomenon is that true love endows a man with superhuman qualities, and Weegee is truly in love with New York. Not the New York that you and I know, but the New York that he has known, first as a poor immigrant boy and later as a free-lance newspaper photographer specializing in crime and violence. Loving the city, Weegee has been able to live with her in the utmost intimacy." And, later on: "I think that Weegee's subjective portrait of New York must be regarded as a work of creative art, because, although all of the elements were there for anyone to use, no one has ever used them as Weegee has."

On the dedication page, Weegee offered the book not to his parents

or his siblings but "To you, the people of New York." It offered acknowledgment to everyone who had posed for him, willingly or not. He included
the visit to Stieglitz, rewritten slightly, as one of the book's eighteen chapters. The last of those is devoted to practical advice, probably drawn from
his lecturing. It told amateurs how they could follow his lead, break into
freelance life, work fast at a fire or a crime scene, make a sale. He took
his advice down to an almost comically fine level. "At auto accidents where
gasoline is spilled all over the streets," he offered, "don't light a smoke yourself and throw away the lighted match." But a lot of it was illuminating
as well. Avoid fumbling with a light meter, he suggested. "I haven't got
the time for gadgets because all my energy is concentrated on the drama
taking place before my eyes." (Even today, when electronics have eliminated most exposure guesswork, most news photographers would agree.)
And "get all the information you can, don't be afraid to ask questions . . .
be curious. The readers always are." Still are.

Weegee later said the book had been a tough one to sell, because his
high-life-low-life portrait of New York was not well understood by con-
servative book publishers. Every editor who saw it, he said, wanted something more like a tourist guide: "Where's the picture of the sailor in the
rowboat in Central Park? Where's the picture of the Statue of Liberty?
Where's the picture of the Fulton Fish Market?" Murders and fires certainly didn't fit into that category. Sure, Weegee had photographed the
Fulton Fish Market—after half the building had slid into the East River
one night. That wasn't the cozy yet marvelously authentic workingman's
scene editors were looking for.

You have to wonder whether that was the real problem, though, given
that high-life-low-life stories were already a staple of the papers. It seems
likelier that publishers were simply balking at the prospect of a photo
book by a semifamous newsman. Rationing made it difficult, during the
war, to produce any printed matter not deemed essential, let alone something that required high-quality paper stock. By 1943, Random House
was producing many of its books on a bad grade of pulp, with a V-for-
Victory logo and an apologetic note on the copyright page. The Book-of-
the-Month Club had its membership capped "for the duration," to keep
press runs down. The publishers of *The New Yorker* found it so difficult
to find enough paper that they seriously considered dropping back to

biweekly publication. Committing to a big picture book, and printing it right, would have made any publisher uneasy.

Weegee's mock-up of the book circulated through publishing offices that summer. At one (he claimed), it was briefly lost, then turned up in the ladies' room. Eventually, though, it found his way to a firm called Duell, Sloan and Pearce. It had opened for business just six years earlier, and already it had a solid author list, including Erskine Caldwell, John O'Hara, E. E. Cummings, and Wallace Stegner. The house was interested in the high-life-low-life world where Weegee operated. Charles Pearce, its cofounder, had just published Joseph Mitchell's second book, *McSorley's Wonderful Saloon*, and had recently taken a stab at persuading Joe Gould, the mad bohemian who had achieved local fame after Mitchell profiled him, to publish a portion of the multimillion-word oral history of the world that he had purportedly been compiling.* (Pearce didn't get that manuscript, because Gould himself hadn't actually written most of it down.) Duell, Sloan and Pearce also had some expertise when it came to photography books. It had been the publisher for the annual collections put out by the magazine *U.S. Camera*, and had gotten into a censorship tangle over the 1942 edition, which contained nudes and was banned in Boston. Weegee later spun a yarn about wearing down the resistance of Frank Henry, a nonfiction editor who handled Duell, Sloan's Essential Books imprint, over many lunches and drinks at a Midtown restaurant.

The deal itself was made pretty quickly. Weegee got a respectable $1,625 as an advance against royalties, and in late November 1944 the press release went out: "*Naked City*, New York as seen through Weegee's camera, will be published in January by Essential Books and distributed through Duell, Sloan and Pearce." For unrecorded reasons, though—wartime austerity? plain old schedule shuffling?—publication was delayed, and delayed again. The date was set for the spring, then June 11, then July 18. By early summer, one press account referred to the book as "postponed continually." Weegee, who was used to the

---

* Weegee, later in life, claimed that Mitchell had also profiled him for *The New Yorker*, and that he had, tit for tat, written about Mitchell for *PM*. Neither story ever made it into print. Mitchell, after hanging around Weegee and getting to know him for six months, decided he couldn't make the story work. The manuscript, if the story ever got that far, is neither in Mitchell's files nor in *The New Yorker*'s archives.

rat-a-tat speed and payout of daily publication, seems to have been irritated by the rescheduling, and by the slow grind of book publishing. The project, he said, became "really a job . . . a holy crusade."

It can't have helped that, just a few weeks before the book was finally on track to be published, the newspaper truck drivers' union went on strike. Every paper but *PM*, which had its own labor deal, was producing a tiny fraction of its usual print run. Weegee was probably not selling many photos to the other papers in those weeks, and of course nobody would be running book reviews or author features to publicize *Naked City*.

Although the newspapers were effectively shut down, the radio was not. (This was the same newspaper strike during which Mayor La Guardia cemented his legend by reading the comics pages to the city's kids over WNYC.) Duell, Sloan and Pearce's publicity department did its work well, booking Weegee on *Mary Margaret McBride*. Nearly forgotten now, it was a daytime radio interview program that was as powerful in its time as Oprah Winfrey's TV show was in ours. McBride was a bubbly, middle-aged midwesterner, almost exactly Weegee's age, who affected a country-gal-dazzled-by-the-big-city air. She was no rube, though. She had a daily audience that peaked at about eight million devoted housewives, and she wielded immense selling power for her sponsors. (She also exercised that power to secure a first crack at every guest. She wouldn't book you if you'd been on another show first.) Each weekday, her announcer and cohost, Vincent Connolly, introduced her with the words "It's one o'clock, and here is Mary Margaret McBride . . ." whereupon she picked up the thread and continued the sentence.

". . . Who's always been madly in love with New York City," she began her show on July 11. "But maybe, Weegee, I'm not quite as much in love with it as you are. The way everybody talks about you and this book, this beautiful book, that you've done, I think maybe you not only love it better than I do but you know it a doggone sight better than I do." And they were off, for nearly forty-five minutes of talk show banter. In an atypical move for 1945, the show had been prerecorded (on a shellac disc), because it was to air during McBride's vacation.

Weegee was a bit tentative and nervous as the interview began, but McBride's effusiveness and leading questions helped him along, and very quickly he became his usual wry and boastful self ("Well, I used to spell it O-u-i-j-a, but I changed it to W-e-e-g-e-e, to make it easier for the fan mail"). And he played the street-smart anti-intellectual charmer exceptionally well.

> **MCBRIDE:** There is one picture of the opera, two females coming into the opera, and another female watching them. I guarantee that if there ever was satire in the world, that picture is real satire. Maybe you didn't try to be a satirist, but you've done it there, Weegee.
> **WEEGEE:** Listen, what's a satirist? [*Laughter*]
> **MCBRIDE:** A satirist is one who holds the foibles . . .
> **WEEGEE:** [*Deadpan*] Ehh, what's a foible? [*Laughter*]

This led to a good-natured argument between McBride and Connolly about what, exactly, constituted satire. They and Weegee chatted for nearly the full length of the show, McBride breaking away from the interview only to insert her sponsor messages. Weegee served up anecdote after anecdote: the one about processing photos in a subway car, the before-and-after Mott Street explosion, the lonely girl on the Coney Island lifeguard's chair. With a little help from his host, he was able to evoke his pictures on the radio.

It went well enough that, over the next couple of weeks, a pair of WNEW shows called *Crime Club* and *Crime Quiz* put him on as well. So did CBS's *Margaret Arlen Show*, a breakfast-time program with a big national audience. Even WQXR, the classical-music station of the *New York Times*, booked him. His high-life-low-life angle meant that he could find a connection with almost any audience.

A few days after McBride's show aired, Weegee, as he so often had in the past, caught a break around dawn. Early on July 17, the drivers' union and the papers settled their differences, and by the next day, all nine dailies were at the newsstands again. The reviews they ran over the next couple of weeks were, for the most part, positive, if a little perplexed about just how to categorize this book. Was it hard news? Slumming? A new kind of art? Was it about the city, its residents, the pictures themselves, or this night-crawling photographer character?

The newsweeklies, which customarily told stories through personalities, barely discussed the pictures and instead ran brief profiles of the author. *Time* trotted out the O. Henry–with-a-camera comparison and called the book "a first-rate reporter's picture of Manhattan." There's no byline, but the story seems to have been written by someone who knew Weegee firsthand, capturing his speech patterns and taking the usual lighthearted pokes at him. "Weegee now makes about $4,000 a year, and that more than keeps him in cigars," the story said. "He has no other expensive habits. He sees an occasional movie, likes to drop into Sammy's bar on the Bowery once in a while. Otherwise, the money just accumulates, and Weegee stuffs it away here and there. Recently a couple of photographers searched his car, found $1,500. They bought him some war bonds." *Newsweek* went for near mockery, quoting Weegee as he said, "I'm very sens'tiff and artistic, and hate the sight of blood, but I am spellbound by the mystery of murder," and followed that up with a remark by an unnamed colleague: "If he were as sensitive about his personal appearance as he is about other things, he'd be quite a guy." But both magazines admitted, almost grudgingly, that the book had visual power. That they were covering it, and him, at all constituted an endorsement.

You'd think that newspaper book critics would understand Weegee's work, given that they were in the same business, and given that many of them aspired, as he did, to something beyond the column-inch grind. Yet quite a few of them missed the point. The *Herald Tribune*'s Richard Crandell was generally complimentary ("many of them are great news photographs, dealing with those submerged millions of the city") while taking the usual sidelong knocks at Weegee's shabbiness. Crandell seemed to crave those touristy pictures of Central Park that Weegee had refused to include: "His book is curiously bereft of any of the natural or man-made beauty which abounds in New York. Perhaps one does not walk in beauty in the shadows of the elevateds." The *Chicago Tribune*'s critic similarly praised the photographs while scratching his head: "This is not great creative art—but in large part it is good reporting." There was a mostly positive review in the *Hartford Courant*, a brief, chipper tease in the *Los Angeles Times*, a burst of enthusiasm in the *San Francisco Chronicle* and another in the the Toronto *Globe and Mail*. He got raves in the *Washington Post* and the network of papers fed by the Independent Jewish Press Service. The Newspaper Enterprise Association, a syndication service affiliated with Acme, assembled a clever quiz for its subscriber papers, showing a dozen faces from Weegee's photographs and challenging readers to match them with their captions. *Which person is at the circus? Which is watching relatives burn? Which is the swooning Sinatra fan?* The great Harlem Renaissance poet Langston Hughes, in his regular column in the *Chicago Defender*, called it a "wonderful, wonderful book" and added that "it's just about the most dramatic and, at times, amusing collection of photographs ever put together."

Really, though, the big review of *Naked City*, the one that mattered most for both respectability and bookselling, would be that of the *New York Times*. It was written by Russell Maloney, who'd come up at *The New Yorker*, and he got it right. He made fun of the characterization that was quickly becoming tiresome: Weegee, he wrote, "will soon live down the appellation of 'an O. Henry with a camera' which some misguided admirer bestowed on him." He got to the source of *Naked City*'s strength, too. "Weegee has managed to accumulate a number of pictures of recently dead, but none the less very dead, people. He seems very proud of these, but they are not the best things in the book. What you remember are the faces." Maloney also addressed (though did not entirely resolve, even for himself) the question of whether Weegee was more than a member of the working press: "Whether or not he is a good artist, he possesses a good artist's unsentimental outlook."

If there were an award for the backhanded compliment, it would have to have gone to the *New York Post*, the paper with which Weegee had had so many ups and downs. It came from John Adam Knight, the same columnist who'd plugged Weegee's lectures and written about his gold-plated flashgun. "Until a year or so ago," he wrote, "Weegee (Arthur Fellig) was the outstanding newspaper photographer in New York. A freelance specializing in violence and catastrophe by night, his pictures appeared in many newspapers and put to shame the rutted work of most staff photographers. Then a great tragedy occurred. The prissy photography department of the Museum of Modern Art 'discovered' Weegee and hailed him, in effect, as a genius—which he is not, of course."

Knight went on to slag the Photo League, a group he found so distastefully leftist that he refused to use its name, calling it only "a camera club bent on making over this country's government and culture to conform to its own ideas" and its photographers "maladjusted members of this misfit club." Knight's basic stance was that Weegee, a great photojournalist, had begun to believe he was an artist, and that his work had suffered terribly. *Naked City*, Knight suggested, was effectively a tombstone. "The paper shortage denies me the pleasure of describing dozens of these pictures individually. I have space only to urge every one interested to buy the book and learn the lesson that Weegee once knew, that honesty, a genuine interest in people—all people—and a recognition of what constitutes human interest in pictures can make any of you as nearly great as Weegee once was." Maybe it was payback for Weegee's on-again, off-again feud with the *Post*. More likely, Knight was just a grump, perhaps one who had watched Weegee's self-promotion and couldn't accept that there was substance there as well. But although plenty of people had knocked Weegee as a figure of fun or a blowhard, this was new: the first time anyone had publicly suggested that his fame chasing was cutting into the quality of his work.

On publication night, July 18, the swells and the bums seen in the pages of *Naked City* mixed in person at the book party. It was held not at some literary Midtown cocktail bar but down at Sammy's, and Sammy laid on the complimentary booze and platters of pastrami sandwiches and pickles. Weegee signed books and accessorized his police-tailored, zipper-pocket business suit with a black silk top hat, which was not exactly elegant but exactly appropriate.

PM sent Arthur Leipzig and a reporter named Tom O'Connor to cover the bash and ran a congratulatory story the next day. "Last night Weegee the Famous had a large and varied assortment of book critics, photographers, photographic editors, reporters, cops, prostitutes, grifters, stenographers and other admirers or imbibers of free liquor down to a slumming party at Sammy's Bowery Follies, in honor of Weegee and his book," O'Connor wrote. "Everybody thought it was great fun. Weegee was the perfect host, and even had his shoes shined. But he forgot to bring his camera, and thereby missed what would have been a great picture for his next book: the cluster of ragged, dirty, sag-cheeked down-and-outers who stood outside the door of Sammy's, eyeing the full platters and the full bottles and the stuffing and guzzling of Weegee's guests at Weegee's slumming party, and begging anyone who came near the door to steal them a sandwich."

Was *PM* just funning around, or was O'Connor, like John Adam Knight in the *Post*, suggesting that Weegee was losing his way? You might

Celebrating the publication of Naked City *at Sammy's Bowery Follies in July 1945.*

guess the latter, except that *PM* also ran not one but two positive reviews. Its editor, John P. Lewis, had written a short item the previous day, expressing nothing but affection for Weegee and his book. "I've been through my copy now three times, and every trip there's something new," he said. "Many of them appeared as news pictures in *PM*, and you'll remember some of them—certainly the ones of Joe McWilliams, the Nazi lover, with the rear end of his horse, and Mrs. George Washington Kavanaugh with the late Lady Decies and their jewels at the opera." He omitted that his own paper had rejected "The Critic," but never mind. And then Paul Strand, one of the most respected photographers alive, considered the book at length a few days later. "There is much in the subject of this book which is sensational," he wrote. "But sensationalism is not Weegee's purpose. He is an artist, a man of serious and strong feeling. In the area of life in which he has lived and worked, his photographs truly record the way he sees."

To accompany its (long, thoughtful, and very warm) review of *Naked City* that summer, *Popular Photography* commissioned no less celebrated a figure than Philippe Halsman to make Weegee's portrait. The two knew each other slightly; Halsman had gone to his lectures, which he said had been hilarious if not especially illuminating. Halsman, who had recently photographed Humphrey Bogart and Frank Sinatra for *Life*, found himself curious about Weegee's mix of bravado and sensitivity, and asked him outright: "You sleep during the day, you roam the city by night. Does this kind of life make you happy?" Weegee paused. "No." Halsman asked him why not. "Too little money and too little love," Weegee said. "I don't know why the broads don't go for me. I wash!"

But Halsman also saw the artist inside the shabby suit. "Weegee, why do you take pictures of murder?" he asked. "Listen, friend," Weegee responded, "what I look for in a murder is beauty. When I focus my camera, it's not on the corpse but on the young couple that is holding hands looking on. You see, friend, the real meat of life is beauty." When it came time for the sitting, Halsman, a master of subtle and complex stagings, paid homage to Weegee's own technique by shooting him with a single light source, throwing a film noir shadow across half his face. Weegee didn't ham it up for this one, although he did stick his police press credentials in his hatband, a move he normally disdained ("that's only done in the movies").

Positive or mixed, the reviews of *Naked City* did their job, at least from a commercial standpoint. The book sold well, despite a high cover price of four dollars, about one dollar more than a hardcover novel typically cost. The Chaucer Head Book Shop, a highbrow store on the Upper East Side of New York, filled its window with big prints of his photos and a poster-size book jacket. The Vendome Book Shop, on the West Side, had him in for a book signing. He got into the window at the Fifth Avenue bookstore run by Scribner's, too, after doing a little nudging. "Look, this will bring in people who have never been in a bookstore before," Weegee claimed to have told the managers, who replied, "We don't want that kind of people." Macy's, then a major bookseller, sold its copies fast enough that, at one point, when it needed its stock replenished in a hurry,

Duell, Sloan and Pearce rushed over a carload by taxicab. A second printing followed, then a paperback run.

It didn't quite crack the *Times* best-seller list, but in its first half year,
Naked City sold more than fourteen thousand copies. That plus some
serial-rights sales brought Weegee a bit more than six thousand dollars.
Add that to the amount he was making from newspapers and the wire
and syndication services, plus the paperback reprint (which eventually
sold about twenty-five thousand copies), and the result was, once again,
"a very lush living." He had just turned forty-six and was, alone among
newspaper photographers, a household name in homes both patrician and
proletarian. Shortly thereafter, private recognition arrived in the form
of a courtly and rhyming two-sentence letter, written in an old-fashioned,
Old World hand. "A copy of your 'Naked City' was given to me," wrote
Alfred Stieglitz on September 11, 1945. "My laurel wreath I hand to thee."
Thereafter, even when he knocked other photographers as he puffed up
his own image, Weegee continued to speak humbly about Stieglitz, quoting his advice about capturing the fleeting part of a second and calling
him "truly a great photographer."

Enthusiasm for his work came from the most far-flung places. On
an early morning in October 1945, Weegee had headed to Pier 90 on
the Hudson River, making pictures of Cunard's RMS *Queen Elizabeth*
as it brought nearly fifteen thousand men home from the war. Hundreds
of them stuck their heads out portholes to see the city; thousands more
stood on deck. When they spotted the photographer on the dock, they
began to call to him. "Hey, Weegee!" one shouted. "Wanna buy a camera?"
Even soldiers who'd spent the past two years in the mud of Germany
and France knew who he was.

Fame brings offers of work, and a sudden burst of fame brings a sudden burst of those offers. In the six weeks after his book was published, Weegee was approached with assignments in quick succession for *Seventeen* and *Coronet*, and for a new spin-off of *Harper's Bazaar* called *Junior Bazaar*. He kept up his newspaper work, shooting sailors in town at the end of the war and street photos of the celebrations on V-J Day in August. He was still doing his old bread-and-butter news items, too: one night when a water-main break flooded and undermined Third Avenue, a pillar holding up the elevated train began to sink into the street, and Weegee made a photo that exaggerated the roller-coaster curve of the tracks. A few of his observers at murders and suicides and the like appeared in *Look*, which used them to illustrate a series of stern pop psychology essays called "The Nature of Human Behavior."

Magazine work was both more prestigious and less onerous than gutting out a living the way he had been. It was certainly a lot easier than spending the night rushing around and getting blood on his shoes. Besides, he was now Weegee the Famous, which meant that the glossies offered him a premium rate. *Seventeen*, hardly the most prestigious magazine out there, was willing to pay him one hundred dollars for that single job, as much as he'd sometimes have made for a week of twelve-hour days on Centre Market Place. That kind of work was so much easier than the nightly grind that he was beginning to think about a life without crime.

Weegee must have been a little surprised, though, when he got a telegram reading PLEASE CALL OR COME IN TO SEE MR. LIBERMAN IMMEDI-

ATELY. There was almost nobody else in the magazine world comparable to Alexander Liberman, who had, the previous year, taken over as the art director of *Vogue*, and would eventually rise to run the editorial operation of its parent company, Condé Nast. The magazine he stepped into had already been remade into a showpiece of clean modernism, and Liberman, in his charming yet relentless way, soon began to elevate it further. He was in many ways the antithesis of Weegee, a pan-European aristocrat who wore impeccable (and identical) dark suits every day, and wouldn't have been caught dead eating a hot pastrami sandwich. But perhaps he understood Arthur Fellig a bit: both men's families were Jewish, albeit of very different classes, and both had left eastern Europe as they saw the future there darkening. Weegee recalled, of their first meeting, that Liberman's telephone never stopped ringing, and that Liberman teasingly admonished him that, on a *Vogue* assignment, he couldn't go climbing fire escapes and peering in windows. Liberman stopped answering the phone long enough to make an arrangement with the photographer, a deal Weegee described as two stories a week at seventy-five dollars apiece, under which Weegee could shoot mostly what he pleased and *Vogue* would send him out on the occasional assignment. That rate of production sounds implausibly high, given *Vogue's* bimonthly space and needs. But it's true that Liberman came out of the news business, and *Vogue* had an enormous budget. Perhaps he was willing to spend money to put a newsman on retainer, even if he got only a few great pictures out of the deal.

Weegee had, by the time that telegram was sent, already sold one photograph to *Vogue*, and it had been a showstopper. On V-J Day, a group of street kids in Greenwich Village had wanted to celebrate by building a bonfire. Instead of piling up wood, campfire style, they found a bag of sawdust, poured it out to form a big V for "victory" on the street, soaked it in kerosene, and set it ablaze. Weegee stumbled upon the scene and, as he always had at burning tenements, worked fast. "There was my picture for *Vogue*. I didn't have my tripod with me, I set my camera on an ashcan," he later recounted. The boys stood in the crook of the burning V, and "I had them wave their arms to give it a lot of action." Liberman gave the photo a full page, using it as a frontispiece for a section marking the war's end in *Vogue's* September 1 issue. The credit, in headline-size type, read V-J DAY NEW YORK—PHOTOGRAPHED ESPECIALLY FOR VOGUE

BY WEEGEE. On *Vogue*'s oversize pages, with superior paper and fine print-ing from the Condé Nast plant up in Connecticut, it looked fantastic.

Before the end of the year, he was carrying a letter from Allene Talmey, the fearsome editor who ran *Vogue*'s features department, gaining him admission to fancy events. It took him to the ballet, where he made a fine set of portraits of the prima ballerina Alicia Markova at her backstage dressing table. He also defied a union rule requiring a payoff before photo-graphs could be taken in the auditorium, sneaking a quick frame of Markova onstage at the end of her performance. It was a moment when his police headquarters toughness and speed served him well in a new environment. He even bought himself a tuxedo, about which he related anecdote after jokey anecdote. Among them: the suit was secondhand and greenish with age, bought under wartime restrictions, and socialites and *Vogue* editors purportedly began asking him where they could find similar bottle-green evening wear for their husbands.

He was, he later wrote, toggling with ease among three worlds, "one with *P.M.*, one with Acme and one with *Vogue*." Spiritually, that was true, because his work could be divided thus. For the first, he photographed slices of city life, both violent and less so, that took bank shots off the night's events; for the second, straight hard news, close up; for the third, uptown events at the St. Regis or the Waldorf-Astoria. But tempo-rally, that sentence doesn't quite reflect his life, because by the end of 1944, the deal with *PM* had quietly ended. Neither side said why, and (especially judging by those warm book reviews he got after the split) the parting does not appear to have been rancorous; Weegee continued to publish in *PM* off and on for a couple of years, albeit less frequently than he had before. Possibly his thinning presence in the paper had caused the editors to cut off his stipend. Or perhaps his increasing fame meant that he had other, flashier outlets for his more ambitious photography. It's also plausible that he was just busy producing and then plugging *Naked City* and slacked off.

Besides, *PM* itself was beginning to run out of gas. Ingersoll had been drafted in mid-1942, and while he was overseas, much of the paper's edi-torial energy and coherence had dribbled away. "We're hypothyroid" is how his editor John Lewis put it. Ingersoll claimed that the paper was finally breaking even around the end of the war, but that was true only if you ignored the huge amount of money the business had burned through already, and he was probably bending reality a bit with even that claim. In his 1946 diary, he admitted that it was losing four thousand dollars a week and showed no signs of getting healthier. "Between the high resolve to create a new kind of newspaper and reality, there was a gap ten million dollars wide," he later wrote.

Weegee was still doing work for Acme and peddling to the other dailies, though, and he finally had the upper hand with them when it came to credit. He'd even patched things up with the *Post*. Earlier that year, he had signed a copy of *Naked City* for the *Post*'s Mark Sherwin, putting his CREDIT PHOTO BY WEEGEE THE FAMOUS stamp on the title page and inscribing it "My favorite picture editor who forgets to put this famous trademark under my pictures & thereby tortures my soul!" Now that he really was famous, his pictures would appear over his name, marked "Post Photo by Weegee." The power had shifted, and it was in the paper's interest to grab onto his prestige, instead of the other way around.

It wasn't only newspapers that were drawn to his fame. Finally, after all those decades of trying to find himself some female companionship, and sometimes paying for it, Weegee was getting attention from girls. "I now had women who screwed for the sheer love of it, not the two dollars," he wrote. "They wanted to find out what a genius was like in bed." Philippe Halsman, who'd found Weegee so gloomy over his inability to get a date before *Naked City*, ran into him one day soon after the book was published. "I saw Weegee walking proudly in the street, followed by a young woman carrying his equipment. It is astonishing how fame adds to the sex appeal of a man." Perhaps she was his dream gal, the woman he wisecracked about often: "a girl with a healthy body and a sick mind."

When he was on a pure money job, his proven ability to get a photo on the run made him astonishingly productive, if not exactly an artist. Late in 1945, Cities Service, the oil company later known as Citgo, asked Weegee if he'd do some corporate work: a documentary project about its headquarters, a skyscraper with the dual addresses of 70 Pine Street and 60 Wall Street. It was the tallest building in Lower Manhattan, a vertical near-village, with its own bakery, gym, wine cellar, and library.

Weegee was an odd choice on Cities Service's part. Yes, he was highly visible, the flavor of the month, but that visibility had come for photographs that most corporate-communications people would have considered incredibly harsh. Nonetheless, they wanted him, and Weegee was perfectly happy to cash in—but the cash had to be significant. He asked for, and got, five hundred dollars plus a parking spot (a solid couple of months' wages for an average newspaperman) for the job. He photographed the bakers, the exercisers, the elevator operators, the beauty shop downstairs. In the best of the portraits, a cleaning woman mops the lobby late at night, seen from about a hundred feet off, under one small light that illuminates a corner of an otherwise black frame. In toto, Weegee documented the building's life more than creditably, if a little coarsely. His high-contrast, high-key images of its days and nights are somewhat stark but not bad at all.

The people at Cities Service must have been pleased, because they brought him back for a second round, to make portraits of the company's executives. This time, though, Weegee could not restrain his knack for making visible his feelings about his subjects. "I don't like executives," he wrote, "so I figured I would give them a snow job. I went into the offices . . . and, no matter what they were doing, sleeping or scratching, I took one shot and went out like a flash of lightning." He wasn't kidding: the set of portraits reveals a lot of middle-aged men blinking or talking on the phone or just generally unposed, a couple of them looking nonplussed. They aren't very good photos, although his speedy work did inadvertently reveal some personality. Perhaps because it had paid so much money for the pictures, Cities Service liked the results anyway, and ran them in its corporate magazine.

That Weegee got away with this—doing lame work that was lucrative purely because it came from the hand of Weegee the Famous—was, to him, clearly a goof. After all the years in which he'd been at the mercy of the "dopey editors," now he figured that he could put one over on corporate America. He even got work as an advertising pitchman himself. He showed up in a Graflex ad for the Speed Graphic, and in the catalogue for Burke & James press cameras as well, offering paid testimonials for the two competing companies. He showed up in ads for the Diamond Gadg-it Bag ("keeps everything at my fingertips ready for instant use"), too.

He was back at the Museum of Modern Art on the evening of October 16, for the opening of a retrospective devoted to the great American artist Stuart Davis. A (nice enough, if slightly blurred) photograph of Davis made it into *Vogue* a few weeks later. Much better were the pho-

He was happy to plug cameras, flashbulbs, even the Diamond Gadg-it Bag.

tos he made of the exhibition viewers peering at Davis's abstract paintings. Liberman, for reasons unknown, didn't publish those, and in fact Weegee's ostensible pace of two stories a month for *Vogue* was not working out. Later on, when he recounted his experience there, he spoke about story after story he'd shot for the magazine. A series on rich society partygoers at the St. Regis hotel, which turned into a feature on their dogs. A fashion shoot at Sussman Volk's Jewish delicatessen on Delancey Street, where he'd posed the tall, slim models in front of a backdrop of hanging salamis. (He claimed to have been paid a $202 fee on that one: $2 for the print, $200 for "imagination.") He may indeed have made those pictures; he may well have been paid for them. But better magazines, and especially those of high refinement such as Liberman's *Vogue*, are not as hungry for material as newspapers are. They assign liberally and kill pieces often, making changes both to winnow out the chaff and to perfect the mix. It's possible that Weegee filed every couple of weeks to *Vogue* and that only a small fraction of his output was strong enough to make it into print. It's also possible that he didn't file as often as he said he did, or that he exaggerated the nature of his deal altogether. The numbers, though, don't lie: between 1945 and 1948, he had a mere five new photos appear in *Vogue*, and only the V-J Day portrait and the Markova picture had any real Weegee flair. When he was dispatched all the way to Washington in early 1946 to photograph Senator J. William Fulbright, he turned in a portrait that was competent and publishable but could've been made by any number of people. He later told an interviewer that he quit *Vogue* after two years, which more or less squares with the published record.

This is not to say that his relationship with Liberman was difficult: the editor, asked about Weegee many decades later, lit up warmly at the mention of his name. Nonetheless, he didn't use a lot of Weegee's work, a fact that's all the more surprising when you take a look at his photographs from these years. The pictures he was making in 1946 were often much like that V-J Day photo, and a good portion of them could have been at least candidates for *Vogue*'s pages. They had almost completely superseded the fires and murders. Everyday people photographed in the Weegee manner were his subjects now. He was, to put it simply, wrapping up his career as a police chaser and switching entirely to making pictures of city life. "I had reached the peak," he later wrote, "and I always like to leave something at the peak."

The turning point came in May 1946. He'd briefly been in the hospital, to have a double hernia repaired for the second time. (The fire-department ambulance drivers had kidded him on the way there, saying, "Well, this is one picture you won't make.") Perhaps he was still uncomfortable, or feeling his age, but whatever the reason, when the radio squawked on the night of May 20, he hit the brake instead of the accelerator. "About 8 o'clock at night, riding in the Village, I picked up an alarm. An airplane had crashed into a skyscraper." It was a military plane that had plowed into the tower at 40 Wall Street, killing five people. The previous summer, when a bomber had crashed into the Empire State

Building, Weegee had made great pictures of New Yorkers gawking at the hole in the seventy-ninth floor. This time, he was indifferent. "I could have been there before the ambulance got there, I would really have got the pictures, but I said NO, I did not go." He was through with the chase. He eventually even got rid of the Chevy, which by this time was a seven-year-old junker with rusted-out fenders and vast mileage on the odometer. "I was really through with that sort of picture. My blood bath was over." At a luncheon, he told a writer named Clip Boutell that he was moving on: "No more pictures of murders or accidents or women crying. I've been taking pictures of happiness . . . but not saccharine pictures— just pictures showing the humanity of people." And he ended his years of covering violent crime with a bit of violence of his own. Going up to his room on Centre Market Place, he wrote, "I took the radio and smashed it against the wall," adding, emphatically, that it was "SOMETHING I'VE WANTED TO DO FOR YEARS." He was out.

He took some time to loaf around Washington Square that summer, relying on the continued sales of *Naked City*, but he never quite stopped working. Duell, Sloan and Pearce had agreed to a sequel, and he'd signed a book contract just days before that plane crash on Wall Street. Weegee also agreed to teach a class in Chicago that August, part of a seminar called "The New Vision in Photography." He'd be among the elite of photography there, lecturing alongside the likes of Beaumont Newhall and Berenice Abbott. He went back on the lecture circuit in New York, too, starting with a talk in July at the Photo League, which had moved up a few blocks to East Twenty-Ninth Street. (That lecture comprised slides from *Naked City* and the forthcoming book and, per its promotional materials, "comments in the Weegee manner.") He also spoke at a pair of enthusiast groups, the Manhattan Camera Club and the Brooklyn Camera Club, several times that spring and summer. He'd billed one of the Manhattan talks as an evening devoted to "psychic photography," and two attendees walked out in the middle, disappointed that the séance they had expected was not taking place.

Even as he got away from the murder beat, he was only too happy to talk about it. While he was in Chicago teaching that class, he concocted a field trip and invited *Life* along. "Weegee Shows How to Photograph a Corpse," appearing in the August 12 issue, followed him in Lincoln Park with a few students, standing over a dummy sprawled on the pavement. Weegee circled the fake cadaver, placed its fedora just so on the sidewalk, and mussed its hair "for authenticity." He even posed for gag photos

As Weegee's fame increased, so did demand for his lectures, where he coached, told stories, joked around, and occasionally demonstrated how to photograph a corpse.

himself as he lay on the concrete, his dead cigar in place, the mannequin appearing to hold his hand. (This seems to have been a standard bit of theater for him. There are pictures of a lecture he gave a year or so earlier in New York that also show him down on the floor in the talkative-shot-gangster role.) "He wanted to hold class on North Clark Street, site of gang killings," wrote *Life*, "but cops chased him off."

His new book, however, was corpse-free. He was sticking entirely to slices of New York City life: concertgoers at the Paramount (again) and the Roxy; patrons at the opera and at Sammy's; public sleepers; interesting street people; an odd-looking man who was polling pedestrians to test competing taglines for Pabst Blue Ribbon beer ("Full-Flavor Blended" was the one that ended up in the ads). A few pictures showed firemen on the job, but they were portrayed, mostly, like other working people, rather than in mid-rescue. When the cops appeared, they, too, were just being themselves, one of them working an early-morning shift as the dawn broke behind him. They joined Max the bagel baker, making his morning deliveries, and a trio of dance-hall hostesses waiting for customers to turn up. Visits to Harlem produced pictures of an occult religion shop on Lenox Avenue, its shelves stocked with jars of "Hindu magnet incense" and the like. There were some spot-news pictures, but they were more along the lines of the ones he made on a day in September 1942 when a truck full of live turkeys and chickens spilled its cargo near the corner of Elizabeth and Grand Streets. It had made for a scene straight out of a Harold Lloyd movie as the driver ran around trying to recapture the birds.

Most of the pictures he compiled for the new book showed underclass New Yorkers living their lives at various degrees of discomfort. Sleepers on park benches, in stairwells, on sidewalks, mingled with photos of the flophouse signs advertising rooms for thirty cents (a bottom-end price even then). One set of frames showed four different men on different nights sleeping in the same doorway at Hudson and Duane Streets. The spot was directly across the street from *PM*'s new offices in Lower Manhattan, which is probably how Weegee had happened upon it. Another showed a foursome one midnight as they hauled a bedspring and mattress across Washington Square Park. They told Weegee they were looking for an apartment; "I asked them who wasn't," he wrote, "as I wished them good luck."

Those kinds of scenes were beginning to draw him away to Greenwich Village, a short walk and a long cultural distance from Centre Market Place. We think of the postwar scene there now as a bohemian ideal, at the peak of the neighborhood's golden era of painters with Vandyke beards and hip interpretive-dance gals in leotards and berets. In fact, even its silver age was nearly past. A good three decades earlier, residents had already been grumbling that "Greenwich Village isn't what it used to be." Tourists who wanted to sample *la vie bohème* were everywhere. Yet the raffishness and artiness of the neighborhood had not been wiped out entirely, in part because the Depression and then wartime rent controls had helped keep the buildings shabby and the rents down.

Weegee was already making rounds through there regularly and was in the habit of picking up messages and mail at Julius', the ancient saloon on West Tenth Street that later became a landmark gay bar. He found all kinds of subculture moments to shoot in the Village, including an apartment-building subcellar where a clique of nightclub musicians would continue to jam after their evening gigs ended. There they'd smoke and drink and play until sunup, their girlfriends joining them along the way to listen and broil hamburgers in a skillet tucked into the building's coal furnace. It made a gorgeous photo essay, a great high-life-low-life, capturing the truth of late-night Village culture and also delivering it in a way any square could appreciate.

Jazz, and specifically jazz clubs, often supplied Weegee with material in this era. In 1946, Bunk Johnson, the Dixieland-era New Orleans trumpeter, came to town to play a few nights. It was something of a moment in jazz circles; Johnson had been an early contemporary of Louis Armstrong, but he had fallen into complete obscurity and was working as a manual laborer until he was rediscovered in the mid-1940s. (When the world caught up to him, he had not played in more than a decade, because he had no horn and no front teeth. Sidney Bechet arranged for some pro bono dentures.) Weegee made moody pictures of Johnson and the (mixed-race but mostly white) crowd grooving along with him at the Stuyvesant Casino, a club on Second Avenue near St. Marks Place.

That stretch of Second Avenue, though, was more famous as the Yiddish Rialto, the strip of theaters where eastern European Jews went to hear their mother tongue onstage and on-screen. Weegee repeatedly photographed the actors at work, catching their strong-featured, expressive faces. Then he followed them offstage, depicting them in their off-hours at their customary hangout, the Café Royal. One of Weegee's best photos from the restaurant shows nothing more complicated than a black-haired woman hoisting a damp tea bag out of a glass. Some of his prints are cropped to show nothing but the tea bag, the glass, and the woman's hand. But this simple scene, almost a still life, has transporting powers, especially for New Yorkers of Weegee's generation. *Glezele tei*, tea in a

*At the Café Royal on Second Avenue, aka the "Yiddish Rialto,"
even something as simple as a tea bag now evokes a lost world.*

glass (sometimes held in a nickel-silver zarf) rather than a china cup, was
and is a mark of old-country Jews from Russia and eastern Europe.

The book containing all this was, like *Naked City* before it, delayed.
Scheduled first for August, then bumped to the fall, it had been teed up
with excerpts in *Minicam Photography* and in *Look*, which ran four pages
of generously proportioned photos in its July 23 issue. Weegee occupied
his autumn with some early promotion, including a trip to the Boston
Book Fair at Symphony Hall the week of October 14. There he gave his
slide lecture, "looking very respectable in a new suit and new shoes," as a
visitor put it, adding that "Privately, however, Weegee confessed that he
was 'through with documenting the sordid side of life and was going to

concentrate on beauty and young love.'" As for his own attachments, he still had some kind of friendly relationship going with Wilma Wilcox. She had stepped up as the Photo League's darkroom manager, and the two had worked together late that summer on an event billed as a "beer-and-pretzel party."

There was less writing in the new book than there had been in *Naked City*. The pictures did virtually all the storytelling, and although there were occasional longueurs, where certain images weren't played big enough to have great individual impact, the book still had enormous power. It was at least as successful, artistically, as its predecessor—particularly when you grasped that it represented perhaps two years' collected work against the previous book's fifteen. In keeping with the warmer tone, Weegee dedicated it not to the city as a whole but to his mother. If one of its photos functioned as a mission statement, it was the frontispiece portrait of Weegee himself. It had been taken by a young friend of his, a woman named Jean Polacheck, and it showed Weegee asleep on a park bench. "I like this picture of myself because it's real, and I think it's an improvement over the usual pictures of authors—the kind where the author poses with pipe and book in hand and the usual dog by the fireplace—not a care in the world, not even a worry about royalties or sales of movie rights." Last time out, his opening self-portrait had been one of a man at work, wielding his Speed Graphic almost as a shield; this time, he was one of his favorite subjects, a city dweller caught unaware, dozing by day in Washington Square.

Weegee's People was published on November 12, and it was received at least as well as *Naked City* had been. Beaumont Newhall himself wrote about it in the *Saturday Review*, praising everything about it except the quality of the rotogravure printing, which he found lacking. The *Herald Tribune* called it "on the whole better" than its predecessor, though the critic couldn't resist a few of the usual side-eye compliments, making reference to Weegee's "wheezing genius." The St. Paul *Pioneer Press* opened its brief enthusiastic review with the sentence "Weegee's happy now." The African American *Amsterdam News* published a rave, noting that Weegee had found himself "in a mellow mood" and remarking on his ability to make social conscience photographs without seeming to be trying. Bruce Downes, the editor of *Popular Photography*, wrote his magazine's very long, extremely positive review himself. Langston Hughes, who'd offered praise the previous year for *Naked City*, put *Weegee's People* first on his list of favorite books of the year.

In a lucky bit of timing, Weegee got some unrelated press the next week, when he won two awards in the annual Graflex photo contest, one of them for that turkey picture that had gone into the new book. "Weegee, as might have been expected," noted one columnist, "won in Class I, humor." (A *Chicago Tribune* staff photographer named Swain Scalf got one of the other prizes that year for a remarkably close rip-off of Weegee's swooning Sinatra fan.)

The book party was at Sammy's again, on the night of November 11. Weegee's friends Lee Sievan and Simon Nathan were both there, taking photographs. Weegee put on his tuxedo, which he'd taken to wearing anywhere he could, once joking that he did so until the cuffs had worn down to the second button. It was still quite a sight to some of the Sammy's regulars who had never seen him dressed up before. And although he spent part of the evening without a camera in his hand, he did shoot some film—only this time, it was moving-picture film. A few bits of the party were also filmed by WCBS for use on that very new medium called television.

Weegee had actually acquired a 16-millimeter movie camera a couple of years earlier, during the prime of his *PM* run. He seems mostly to have just noodled around with it at first. The (soundless) film from his book launch party reveals the crowded, raucous spirit of Sammy's, with Bowery characters and social figures intermingling in just the right proportions. Joe Gould turned up, toothless and shaggy, making his only known appearance in moving pictures. So did Mrs. Kavanaugh, with merely an elaborate hat instead of a diamond tiara. Weegee practically mauled her by way of greeting, with a big, overenthusiastic smooch.

In fact, he'd begun to get it into his head that moving pictures were his next big plan. By early 1947, he'd stripped his apartment on Centre Market Place of all the newspaper clutter on the walls, apart from a single tacked-up tear sheet of "The Critic." Reels of movie film, haphazardly stacked up, replaced the piles of pictures on his desk. As he made a long round of promotional appearances for the book, he told *PM* flatly that his "next venture will be moviemaking." *U.S. Camera*, too, said Weegee had turned his eye toward Hollywood. Otherwise, though, the promotional whirl was much like the one for *Naked City*, although on a larger scale, because the previous book's success had given Fellig's public profile such a boost. Dowling's, a big photo-equipment store on Fifth Avenue, had him in for a book signing and put up a little show of his prints. Weegee made at least one more promotional trip out of town, to Detroit. Duell, Sloan bought display ads for the book in the New York papers. And at one of his appearances, a woman named Margaret Atwood lined up to have her copy of the book inscribed. Weegee chatted her up, tossing out a line: "Are you single, footloose, and free, Babe? I'm going to take you under my wing." She bantered back, "Photographically speaking only."

Twelve weeks later, they were at the Municipal Building on Centre Street, exchanging rings.

She was a New Hampshire farmer's daughter born Margaret Gluck, and she may have been footloose, but she was not one of the arty young Greenwich Village types Weegee had been eyeing lately. She was forty-six, and for twenty-two of those years she'd been married to a significantly older man named Edward Atwood. Edward had been a school principal when they got together, and Margaret had been a secretary, but the couple acquired a portfolio of real estate that eventually became their livelihood. (They did not have children.) By mid-1946 they were living in a first-rate town house on Marlborough Street in Boston, he managing their properties, she working as a real estate agent. Then, on September 18, 1946, Edward had died, at sixty.

In November, Margaret was waiting in line at Weegee's book signing, and by February she was in New York, staying at the Hotel Breslin and preparing for her second wedding. She joked that, having bought Weegee's book, she was marrying him to get her money back. And if Weegee was given to bending reality to create the picture he wanted, she did a little reorganization of her own. In the process of reestablishing herself in New York, she clipped ten years off her age, a fiction she maintained from then on.

They had their prewedding breakfast not at some romantic soft-lit hotel restaurant but at Sammy's. It was a Friday, February 28, chilly and cloudy. Of course there were photographers. Weegee's Acme photographer colleagues Bert Brandt and Edward Jerry, with a reporter named Marc Parsons, came along to cover the wedding as a news event. So did the *Post*'s Anthony Calvacca and Jay Nelson Tuck, and *PM*'s Morris Gordon. Weegee's friend and occasional darkroom aide Lee Sievan joined them with her husband, the painter Maurice Sievan. Wilma Wilcox, Weegee's quiet on-again, off-again girlfriend who'd moved to New York to be with him, does not appear to have been there, and she never recorded her reaction to his marriage, which had to have been disappointing to her. "Weegee, of course, directed the photographers," wrote *Popular Photography*, "to make sure they showed the worst," noting that he kept interrupting the ceremony to make sure each significant moment had been caught on film.

They were posey, hokey pictures, of a type that wedding photographers still make sometimes—scenes in which, for example, Weegee pointed at the sign at City Hall noting the two-dollar fee, indicating that his bride ought to pay up. Margaret played along, grinning throughout, and she dressed the part of the madcap heiress, too, in a leopard-print fur coat and elaborate updo and hat. "A Brooklyn girl at heart, even if she does come from Boston," Weegee told Parsons. "She's a sweet girl and I like her for herself. Besides, she's lousy with money." At the judge's lectern, a little before noon, Weegee set his lit cigar down on the edge for long enough to exchange rings and say, "I do," then held up the bride's hand. "Look at them rings!" he said to the assembled reporters. "Almost real gold! You can see she finally hooked me." Lee Sievan snapped the moment, Margaret and her new husband signed the marriage certificate, and all the photographers caught the newlyweds' kiss, which the *Post* called "unrivaled by anyone except perhaps a grizzly bear trying to bust open a hollow tree full of honey." In his ardor, the bridegroom knocked off Margaret's hat and earrings.

Once she had pulled herself back together, the Felligs and their press gaggle of guests celebrated in a way that will be familiar to any Manhattanite who has ever been called for jury duty. The courts and municipal complex of the city stand right at the edge of Chinatown, and the wedding party began a slow crawl through its barrooms, the guests dropping off one by one, until the stalwarts wound up at the China Lane Restaurant, a basement joint on Mott Street. It was perhaps thirty steps from the site of the putatively psychic water-main-break photo Weegee had made three years earlier, the one he talked up in every interview.

The couple did not head off on a honeymoon, for the maddest reason

Weegee and Margaret Atwood arrive at their new apartment after their wedding, February 28, 1947.

possible. "I gotta cut my movie," Weegee said. He'd shot all of thirty minutes of raw film by then, a sizable percentage of it at his own book party, but he was eager to get on to the next thing, no matter the feelings of his spirited new bride. Instead they went back to their not-a-honeymoon suite that night and posed for more photos. In one, she puts on a glum look as he settles in at his film-editing console, and in the other, they climb into their twin beds as Weegee pretends to toss a shoe over his shoulder. He had already converted part of the apartment into a darkroom. "He plans to spend a year working on [the movie]," wrote *Popular Photography*, "and, as usual, [he] turned up with a typical epigram to describe it. 'This movie,' says Weegee, 'is going to finish where everyone else has started.'" An ambitious sentiment, assuming that he meant the opposite.

That apartment where they resettled, significantly, was not on Centre Market Place. "We give up the dump," Weegee said proudly that day. Instead of living in a seventeen-dollar-a-month hovel, the couple took a place in Midtown, at the Hotel Elmwood near Rockefeller Center, paying two hundred dollars. He also took a room on West Forty-Sixth Street, most likely to use as a studio. The lease for the room on Centre Market Place went to an acquaintance, Lawrence Racies, a reporter for CBS. Weegee gave him the police radio that had been installed in the Chevy, too, a significantly expensive gesture. The new apartment "cost me plenty of chips, but I can afford it," he said. "I'm going on a radio program. The Poor Man's Rembrandt is going to be the Poor Man's Oscar Levant."

At any rate, he was going to try. Weegee had just signed up to be a panelist on a talk show devoted to the mayhem he had just quit photographing. Called *Racketbusters Roundtable*, the program was intended to tell (per the tagline) "stories of unusual crimes told by insiders for you listeners who are interested in the story *behind* the crime." Two prosecutors, one former G-man, and a moderator, plus the self-described "world's greatest living photographer," recorded a chatty series of war stories about charred mobster corpses and confidence-man bilking. The guys were supposed to try to one-up each other, and the moderator declared a winner at the end of each segment.

Not a bad idea, but it didn't quite jell. Weegee was, uncharacteristically, the weakest raconteur in the group. His anecdotes (somewhat like his pictures) were usually built around a single quick, blunt joke rather than a long, slow buildup, and the lawyers on the panel were far better storytellers than he. (The best of all was probably Burton Turkus, the assistant DA who'd busted up Murder Incorporated.) The premiere was recorded in April 1947 for the Mutual Broadcasting System, and aired on May 29, in prime time on a major local station, WHN. It was an entertaining enough program, intended as a one-off and then picked up for several more episodes later that summer. But perhaps owing to Weegee's lackluster turn on the pilot, he was replaced in later installments by the *World-Telegram* reporter Harry Feeney, the very man who had coined the term *Murder Incorporated* many years earlier.

Weegee may have been casting an eye toward broadcasting and movies, but the work he started doing around this time took a new direction, one that would dominate his later career. It began when he met a young photographer named John Morrin, who had a studio on the parlor floor of a big West Fifty-Seventh Street town house. Morrin was establishing a reputation as a photographer of nudes and girlie pictures, and had begun teaching "classes" on the side—essentially sessions where a few guys could come in and shoot a topless model, her lower body draped to avoid indecency charges. He advertised the course in the *World-Telegram*, under the name Figure Photography by George. (There was no George.) As Morrin recalled it, fifteen or so students would show up, a couple of whom sometimes had to be dissuaded from lying down on the floor to shoot up the model's skirt. When Morrin mentioned these sessions to Weegee, he practically begged to step in as a teacher, at no charge. Morrin cautioned him against getting handsy with the models, and from then on, he said, "Weegee became the surrogate Mr. George." Fellig had, of course, a standing interest in looking at nude girls. Since he didn't have model releases, he wasn't even shooting for publication: he had to cede his film to Morrin at the end of each session. But while he was there, he also (according to Morrin) started doing something new: playing around with lenses and filters to bend and twist the images he was making.

Around the beginning of 1947, he went back to the pictures he'd shot for *Vogue* at the Stuart Davis opening at the Museum of Modern Art. He told people that he found himself irritated at the fatuousness he was seeing among those elite New Yorkers, and decided that he hadn't been able to capture the museumgoers' essence with straight photographs. So he took that set of negatives into the darkroom, applied some of the methods he'd been playing around with at Morrin's studio, and reprinted them as deliberately distorted images. In this first attempt, he appears to have used simple techniques, flexing the photo paper or tilting the enlarger easel, stretching out the figures or making them seem to be peering around corners. They were fun-house-mirror portraits, but they came from a chichi event rather than the Coney Island Midway. Among the twisted was, appropriately enough, Salvador Dalí.

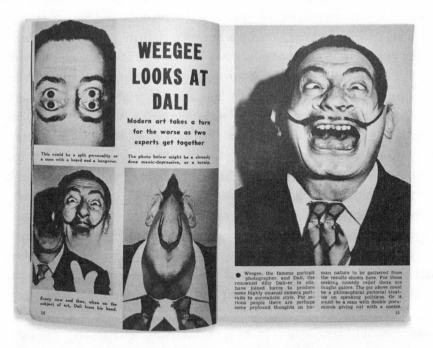

Weegee's distortion photos ran wherever he could place them, from Vogue *to the seediest pulp. This spread appeared in a men's magazine called* Scoop! *in December 1953.*

They first appeared in the second issue of a small, smart monthly magazine called '47: *The Magazine of the Year*. It's not widely known today, but during its short life it was well regarded, and it is remembered in part because it ran a Ralph Ellison short story that turned out to be an early excerpt of *Invisible Man*. (The magazine became '48 partway through its fifteen months of existence, torturing library cataloguers everywhere.) In '47, Weegee was not O. Henry but "Puck with a Camera," and a crusader at that. "To him," a writer named Jacquelyn Judge observed, "these men and women at the Museum were people who needed others, yes; but only as a background against which they might act. Weegee does not regard this Dalí-peopled world with affection . . . He watched what might be called a fruition of that culture—an Event in the Art World. And he did not like what he saw." He did, however, like the distortion effects, and he began to incorporate them not only into his still pictures but also into the movie he was shooting.

He was not the first to try it. The great photographer André Kertész had also distorted photographs in the darkroom, and heavily manipulated pictures had been a staple of the pictorialism movement, popular thirty years earlier as fine-art photography was just getting on its feet. And to most observers, this would seem to be a strange turn for Weegee. The photographer who'd made his name as a true-to-life shooter, one who gave urban darkness to newspaper readers hard and straight up, without the slightest bit of dilution, had taken to the idea of deliberately messing with his pictures. He and his admirers always believed, despite the occasional staging of a scene, that his work exuded power because it was more real than anyone's. Now he was pulling away into bizarre territory, a hybrid of photography and illustration.

But think about it another way. Every good photo, Weegee knew, required a modest level of darkroom work to look natural. All printers routinely lighten certain areas with the technique known as dodging, and intensify others by another method called burning-in. (Weegee's Coney Island crowd photo, to take one example, is full of glare and requires a dose of each.) His best pictures also sometimes needed some extra on-the-spot manipulation: the kids on the fire escape needed to be bribed with ice cream and shot in advance, and the ladies at the opera needed to be joined by their observer. Weegee was, with those setups, playing fast and loose with the facts to make a photo truthful. An even more pronounced way of doing that, one could argue (and he did argue), was to skew the image itself. You see a fake smile on an observer at an event? Turn it into a rictus that dominates his face. You want Salvador Dalí to become a Dalí painting? Stretch him out like a melted watch. If the idea is to make a point, why not hit that point as hard as you can? And with his darkroom facility, he could manipulate images in ways that few other photographers could. Caricaturing people, especially famous people, seems to have started as a side project, but in the next few years it would be anything but.

Edward Steichen, an early associate of Stieglitz and a giant in his own right, stepped in to run the photography department of MoMA in 1947, replacing Beaumont Newhall. (A couple of years later, Steichen's *Family of Man* exhibition would be the biggest thing in the art world.) Steichen was even more committed to treating press work as serious art than the Newhalls had been, and he and Weegee were friendly. Weegee brought him his early distortions for a look, and reported, "He got very excited. 'You're really creating with your camera, Weegee,' he said. 'You are now using your camera as a creative tool.'" Whether Steichen was merely being polite or expressing real enthusiasm is hard to gauge. Weegee, though, took it as the latter. "Feeling very much encouraged I decided to leave the world of reality for the one of fantasy." Or, as he put it to a reporter: "Steichen says it's a new era in photography, and Steichen is the greatest photographer in the world. Next to Weegee, that is."

As for how he did it? Weegee made a game of keeping that secret, telling one reporter that he expected to make a fortune licensing his techniques for special effects. But it's pretty evident that most of the first distortions were made from straight negatives and altered in the dark-room, and others, especially later ones, were shot through distorting lenses in the first place. At this early stage, they were likely made with a clear glass or Lucite cylinder placed in front of the lens crosswise, functioning as a crude version of an anamorphic lens. Others seem to have been made by tilting or warping the photo paper during printing.

As his treatment of those MoMA pictures reveals, Weegee may have had a conflicted relationship with the rich and powerful, but he was only too happy to make deals with them. In the spring of 1947, the contract that would change his life appeared on his doorstep, and it had gotten there almost entirely by accident, via a fellow newspaperman who'd found success in the movie business on the West Coast.

Mark Hellinger had been a beloved public character for a generation of New Yorkers, one who had come up through the daily press in the twenties and thirties, as a writer on the *Daily News* and then the *Daily Mirror.* He'd had more literary aspirations than most newspapermen, though, filling his column inches with short stories rather than the expected gossip. By 1939, he was out in California making movies, and in the next few years, he produced quite a few, including *High Sierra* (a major success, starring Humphrey Bogart) and *The Horn Blows at Midnight* (a notorious turkey, with Jack Benny).

In early 1947, Hellinger was beginning work on his latest film, which was about the murder investigators of the New York City Police Department and was going to be titled *Homicide.* He registered the title with the Motion Picture Association of America, as was customary, to avoid conflicts with other studios—only to find that Warner Bros. had, rather sneakily, grabbed the title *Homicide Bureau* and begun production on a similar film the day after Hellinger's was announced. Moreover, 20th Century–Fox had already registered a similar title, *Home Sweet Homicide*, and lodged a complaint of its own. After a little squawking, Hellinger offered the MPAA a new title, *New York Story*, but that ran into a clash as well.

The squabble lasted six months, as principal filming drew near, until the screenwriter Malvin Wald offered a solution. He handed a copy of Weegee's *Naked City* to Hellinger and suggested acquiring the title. "I like it," Hellinger told Wald. "And it will look good on the marquees." Hellinger called Weegee and explained that the book itself didn't suggest a movie but the name did. On May 9, 1947, he made an offer, contingent on MPAA acceptance of the replacement title. Weegee's attorney brother, Elias Felig, and the representatives of Duell, Sloan and Pearce drew up the deal within a few days. On May 29, the press release went out: "*The Naked City* will replace *Homicide* as the title of Mark Hellinger's production for Universal-International release. Director Jules Dassin starts pre-production filming in New York today . . . Hellinger acquired the title of *The Naked City* from Weegee, famous New York police photographer who published a noted book of New York camera studies under that title two years ago." (The addition of *The* to the film's title seems to have been a whim; Hellinger noted in a memo that he had "no preference" regarding the article's use.) Hellinger paid $3,500 for the rights to the name, a portion of which went to Duell, Sloan and Pearce, and he put Weegee on the film's payroll at $100 per week. There, as "technical adviser," his main job was to take still pictures on the set. Altogether, he got $2,100 out of the deal.

Dassin and Hellinger wanted to do something highly unusual with *The Naked City*: they'd been persuaded by Wald to shoot the film on the streets of New York, a choice that sounds ordinary today but had been attempted only a handful of times since the advent of talking pictures. With the prospect of extraneous noise, of crowds, of traffic, of bureaucracy and bribery, of the rain delays that Los Angeles never had—why bother? In fact, the film did hit some of those snags once production began. But, of course, there was one great benefit: absolute visual authenticity, especially as the climactic chase sequence played out on the (real) walkway and towers of the Williamsburg Bridge. The street crowds did indeed get in the way during filming, but Hellinger's team figured out a variety of ways to manage them. Sometimes the cameras were hidden, in vans or fake phone booths. For a while, the producers hired a professional juggler to put on a show at a distance from the actors, to distract pedestrians. Universal said that two hundred thousand spectators had turned out to watch the filming take place, and even if you treat that number as a press-agent exaggeration, clearly this was a significant event.

Weegee, in addition to taking production photos, spent significant time nudging Hellinger to put him in the movie. In his words:

> I suggested to Mark Hellinger—who's a newspaperman—I says, "Look, you oughta have a photographer in the picture." He says, "Nope, I don't want no photographer." I says, "Look, it doesn't make sense. Here's the scene. A girl's been murdered. Barry Fitzgerald arrives in a police car to look [it] over. There would be photographers." So they said, "We'll get an actor."
>
> And they said, "Do you mind lending us your Speed Graphic?" I says, "I certainly *do* mind!" I says, "Who have you got for this actor?" They had a guy picked out who played Arabian parts. He was gonna be this photographer. I says, "Oh, no! If you want a photographer, and if you want my camera"—I had it with—"*I'm* gonna be the photographer."

Sure enough, he was. Weegee appears on-screen for only a couple of seconds, half-obscured in a crowd, but he's there: as Fitzgerald, the film's star, steps out of a car, a familiar-looking newspaperman jumps in front of him and takes his picture. In his usual fashion, Weegee, or the studio press office, got *Harper's Bazaar* to run a page about his role in the film, including an uncredited photo of him. It's probably by Lee Sievan, who was also taking pictures on the set. The studio had Weegee do some press for the film, too, including a guest spot on Tex McCrary and Jinx Falkenburg's popular WNBC morning radio show *Hi! Jinx*.

Clearly, he was getting ideas about life after night crawling. He loved media attention, and Hellinger was something of the man he wished to be, a newspaper working stiff who'd become rich and famous. (Never mind that he was far more polished than Weegee.) A whole generation of poor Lower East Side New Yorkers had gone out to California seeking fortune, and some of them had made it. (Jimmy Cagney, to take one random example, had grown up a few blocks from Weegee.) Out of either hubris or obliviousness, he did not think he was too old to start a movie career at forty-eight.

Hellinger himself provided the film's voice-over, with its famous closing line "There are eight million stories in the naked city. This has been one of them." He also gave the movie a poignant and hard-to-resist backstory when, in December 1947, he reviewed the final cut at home in Los Angeles and then died of a heart attack a few days later at the age of forty-four. When the film was released the following March 4, its mixed-to-positive reviews may have been warmed up some by the widespread affection for Hellinger himself.

Weegee had spent some of that year working on his own movie, which had grown to about an hour's worth of footage and soon got a title, *Weegee's New York*. Roughly half of it was straight documentary film, more or less in the same idiom as his *PM* work had been, except in color rather than black and white. (He said he shot some of it on the same locations where *The Naked City* had been made, after watching Dassin and his crew do their work.) A section of *Weegee's New York*, made in daylight with the camera presumably hidden, shows couples necking on the Coney Island beach. About half of the footage was his "fantasy work," incorporating distortion and abstraction: the flicker of city lights, of the skyline triple-exposed in different colors. Weegee often told the story that the Eastman Kodak lab had returned a couple of the early reels, suggesting that he get his camera checked and apologizing for its inability to process his images. (As Weegee repeated the anecdote over the years, he sometimes claimed that he'd kept sending in the strange footage and conned Kodak into continuing to process his film for free.) He left out another part of the tale: Kodak had also elected not to return twenty-nine feet of film because it contained "pictures which in our judgment cannot be legally returned to you." That almost surely referred to nudity. The Comstock laws were still in force, and it was against the law to send images of a sexual nature through the mails.

Weegee had little idea how to assemble a finished film from raw footage, despite his wedding-day boasts, but he soon found someone who did. Amos Vogel, who later cofounded the New York Film Festival, was running a film society called Cinema 16, one that allowed adventurous young moviemakers to show their work to Americans for the first time. (Among them, over the years, were Luis Buñuel and John Cassavetes.) Vogel later said that Weegee, with no knowledge of how to edit film, had shown up to meet him with a bag of reels. Vogel added music and cut it all together into a watchable, if plotless, movie. It was, Vogel said, the only film he ever edited for anyone. He's probably responsible for the shortened version that is most often seen, which runs to about twenty minutes, and today Vogel is sometimes credited as the codirector. He also, after signing an exclusive deal with Weegee at the end of 1947, became the film's distributor for a year.

MoMA held a screening of *Weegee's New York* in mid-January, and a press viewing and a short run at the New School were sponsored by the American Society of Magazine Photographers a few weeks later. The response was measured, mixed, even confused. John Adam Knight, the same columnist who'd criticized Weegee so harshly for straying from his night-beat orthodoxy into artiness, reacted even more sourly this time, calling it "doodling done with a movie camera" and "a conglomeration of novel effects—novel, that is, if you have not seen them too often—yet, paradoxical as it may seem, its greatest shortcoming is lack of imagination." There were a few warmer responses in print, but not many. *PM*, by then running on fumes, published a friendly review that sums up the general bafflement: "I'm not guessing what the verdict will be. It may be as Bruce Downes, editor of *Photo Arts*, said: '. . . a contribution to photographic techniques . . . which will go down in history as an advance.' Or it may be the verdict of the Eastman Kodak Co. when they processed the strange second-reel shapes and colors: 'We suggest you stop exposing film.' At any rate, nobody's going to be bored." Basically, there was a lot of head-scratching along the lines of "What's he *doing?*"

Yet Weegee did indeed have a plan, because the time he had spent on Dassin and Hellinger's movie set had only intensified his interest in Hollywood. "O boy, me for California," he told a reporter. "Ya got climate, ya got a future—and ya got some mighty pretty women. Ya also got Weegee, if I can find a hall bedroom." In the spring of 1948, the Felligs gave up their apartment at the Elmwood and headed west, leaving the Naked City behind in favor of the Big Orange.

They exited the train to be greeted by yet another group of half a dozen
photographers—or, at any rate, Weegee did, in the flagrantly posed
publicity shots that *Popular Photography* ran. (Margaret was absent
from the pictures, though not out of the picture.) Nearly penniless at
Ellis Island in 1909, Usher Fellig had been handed an orange, which he
had to figure out how to peel and eat. Arriving by train in Los Angeles
thirty-nine years later (or pretending to), with a different name, a well-
off new wife, and a couple of good books under his belt, he got not one
but two oranges, handed up to him by pretty actress-models who certainly
had been hired for the scene. America!

He brought to Los Angeles the attitude that was then customary
among New Yorkers in California: love for the weather, contempt for the
restaurants, astonishment at the women, disdain for the shallowness—
and, in some ways, a new immigrant's naïveté all over again. Among his
first stops was at the famous corner of Hollywood Boulevard and Vine
Street, where he gawked and compared the goings-on to those in Times
Square. He marveled at little things, such as the ads carried on the benches
where streetcar and bus riders waited: they didn't have those in New York.
Nor did New York have drive-in restaurants, or street-corner phone
booths (yet), or big drugstores that sold everything from steaks to motor
oil. Very soon, he started referring to Hollywood with worldly disdain,
calling it "Land of the Zombies."

After a brief stay at the Knickerbocker Hotel ("where the rent for
one night was more than I had spent for a whole month for my room at

the back of Manhattan Police Headquarters"), he and Margaret took a place at 6606 St. Francis Terrace, a very short walk from Hollywood and Vine. The neighborhood was lively, not surging with energy like a New York street but definitely bustling, and St. Francis Terrace itself was charming: a dual row of modern bungalows, on a small side street half a block away from, and running parallel to, Hollywood Boulevard. He even broke down and installed a telephone, so he could do business with the studios. "You can't be cute in Hollywood the way you can in New York," he explained.

At parties, he began cultivating a California eccentricity of dress, pairing the tuxedo he'd been so proud of with a plaid sport shirt, sans tie. He wrote that Gene Kelly threw a bash to mark his arrival, most likely an event arranged by publicists. Almost immediately, he arranged for *Weegee's New York* to be run in the screening room at Universal-International Pictures for friends and technicians, and lobbed an after-the-fact gossip item about the event into the papers. (He was known at Universal already, because that was the studio that had distributed Hellinger's *Naked City*.) He followed up that screening with two more public viewings of the film, both sponsored by the American Society of Magazine Photographers, at the El Patio Theater on Hollywood Boulevard. That spring, he said he'd commissioned a new score from someone he referred to only as "Hollywood's most famous composer," although, if it was indeed written, it never got attached to the film in recorded form. There were also some cuts so the movie could clear the New York State Censorship Board.

He'd also agreed to appear at a screening back in New York, at Amos Vogel's Cinema 16 society that June 2, but he blew it off and failed to send a print of the film. Vogel, left in the lurch after advertising the event, was furious. "You know we can sue you," he wrote in a series of increasingly irritated letters, and "You have given us a raw deal." Weegee had to smooth things over when he was back in New York briefly that July.

It is not surprising that Weegee wanted to be a filmmaker. That would've been a natural extension of his photographic work. Besides, there was a long-standing pipeline from New York newspaper and magazine offices to studio back lots, where press writers become screenwriters (e.g., Ben Hecht, Dorothy Parker). What most of those newspaper folk did not try, and what Weegee intended to do, was to become not a below-the-line expense but an on-screen star.

He finally admitted it, after a little coaxing, in an interview in May 1948. *Do you want to be a camera operator?* the reporter asked him. "No. The camera men have a union and I can't get in it. Too crowded." *You could do some of the trick photography you've been trying,* he was told. "Maybe." And then, finally: "If you want to know the truth, I want to act." The incredulous reporter then sought out Don Taylor, one of the stars of *Naked City.* "Honest, he's not kidding," Taylor confirmed. "He doesn't want to be behind a camera. He wants to be in front of one."

By the end of the summer, Weegee had himself an agent, Ingo Preminger. He, like Weegee, was an Austrian Jewish immigrant, but his family had been much better off in the old country than the Felligs had been. His brother was the prominent director Otto Preminger, who'd just had a big success with *Laura.* Later on, Ingo would also be a fairly prominent Hollywood player, producing the film *M*A*S*H* and representing Maureen O'Hara and Paul Henreid. (And an old pal named Johnny Banner, who ended up playing Sergeant Schultz—"I know nothing!"—on *Hogan's Heroes.*) But at this stage, Preminger, too, was new in town, and his client list included a lot of off-screen talent such as directors and screenwriters, including two of the blacklisted men known as the Hollywood Ten. He also represented directors of photography, which may be how Weegee connected with him.

By August, Preminger and his new client had lined up a bit part in a light Cary Grant comedy called *Every Girl Should Be Married,* for which Weegee was paid $250. He played a photographer who snaps people on the street and then sells them pictures for 25 cents, rather as he had during his "kidnapping" days on the Lower East Side. In the film, he catches a newsworthy photo of a kissing couple, whereupon a passerby says he should sell it to the papers for $25 instead of to the couple for a quarter. Weegee responds with his one line: "Well, let's get going!" In the finished movie, it's not even his voice. The studio dubbed it, probably to evict Weegee's New York honk from a film made and set in San Francisco. A shame, because he said he'd practiced his delivery for a week before-hand.

That September, Weegee also told Walter Winchell that, for his next act, he'd be getting a thousand dollars a week to play a bartender in

After moving to Hollywood, Weegee's first movie role was in the Cary Grant pic-ture Every Girl Should Be Married. *He had one line, and the studio dubbed it.*

the forthcoming *Anna Lucasta*, a hit play that was being adapted for the screen (for the first of four times) with Paulette Goddard in the bad-girl lead role. But he'd spoken too soon and lost the part to another actor. "He knew somebody," Weegee later offered as an excuse.

These jobs weren't much, but they got him on his way, and made him a little money. In October, supported by a letter of intent from an RKO Radio Pictures talent executive named Ben Piazza, he got his Screen Actors Guild card. Weegee signed a letter of his own, too, saying, "I am joining the Guild to do bits and parts, and have no intention of doing extra work" (meaning work as a film extra, not additional labor). He was, Piazza explained, about to take another small role, in a Robert Wise film called *The Set-Up*, as the timekeeper at a boxing match. This time, he got fifty-five dollars a day, the Guild minimum, and because the bout extends through nearly the entire second half of the movie, he got eight days of work during which time, he said, "I couldn't change my shirt."

It's a well-made movie, a luminously shot film noir about a crooked fight. Weegee has about eight seconds of face time and exactly five words of dialogue ("six . . . seven . . . eight . . . nine . . . ten!"), plus another half minute or so during the opening credits, which are superimposed on a shot of the back of his head. He's incidental to the film, but he sold his presence there as a significant one—and of course he had his camera in hand on the set. RKO had its own photographer, Ernie Bachrach, making promotional stills, but Weegee shot a bunch of pictures of his own. Possibly through his newfound friendship with Leonard Shannon, one of RKO's publicity men, he got a set of those into a new (short-lived) Los Angeles tabloid, the *Mirror*. The paper headlined it BIG TOWN WEEGEE GOES HOLLYWOOD.

Access to the movie business, with all its artifice, provided him with lots of photographic opportunities. A wig on its block for a final backstage trim, men and women costumed for jungle movies, the racks and racks of mannequins (mannequins again!) in the wardrobe department— all had that uncanny quality he'd sought to get into his pictures in New York. He also made two more films of his own. One was a companion to *Weegee's New York* that, at least at this point, he called *Land of Zombies*; the other was titled *San Francisco*.* He told people that his distortion techniques involved "the subconscious camera," adopting the then-voguish language of Freudian analysis, going so far as to have WEEGEE'S SUB-CONSCIOUS MOVIE CAMERA painted on a carrying case. Although his movie-star dreams were beyond unrealistic, he was getting a foothold.

What wasn't working so well was his marriage to Margaret, even though it was barely a year old. Ida Wyman, who'd known Weegee in New York when she was an Acme printer, was now a working photographer, and when she went to Hollywood on an assignment she dropped by the couple's place to say hello. Margaret, Wyman recalls, seemed cheery at first but turned glum when the two women were alone, admitting that Weegee was impossible to live with, needy, "a big baby." Atwood, after all, had given up her previous life and moved across the country with him, and she wasn't getting much in return. By December 1948, the couple was still living on St. Francis Terrace, but Weegee was sufficiently dis-

---

* Both films are believed lost.

engaged from his marriage to write Wilma Wilcox, who was by now living in Greenwich Village.

> Dear Vilma [*sic*]
> Please excuse me for not writing to you. I have no excuses except that I have so many problems to solve. Some have solved themselves already . . . expect to be in New York around April with good news . . . (not forgetting the money which you so kindly lend [*sic*] me) Enclosed find clipping from the LOS ANGELES MIRROR expect a big story about myself in the Sunday NEW YORK STAR . . .
>
> That's about all. I don't have to write my feelings about you through the mails . . . it needs a more personal touch . . . I see a lot of LEONARD and he makes a good courier. So that's about all.
>   XXXXXXXXXXXXXXXXXXXXXX
>   W.

It's an extraordinary document, bathetic and self-aggrandizing and callous, but also touching and emotionally open. It pretty clearly is the work of a man whose current relationship is out of gas and who is pining for both his old home and his old girlfriend. (He also owes her money, brags about his good press, and misspells her name.) He marked the envelope with the St. Francis Terrace address stamp and then scratched it out. Was he taking care that a letter sent to Wilma would not be returned to his home address? Or had he already left his wife? Either way, he was moving on. Wilma kept the letter for the rest of her life.

It's not clear how often he left town during his Los Angeles years, but it doesn't seem to have been often. He probably did visit New York in the spring of 1949, because his mother died in Brooklyn that March. Otherwise, in between movie jobs, Weegee was busy reconstructing a version of his after-dark New York life—but without the bloodshed. He joined the press gaggle at all sorts of film-business events, especially premieres, where he made countless watching-the-watchers pictures. One set of them is similar to the series about the swooning Sinatra bobbysoxer, but instead ends in sobs rather than ecstasy, as the celebrity, whose face we never see, skips the rope line. Weegee called it "An American Tragedy: No Autograph." Other times, at premieres and parties, he actually did find himself chatting with stars. The very young Tony Curtis and the aging Errol Flynn both make appearances in Weegee's photos from this period, and Weegee himself does as well, standing next to both men. He cropped himself out of some of the prints, probably the versions he printed to sell.

Late in the summer of 1949, his work appeared in a group show at Los Angeles's Fraymart Gallery, a small, newish space. (Later, under the name Paul Kantor Gallery, it became an art-world powerhouse, but at this point it was just a little room on Melrose Avenue.) The gallery screened *Weegee's New York*, too. It was, however, an exhibition looking backward, not ahead: the pictures on the walls were his greatest New York hits, including "The Critic" and "I Cried When I Took This Picture."

What did lie ahead, for Weegee, was more trick photography, this time in a major studio release. In July 1949, he signed a contract with M-G-M to deploy his distortion lenses in a studio comedy called *The Yellow Cab Man*. The film was a vehicle for the comedian and clown Red Skelton, and its plot is inescapably dumb. Skelton plays an absentminded and accident-prone genius who's come up with a springy, unbreakable material that he calls Elastiglass. Through the machinations of the script, he spends most of the film working as a taxi driver while trying to prove his invention's lifesaving value when it's made into a windshield. (There's a bunch of interplay involving stuff bounced off car windows, scheming lawyers, and a plot-pivot murder that seems to leave nobody even slightly emotionally affected.) A little past the halfway point of the film, Skelton's character is drugged by a couple of bad guys who are trying to pry the secrets of his invention out of him, leading to a surreal dream sequence. For about a minute, stretched-out cars and trucks, shot through Weegee's distortion lens, zing around the screen. Weegee was paid $4,500, roughly a year's income back in his newspaper days, for five days' work. The sum seems to have astonished him, and he spoke about it later almost as if he'd pulled off a kind of aboveboard grift. He also shot a brief scene playing a cabbie, cut from the film, for which he got an extra $250.

Weegee, perhaps inspired by the film's script, began calling his own invention the Elastic Lens. The first firm he had approached to manufacture it for him had written him off as a nut, so he'd ordered various optical elements ground separately and put them together himself. He used the lens (or, more likely, lenses) in all sorts of imaginative ways. He distorted pictures of L.A.'s City Hall and sold them to the Los Angeles *Examiner*, and he got a similar set of photos of NBC headquarters into a smaller paper called the Hollywood *Citizen-News*. Having seen the Cadillac limousines in which film executives and stars traveled, he photographed and played around with the marque's V-shaped insignia: doubling it on the hood, or applying it to the back of a movie mogul's bald head, or tucking it into an actress's cleavage.

He also found incongruities that did not require special lenses. Back in New York, he'd always shot funny animal stories for the *Sun* and other papers. Now movie sets, with their performing chimps and plaster prop snakes, supplied antic new opportunities. So did Los Angeles's preponderance of funny, tasteless neon. Weegee was particularly taken with the signage advertising colonic irrigation, which was then (and has once again become) a voguish, quackish health treatment. One pair of placards read DIERKER COLONICS / PARKING IN REAR.

That summer, he got another RKO job calling for the Elastic Lens, on a film called *Footlight Varieties*. It was not a narrative film but rather a set of sketches, introduced by an emcee who happens to be Jack Paar, the future star of the *Tonight* show. *Footlight Varieties* appears to have been made in response to the new crop of TV variety programs (which drew on old vaudeville formats) that had begun to threaten the feature-film business. Indeed, the segment involving Weegee's footage was about the growing influence of television, and is actually seen on a TV set next to Paar. Most of that minute or so of film looks like the dream sequence from *The Yellow Cab Man*, showing distorted cars as they roll through Los Angeles traffic, although there are also a couple of elongated gals in swimsuits. The film came and went with little attention, and its only lasting impact was as an audition tape for Jack Paar, who is jaunty and animated as he delivers one thin, awkward joke after another.

The Felligs do not appear to have had money worries, Margaret with her inheritance and Weegee with his movie income. Their marriage, though, was effectively over by the end of 1949. His relentless chasing of women must have irritated his wife, although it's entirely plausible that he was not cheating on her, because she confided to a friend that he had become impotent. He fell hard for a stunt girl working on *Tarzan's Peril*, and made portraits of her (and other pictures on the set of the film, some of them great), but she wasn't interested in a romance.* The only lingering thing he got out of that film was an anecdote about one of the stars, Cheeta the chimp. The animal was playing a female but was male, and was not having the problems that Weegee was, because Cheeta once brought the production to a sudden halt when he sprung an extremely obvious erection. It took a mild tranquilizer and a swipe of black paint before filming could resume.

Around that time—the exact date is hard to pin down, but it was around 1950—Weegee began listing his address as a residential hotel nearby on North Hudson Avenue, and soon after that at yet another place, on Selma Avenue. (All three of his Los Angeles addresses were within a very small walkable range, within about five blocks. He and Margaret may have bought a car in Los Angeles—he was photographed behind the wheel once while he lived there—but he was still living on foot like a New Yorker. A very high proportion of his photographs from Los Angeles were made near home.) That fall, Margaret bought a business, a Laundromat on North Vermont Avenue, and she did so as "Margaret Atwood," rather than "Margaret Atwood Fellig." The Felligs do not appear to have formally divorced; they apparently just went their separate ways.† But among Weegee's papers, there is a copy of a pawnshop receipt, dated December 21, 1950, for a ring. The shop is around the corner from the Selma Avenue address, and it's hard not to conclude that it's for his wedding band. He got three dollars for it.

As much as he was drawn to the glittery Hollywood scene, Weegee was really more comfortable at the pawnshops-and-residential-hotels end of city life. The pictures he took of (for example) the services at the Peniel Mission, near Skid Row in downtown Los Angeles, are quite similar to those he made in the Bowery soup kitchens of New York. He had the same sympathy for the broken-down men and women on view, and the same knack for finding their stories in their faces. The Los Angeles folks are sometimes more lightly dressed, but that's about the only difference.

---

* According to Weegee, he invited her to his studio to pick up her prints, readying the place with soft music and chilled champagne; she arrived with three bodyguards, took her photos, and left immediately.
† It is difficult to prove a negative, but there is no divorce on record in Los Angeles County (where the Felligs lived), San Bernardino County (where Margaret lived on her own later), Reno (where many Americans traveled for quickie divorces in that era), or New York City. Margaret Atwood Fellig's death certificate, from 1989, says that she is not a divorcée but a widow.

Mannequins: Weegee with friends in a promotional store-window display at the L.A. Camera Exchange, 1951.

One memorable portrait of Peter Howard, a local character known as "Peter the Hermit" who grubbed out a living by posing stoically with tourists for photographs outside Grauman's Chinese Theatre, could easily have been made in Greenwich Village if you ignored Peter's clean all-white outfit. Weegee even found (and began to photograph the habitués of) a seedy

Backstage at a Los Angeles strip club, 1951. She's painted glitter-gold; the guy in the background would prefer that you didn't notice him there.

downtown saloon with a piano, a place that could stand in as a less ebullient Sammy's. He may have liked meeting Tony Curtis and taking funny pictures of Francis the Talking Mule and Cheeta and Trigger, but he was more at ease among the down-and-out, and his next two jobs allowed him to have it both ways for a while.

The first of those gigs started in early 1950, when a publicity executive of Universal-International Pictures got in touch with him. The studio had a movie coming out called *The Sleeping City*, starring Richard Conte. It was a particularly atmospheric film noir, one of those movies that drew visual style from tabloid photography and thus from Weegee himself. It had, like *The Naked City*, been shot on location in New York, in Bellevue Hospital. (The plot involved a murdered doctor.) In March 1950, Universal's promotions department—it was, unsettlingly, called the "exploitation department" back then—started preparations for its release. An executive named Frank McFadden cooked up the idea of hiring Weegee and sending him on a tour of fifteen cities, where he would spend a few days documenting each as it slept, in partnership with each city's local paper.

It was a clever scheme, beneficial to all. The dailies would get a bunch of free work out of the most famous newspaper photographer alive; the studio would get substantial space in print, salted with mentions of *The Sleeping City*; and Weegee would be paid well, getting $250 a week plus expenses. "We have concocted a story that Weegee is coming into each town to take pictures of 'the sleeping city' because he is gathering material for a book which shows various facets of a city while asleep," Universal's Al Horwits, another promotions man, explained to his colleagues in an internal memo. "In addition he will say that he was one of the technical advisors on *The Sleeping City*, which gave him the idea for these photographs." Weegee, he noted, was eager to shoot some infrared pictures of sleepers on the beach at Coney Island. The rest of the Universal team agreed, with a caveat that one of them scribbled on the memo: "Limit expenses."

The film's release was eventually moved to the fall, but the plan to hire Weegee was retained, and Universal picked up the thread and expanded upon it that August. "Check [with] Weegee to see if he can represent a legitimate photography association for presentation of an award of merit to the top rated CBS *Crime Photographer* program," Universal's Charles Simonelli wrote a colleague via telex from New York. "*Sleeping City* will receive number of plugs in interview during radio show." A photo-contest tie-in cosponsored with the Peerless chain of New York camera stores was arranged, calling for photographers to submit pictures of the city's citizens at night, to be judged by Weegee. A few days later, on

September 5, Weegee got on an American Airlines flight to New York, where Universal put him up at the Taft Hotel for the first two weeks of his tour. He traveled alone, without Margaret. It's not recorded whether he caught up with Wilma in New York.

Through the week of September 11, his pictures appeared in the *Post*, teeing up the film's release. Most of his time that week, though, was spent as raconteur, on radio and television. He appeared on a charmingly unstructured local TV program called *Johnny Olson's Rumpus Room*. (Yes, that's the same Johnny Olson who got famous a couple of decades later for his "Come on down!" command on *The Price Is Right*.) Weegee revisited Mary Margaret McBride and also sat down with the talk-radio pioneer Barry Gray. On September 13, he did three local television segments in one afternoon. In the next few days, there were three more, including one that was broadcast nationally: a Friday night prime-time talk show on NBC called *We the People*. They were almost surely all similar appearances, and the trade papers reported that Weegee had created a prefab spiel to unspool. "A 10-minute television show featuring Arthur 'Weegee' Fellig, nationally-known photographer, will be used in key cities during the coming weeks to help promote openings of Universal-International's *The Sleeping City*," one of them read. "'Weegee,' author of several books on still photography . . . will do a commentary type of show using samples of photographs taken with his specially constructed 'elastic lens.'" Weegee had also signed a couple of side deals to promote Schlitz beer and the television sets made by the colorful huckster Earl "Madman" Muntz, and he made a point of bringing up Muntz in broadcast interviews. He claimed that he tried sneaking Schlitz bottles into the pictures, their labels facing out, although the published photos don't support that tale.

The Sleeping City opened at the Paramount on September 20, to pretty good reviews, but by that time, Weegee had moved on to Boston, for more interviews and a night of being escorted around by two detectives to take photos. Boston in those days had a reputation as a prim place, bereft of interesting vice, and the evening was indeed a bust. He took a few distortion pictures, "left the film with the Boston *Globe* to be developed, and beat it," he later explained. "I was glad to leave . . . the dead spot of America." A *Globe* columnist interviewed him, so he was able to dispatch his responsibilities to Universal, and he got a plug for his Elastic Lens into the interview. No Muntz or Schlitz, however.

He did better when he got to Chicago, a town with more Rabelaisian tastes. There he did a day of radio, followed by a night's shooting on Skid Row and in strip clubs plus an unsuccessful attempt to get Universal's young female press representative to spend the night in his hotel room. The pictures, though, were a success this time, and the *Chicago Herald-American* ran a full page of them, plus one staff photographer's portrait of Weegee at work. For the accompanying copy, he told the editors that he'd have liked to cover Chicago in the Al Capone days, and commented on how good-looking Chicago women were. The *Tribune* interviewed him, twice.

He'd figured out the game now and repeated the success in each subsequent city. Four papers in Washington, D.C., picked up his photos or ran items. In Cleveland, a fire and a burglary, plus some street sleepers, ended up in the *Press*. In Minneapolis a few days later, Weegee happened upon a guy being tossed out of a notorious dive called the Persian Palms and photographed him (and a spatter of his blood) on the sidewalk. The *Minneapolis Star* went for those and a lot more, giving him most of a page. Its rival the *Tribune* ran a story about his distortions, with a passing mention of the movie, a few weeks later. In nearby St. Paul, he did a similar set of rounds for the *Pioneer Press*. The *Milwaukee Sentinel* ran a set of pictures on September 25, from a strip club, a local mission, and a disturbing moment in which a woman was being knocked down by two men on a street corner by a filling station. He went out shooting for the *St. Louis Star-Times*, and Weegee later said he insisted on making a picture of a sleeping drunk while he was in town just so he could call it "The Spirits of St. Louis." He went through Atlanta, too, where the *Atlanta Constitution* ran a brief teaser about his night.

City by city, he was stacking up credits. Denver turned out to be a great town for him, as he caught a sleeping man in a cowboy hat at the local bus terminal, a mother and baby dozing at Union Station, and a smattering of arrests and more drunk-tank pictures. The *Rocky Mountain News* ran those, although it declined to use a racier set of photos Weegee had caught showing a deeply clinched couple in the doorway of La Popular, a Mexican restaurant on a gone-to-seed section of Larimer

A disturbing image made on a Milwaukee sidewalk in September 1950. "Did she fall or was she pushed," Weegee's caption asked. "At 4 a.m. at 6th and Juneau I saw two men and a woman talking excitedly. Next thing I knew she was on the pavement."

Street.* Weegee said he drove around the block and rephotographed them several times, and there are indeed several frames. The couple had inadvertently posed next to a painted sign reading HOT TAMALES.†

---

* La Popular is still in business about three blocks away from this location, and the district, once fashionable and then down-at-heel, has become stylish again.
† In Weegee's files from the trip, he retained a model release from a young woman, Dorothy Oswald, who lived a short drive or a modest walk from La Popular. Did he plant the HOT TAMALES couple next to the

New Orleans, being a place with its share of late-night misbehavior, produced what were probably the best pictures of the trip, including a fine backstage moment at a Bourbon Street strip club and a man sleeping on the floor of a filthy jail cell in the Third Precinct, which Weegee (in the afternoon daily the *New Orleans Item*) called "the Vieux Carré Country Club." The police ride-along there ("like old times . . . tonic to my soul") even supplied a moment right out of his earliest Lower East Side days, when they encountered a "cute little blonde in panties and brassiere, stretched out on the floor as the ambulance doctor tried to revive her. She had had a spat with her boy friend, locked herself in the bathroom and taken poison." (She survived.) At another burlesque club, the star—she went by the name Cup Cake—took to Weegee, autographing one of her G-strings and giving it to him as a souvenir. He befriended another dancer, Amy Warrens, and told her to come to Hollywood.

He spent a bit over six weeks on the tour, charging everything from sandwiches to flashbulbs to the studio's accounts and claiming that he'd stayed one step ahead of the company's bean counters and their "limit expenses" notation. It didn't matter: Universal's exploitation department was overjoyed. By Hollywood standards, Weegee's ostensibly extravagant spending was barely noticeable. The tour cost Universal a little more than six thousand dollars plus his stipend, not even 10 percent of the movie's promotion budget, and Simonelli wrote his colleagues that it "met with tremendous success." Weegee thought he was soaking the studio; in fact, Universal had gotten a bargain.

This project occupied a strange, telling space. It lay in a netherworld between actual newspapering and conventional public relations, because Weegee was neither photographing whatever he wanted nor shooting to order from a script. It's territory that today's journalists know well, usually falling under the label "sponsored content," where an advertiser or PR firm exercises control over a story but gives it the appearance of journalism. That tour may have marked the moment when Weegee the nightcrawling newspaperman who had to beat everyone else to the scene finally disappeared for good. Now he was Weegee the Famous full time, starring as himself.

---

sign? Possibly, although the photos were made at a distance, seemingly from the street, which suggests that he really did just catch them there.

Back in Los Angeles, he had two more movie jobs come his way, both in more sophisticated films than he'd cracked so far. One was a moment's work, a two-word appearance as a murder suspect in the American remake of Fritz Lang's Expressionist classic *M*. The other was more substantial, and it genuinely, rather than purportedly, drew on Weegee's expertise. *Skid Row* (the working title) was to star Sterling Hayden as a minister who'd fallen from his faith and ended up homeless. Weegee was contracted not to shoot stills on the set and thus show the movie to the world but, instead, to bring the outside world onto the movie set: his pictures of missions and jail cells were used to create the production design of the film itself. Many were the pictures he had taken on the *Sleeping City* tour, from Denver and New Orleans and the like, but quite a few were also made locally. "The Los Angeles drunk tank will be duplicated in this picture exactly," he told a reporter from the New York *Daily News* who was visiting the studio in California. "I'll see to it. I'll see to it that the language is good. In one scene they used the word 'dishwasher.' I told them to change it to 'pearldiver,' which is Skid Row lingo." Although it didn't work out, he even tried to get his burlesque dancer friend Amy Warrens to come in from New Orleans for a bit part on the film.

Once again, Weegee's consultancy included an on-screen role of his own, although this one was even smaller than the last. He didn't get to do much more than mumble in a crowd scene. Oddly enough, when the film was released under its final name, *Journey into Light*, he did show

Shooting on the set of Journey into Light, *probably in early 1951.*

up on a lobby poster, peering out through a group of flophouse dwellers. He somehow seems a little bit more present in this film than he does in the others he made, maybe because the milieu is so much like that of his photographs, and because the Los Angeles jail scenes drew so heavily on his pictures of the real thing.

All the same, Weegee was self-aware enough to know the truth: Hollywood was not working out for him. In not quite three years, he'd worked on a handful of movies and accumulated perhaps ninety seconds of screen time all told, with barely enough lines of dialogue to fill a single page. He'd been well paid for his trick-lens rentals, but that work was inconsistent, providing neither the level of attention and artistic engagement to which he'd grown accustomed nor the repeat business that would make him rich. Whatever was left of his marriage wasn't keeping him in Los Angeles. Nor was his photography itself, although he could have made a decent and very dull living shooting stills on movie sets. "I was pretty sick of Hollywood," he explained. "My tour of the country had given me the taste of real life again." He missed the snap and speed (and pastrami) of New York. In December 1951, he left Hollywood essentially for good.*

He not only came back to Manhattan but moved directly into its beating heart, Times Square. He took a small apartment at 250 West Forty-Seventh Street, a walk-up marginally less grim than the room on Centre Market Place had been, paying (as of a couple of years later) $24.15 a month. He also signed up with the Columbia Lecture Bureau, joining a big roster of touring speakers that ranged from the powerful *New York Times* columnist James Reston to the folklorist Alan Lomax. Weegee was accustomed to New York audiences of fellow photographers and artists and publishing people, and occasionally the groups of club ladies to whom Columbia sent him complained that his talks were "too risqué." Other nights were more successful, though, including one when, he claimed, nine hundred people attended. Another night in San Diego, an intense and arty young woman took him home afterward and shared a shower with him. "I believe in clean living," he later wisecracked. And the bureau sold him enthusiastically, albeit mostly on his past work. RIDE WITH WEEGEE ON HIS THRILLING HUNT FOR PICTURES OF FIRES, CRIMES AND HUMAN INTEREST STORIES, its flyer went. "Sit beside him in his car as he races through the streets of a large metropolis . . . Laugh to the stories of the dozens of human, comic, and tragi-comic incidents that are all in a day's work for him." He earned up to five hundred dollars per night, depending on the size of the room.

He probably couldn't have gone back to newspaper work even if he'd wanted to, because the New York papers were beginning to change. Although he'd left town only in 1948, his habits were really those of the Depression, when there was a lot of opportunity to live around the margins. Most of the mainstream newspapers had been packed with small items of local interest, hand-gathered in the artisanal way he'd learned

---

* A small item in the *Herald Tribune* of August 23, 1953, says that he took on one more movie consulting job after this date, on a picture called *Vice Squad*.

on the street. By the early fifties, though, the world was shrinking, knitted together by faster communication, and that village-town-crier approach was starting to fade. The New York *Daily News*, although it had always been wealthier than its competitors, had before the war been an almost entirely local outlet, with (as one contributor put it) "no foreign news at all except for an occasional story about the Prince of Wales falling off his horse." Now it was covering not just three baseball teams and the cops but also the atom bomb, the Cold War, and the United Nations. (Weegee made fun of these international aspirations, joking about papers that covered "the blintzes crisis in Bulgaria" and "the tense halavah shortage in Turkey.") The business was beginning to become professionalized, with more and more reporters who were college graduates. Two of the newspapers that had published Weegee's work were gone altogether: *PM*, after being sold and briefly relaunching as the *New York Star*, had gone out of business in 1949, and the *Sun* had died and merged into the *World-Telegram* in 1950. The nine dailies were now seven, and a bigger shakeout lay ahead.

New York itself was also starting to become a different place, one that was going to be harder for Weegee to navigate. Its economy was humming along, even as its middle-class residents began to flow out to new suburbs in Long Island and New Jersey. Relatively little housing had been built during the war, but now enormous white-brick apartment houses were starting to spring up all over Manhattan, especially on Third Avenue, where developers anticipated a boom once its grimy old elevated train was demolished. (The Third Avenue el came down in 1955, and they were correct.) The most striking changes were in Weegee's old neighborhood, as the Lower East Side began to experience the heavy hand of "urban renewal." Blocks of tenements were torn down and replaced with gridded brick superblocks of towers surrounded by narrow lawns. The new housing projects were crisp and modern inside, at least when they were new, but they also were entirely inward-turning. Many of the tenements had candy stores and stoops at the street level, where residents would chat, hang out, exchange gossip. The shape of the new buildings engineered all those interactions away, and although they were initially pleasant, they turned silent after dark. They were deliberately disengaged from street life.

The exception was Greenwich Village, which (for a variety of reasons involving racial makeup, money, class, and geology) had mostly been left alone. There, in what was largely an Italian lower-middle-class neighborhood, the bohemian culture that had existed for half a century was hanging on. In fact, it was actively growing, fed by a new wave of young people loosely coalesced around the poets of the Beat Generation. (Espresso fed poetry, in the Italian coffeehouses of the Village and in their counterparts in San Francisco's North Beach.) He'd already begun spending time there while working on *Weegee's People*. Now upon his return to New York, the Village fully replaced the Lower East Side as Weegee's principal urban subject. Because the arty goings-on were of interest to readers nationwide, he could often sell stories about them to the glossy monthlies. The magazine business, in the fifties, was about as rich as it would ever be, and it had enough niches to support him comfortably.

Below the level of the giants such as *Life* and *Look*, there was an entire universe, nearly vanished now, of newsstand magazines aimed generally at men. Many were digest-size, some bigger, most pitched at a blue-collar audience. Apart from a few how-to titles along the lines of *Popular Mechanics*, they were unlike most of today's magazines, which deal largely in consumer aspiration. Instead, they told stories in the Junior Hemingway mode, about war exploits and bedding women and hunting in the jungle and bar crawling in New Orleans. Dan Merrin, who edited lots of them for a company called Mutual Magazine Corporation,* recalls that his readers would always respond to a good story about snakes.

There were swimsuit and topless pictures in these magazines, but no full-frontal nudity, which would have been prosecutable. Their names (*Stag, Eye, Candid, Brief*) gave off clouds of testosterone. The launch of *Playboy*, in December 1953, recast this business slightly, as publishers scrambled to copy its more openly sexualized, slicker, upscale entertainment-for-men formula with new titles such as *Rogue* and *Swank* and *Sir!* Bob Harrison, who had long ago been a reporter on the *Evening Graphic*, started his own series of sensation-driven magazines for men— *Titter, Eyeful*, and *Wink*—and then created the mother of all gossip magazines, *Confidential*. Harrison, who was enthusiastic about Weegee's distortion pictures, asked him to make all sorts of lewd ones, calling for

---

* Martin Goodman, publisher of Mutual Magazine, also owned an imprint called Timely Comics. Eventually, and through several successor owners, it took the name of its first and most successful title, Marvel. Spider-Man was born there in 1961.

a woman with four breasts, another with two bottoms, and still another with, in Weegee's unsettlingly crude description, "two snappers and two G-strings, one for her husband and one for her boy friend."

Then there were the publications that were ostensibly about picture-taking itself. These had titles such as *Art Photography* and *Glamour Photography*, and they also ran a lot of boudoir and bikini pictures, many of them nudes. They were full of explanatory copy, telling budding photographers how to scout college campuses for coed models, or how to get good pictures of a girl on a log in a forest. Maybe some readers were buying these magazines for the shutter-speed advice, but a lot more weren't.

The upshot of this was that a big new market had opened: slick-paper magazines that showed edgy subjects and sexy girls, both of which had long been interests of Weegee's. And Greenwich Village supplied attractive young women who—if we believe his bragging—were easier than their predecessors to coax into both studio and bed. "I'm looking for a little lost creature from another planet," Weegee said, "one who comes into a room like a mild, tiny ghost." And that familiar refrain again: "I'm looking for a girl with a healthy body and a sick mind." A flighty bohemian given to poetry readings and body-conscious interpretive dance just might fill all those criteria. His friend Peter Martin observed the double-edged nature of that desire: "There were many of those sweet young things who were delighted to be seen in his company, hoping that some of his fame or knowledge might rub off. They had a tendency, however, to feel safe in groups. At parties, he would be surrounded; but as the crowd dispersed, he often found himself alone," and that was how the evening would end.

Not always, though. Judith Malina, the founder of the Living Theatre, got to know Weegee in the early fifties, when both were regulars at the San Remo bar, a popular late-night hangout on Bleecker Street. "We were there probably till 4 o'clock every morning," she recalled in 2014, "and then different people went home with different people. I didn't usually go home with Weegee, but Weegee found girls, because he was a very attractive talker, and he took good photographs. He was very funny—he was funny-looking, he was funny-sounding, he was humorous. And a charming man. Between the two virtues of being a charming talker and being a good photographer, he had a lot of success with the ladies." Besides, he had something to offer. The actresses in her company, Malina recalls, "were a pretty wild bunch, and always in need of photographs."

Malina, though she was certainly a free spirit herself, went to Weegee's apartment only once. "It was a running-around-the-table situation, you know? So I didn't go back. His apartment was a filthy mess. A comfortable mess—we were all a little messy then." The two kept in touch, though, and as they grew friendly, she eventually agreed to pose nude. "It was his idea from the time he met me, but I didn't want to do it! And then after a while we got closer, and I said, all right, but only if you keep your hands off me. No, uh, itchy business." They went to her apartment rather than his, so she could control the situation. (She had lights set up in the living room, for the theater performances her company sometimes staged at home, so it made a fine photo studio.) He chattered away as he worked, perhaps because he was outside his comfort zone. "It was like being inside his monologue—he talked a mile a minute." She took a while to get comfortable and disrobe. "I'm not a shy woman about that— I'm a nudie actress—but I was afraid I'd face a scene again of running around the table." Nevertheless, Weegee was, as she put it, "very good about it."

Those portraits stayed with Weegee and Malina—they show too much skin to have been publishable, even if he or she had wanted them to be—but the growing magazine market did offer him lots of places to sell girlie pictures as well as his press photos. As early as the fall of 1952, he had a photo essay published in a low-pitched men's magazine called *Night and Day*. Headlined "After Sundown," it was a repackaging of photos from the *Sleeping City* tour, this time framed as a study of America after dark, with nary a mention of the movie. It was a little incongruous alongside the magazine's "Bust of the Year" awards, but the pictures were as strong as they'd been in the newspapers. A year later, *Art Photography* bought essentially the same story with a different picture selection, reframing it as "Weegee, U.S.A." Another magazine, *Tab*, reused a handful of Weegee's old newspaper photos to illustrate a story about juvenile delinquency in "sin clubs," adding captions that were vague enough to imply that the images were new.

That idea—repackaging Weegee's past two decades' freelance work for resale, several times over—helped carry him through the next five years in New York. He was still taking lots of pictures, to be sure, but they weren't off the news anymore. In magazine after magazine, his old work reappeared, sometimes mixed with a few new shots. Usually, though not always, his name was prominent, often on the cover. (He brought prestige to these publications, which did not often get the chance to hire anyone certified by the Museum of Modern Art.) For quite a few of the stories, he used his distortion techniques on his older pictures, and thus added a second layer of repackaging, along the lines of "here's Weegee, now with new secret techniques!" *Night and Day*, over several issues in 1953 and 1954, bought the *Sleeping City* pictures of New Orleans, a batch of distortions, and then several other sets of older photographs, pairing them with new copy to tie them together. The editors occasionally ran two Weegee stories in an issue.

Did it pay? Passably. Dan Merrin, the editor who bought Weegee's pictures for, among others, *Eye* and *Brief* and *Focus*, explains today that the rate was about three hundred dollars for a multipage story. But because his company published in so many niches, he could even go up against larger houses if there was something he really wanted. "If I was in competition with *Life* magazine, *Life* could obviously outbid me. I would pay a base minimum, maybe $300 for something that was extremely good, and I'd work out a deal to buy three rights—one for *Eye*, one for *Male*, one for *Stag*—and the cumulative price would be more than *Life* would be paying for single use." That got Merrin into the game with prominent glamour photographers such as Andre de Dienes, who'd made his name by spotting Norma Jeane Baker before she became Marilyn Monroe. In 1953 alone, Merrin ran five sets of photos by Weegee in *Eye*, and several others in Mutual Magazine's other titles. One, in *Stag*, was entirely about Weegee's Murder Inc. days, and it didn't contain a single picture less than ten years old. In Merrin's universe, he recalls, Weegee was a known figure but also "an oddity."

When an editor at *Brief* asked Weegee to reprise his movie-theater infrared series, with pictures of moviegoers "eating, sleeping, and making love," he happily agreed, before discovering that the editor needed pictures in a matter of days. That put him in a jam, because those movie-theater moments had to happen and did not conform to a schedule. Getting the "eating" pictures was easy—everyone eats at the movies, and Weegee made some great pictures of kids blowing bubblegum bubbles—as was "sleeping." But catching couples necking in the dark was rarer, and "It was a $300 assignment, and with the resale rights I could really do business," So Wee-gee resorted to stocking the pond again, coaxing a few couples to pose.

One of those couples appears in *Brief*. A second had been at a 3-D movie, and the cardboard glasses add an extra level of eeriness to the scene. Also, the woman in the latter set wears a gauzy blouse that has turned see-through under the infrared flash, revealing her bra and a little skin and giving the scene much more of a sexual charge. Weegee later said that some of the models were hired from the Art Students League of New York.

A third couple are also wearing 3-D glasses, and they were not hired hands but friends of Weegee's. Al Levin was a photo-equipment marketer, working for Nikon as its cameras began trickling into America. (Levin was widely liked in the business, and is one of a few people most reponsible for changing the perception of Japanese cameras from junk to gem.) He brought his girlfriend Joan Loew to a Manhattan movie house, and the two went up to the balcony with Weegee, where they obliged him with some kissing as he shot away. Joan Loew became Joan Levin a few months later (and is now Joan Gropper; she remarried after Al died in 1999), and she recalls Weegee as a rather gentle guy, perpetually covered in dropped cigar ashes. "He really had mostly his work," Gropper says. "He didn't have a lot of friends, but Al was a friend." Weegee liked the Levins enough that he was able to set aside a general distaste he had for wedding photography and lend a hand when they got married. As a result, she has possibly the world's only wedding album that's full of trick-lens distortion pictures. Weegee shot their son's bar mitzvah, too.

Weegee's entrée into this world of magazine work may have been quicker and smoother because he'd found himself an agent. Erika Stone, whom he knew from the Photo League, and her friend Anita Beer in 1953 opened a small agency called Photo-Representatives, and he was among its first clients. Both women were photographers in their own right, and the agency was, Stone recalls, a way for them to stabilize their income in between freelance jobs. They had had their doubts about signing him, but he was the most prominent name at the agency, and it turned out to be a good partnership. His newspaper background meant that he showed up when he was supposed to show up and turned in assigned work on time. Her only headache, she noted later, was that "when we took him along to meet editors, he usually told off-color stories."

He'd also met a graphic designer named Mel Harris, who was able to do for him in print what Amos Vogel had done on his movies: shape a heap of pictures into a readable, consumable, salable product. Harris was the cofounder with two partners of a firm called Designers 3, doing layout and illustrations for publishers and ad agencies. He encountered Weegee randomly one day in a camera shop on Sixth Avenue, where they chatted about the prospect of collaborating sometime. "At two a.m. the next morning," Harris later recalled, "Weegee deposited two thousand photographs on the floor of my house."

That late-night arrival may have been a little color that Harris injected into the story himself, though it is not out of the question—Weegee was known to call people, even those with families, at all hours. However their relationship began, Weegee was indeed a presence in the Harris household for months thereafter. There's a photograph of the family living room in which the carpet is swamped with hundreds of Weegee's black-and-white glossy prints, and Harris's daughter Joan recalls that the scene lingered for months as the book came together. "My mother was very indulgent," she says. "We really did live like that." The two men worked at the kitchen table, Harris doing the cropping and paste-up.

Weegee was impatient to get the book done and get paid, and he grew somewhat frustrated at Harris's deliberative way of working. "Mel fancied himself a writer," their literary agent Stanley Colbert recalled later, "and would take days dreaming up captions for the photos to be included in the book. Weegee couldn't care less about the captions. He wanted publication." But he'd also keep bobbing up with extra photos he wanted to include. "It was not unusual," Colbert continued, "to get midnight or later phone calls from Weegee, complaining about the time Mel was taking to get the book together and off to the publisher, to be followed by a call from Mel, complaining about Weegee's complaining."

The writing in *Naked Hollywood* sounds less like Weegee's speech than his other books do, suggesting that Harris did do most of that work. But the spirit is fully Weegee, and fully Los Angeles. The material is bawdier, the joke pictures coarser, than in the New York books. Weegee, mimicking the success he'd had with his top-hatted operagoers back in 1940, shot many of his movie stars from behind, or with their faces obscured behind microphones, and the captions are often slightly oblique. Especially at our distance, when (for example) Cecil B. DeMille and Ann Sheridan are less

Weegee and his coauthor Mel Harris at work on Naked Hollywood *in the Harris apartment, ca. 1952.*

instantly recognizable than they were at the time, there's a fun can-you-name-this-celebrity aspect to the book. Weegee also slipped in a few photos that weren't from Hollywood at all: the portrait of Peter the Hermit on Hollywood Boulevard shares a page with a photo of Joe Gould made in New York, probably because their long, scraggly beards paired up so nicely.

Yet *Naked Hollywood* is a project whose contents did not quite hang together, and still do not. For every great photo, of which there are quite a lot, there's a jokey manipulated image of, say, a beachgoer with his head on backward, or a leering look at a starlet inadvertently showing too much cleavage. (Marilyn Monroe and Zsa Zsa Gabor both appear with low necklines, each of them leaning forward, over a caption reading "Spheres of Influence.) Two of the best portraits Weegee ever made, of the columnists Hedda Hopper and Louella Parsons, appear in *Naked Hollywood*. The pictures of showgirls backstage, napping or getting dressed, are superb, probably the best work in the book. But there also are several not very distinguished pictures of, to put it plainly, women showing their breasts and their asses. Sometimes, Weegee said, he used a particularly penetrating light that he called the Weegee Nippletickler. The distortions are often of female bodies, and quite a few of them slip over a line past titillating and into crass. They're (a very weird variety of) T and A. As the art historian Miles Orvell once put it concisely, "In *Naked City*, naked means a revelation of the real city. In *Naked Hollywood*, it's just bare behinds." For significant swaths of the book that's true.

Harris and Weegee had the dummy book pasted up by the middle of June 1952, when Stanley Colbert sent it to a small, well-regarded house called Pellegrini & Cudahy. "To our way of thinking," Colbert offered in his pitch, "this book is the sharpest satire ever done on the people and places in Hollywood." They all made a deal within a couple of weeks, with an eye toward publication early the next year to correspond with Lillian Ross's *Picture*, a (pictureless) landmark book about Hollywood by Weegee's onetime *PM* colleague. Weegee and Harris split an advance of a thousand dollars, with a solid royalty rate, and Harris got an extra hundred for the layout job and jacket design. Colbert also later recalled that he got *Naked City* reissued, and that Weegee inscribed a copy to him with effusive thanks, saying, "Now I can eat again regularly."

They also were able to arrange for a second small tie-in book that could be promoted along with *Naked Hollywood*. Designers 3, Harris's firm, had a working relationship with the ad agency representing Westinghouse, one of the largest makers of flashbulbs. So Harris and Weegee produced a small paperback called *Weegee's Secrets of Shooting with Photoflash*, "as told to Mel Harris." A pocket-size booklet of sixty-four pages, it was mostly a how-to manual with a number of digressions into Weegee's exploits and anecdotes, including yet another retelling of the story behind "The Critic." But there is a lot of useful photo advice in there as well, about how to make good pictures at parties and avoid flash glare. (There's a fine section on photographing children, with some sample pictures. Mel Harris's two-year-old daughter, Francine, posed for Weegee with her pet parakeet, and Bobby Seebacher, the son of a reporter friend of Weegee's, appeared in his high chair, tangling gleefully with a plate of spaghetti.) It was certainly worth the seventy-five-cent cover price Westinghouse put on it—reduced to a quarter if you supplied the paper sleeve from a flashbulb purchase—and Pellegrini & Cudahy and Westinghouse attempted to knit together publicity for the two books. Their synergistic plan turned out to be a fizzle, though, because each expected the other to pay for the ads and displays.

Naked Hollywood was published in March 1953, right behind Lillian Ross's *Picture*, to a response that was mixed at best. The *New York Post*'s John Adam Knight, who had been cranky about *Weegee's New York*, was flatly dismissive this time. "Like reading an obituary," he wrote. "Its pictures appear to prove that the not inconsiderable talent he once had is now as dead as the dinosaur." *Modern Photography* was basically kind, but knocked the distortions, saying "it's questionable whether there was any need for them in *Naked Hollywood*." The *Chicago Tribune* probably spoke for most critics when it called the book "indescribable, but fascinating at times in a vulgar way." Most of the New York papers mentioned the book neutrally, with a teaser but no review—the telltale sign of a disappointing release by an author they otherwise respected and did not want to knock down. One Maine bookseller returned his sample copy to Pellegrini & Cudahy, disgustedly saying, "I want it neither in the shop nor at home. How low can publishing get?"

Pellegrini & Cudahy had trouble selling paperback (then called "reprint") rights, too, because of the book's racier photos. Reprint publishers had a reputation for pulp seaminess, and cultural conservatives were feeling their dudgeon in the McCarthy years. "In view of the . . . current frame of mind of wholesalers, local censorship groups, etc. I just don't think we would be able to get away with it" is how a Pocket Books editor put it in his turndown to Pellegrini & Cudahy. "And so I think we had better to leave it to you fortunate high-priced publishers who are not subjected to the same restrictions." Only two years later, after McCarthy was gone, did a smaller paperback house, Berkley Books, make a go of it— and in fact Berkley may have felt emboldened by then, because its editors deleted a few photos and added others, making the book a bit more salacious rather than less.

The pictures did, at least, engage one persistent young magazine editor who didn't mind going up against obscenity laws. A couple of months after the book's publication, on July 27, 1953, Hugh Hefner—then preparing his first issue of *Stag Party*, soon to be renamed *Playboy*—sent a very irritated letter to Pellegrini & Cudahy's publicity director. "I don't

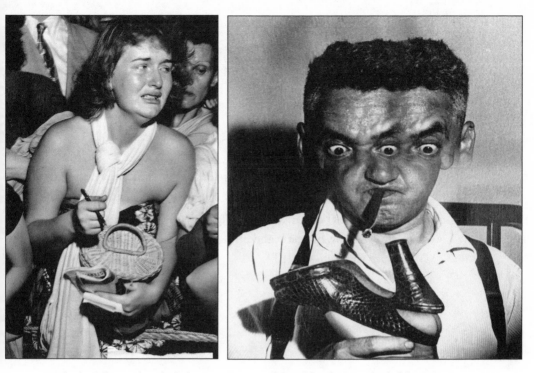

Naked Hollywood *included great Weegee photos like this one (titled "An American Tragedy: No Autograph") and sillier ones like this self-portrait (titled "Talent Scout").*

know what's going on at your offices, but someone is apparently throwing our letters in the circular file on the floor," he wrote. (As it turned out, he had been writing to the publisher's old address, and his letters hadn't been forwarded.) He went on to explain that he'd been trying to get glossies of seven of Weegee's photos—the ones in the book that revealed the most skin—for a feature to run in his new magazine. "Whether your answer is 'yes,' 'no,' or 'drop dead,' I'd very much appreciate an answer," he wound up. Once he finally connected with the publisher, he did indeed run a group of them (all distortions, all showing bare breasts, plus a thumbnail image of Weegee's own distorted mug) the following year, in one of the first issues of *Playboy.*

Naked Hollywood was, itself, very much like Weegee's time in Los Angeles. It is semisuccessful, handsomely put together but made from base material, and ultimately a little disappointing. Weegee, some time later, flatly dismissed it to Louis Stettner, calling it "a bad book." Perhaps Mel Harris suspected as much, because his short introduction to the volume (signed with his name rather than Weegee's) ends on a tongue-in-cheek remark about the innate problems of the material that follows. He was almost surely thinking about the distortion photos when he wrote:

> There are more misconceptions haunting Hollywood than there are stars. This little book attempts to exorcise those misconceptions. It has always been felt that the camera infallibly mirrored reality. Inevitably then, the word corroborated by the picture must impart to this book the rare quality of presenting the facts as they are—simply, honestly and objectively.
>
> We regret that it has failed.

The Concord Camera Circle was not really a club, at least not the kind where you join and pay dues. It was a loose association of amateur and professional photographers who met up on weekends, at sessions much like the ones Weegee had begun attending at John Morrin's loft a few years earlier. This one, though, was the side project of a successful Jamaican jazz musician named Cass Carr, a bassist and bandleader living in Harlem and playing in clubs at night. Because his days were free, he'd picked up a camera back in the thirties to occupy himself, and he soon gathered up a group of like-minded folks at the local YMCA.

By 1952, he had a studio on Forty-Seventh Street just down the block from Weegee's, and, like Morrin, he ran a weekend business that he'd advertise in the classifieds. Carr would hire a couple of models for the day, and a group of young photographers, nearly all male, would each chip in four or five dollars in exchange for the chance to shoot all the film they could. A few were probably looking to sell their work to that new crop of men's magazines, but others were simply having fun taking pictures. There were many such camera clubs, and Cass's was one of the better-known ones. It's been suggested that some of the attendees were just voyeurs, and never bothered to put film in their cameras, but most took the sessions at least somewhat seriously, and caches of their pictures still occasionally resurface from attics and basements.

Aside from his studio sessions, Carr also ran trips out of the city, advertising them in the *New York Post*. Each participant's eight dollars or so included not only the modeling fee but also a chartered bus ride, a box lunch from a Chinese restaurant, and an afternoon on the dunes of Long Island or in a field upstate. Sometimes he'd have sixty people on the trip. It was a perfect fit for Weegee, and because he was Weegee the Famous, he was not a mere participant but an attraction as well. "Guest artist: Weegee" began to appear in Carr's ads.

The price went to ten dollars if the model was a name, and in 1952 Carr's best draw was the young Bettie Page. She was living nearby on West Forty-Sixth Street, just around the corner from Weegee himself, and was at the beginning of her pinup career. Page would eventually become known as the most photographed woman of the 1950s, famous for both cheesecake and racier bondage stuff, in both still and moving pictures. She was also friendly and accessible, and tough enough to hold her own with a roomful of randy men. At this stage, though, she had just started making enough money as a model to quit her day job as a secretary. Weegee photographed her multiple times, on multiple occasions, both in the studio and out of town. At least once, on a shoot where she was posing in a bathtub, he tried to climb in with her, ostensibly to improve his camera angle. "Out, Weegee, out!" she shouted at him.

Weegee's studio pictures of Bettie are fun, and they do get at her exuberance and expressiveness, but they look like a lot of other bathing-suit pictures of her. (Which is not surprising; after all, there was a scrum of guys in the room, every one shooting from the same angle.) Still, there are a few that get beyond the familiar, and they, of course, are the ones in which Weegee was once again watching the watchers. In 1952, he made one portrait of Page that stands with his best pictures. It shows her from behind, in her sparkly hand-sewn bikini, as she faces half a dozen men with cameras. We don't see her face, and it doesn't matter. Her shoulders and stance convey her strength and extroversion without downplaying her ooh-la-la body, nearly silhouetted by the studio lights. The photographers themselves are nearly faceless, because their equipment blocks their eyes, and their bodies mostly fall back into the shadows. Most of what you see of them is a phalanx of lenses boring in on Bettie as she stands alone.

At least once, the nudity at these sessions caught up with Carr and his customers. It was on July 27, 1952, the latest in a series of those weekend day trips that had begun in May and taken them to Fire Island and Connecticut, among other places. This one was headed to a farmer's field in South Salem, New York, a village in Westchester County near the Con-

Weegee made many pinup pictures of Bettie Page, but when he turned around and saw the other cameras, an ordinary photo shoot turned into something more.

necticut border. There were four nude models that day, plus two more who were clothed, and twenty-three photographers, including Weegee. The local sheriff John Hoy had been plotting for a couple of weeks to put an end to these outings, and he and his deputies lay in wait for the club, hiding in the bushes with walkie-talkies.

After Page had been posing with the other models for a while, she took a break, ducking into the bushes for a quick pee, not knowing that she was right by one of the hidden cops. That was when the law enforcement party swooped in, guns drawn, as one deputy ran a movie camera to record the raid. Carr and three others were arrested, and everyone was ticketed. The models were charged with indecent exposure, and the photographers' film was confiscated. Carr ended up paying fifty dollars and lost the one hundred dollars he had on him to cover the day's costs. Weegee got out of there with a five-dollar fine.

Carr didn't stop his trips, but (perhaps because he had more to lose than the white members of his club did) he grew more cautious, discouraging nudity during future sessions. "Guest artist Weegee," unfazed, kept tagging along with him for years. Jonny Wilson, who regularly modeled for the Concord Camera Circle, remembers going to Fire Island the following July, and the head count topped eighty people that day. In these settings, Wilson recalls, Weegee kept his ogling in check, but it was obvious to her that he liked being around the models. "He was professional with me," she recalls, then pauses. "And I could see that he was watering at the mouth."

As the role of Weegee the Famous took over his career and as the high-profile assignments remained fairly scarce, he played the part of himself with more and more bravado. In February of that year (just to take one example among many), you could find him at the Grand Central Palace, a convention hall on the East Side, at a promotional event for Westinghouse, signing copies of the *Weegee's Secrets* booklet or just tossing them into the crowd as freebies. At one such event he was seated on a prop gilded throne, playing the superstar to the hilt, complete with Speed Graphic and cigar. During some shows, he would work the convention floor, chatting up manufacturers and persuading them to send him free gear in exchange for mentioning it in interviews. At the back of *Naked Hollywood*, there's a paragraph of what are surely payback credits, mentioning Wollensak lenses and several other makers of photo equipment by name. When an acquaintance once asked Weegee about the camera he carried that day instead of a Speed Graphic, he shrugged, saying, "Whoever pays me the most to use their camera, that's the one I use."

That spring, Sid Kaplan met Weegee at one of those trade shows, where he had some work in a small exhibition. Kaplan was still in school, not yet really into his great career as a photo printer and photographer. To him, he says, meeting Weegee was like walking up to Babe Ruth. "I was fourteen. And he sort of picked my work on the wall, and he started telling me, 'These pictures are great, you got a good future, keep the good work up. Piling the shit up.'" Then a pause. "And then he says, 'Kid, you ever thought about stamp collecting?'" A put-down, sure, but one from a fellow Lower East Side wisenheimer who knew his audience, and despite the awkward start a loose, long friendship began.

Kaplan remembers that, in the 1950s, Weegee's lectures began to focus more and more on the work he made with the Elastic Lens. "He used to go in front of audiences and talk about all the distortions, and the big thing that he kept was the secret of how he'd do these things," Kaplan recalls. "Like everybody wanted to know!" he says, laughing. Then Weegee would turn it into a game, asking other photographers to offer theories. "He'd ask, *What do you think?* And they'd come up with ideas." Weegee would respond, "No, no, that ain't it." Kaplan thinks that Weegee may even have been fishing for new ideas and methods that way.

His distortion techniques did indeed broaden and improve through the early and mid-1950s. At some point around 1955—when, Weegee later recalled, his ability to go out and shoot was briefly limited because he'd burned his hand on a hot flashbulb—he picked up a dime-store kaleidoscope, removed the little color chips at its far end, and stuck it in front of his lens. The pictures he made through it fractured single images into snowflake-like arrays of six, giving him new ideas. Soon enough, he had constructed more sophisticated versions of that cheap kaleidoscope, with better mirrors at different angles, fitted more precisely to the camera lens.* He also tried out a periscope-like construction that, oddly, was intended to make an image from the direct point of view of the flashgun rather than the lens. This rather silly idea doesn't appear to have gone anywhere, although he made a case for it, saying, "I wanted to know what the [flashbulb] holder saw. After all it contributed to the photograph, it should certainly be given an opportunity to express its focus." Only a man whose work had been so intimately tied to the effects of camera flash would have thought of it as a personifiable character.

Maybe it was just all that time he spent around camera makers, maybe it was a sense that he had to jump-start his career, but he did make one big change in 1954. The occasion was a bad moment backstage on Ed Sullivan's show, when he was photographing the singer Julius La Rosa. As the photography writer John Wolbarst described the scene:

> He arrived at the studio in the midst of a dress rehearsal being shown on a closed circuit. Seeing what he considered an excellent shot, he aimed his Speed Graphic and fired his first flashbulb of

---

* In later references, including his autobiography, he refers to one of these setups as the "Weegeescope," and thanks an optical firm called Schnur & Appel for help with its creation.

the day. The effect was stupendous, but not exactly what he had intended. While viewers of the closed circuit screens tried to regain their vision, and camera operators cried "murder" or the TV studio equivalent, the Ed Sullivan show took an unscheduled intermission.

A good story, and it is true that the old-fashioned Speed Graphic was falling out of favor then. Its cumbersome mechanics and single-shot film were simply outclassed, for most work, by the 35-millimeter and medium-format cameras coming out of Germany and Japan. So Weegee, master of the flash, began learning to shoot with available light and a Nikon rangefinder. "Some people said it couldn't happen," Wolbarst wrote. "Others still can't believe it."

Now, Weegee's narrative here is at least a little bit concocted, because the pictures he shot of La Rosa that day were not in fact made with a Speed Graphic, and he had already started using more modern equipment while he was in California. But it is true that, around this time, Weegee did begin shooting 35-millimeter and medium-format film consistently, although he didn't abandon his big press camera altogether. What's driving this account, almost surely, was his desire to get himself a free-bie. Given that he appeared in posed publicity pictures with his Nikon, he had likely been given one by his friend Al Levin (the same Al Levin who'd posed at the movie theater with his future wife, Joan) and one of them pitched *Modern Photography* a promotional story. Neither Weegee nor Nikon would have said no to a friendly spread in the press.

Not long after this, Weegee also started making his kaleidoscope pictures with the hot new photo tool of the era, the Polaroid Land camera, whose instant-developing film could not have been more precisely created to ignite his interest. Imagine if you'd spent your whole early career racing to get a picture to the darkroom minutes before the competition did: now here was a camera that eliminated that need entirely. Donald Dery, a Polaroid publicity executive, recalls that the reaction at the company's Massachusetts headquarters was barely tepid. "We didn't consider him an artist of the caliber we wanted to work with," he recalls. But Weegee, at least occasionally, did use his Polaroid camera to return to his formative subjects. There still exists a cache of Polaroid pictures he made at car crashes in New York, probably shot on the fly as he happened upon them.

The distortions and other experimental photos were taking more and more of his time, but he was still working the streets of Greenwich Village, collecting photographs for what he thought might be a book. Rent parties and street musicians, scenes at the San Remo, even James Dean, caught in the background of a picture shortly before fame hit him. One evening in 1954, Weegee photographed Maxwell Bodenheim, the aged bohemian poet now down on his luck. Bodenheim was murdered with his wife, Ruth Fagin, the next day, whereupon Weegee went back and caught Ruth's corpse being removed from the rented room where the two had died. Weegee's pair of photographs melded his crime-scene past with his Greenwich Village present.

In the spring of 1954, on a sidewalk off Seventh Avenue South, Weegee ran into Helen Gee. She was about to open a café called Limelight, and it was going to be the premier (and only) gallery exhibiting serious photography in New York. Gee was at the forefront of the widening interest in the camera and its practitioners, cultivating Robert Frank, Leon Levinstein, and many others early in their careers. She was, like a lot of people, put off by Weegee when they first met. In her case, it was justifiable, because she'd been with her eleven-year-old daughter, Li-lan, at the time, and "I'd noticed as we talked that he kept looking her over, a lecherous gleam in his eye. He called a few days later, asking to photograph her in the nude. I hung up."

Gee didn't like Weegee, but she did admire his work, and once she got her gallery open he began dropping by, simultaneously holding her interest and making a nuisance of himself. When he caught the actors Rod Steiger and Claire Bloom on film holding hands, they complained to Gee, and another well-known customer got so irate about being photographed one night that he threatened to smash Weegee's camera. Gee had to ban unauthorized picture-taking from a room that was supposed to be a temple of that very form.

The prohibition stuck for a while, but one night some months later, Weegee sneaked back in when Gee was out of town and posed a young black-clad model in the café with a stuffed crow on her head. (The idea was to create a putatively unstaged moment of Village wackiness.) The photograph appeared along with more than a dozen others in the magazine *Night and Day* in June 1955, and although the story was respectful, with some genuinely good atmospheric portraits made at the San Remo and elsewhere, Gee was, she wrote, "furious." She had been working herself to exhaustion creating a haven for serious-minded Villagers and attempting to keep it solvent, and the gawking *Night and Day* reader, skulking in to check out the easy bohemian girls, was exactly the kind of visitor she feared. She had to eject a couple of flashers soon after the story was published, and she blamed Weegee, banning him from the room for a year thereafter. When Gee finally let him back in, they discussed an exhibition, whereupon he insisted on showing the most inelegant of the distortions rather than the newspaper work that interested her. "You're missing the boat. These broads with five tits will be a sensation,"

At the Limelight, the pioneering photography gallery on Seventh Avenue South, Weegee posed a young woman with a crow on her head for a magazine story about Greenwich Village beatnik eccentricity. The gallery's owner, Helen Gee, was not amused.

he told her. "Nobody's done anything like it." Gee was not interested in being the first, and they parted ways.

It was a situation that he more and more frequently found himself in. Respected for his old crime and newspaper pictures, he could rarely interest anyone consistently in his new body of work. Over and over, those smaller magazines, the ones with names such as *Candid* and *Tab* and *Stag*, would run a story or two—a spread of city pictures, and maybe one new set of distortions after that—and then the relationship would peter out for lack of new material. Once in a while a magazine outside his usual purview would buy them as a one-off, as the auto magazine *Cars* did in 1953. ("I sign all my pictures 'Weegee, 1968,'" he told the writer. "That's because I'm fifteen years ahead of my time.") The distortions were treated as a curio: *that wacky screwy Weegee!* They were sold on his celebrity rather than on their strength.

This is not to say nobody appreciated them, particularly after Weegee hit on a couple of new variations. In 1955, he began a new method of manipulating images, making prints through textured glass and rippled sheets of plastic instead of using the Elastic Lens or the kaleidoscope, and he began applying these techniques to portraits of the famous. Effectively,

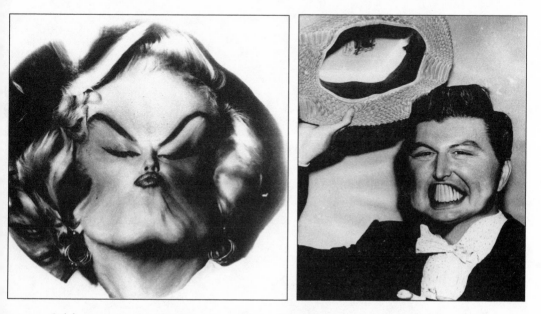

Celebrity caricature: Marilyn turned into a bat, Liberace into a piano keyboard.

he was turning himself into a caricaturist, exaggerating features to emphasize or tweak the personae of public figures. Because he was suddenly
messing with familiar faces, there was a fresh hook for editors. Photo-
Representatives took the first batch of celebrity caricatures to *Vogue*,
and they restored (if only briefly) his connection with Alexander Liberman, who ran two pages of them in July 1955. The toothy smile of Liberace became a nest of big white slabs, pretty nearly approximating piano
keys. Jackie Gleason's curled lip became even more of a smirk-smile than
it was on the small screen. Marilyn Monroe's mass of blonde curls became
even more massive, her pursed lips bat-like. "What I've actually done,"
Weegee crowed to *Vogue*'s uncredited writer, "is done the impossible."

He hadn't, but the caricatures were consistently salable. He made more of
them on assignment for *Look* in 1956, and they won an award from the
Art Directors Club. Another *Look* assignment called for Weegee to warp
the season's new women's hats, which had been shot by another photographer, Tony Vaccaro. Even *TV Guide* went for a couple of pages of
twisted-up celebrity faces. All those stories were in full color—Weegee
had hooked up with a lab called Authenticolor, whose owner, Mike Lavelle,
could handle the complex darkroom processes that he couldn't—and
even if the hat pictures were not exactly for the ages, they were fun and
vibrant on the page. A jazz bandleader named Hugo Montenegro used
one of the better color distortions for an album cover. A smaller magazine, *Pageant*, bought a spread of Weegee's celebrity caricatures as well.
Still, that was not really enough to match the "very lush living" he had once
been able to sustain, and he was consistently short of money. Around
this time, he sold Mel Harris his half of the rights to *Naked Hollywood*,
figuring that the book had run its course. Amos Vogel bought *Weegee's
New York* from him outright, too, for all of $150.

Perhaps seeking to cover the gap, he started pitching himself to advertising agencies. This was not an outlandish idea, despite his reputation
for pictures that most admen would have considered far too gory for their
use. After all, the tour for *The Sleeping City* had been promotional photography, as was his photo essay on the Cities Service Building. He was
certainly capable of doing commercial work, and an ad that Designers 3
produced in 1954 using one of his photos got him an award from the

American Institute for Graphic Arts. Another one, for an industry trade group called the National Electrical Contractors Association, used a Weegee-warped photo of a skyscraper over the cutline STRAIGHTEN OUT YOUR ELECTRICAL SYSTEM. Still another, for University Loudspeakers, emphasized the product's sonic fidelity by pairing a distorted image of a violinist and its undistorted source.

He also later claimed to have worked on projects for Ballantine Ale, Canada Dry, and Maidenform, and perhaps he did indeed sell pictures to their agencies. But if those ads actually made it into print, they are unidentifiable, and not visibly Weegeeish. By his own admission, he treated these jobs as moneymakers that were somewhat beneath him, choosing people nearly at random off the street and paying them a few bucks to pose as regular-Joe models for the agencies' scripted scenarios. One suspects that the agencies paid his fees and did not invite him back, and no lasting relationships developed. Besides, given that it was usually anonymous, ad work would never be emotionally satisfying to Weegee the Famous.

Occasionally, though, he would still find himself in a setting that provided first-rate editorial pictures, and he could rise to his old level. Over the course of a few nights in 1954 and 1955, Weegee got himself backstage access to a jazz club on West Fifty-Second Street called Basin Street. There he photographed none other than Louis Armstrong. Imagine it: the great American vernacular photographer and the great American vernacular musician, kibitzing and riffing backstage. They were, despite their disparate backgrounds, weirdly alike: children of extreme poverty and disenfranchisement, early dropouts from school who had become well-read adults and took their respective arts to astonishing levels of expression. (They even had similar writing styles, with the odd habit of EMPHASIZING several KEY WORDS in each sentence with capital letters.) The Armstrong pictures show the great musician backstage cooling off with a handkerchief tied around his head, onstage in full-throated performance, and hanging around with the singer Gary Crosby, who dropped in one evening after he and Armstrong had made an appearance on Ed Sullivan's CBS show. There's even a photo of Weegee and Armstrong in which the two clown unselfconciously, as Weegee pretends to play the trumpet, both men's eyes bugged. The series is an unusual visit with one of America's most impor-

Backstage at Basin Street, a jazz club on West 51st Street, in 1954.

tant cultural figures, seemingly unaffected by the camera and wide open in a way that celebrities today rarely are. There are certainly many great pictures of Armstrong by other photographers, but relatively few show him with his guard down as these do.

Weegee also, in mid-1956, received a lively and clever assignment from *Popular Photography* to use his caricature methods to make portraits of his professional peers. And what a set of subjects he cadged: Alfred Eisenstaedt, Yousuf Karsh, and Philippe Halsman, plus a less well-known commercial photographer named Victor Keppler. The sessions were loose and funny. Halsman, by now an old friend, showed off some recent work, a magazine cover portrait of Jayne Mansfield dressed as Joan of Arc. (Weegee had two responses: shock at the vast number of frames Halsman had exposed and the fact that he'd covered her up with an armor breastplate.) Eisenstaedt's session was at *Life*'s offices, and it went awkwardly because of an equipment failure. Gordon Parks and Eliot Elisofon, two other photography giants who happened to be in the building, were called over to lend a hand with the gear, but Weegee had to come back to reshoot a week later. He and Eisenstaedt didn't solidly connect in person, judging by the exchange that took place when Weegee tried to get his model to smile big.

WEEGEE: Make like Liberace!
EISENSTAEDT: Who's Liberace?

Nonetheless, the straight photos he made were pretty strong. Eisenstaedt did, in fact, supply a big, toothy grin, in imitation of Weegee's imitation of Liberace, and the others were similarly obliging. The caricatures, which are kinder than a lot of the celebrity ones, turned Eisenstaedt even toothier, Karsh squared-off and stern, Keppler goofy, and Halsman puckish. They're pleasingly odd pictures, certainly among the best of Weegee's distortion work. The accompanying copy (unsigned, and thus probably by editor Bruce Downes) said that Weegee was still keeping to his old schedule. "He toils away through the New York night in a locked, secret room like a troll in an old German fable. A coffeemaker maintains him through the long hours—'the time of fantasy' he calls it—while the rest of the city sleeps."

In between the more prestigious jobs like these, the girlie magazines kept providing Weegee with a modest living, and in late 1956, he even helped get one off the ground himself. Called *Photographers Showplace*, it was yet another hybrid of the men's and photo magazine formulas, and the first issue showed a reclining Jayne Mansfield—sans armor plate—on the cover. It had been launched by Michael St. John, whose family business, St. John Publications, was another of those second-tier houses putting out comic books and men's titles. (*Manhunt* and *Nugget* were among the most successful.) Weegee not only served as a contributor but was listed as "photo editor" on the masthead.

The first issue, while heavily dependent on standard-issue cheesecake photos, does contain a few surprises, because either Weegee or the magazine's actual editor, Roy Ald, hit on the idea of asking for contributions from stars who were good amateur photographers. Thus the cover could tout, for example, the ALL-EXCLUSIVE GUEST PHOTOGRAPHER SAMMY DAVIS JR. Ald also bought a portfolio shot by Christine Jorgensen, then a very famous person for having just undergone sex-reassignment surgery.

It was just one more glancing collision between Weegee the Famous and actual fame—and the Sammy Davis photos, in particular, are not bad at all.

Weegee clearly used his role as photo editor as an excuse to publish as much of his own work as he could. The first issue of *Photographers Showplace* contains a large portfolio of his distortions with wry captions, offered as "a hilarious new photo-book called 'Weegee's Women.'" A couple of his pictures are tucked anonymously into other stories—for which, he later said, "I paid myself extra." For a large feature in the second issue, a woman's nude body was painted in black-and-white stripes, and a photographer named James Pappas posed her alongside snippets of prose taken from a book about the African habitat of the zebra. (For the phrase "indolent and slothful in the sun," she relaxed. For "instant alertness to alien sounds," she perked up.) As photo editor, Weegee was the one directing the session rather than holding the camera, but he got a photo into the magazine that showed himself wielding a paintbrush.

Despite these weird little bits of creativity, *Photographers Showplace* was evidently not able to bite off enough of the *Playboy* audience to survive. It lasted four issues over less than two years, its brief life distinguished chiefly by one of the first appearances of Weegee's kaleidoscope photos in print.

He did have the Elastic Lens, and that could still get him some prestigious film work. The late fifties were a moment when, challenged by television, movie studios were looking for new technologies to offer filmgoers a unique widescreen experience. Those systems had all had bigsounding names: CinemaScope, VistaVision, Ultra Panavision 70. The most ambitious of all, probably, was called Cinerama. It called for three projectors to roll three reels of film, all precisely synchronized and aimed at an immense and deeply curved screen. The point was to immerse audiences in the movie, and although the technology never took off—it was just too complicated to make and show most movies this way—it did linger for several showy years.

Arguably the best demonstration of Cinerama (or, strictly speaking, a variant thereof called Cinemiracle) was *Windjammer*, a luxe documentary of a journey by sail across the Atlantic. Louis de Rochemont, the producer, had big plans for the Cinerama system, and financed this very expensive and complex film to demonstrate its abilities. Over 238 days, the three-masted full-rigged ship *Christian Radich* made its way from Oslo down past the Portuguese coast and out into the Atlantic, across to the Caribbean, up the eastern seaboard of the United States, and back to Norway. The producer's son, Louis de Rochemont III, directed the film, and it was an immense job. The madly complex camera weighed five hundred pounds, plus another thousand once it was encased in a watertight steel compartment called a blimp. The gear constantly had to be cleaned of corrosive saltwater, and the lighting man received shocks, more than once, from wet electrical gear. Despite all that, they did manage to make a completely watchable movie. The sailors are handsome young blond Scandinavians, and the shots of waves breaking over the bow and fjords looming into view, set to a score by Morton Gould, are genuinely thrilling.

Weegee did not, needless to say, spend those eight months at sea. But the ship touched port in New York for a couple of days, and at that point in the film, audiences see an antic montage of midcentury Manhattan, meticulously shot through the kaleidoscope and the Elastic Lens. The blond boys drop into a nightclub, Jimmy Ryan's, to hear Wilbur de Paris's jazz band. Times Square's neon lights spin and dance around the sailors. So do the skyline, the Statue of Liberty, and streams of traffic. Scrunched-up cars make an appearance as they had in *The Yellow Cab Man*, this time in much crisper definition and full color. Like *Weegee's New York*, *Windjammer* is a mostly visual experience with not a vast amount to say, but it says it in a way that keeps you watching, and it got an outsize amount of attention when it was released in April 1958, including some kind of murmuring from the critics about Weegee's montage.

The project came at a good time, because Weegee, in addition to needing money, was feeling his age. Around 1957, he was diagnosed with diabetes. Although it did not much affect his everyday work right away, beyond requiring what he called "the white pills," he spent at least a short stretch in the hospital. His constant smoking and pastrami consumption could not have helped his physical state, either. Old friends began to step up to help: Louis Stettner made sure that Weegee's prescriptions were filled. Sid Kaplan, who'd met Weegee as a teenager at that trade show a few years earlier, was by now working as Stettner's assistant and remembers running bottles of medicine across town to Weegee on Forty-Seventh Street.

At work on a New York montage of kaleidoscopic effects for the 1958 feature film Windjammer.

But the person Weegee gradually came to rely on most was Wilma Wilcox. The two had picked up again after he moved back to New York, although exactly how quickly they reconnected is a little hazy. Wilma later said that they lived together continually after he returned; friends suggest that he drifted in with her somewhat gradually, over time. She had been in an apartment on City Island, in the Bronx, but eventually resettled on Cherry Street, on the Lower East Side, just a few blocks from one of the tenements where Weegee had grown up. When he wrote to her from out of town, he'd mail her in care of his own Forty-Seventh Street address, or at her office in Midtown, or at the Cherry Street apartment, where he lived at least part-time. She would stop by the Times Square place, pay the bills for him if he was traveling, handle the rent. In 1958, he gave up the Forty-Seventh Street studio for good.

A little slice of his life in 1956 (though none of Wilma's) can be glimpsed through the lens of Lou Stoumen, a fine filmmaker-photographer who made a creditable stab at laying out the entire history of photography in a documentary movie. *The Naked Eye* was his title, and the distinguished Hollywood actor Raymond Massey supplied the baritone voice-over. (Its aesthetics aside, *The Naked Eye* is also remembered as the first modern Hollywood film to show full nudity, which arrived wearing the fig leaf of Art.) Stoumen focused on a few contemporary photographers, notably Alfred Eisenstaedt, Margaret Bourke-White, Edward Weston—and Weegee. "A kind of photographic primitive, and an amateur at heart," Massey calls him, faux-chuckling as he first pronounces "Weegee." We see our man yawning and stretching as he rises from his cot, fully dressed, in his cluttered studio. "Weegee's day begins usually in the late afternoon, in his combination darkroom and bed, just off Times Square," Massey says. "He lights up last night's cigar butt and sets about his day's work." He's soon tromping around the Lower East Side with his Speed Graphic in hand as he "begins a working day down on the Bowery," negotiating to buy a used overcoat from a random man on the street. He visits Sammy's, "a place that Weegee helped to make famous with his pictures," and we hear that he covers the cops, murders, fires, Sinatra at the Paramount. Stoumen, like so many other people who observed Weegee over the years, begins by framing him as a cartoon character, and by the end has almost accidentally made a persuasive case that he is anything but.

He was still respected, albeit almost always for the work he wasn't doing anymore. Increasingly, Weegee had become an oldies act, and the distortions were the new album that nobody wanted to hear. But he could always depend on his greatest hits, and he talked about them whenever he was asked to do so. Appearing on the interview show *Night Beat* in 1957, he told substitute host John Wingate a bunch of his old stories, and dropped the names of some cameras he'd gotten for free. He even made an appearance on *Tonight* that year, during the multiple-host twilight between its first and second permanent stars, Steve Allen and

Jack Paar. When Steichen included Weegee in a Museum of Modern Art show called *Seventy Photographers Look at New York* in 1957, Weegee had a dozen great pictures on the walls. The newest of them, though, was from 1945.

For every sophisticated project like that, though, there was some grubby, coarse job to be had, and Weegee seems never to have turned one down. For a magazine called *Slick* ("Fun for Men"), he shot the actress Maila Nurmi, best known as the scream queen Vampira, and distorted her bombshell figure to become, variously, extra-skinny, extra-busty, extra-hippy. He also did a number of stories with a magazine—actually, a pair of magazines—published by a small outfit called Periodical House. They were called *Hi* and *Ho!*, and each was half the width of a standard magazine, the idea being that they could be kept in an inside jacket pocket, out of the sight of wives and girlfriends. They were magazines for the raincoat crowd, full of peekaboo photos and smirky *tee-hee* cartoons, with a regular salting of Weegee's caricatures and Greenwich Village photos to add a little name-brand class.

In 1957, he and his distortions were featured in the *National Enquirer*, which was at least as downscale and fringy as it is today, except with more stories about two-headed animals and the like. MODERN WOMEN AREN'T HUMAN!... IF YOU DON'T BELIEVE IT THIS MAN TELLS WHY, the front page blared. The interviewer, Bob Lichello, let Weegee rattle on for a bit, and the conversation includes a lot about his career, including the story of the Gladys MacKnight murder, back in 1936, that jumpstarted his career. Lichello was clearly appalled at the seediness of Weegee's apartment, writing that "it was the room of an old man living on a meager social security check, or a rum pot who works a panhandling route." The worst of it, though, is some dark-edged talk about women. Weegee called them "the greatest fraud since Ponzi," and offered this about marriage:

> The most hazardous part of a cop's job is when he comes home. They all live in Queens and eat corn beef and cabbage. The little woman is fixing it. He's been on a raid of dirty books and pictures . . . Well, he goes home . . . studying the French postcards and tells the woman, "Let's try something new." Being a frigid inhibited dope, a human frigidaire, she takes hubby's gun and shoots him dead with one shot.

Weegee's least sympathetic views of the opposite sex had found their outlet.

A much friendlier Weegee poked his head into view in *Popular Photography* a few months later. A reporter named Les Barry accompanied him when he visited the circus at Madison Square Garden, and even though Weegee's days of photographer-as-clown were long past, Barry was amazed to see that everyone backstage knew him. "I anticipated an evening of lessons in split-second photography," Barry wrote. "I got an evening of lessons in photographic public relations . . . Weegee had a word for practically every member of the circus." When he accidentally pulled a button off his coat, a circus seamstress stitched it back on for him. Barry noted that Weegee shot all of eight frames all evening, and only two in a couple of hours backstage. (He had retained his old habits from the days of using individual film holders, even though he had switched to shooting roll film.) He asked why those two people were worth photographing.

An interviewer for the National Enquirer *in 1957 found Weegee fascinating and his apartment disgusting.*

"They were ready," Weegee explained. "They were relaxed, and their costumes fitted them like they belonged on them."

While *The Naked Eye* was helping with Weegee's visibility and *Windjammer* was getting good notices, another moviemaker came calling, although he was one with less cachet than Lou Stoumen or Louis de Rochemont. Dick Randall was a former television-quiz-show and gag writer who operated around the edges of the film business, and he was at least as colorful a character as Weegee was, with an apartment on Fifty-Seventh Street where actresses (real and aspiring) could be found drifting in and out. Randall was not a Hollywood studio creature; he worked in Europe and Britain and New York and almost anywhere where he could cobble together a few bucks to make a low-budget grind-house film. Randall's wife, Corliss, remembers that he'd work with little clutches of small investors, such as dentists and grocery-store clerks. The first time Weegee visited Randall, he said, he encountered a bustling office where the producer was dashing about and fretting over an urgent retouching job, shouting, "I *must* get that tit painted out!"

Randall had not yet quite developed into the trash-meister who would later make *Four Times That Night* and *Snake Fist Fighter*. He was just getting his business going, teaming up with a gawky comedian named Sammy Petrillo (mildly famous at the time for looking and sounding uncannily like Jerry Lewis) and a TV director named Frank Warren to make a film at Expo 58, the world's fair in Brussels, that summer. Another friend of Randall's, named Sigmund Lasker, came on as a producer—he was one of those enthusiastic amateurs when it came to movies, a professor of medicine from New York—and the group persuaded Steve Allen to write the music and George Jessel to do the voice-overs. The film itself, titled *Holiday in Brussels*, was a quasi-documentary about the fair with a romance plot overlaid upon it, and Weegee makes an appearance as a Chaplinesque tramp. It was (judging by secondary sources; no copy appears to have survived) a decent enough film, and perhaps owing to the Steve Allen connection, it made it onto NBC in 1958, giving a taste of the fair to Americans who couldn't get there.

Weegee loved the trip. "The World's Fair is wonderful, the trip was wonderful, this is the most wonderful experience in the whole world," he wrote back to Wilma in New York. Owing to his press credentials at the fair, access was mostly free. He went up in a small open-cockpit plane with Lasker to take aerial photos of the fair, scaring the doctor half to death. At the American pavilion, he was amused to find outposts of the Brass Rail, a midpriced New York restaurant chain, and Howard Johnson's. Elsa Dorfman (then a student at Tufts, later a prominent portrait photographer in Cambridge, Massachusetts) was working at the HoJo that summer and encountered Weegee at one of her tables. He was with Don George, a songwriter who'd had a recent hit with a remake of "The Yellow Rose of Texas" and was now working on *Holiday in Brussels*. Dorfman had no idea who Weegee was. "I was an adorable junior in college," she recalls. "He said, 'Come to bed with me! Come to bed with me.'" She turned him down, and only later figured out who that sloppy guy had been. "I missed my chance!" she says today, giggling merrily at the thought of it. "I could've had some fun."

Weegee also made a habit of going by the Israeli pavilion for the gefilte fish and kosher goulash on offer there, which were reminiscent of the Lower East Side deli food he was used to. On one visit, he was shocked when an Israeli attendant offered him cream in his coffee after a meal that included meat. "I called for the manager and explained that . . . it was against the Kosher dietary laws," Weegee later recalled. And then, deadpan: "He was much surprised, and promised to look it up." As secular and undomesticated a life as Weegee had lived, he was still the child of an almost-rabbi, and such a basic transgression got his back up. The food at the Israeli exhibit was good, though, and he joked to Wilma that she should come over to Brussels and pick up "the secret formulas."

On his return to New York in August, he met an old colleague, the *Post*'s Arty Pomerantz, to catch up, and accidentally found himself on a hard-news story for the first time in a while. Pomerantz's parked car was sideswiped by a driver who did not stop, and the two photographers and a reporter friend found themselves in a high-speed chase across Manhattan, trying to cut off the guy who'd been responsible. (They got the guy, and of course the story made the *Post*.) But Weegee was no longer a professional news chaser, no matter how he'd been portrayed in Stoumen's film, and the Brussels jaunt had hinted at a fresh market for his work: independently made movies shot in Europe. They were typically smaller than Hollywood productions, with lower bars to entry and smaller budgets, and he found opportunity there. Just a few weeks later, he was in Munich, adding kaleidoscope effects to a fairy-tale movie, a Grimm

Brothers adaptation called *The Magic Fountain*. It was a smallish film, the passion project side hustle of a Chicago adman named Allan David. Once again, Weegee suited up for a bit part, and Fellig-as-elf, given his portly frame and knobby features, was oddly suited to the costume.

Much as he had been upon arriving in Hollywood a decade earlier, he was a bit of a naïf in West Germany. His notes to Wilma back in New York indicated that the smokes weren't to his liking—he asked her to ship over cartons of Philip Morris cigarettes and his favored cigars—but that he was finding it easy to learn German (unsurprising, given that he spoke it as a child, and his Yiddish surely helped him along). Paul Mason, who worked on *The Magic Fountain*, remembers that Weegee couldn't stop himself from tweaking the Munich restaurateurs when he went to dinner, pointedly asking for a kosher meal.

He was skating at the edge of insolvency, though, anxiously chasing down payments that would cover his expenses and shooting pictures for a little advertising job while he was there. While making the film, he lived on borrowed money from the screenwriter until an insurance check arrived. The filming, he told Wilma, would "take a couple of months, I think, and it looks like I'll have to come back to Germany to finish it. SO . . . PACK YOUR BAGS." Then, a few days later: "Looks like the picture won't be finished on time, it rains every day & we can't find two midgets. So it looks like I'll be here at least two more weeks." While he was there, he chatted up the vice president of Cinemiracle, who suggested he'd have some more work available soon. Again Weegee told Wilma she could come to Europe if she wanted: he would work on the movie, and she could shoot the stills and draw a second payment. (She does not appear to have made the trip.) While in Munich, he even—probably through Don George—met one evening with the great Duke Ellington. They fell into an intriguing though fruitless chat about making a documentary.

Although Wilma was the person with whom he had the deepest human connection, especially in this later part of his life, their relationship was not frictionless. During these European jaunts, Weegee was constantly asking her to pack up and ship him cameras, lenses, prescription medication, cigars, even instant coffee and nondairy creamer. At least once she got fed up with serving as his unpaid assistant and sent him a letter saying she felt used. Weegee wrote back that he was "shocked," saying, "You have spoiled my whole stay in Germany . . . What do you mean using you—is being a friend, does that mean using you." And then: "I still have plans for you (in spite of your nasty letter) for future picture in Germany etc. . . . I wish you was here with me, also there is plenty of work you could do and get paid for." He signed the letter "Confused and BEWILDERED and BEWITCHED / Weegee. P.S. Save your broomsticks for witch part in movie." A postcard followed the next day, showing a view of the Marienplatz and reading, "Dear Wilma, This is how Germany looked to me, till you broke the spell with your BITCHY letter." Their discord did not last: Wilma continued to act as his New York supplier, and Wee-gee's subsequent letters to her, while requesting no less help, do at least seem a little more grateful.

A lot of the work he was chasing didn't pan out, and it often seemed as if he just couldn't catch a break. A successful television series adapted from the film of *Naked City* brought Weegee no real attention, and if he got any money for the TV rights to his title, it wasn't much. He'd been in talks regarding a documentary about himself, for which he'd go entirely around the world taking pictures, but the producer went broke. A trip to Havana at the very end of 1958 was scuttled when the Batista regime fell and Fidel Castro took over, leaving Weegee stranded at his sister Molly's house in Miami. In still another Zelig proximity moment, he got pretty far into a conversation with Sherwood Schwartz, the future producer of *Gilligan's Island* and *The Brady Bunch*, about doing a panel show on CBS.* He also had conversations with a French team about making a movie called *Naked Paris*, a kind of loose sequel to *Weegee's New York*, but the idea disintegrated after a few months.

So did a collaboration with no less a filmmaker than John Huston, who was about to make the biographical film *Freud: The Secret Passion*. While in Paris, Weegee met with the actor Ernest Anderson, who had worked with Huston and who made the approach on his behalf. Although the conversation got as far as "dickering" with Huston himself, the col-laboration didn't happen. In April 1960, Weegee had to send Wilma a few hundred dollars from Paris to get two cameras out of hock, includ-ing one of his Speed Graphics. He could get press—Art Buchwald, then

---

* In his letters home to Wilma, Weegee does not name the panel show he's discussing, but he mentions that the writer is about to launch a play in Chicago called *Mr. & Mrs.*, and Schwartz was indeed its author. The panel show did not go anywhere; the play became a TV movie, in 1964, starring Lucille Ball and Bob Hope.

the Paris correspondent for the *Herald Tribune*, wrote a droll column about him—but he was barely making a living.

One thing that did pay a little, at least, was his next book. After all those lectures in which he teasingly half-revealed his distortion methods, he'd decided it was time to tell all, or nearly all. Roy Ald, the editor he'd worked with at *Photographers Showplace*, cowrote the manuscript, putting Weegee's procedures into clear how-to prose, and *Weegee's Creative Camera* was published in March 1959.* The cover implied a great treasure within: "The world-famous photographer reveals for the first time the well-guarded secrets behind his highly imaginative and startling pictures." Detailed passages show how to make a custom kaleidoscope and fit it to a camera lens. Others show how Weegee used a knobby pressed-glass coffee cup, sawn in half, to distort buildings and people. Still others demonstrate how to use textured glass or bent and rippled plastic to produce various warps, twists, and other effects. (Weegee instructs readers to make the plastic flexible by immersing it in a pan of boiling water, and suggests that readers buy a hot plate to do so. He was so undomesticated that it didn't occur to him that most homes had a stove.) There are also some very detailed yet clear technical instructions about how to print images while bending the paper, involving some manipulation of a darkroom easel that's sawn in half and an extra-bright bulb in the enlarger. It was really a book for ambitious darkroom hobbyists and pros, and it left out the single most significant trick Weegee employed—that of a slit down the corner of the enlarger bellows, above the lens, through which he could insert and remove those pieces of wavy glass. The text did, however, give up most of his "secrets." The trouble was that, yet again, not many people cared enough about those secrets, and the book arrived to little press attention outside the trade.

By the time *Weegee's Creative Camera* was in stores, Weegee was traveling again, this time to Las Vegas, where he was making a promotional film for Wilbur Clark's Desert Inn. The press representative for the hotel was an old friend, and Weegee received the key to the city while he was there. "This is a fantastic city," he wrote. "Everything is open 24 hours a day." But he was also too broke to pay his income taxes that spring, and

---

* He also made a short instructional movie in the same vein, *Wee Gee's Camera Magic*, which was released the next year by Castle Films.

while he was in Las Vegas, he was chasing another check (for a short promo film he'd made for the City of Pittsburgh) to do so. Then it was off to Los Angeles, trying to make the Sherwood Schwartz panel show happen. He was there for the whole summer, working on a script for the show, giving a lecture here and there, and reactivating his lapsed California driver's license. He was still friendly enough with his not-exactly-ex-wife, Margaret, to stay with her at her house in North Hollywood.

Then it was back to London, where he settled in at the Mapleton Hotel. There he smuggled an enlarger into his bathroom and at least once flooded his downstairs neighbor's room while washing prints. It was a productive if makeshift arrangement, at least, allowing him to sell a few caricatures to the *Daily Mirror*, Britain's largest-circulation paper. Whereas he'd already worn out his welcome pushing distortion shots on New York City photo editors, the English press was a newly receptive audience. He was able to position them once again as novelties, and he made the rounds, selling a couple to the *Sunday Graphic*, some to the *Times*, a few across the Channel to *Paris-Match*. He got himself a proper British suit (tailored extra-generously, like his American ones, to barely skim his body) and even a bowler hat. When he visited Trafalgar Square, he wanted to make a picture of himself in the manner of the statue of Lord Nelson, surrounded by pigeons, and poured a bit of bird feed into the brim of the bowler to entice them in. (The birds obliged, perching on his head.) He later wrote that he signed a five-hundred-dollar-a-week contract with the British *Daily Mirror* to shoot society and royalty, but the published record reveals that it was a brief assignment, not a continuing deal. His work appeared in the paper four times over a couple of months.

Only once in this five-year stretch of globe-trotting did he pause and stay in New York for any extended amount of time, and while he was there he was writing. He'd taken a job as a columnist for a short-lived newspaper called the *New York Item*, producing sloppily written columns for a couple of months that mixed his anecdotes with blatant promotional plugging. That job came and went pretty quickly, but what he began work on in earnest was a memoir. Maybe the bit of attention he got from *Weegee's Creative Camera* had whetted his appetite to write at length once more; maybe it was that his ability to talk about himself was boundless. More likely, he treated the memoir as a promotional exercise. Whatever the reason, in 1960 he tape-recorded and typed out a long string of yarns, anecdotes, and memories.

Weegee by Weegee, which he put together from those transcripts and manuscript pages, is a full-on performance, a fast read that shows off his best and worst instincts in full measure. Although he got a certain amount of help from his editor in shaping and cutting, the prose is all Weegee's. It's entertaining; digressive; boastful; full of straight facts, bald exaggerations, and tall tales; often illuminating; occasionally revealing; sometimes illusory; and now and then just peculiar. He is at once gentle and crude, at once sensitive and crass, often showing both sides in the space of a single paragraph. There are pages and pages of stories about his sex life: losing his virginity on a rooftop in the 1910s, regular visits to whorehouses in the 1920s, picking up girls who hustled him for meals and money in the 1930s, bedding young bohemian women later on. He explains that he likes a girl with "a small top and a big bottom," denigrates dilettante photographers who don't commit to their art, and almost plaintively makes the case for his continued relevance.

Yet it is an oddly opaque book. He gives the illusion of emotional openness, admitting to a fierce inferiority complex, but speaks surprisingly little about anyone but himself and the famous people he's met and photographed. His family is barely present. He misstates the number of brothers and sisters he has. He completely omits Margaret and his brief marriage, and he never mentions Wilma, either. Yet the reader is taken through that same experience that virtually everyone who ever met Weegee recounts—that the more time you spent with him, the more his charm and eccentric enthusiasm overcame his slovenliness and crudeness. His rattly tales of chasing news are irresistible. What he did with acquaintances in person he was now doing for readers of his autobiography on the page. By the end, even as he seems mildly appalling, he wins you over. He seems fun.

An essay by Bruce Downes, editor of *Popular Photography*, opens the book, and it is ostensibly framed as an appreciation. It is in fact anything but, and it starts off with the most backhanded of compliments: Weegee, Downes says, "began his odd-ball career as a plodding freelance photographer who by his imagination and showmanship bootstrapped himself to eminence." He continues in a familiar vein, about Weegee's honest-if-unrefined quality, his hard lighting, his speed, his murder pictures. He mentions the amazing run of mannequin photos, with a parenthetical note reading "attention psychoanalysts!" (Downes was right about that one.) And then the last paragraph is a shiv between the ribs: "All of that ended when Weegee got his first look at modern art and his first taste of fame. Then the innocence vanished and Weegee traded his radio prowl car for a mess of mirrors in a futile effort to make photographs look like modern art. The years of the kaleidoscope and the distortion devices have netted nothing but gimmicks." The book is surely the only autobiography that opens with a "tribute" that calls its subject a has-been.

Why on earth did Weegee include this essay, unedited, in a book that was meant to reboot his career? One can point only to that inferiority complex he mentions, and perhaps to his deep-set desire to be accepted by the photo-world elite. That fall, he kept busy sending copies off to those insiders, or directing Wilma to do so while he was out of the country. "Most important," he told her, was that she send one to a publicity man at Polaroid—Weegee's latest attempt to cadge a steady supply of free film.

The John Huston project didn't work out, but Weegee could always get work with Dick Randall. Back in the United States as the new decade began, he took a job on *Shangri-La*, a Randall picture set at a nudist camp. As he wrote, "$50,000 was put up by the racket boys, bookies, cabbies, waiters, etc." It is a film so deep down the food chain that the opening credits end with a note reading, "We regret that this film has NO Director. We couldn't find one to keep his mind on the job!" B-movie researchers have attached a name to the film, and it's not a he but a she, the schlock-film pioneer Doris Wishman.

The film stars Sammy Petrillo, the Jerry Lewis look-alike with whom Weegee had worked on *Holiday in Brussels*. Petrillo's character stalks a pair of young nudist women as they arrive at their club and undress, then rather creepily follows them as they go on a vacation and then off to another camp, whereupon he finally lays off the skulking and joins up to become a nudist himself. The comedian recorded a voice-over that at least tries to stitch together the visual segments, which include a few scraps of his nightclub shtick, some physical comedy, swimsuit scenes at Florida's Cypress Gardens theme park, and more than a half hour of topless young women swimming and playing handball and riding horses and doing various other bouncy activities. In the last ten minutes of the film, Petrillo emcees a nudist beauty contest. Really, though, the project is nearly plotless, nearly scriptless, barely a movie.

Wishman did most of her shooting at a naturist camp in New Jersey, adding a few scenes in Florida, and a couple in Washington, D.C., where the (clothed) young women go to ogle the Washington Monument. Weegee took a cameo on-screen, too, as the manager of a D.C. wax museum. (More mannequins.) He shucked his clothes for the making of the nudist camp scenes, wearing nothing but his Hasselblad. He also contributed his customary round of trick-photography shots, although here they seem tacked on at the last second, with no attempt to integrate them into what's going on. Weegee was most likely there for the paycheck and the live nude girls. He'd been a voyeur from the beginning, and he was hardly about to say no to a months-long job that provided little else.

In fact, the project was so enticing to him that about a year later, in Britain, he joined up for *another* nudist-camp exploitation movie, this one called *My Bare Lady*. It, too, has a beauty-contest scene, and this time Weegee plays one of the judges. Shot at a resort called the North Kent Sun Club, near the Hampshire village of Brockenhurst, it is perhaps ever so slightly more put-together than *Shangri-La*. Yet it, too, exists mostly to connect a lot of scenes of frolicking naked bodies around the pool and some monologues in defense of the underdressed life. (Yes, there is volleyball.) Weegee has one line, delivered to one of the other judges, who's nervous about the job: "Don't worry about it. Men are always judging women anyway, so this oughta be right up your alley." Weegee is himself unclothed, but he's sitting behind a substantial table, sparing us the details.

If those two movies existed at the bottom of the barrel, the next one sat a couple of floors below. It was the brainchild, if you can call it that, of Sherman Price, a cameraman on *Shangri-La* who was also an operator of a different sort. "Sherman was always involved in something," remembers Ralph Toporoff, who worked for him as an assistant director. "He was doing something for the U.S. Navy that dealt with tracking ships— always something like that. But I thought, after listening to all these things he was doing, that he was a confidence man!" Turned out that Price was indeed a filmmaker, and late that year, he had gotten Randall to put some money into a film he wanted to make in Paris. The working title was *Europe or Bust!*—the producer had to leave town in a hurry partway through filming, and Toporoff remembers two guys showing up at the hotel shortly thereafter trying to chase money he owed them—and Price hired Weegee not as a bit player or technical director but as the star. He'd finally get to be the top-line actor he'd always wanted to be. Weegee

Judging a nudist-camp beauty contest in My Bare Lady, *a low-rent British film shot in 1962.*

himself sketched out a scenario that Price expanded into the script. He even got the film retitled to incorporate his name: *Europe or Bust!* became *The Imp-Probable Mr. Weegee.*

The film they all made together in the fall of 1962 is, in the kindest possible reading, weird. It opens in a police station, where three women (who disrobe for no reason as they speak to the cops) are being interviewed. One policeman swishes around making catty remarks; presumably, the big laff riot is that he's gay. The women have been brought in to identify a shadowy figure who's been seen committing sexual acts with a store-window dummy. The mystery man turns out, of course, to be Weegee, a portrait of the artist as a dirty old man, down to the raincoat.

Then the scene flashes back to a montage about real-life Weegee, his nights in the Chevy, his crime scenes and fires, his sojourn in Hollywood. Then it goes forward again, through a few impressionistic street scenes in New York (including somewhat more artsy footage that looks like Weegee might have shot it) and then to Paris, where we meet Weegee as a sad-sack present-day version of himself, looking for love and contemplating the end—whereupon he meets and falls in love with that mannequin as it's unloaded from a freighter. His affection for "her" turns his life around. He spends the next hour on-screen chasing the dummy around Paris, as if it's a fugitive lover. Along the way, there are gratuitous scenes of young women in bubble baths, sitting around in elaborate lingerie, shaving their legs, and filming scenes in a television studio where they, without provocation, just decide to strip down. (Several of the actresses in the film were moonlighting showgirls from the Crazy Horse, the high-end Paris cabaret.) If this all sounds disjointed and bizarre, that's because it is.

Nothing that goes on connects to anything else. Weegee is in just about every scene, with raincoat and cigar and camera case, leering and mugging and emoting like mad. In one segment, he's in a bathtub that overflows, dripping water on the lightly clad woman in the room below, a tableau that was surely inspired by his darkroom incident at the Mapleton. He didn't squeeze in any Elastic Lens trickery, but he did get Price to shoot him on a Montmartre street corner, selling prints of his distortions, in a scene that's pretty nearly a commercial for Weegee's recent work. The former Arthur Fellig was, as never before, playing the simultaneous parts of Weegee the Famous, cosmopolitan bon vivant, and European movie star.

Where did this bonkers film originate? At least partly with Weegee himself, and specifically with that sort-of appreciation Bruce Downes included in Weegee's autobiography. "Here's how it all started," Weegee explained in an essay shortly thereafter. "Bruce in his TRIBUTE??????????? mentioned my many pictures of display window manikins (ATTENTION PSYCHOANALYSTS)." Weegee subsequently got to talking about it with Dick Randall, who "decided to do a movie on my strange fascination for MANIKINS." Weegee coaxed an advance out of Randall, and soon enough he was back in Paris. He stayed, as did Sherman Price, at the Hotel La Louisiane, a hotel that attracted artists, jazz musicians, and other creative people.

Ralph Toporoff was living there, too, and that's how he ended up working with Price. "My job," he recalls, "was to pick up the women at the Crazy Horse and bring them to the set" after the early-evening show at the club each night. "And I was in charge of bubble baths. They gave me a manual eggbeater. So I had to arrive with the girls, get 'em into the

In 1962, Weegee finally did get to make a movie where he was the star—a very strange, trashy film called The Imp-Probable Mr. Weegee.

room, they'd get undressed, I'd be madly eggbeating the tub, they'd jump in, Weegee would be doing his bit. And then I had to dry them off, get them back in the car, and bring them back to the Crazy Horse for the midnight show."

It was an almost comically low-rent production. At one point in mid-shoot, everything suddenly halted because the rented Arriflex cameras were seized for nonpayment. There was another pause when Weegee, who'd been riding a deliveryman's tricycle during one scene, fell off and was injured. He spent a week in bed, as Toporoff brought him chicken soup from one of the few good Jewish delis in Paris. Filming staggered to the finish line around the end of the year, and not without difficulty: Weegee had been scheduled to leave for London, and a few scenes remained unfinished. He sold Price his hat and coat (at a shakedown price) so the film could be finished with a body double.

He had good reason to leave on time, though. Where as Sherman Price occupied the absolute basement of the film world, Weegee's next project was with a man who was working at its zenith. Stanley Kubrick, coming off the successes of *Lolita* and *Spartacus*, had begun the meticulous production of his next movie, a black comedy starring Peter Sellers about a Cold War scenario that goes very wrong. Kubrick was rapidly becoming one of the best-regarded filmmakers in the world, but his early life had been spent with a Speed Graphic in his hand rather than a Bolex. He'd worked as a press photographer from the age of seventeen, principally for *Look* magazine, making extraordinarily good photographs that owed some of their look to Weegee's. He even shot a few with infrared film. The two men had crossed paths regularly—"I knew him around," Weegee later explained—and Kubrick had been attentive to Weegee's work and career. As *Dr. Strangelove or: How I Learned to Stop Worrying and Love the Bomb* began filming at Shepperton Studios, Kubrick found himself able to, after a fashion, repay the artistic debt, and he hired Weegee to work on the set, taking still pictures—but not the stills that anyone would have made, which were left to Columbia's in-house photographers. As Weegee explained:

> Stanley says to me, "Look, all the photographers nowadays, they're using available light," and so forth. He doesn't quite like it. He's a nut on sharp pictures. He says, "Weegee, when you make pictures for *Naked City* they were very crude. You had the flash bulb right on the camera. This is ... If you took pictures like this nowadays they'd laugh at you. But I want it like that." So you'll notice I'm the only one that makes flash pictures. I don't have to actually. But I do it to make Stanley happy.

The production notes do not list Weegee as a set photographer, but there's a £750 fee in the records for an unnamed "technical advisor," and that's almost surely Weegee. He loved the experience: staying at the Mapleton again, he had a luxury car taking him to and from Shepperton every day and free rein on the set. It was supposed to be a one-month residency, but given Kubrick's slow and madly obsessive work habits and an A-lister's budget it was extended to three.

The pictures turned out to be superb. They're the last truly great body of work Weegee made in his life, a real return to strength. They had that intense caught-in-action strangeness, the otherworldly is-this-real quality that suffused his best nighttime New York photos. And because the principal film set on which he was working was Kubrick's War Room, the backgrounds are nearly black, tailor-made for him. He documented Kubrick in action from every angle: as the director was framing shots, climbing on stepladders, lying on his back with a movie camera in hand, and, in one case, peering through a tiny peephole in a curtain on the set. Once again, the voyeur photographed the watcher—and was there ever a more acutely focused watcher than Stanley Kubrick?

On the set of Stanley Kubrick's Dr. Strangelove, *Weegee made his last great set of photographs, documenting the director and Peter Sellers at work and the climactic pie-fight scene in the War Room that was dropped from the film's final cut.*

Inadvertently, he also showed the world a part of the film that most of us cannot otherwise see. *Dr. Strangelove* was meant to end with an enormous slapstick pie fight in the War Room, and the scene was filmed as Weegee snapped away, his Rolleiflex sealed in a case built for underwater photography. Everyone, including the photographer, ended up covered in custard. Kubrick later decided that it was too glib a finale for a story about nuclear annihilation, and he rewrote and reshot the ending. The unused scene went into the vaults,* and only from Weegee's pictures can we get a sense of how it looked.

Peter Sellers had three roles in the picture, and the scenes in which he played Dr. Strangelove were scheduled toward the end of principal filming. By the time they came around, Sellers had been watching Weegee at work for weeks. He found him fascinating, as anyone obsessed with accents and eccentricities would, and he not only observed Weegee but absorbed him. A few months later, on Steve Allen's TV show, Allen asked Sellers about Strangelove's peculiar high-pitched German-accented English, and Sellers told him where the accent came from.

> I was stuck, you see, because I didn't want to do sort of a normal English broken-German-accent thing. So on the set was a little photographer from New York, a very cute little fellow called Weegee—you must've heard of him. And he had a little voice, like this, used to [and here Sellers steps into an uncanny impression of Weegee's voice] walk around the set talking like this most of the time. He'd say, *"I'm looking for a girl with a beautiful body and a sick mind!"*
>
> And I got an idea, I was really stuck for this . . . I put a German accent on top of that, and I suddenly got [in Strangelove's voice] *dis thing, you know, where—going up here and* . . . so I got him into Dr. Strangelove. So really it's Weegee. I don't know if he knows it.

Of all the Zelig moments in Weegee's latter years, this has to be the most extraordinary: that his very voice is infused into one of the great

---

* Often said to have been destroyed, the pie-fight footage does exist. It was shown in public once, in 1999, at the National Film Theatre in London.

tour-de-force performances ever put on-screen. Sellers even liked Weegee enough to interview him (judging by a couple of lines in the conversation, it was intended to air on the BBC) around the time filming ended. Sellers was absolutely neutral and laconic, hanging back to let Weegee rush in and fill the pauses. Weegee chattered on about knowing Kubrick as a youngster and told yarns about his recent work at the nudist camp. "Where do you put your filters?" deadpanned Sellers in response. "I don't use filters!" Weegee cheerily replied, adding that his fellow nudists had granted him special dispensation to carry a little camera case, but that he used it only for his cigars.

Weegee continued to work in London for a few months after *Dr. Strangelove* wrapped, chasing a deal with Granada Television that fell apart. "Very discouraging as I had banked so much on this," he told Wilma. "They tried hard but at the last moment a sponsor withdrew. So I have give[n] them till the end of this week, then I take my films back from them. Meanwhile my TECHNIQUE is at its peak. All technical PROBLEMS have been solved except the problem of money, as I have reached the rock bottom." He also (with a writer named Gerry Speck) produced a second how-to book, a near clone of the one he'd done five years earlier. Published by the British firm Ward, Lock & Company, it was titled *Weegee's Creative Photography*. He continued to keep after the local photo editors, selling still more one-off versions of the here's-Weegee-with-a-wacky-new-distortion-technique story: to the *Sunday Telegraph*, the *South Wales Echo*, the Edinburgh *Evening News and Dispatch*, a few newspapers and magazines on the Continent. The European press tended to buy the celebrity caricatures, particularly those of the Cold War's leaders. Charles de Gaulle got an exaggerated nose; Nikita Khrushchev, a big Conehead noggin; Konrad Adenauer, a dour, turned-down frown; Jack Kennedy, a toothy grin.

Before he left Britain, he fell in with a bit of Cold War activity himself. The USSR in the early sixties was beginning to expand its efforts to sell consumer goods in the West, and two Britons, Fanny James and her nephew, Rafael Hyams, set up an importing company called Technical and Optical Equipment (Ltd.) to bring in Russian clothing and electronics. Before long, they began to look at the Soviet cameras made by Zenit, which could hold their own against many German and Japanese products.

In September 1963, Weegee met up with Fanny James—he called her "Auntie"—and they struck a deal that would cover his London expenses while he did some promotion for her company. A few days later, he appeared at a Russian camera sales event at the curiously named Owen Owen department store in Coventry, and did an interview about Russian cameras on BBC Radio. He also photographed the bronze equestrian statue of Lady Godiva that stands in the center of Coventry, and applied the Elastic Lens to stretch her horse out into a racing Thoroughbred. The Coventry *Express*, charmed by the unusual treatment of a familiar scene, put it on the front page, along with a bit of Weegee's boasting ("a cameraman who can command £2,000 a picture") and a plug ("he took it with a Zenit camera during his visit to Coventry this week to promote Russian Camera Week"). Russian Camera Week must have been a success because, less than a month later—in what was the most audacious of his "I'll go anywhere for a freebie" moves—Weegee joined Auntie, Rafael Hyams, and their T.O.E. colleague Charles Saunders on a trip to Moscow. He invited Wilma, but she didn't go.

Weegee was not political enough a creature to be unnerved by the surveillance state he saw there. In fact, he seems barely to have noticed it, although he appreciated the pretty young interpreter-and-monitor women assigned to the group. A Russian camera club invited him to deliver his slide lecture, which, owing to the nudes and abstractions that were unacceptable in the Socialist Realism canon, caused a mild stir. He toured the camera factory, which he found impressive; stayed in the overseas-currency-accepting Ukrainia Hotel on Auntie's bill; and made a side trip to Leningrad, where he visited the Hermitage and took in (and photographed) a concert at the Philharmonia. When asked about the trip on his return, he straight-facedly told an interviewer that he'd found Moscow less oppressive than Paris, where the elevators were constantly breaking down and "the storekeepers are very mercenary and shortchange artists." The only things he found wanting in the USSR were the monotonous food ("every menu is the same in every hotel") and the lack of nightclubs.

The junket came to an end in the early fall, and a Hong Kong follow-up did not pan out. By the end of October, he was back in London, and soon after that in New York, essentially for good. And if his return to New York in the early 1950s had been a mild culture shock, he was now, and increasingly, in a city not his own. Even more swaths of the Lower East Side had been demolished for housing projects, and quasi-luxury high-rises were going up everywhere. "In the new apartment houses they build on the East Side," he half-joked, "a hundred and ninety-nine dollars a month, you get a clothes closet to live in. And if a neighbor is gonna murder his wife, you can hear." Even as the city got more expensive, its structure was breaking down, its subway system falling apart, its crime rate spiking after three decades' decline. There were few if any seventeen-dollar-a-month walk-ups to be had, and he was less physically robust than he had been. His agency, Photo-Representatives, had gone out of business after Erika Stone married and had children and cut back on her work. He once suggested that there was so much housing being built for the underprivileged that the city was going to have to start importing poor people to fill it up. He had had a mixed relationship with the tenements, calling them "lousy" but also arguing that the cold-water flat had been, in its way, a great invention. The Village, he said, "was all right until NYU came in. It's a lawyer factory. Worst influence in the world," he told one interviewer. "You know what I'd like to do? Take NYU out to Yucca Flats [sic] and use it as a target for H-bombs." And, he admitted, "I feel out of place . . . I belong to a different age."

His lifeline was once again Wilma Wilcox, whose diligence and steadiness in her own career had allowed her to accumulate a nest egg. She had done work for a number of social service agencies over the years, including the Salvation Army and the pioneering Freudian analyst Theodor Reik's clinic. Now she had a pension coming her way, and by 1964, she had accumulated enough of a down payment to buy a brownstone, at 451 West Forty-Seventh Street, in the neighborhood known as Hell's Kitchen. It was a little battered, hardly luxurious, but it was a big, solidly built house, and Weegee and his boxes and heaps of camera equipment and photographs settled into a room on the ground floor, with a darkroom one flight up. Once they'd moved in, Wilma continued a project she'd begun years before, sorting and indexing his work. For the first time in years, he had a phone number, listed in the White Pages not under Fellig but under Weegee. He and Wilcox even came up with a wry name for the familiar images, such as "The Critic" and "Their First Murder," that were most often republished: the "Forty Famous Pictures." Wilma tried to get him to move beyond those, to talk up other photos and try to make something of them, without success.

Each weekend that summer, the two headed out to photograph the New York World's Fair in Flushing Meadows, where he made good negatives and clever distortions as she lugged the tripod and a picnic basket. He photographed the fountains and the fairgoers, Wilma later said, "showing the effects that he had worked out in his mind, and also in his techniques, to express what he could see imaginatively." He was still secretive about his custom optics, even after all this time, and took steps toward discretion as he worked. "People were as curious as they could be, of course," Wilma recalled, "and he carefully covered things over." When making the straight pictures, though, he was still bound up in his own jokes. On a script he had prepared for a series of world's fair images, he included the following setup: "Pose a cop running to patrol car pointing upward at car on roller coaster. Caption: 'Quick, follow that car.'" As he had on the *Sleeping City* tour—remember the drunk he photographed in St. Louis—and in too much of *Naked Hollywood*, he was falling back into the slack habit of making gag pictures to fulfill punch lines; they would never stand on their own. But other pictures he made at the fair were better (including some kaleidoscope pictures), and the set was distributed nationally via United Press International, the descendant of the old Acme service.

Other, odd bits of business came his way in these years. One company made a line of naughty greeting cards with a female distortion photo on the front of each and a jokey caption within ("Hope you'll soon be your old self again! Get well soon!"). Weegee tried to get Allan David to go in on a deal to turn his distortions into trippy posters for dorm rooms, but it didn't come together. He also tried to make his way to Tokyo, to tool around the camera business in Japan as he had in Moscow, but no sponsor presented itself. He created a plan in partnership with a company called Phototechnics, Inc., to commercialize his distortion methods, with an eye toward making optical toys and producing caricature books. None of it worked out.

Occasionally, he'd help out an acquaintance with glossy headshots. In May 1966, Ruth Buzzi, then a young comic actress working in New

At Expo 58, in Belgium, Weegee made pictures, ate at the Israeli pavilion, and appeared in a film called Holiday in Brussels.

York theater, met him via letter, then came by for a portrait session. "We talked about the type of roles I wanted to play," Buzzi remembers, "and he had some great suggestions. One of my favorite characters was Agnes Gooch, from *Auntie Mame*. I had played that role in college, and I deliberately made myself as dorky-looking as possible. I pulled my hair back into a bun on the back of my head to emphasize my long chin. I put a hairnet on and split my bangs into side-waves to further lengthen my already horse-long countenance. I got all dressed up like Agnes Gooch—and Weegee suggested I pose seated in a garbage bin labeled KEEP OUR CITY CLEAN. The picture was great." So great, in fact, that when she mailed it to the producer George Schlatter, who was casting his new show, *Laugh-In*, he burst out laughing, flew her to California for an audition, and hired her that day, establishing her TV career.

During this period—perhaps because his age was making it more difficult for him to get around—Weegee also began to experiment with still photographs of the television screen and made a six-minute montage film out of them, alternating between new pictures and classics from his back catalogue, called *The Idiot Box*. It includes distortions, too, performed in live action: he slowly moves his warping plastic lens over the face of the *Mona Lisa*, for example, causing her smile to purse and her temples to throb (and then follows it up with a shot of a Bayer aspirin bottle). The three-breasted ladies of *Naked Hollywood* also reappear. The plotless film, intended as a spoof of TV-commercial tropes, proceeds according to some logic that is ungraspable by any mind not Weegee's own. But it is curiously soothing to watch.

Often, when an artist can't find the thread anymore, he decides to go back to his roots—to make an album like the ones he'd listened to as a kid, or a short 8-millimeter movie with a handheld camera the way he did back in art school. Weegee, despite his belief in the manipulated photos he was making, knew deep down what people wanted from him: murders and fires and crashes, shot on the fly in the middle of the night. Could he possibly give those another try? Never mind that the almost romantic view of murder in the thirties (gangsters, molls, "honor killings") was being replaced with a bleaker view of street crime (old ladies slugged for their grocery money by lawless teenagers); or that the newspapers used staff photographers and had their own radio cars now; or that the press had become more professionalized and sophisticated; or that the *Daily Mirror* had shut down and three of the remaining six dailies (the *Journal-American*, the *Herald Tribune*, and the *World-Telegram and Sun*) were hanging on by a thread.* Spot-news night crawling had worked once;

---

* Those three all closed in the spring of 1966, merging to form a Frankenstein's newspaper called the *World Journal Tribune*. Known (owing to its acronym) as the Widget, it lasted eight months.

maybe it could again. In the mid-1960s, he approached a friend at the *Post* who was doing night work and arranged to ride along. It was audacious—and unsustainable. The long nights were impossible for a frail old man to handle. It was, Wilcox said later, "just too much, just too strenuous to do anymore." The idea fizzled, like so many others had.

And if reaching back to his glory days of the thirties were not enough, he attempted, in one outlandish scheme, to go all the way back to his childhood. The details come to us through a man named Kingdon Lane, a Manhattan radio-and-TV dealer who had a sideline as a photographer. (The two men had known each other for years, and had often photographed the circus side by side.) In a story that beggars belief—although the photography curator Miles Barth heard it from Lane himself, who had no reason to make it up—Weegee, in his last years, briefly attempted to re-create his very first success with Hypo the pony. This time, the hired animal was, even more implausibly, stabled behind Lane's electronics store on a commercial strip of Madison Avenue near Eighty-Seventh Street. If a lot of Weegee's recent choices had been half-baked (the nudie movies, the attempt to start shooting at night again), this has to have been the most questionable. It probably doesn't need to be said that Hypo's latter-day successor didn't work out any better than Hypo had. The floor of Kingdon Lane's shop survived the brief experience.*

Weegee would still go out, by day or night, when the mood struck him: to Washington Square, especially, where he was just another character you'd spot on a warm day. The increasing openness and pleasure-seeking of the Village, as the sixties got under way, were curiously well matched to his libertinism, and his impressionistic and distorted films fit in with the avant-garde cinema that was being made then. (His "subconscious camera" produced results that were a lot like psychedelia.) He began to give talks and show films at the Bridge Theater, on St. Marks Place, and at the Film-Makers' Cinematheque, an underground cinema (in both senses, because it was in the basement) on West Forty-First Street. At one show in 1966 at the Cinematheque, he projected swirly color slides onto the body of a writhing go-go dancer, to roaring applause.

---

* Barth recalled that the pony may have been stabled in the shop's storeroom. A follow-up conversation with Kingdon Lane's son Barry established that the shop had no back room, and that he was somewhat skeptical about this tale. It does, however, have the ring of something Weegee might try. *Caveat lector.*

(He took color photos of the event, of course, and sold them to a magazine soon thereafter.) He made some noise about patenting the projection device, which he called the Color Box, though little came of that plan. And the artist Yayoi Kusama's "Body-Festival," at which the eccentric Japanese artist painted colorful dots all over several models' bare skin, was made for him, both because it was photographically and sociologically interesting and because lithe young women were taking their clothes off.

Kusama and Weegee came from different artistic planets, and probably could not have communicated in any meaningful way. There was another counterculture star with whom Weegee might've solidly connected, though, and that was Andy Warhol. Both were outsiders, children of immigrants who'd grown up far from power and wealth. Both made their work out of base material, turning car crashes and race riots into the stuff of museum exhibitions. Both of them loved being around celebrities; both had started in commerce and moved out on a limb to make art that didn't look like art; both were unashamed to say they wanted to make money and get famous. And at the end of February 1967, they found themselves in the same room.

The event was a weeklong multimedia festival at the Cinematheque called "Caterpillar Changes," at which both Warhol and Weegee films (among many others) were being screened.* The Velvet Underground, their first album due out the next month, played onstage. Weegee was a bit of an anomaly in that scene, which was very youthful—another program from the Cinematheque around this time was made up of "mystik luv films"—but he was eager to meet Warhol. Warhol was an admirer, too. There are references in his diaries, some years later, to paging through a book of Weegee's photos for research, calling them, in his perpetual deadpan, "so great."

It didn't go well. Weegee, always excitable and perpetually a little awkward when he wasn't on the job, was no match for Warhol's sunglassed detachment. "Warhol snubbed him," explains the photographer Ira Richer, who met Weegee around that time and later became friends with Wilma Wilcox. "I don't think Weegee was the type to be hurtful to people,

---

* The two men had come close to crossing paths before. An ad for the Film-Makers' Cinematheque appearing in the *Village Voice* of April 7, 1966, lists screenings of Warhol's *My Hustler* followed by three Weegee films later in the week.

Two of a kind: Warhol and Weegee. They should have had a lot to talk about, but their meeting did not go well.

and Warhol, who was a master of cliques, was probably unrelatable to him at that time. It was another artist who was getting a lot of attention, and personally, not artistically, Warhol could not give him credit." One suspects that Warhol gave his customary flat "hi," posed for a picture, and left it at that. "It was a hurtful meeting," Richer says, adding that, on Wilma's behalf later on, "I took it in an almost morally indignant way."

It was one of two public embarrassments that spring. A few weeks after the Warhol meet-up, Weegee was scheduled to show *Weegee's New York, The Idiot Box,* and three other films that he'd put together from new and old footage. The screening was to be held at the Gallery of Modern Art, a boutique museum funded by the eccentric supermarket heir Huntington Hartford.* It was an upstart institution, headquartered in an outré marble building on Columbus Circle, and it prided itself on providing both an institutional challenge and a public tweak to the Museum of Modern Art, down to its similar name. From April 11 to 16, 1967, Weegee's pictures would hang in the exhibition spaces and his films would roll in the museum's theater, marking his fiftieth year as a photographer. (More or less accurately, if you start with Hypo the pony.) He even made a new distortion photo for the handbill, showing the twelve-story museum building ballooned out of shape and emblazoned with a giant CREDIT PHOTO BY WEEGEE THE FAMOUS stamp. Mailings went out; Weegee was to appear at all twelve film screenings. The opening went fine. The next day did not.

The problem, apparently, was the Coney Island sequence in *Weegee's New York*. There were just a few too many shots of beachgoers' backsides and amorous couples for one deputy curator at the gallery. (Weegee referred to him only as "the Frenchman," and nobody recorded his name.) The unnamed Frenchman suggested cuts, and Weegee countered with the fully reasonable argument that the film had been screening without incident for nearly two decades. The discussion got heated, and Weegee grabbed his reels and left the museum in a huff. A few hours later, he was back with a station wagon, taking his pictures off the walls. The museum's film curator, Raymond Rohauer, had been away when the argument escalated, and he came back to find his exhibit gone. He tried to talk Weegee back into the fold, without success. The 1922 film *Salomé*, which was also screening that week, was run in place of the Weegee program. "Salami, a broad with her head on a tray," Weegee called it.

In his outrage, he didn't have much recourse. He couldn't reschedule the anniversary program at another museum, because their lineups had been booked months ahead. Instead, he squeezed in a one-night screening that Sunday at the Bleecker Street Cinema, the downtown art house, at 1:45 in the morning. It wasn't nothing, but it constituted a lot less of an anniversary celebration than Weegee had planned.

His ebullience and enthusiasm were beginning to wane. When the photographer Alfred Gescheidt ran into him at a photo show at the New

---

* Hartford, as a dilettante playboy trying on careers in the 1940s, had coincidentally done a brief turn as a reporter for *PM*.

York Coliseum, his old friend looked almost haunted. "Weegee told me that it was just a matter of time for his career to end," Gescheidt wrote, recalling the scene. "As we were standing by an escalator (it was symbolically descending), Weegee looked at me with his large, sad, hooded eyes and said, *Alfred, you must carry on. My shooting days are almost over.*" Gescheidt couldn't tell whether it was just a put-on or a genuinely dark mood; it may have been both. Stettner noticed the same thing in these final years—that Weegee's previously endless well of good humor seemed to be drying up. He'd spent thirty years playing Weegee the Famous, and now, when he needed to lean on that fame most, it was slipping away from him. He had begun to grasp that he had been eaten alive by his own image. "My real name is Arthur Fellig. But I don't even recognize it when I see it. I created this monster, Weegee, and I can't get rid of it," he told an interviewer in 1965. "It's like Dr. Jekyll and Mr. Hyde, and I can't go back to my real identity."

The future he had glimpsed when he visited Alfred Stieglitz back in 1944 was now taking shape in his own life. Still, he was trying to keep up, trying to get out and do some work. When the Chinese New Year came around in early 1967, his friend George Gilbert bumped into him on a cold day in Chinatown as the traditional dragon costumes were paraded through the streets. Weegee was carrying a 16-millimeter Bolex camera and a heavy bag of equipment. *What are you shooting?* Gilbert asked. "The firecrackers and the kids," Weegee replied. "I'm getting it all." Gilbert and his friends headed off to a warm Chinese restaurant; Weegee went back to work.

He began spending more and more time in the darkroom, making piles of distortions and kaleidoscope prints from his old negatives. Next to the enlarger, an enormous bowl slowly filled to the brim with cigar ashes. As Weegee got frailer, he would work there for a couple of hours at a time, taking long breaks during which he'd exit to lie down and rest. He planned another book, a more serious one, and approached his old friend and former Acme editor Harold Blumenfeld, whose wife was a writer, with an idea that they might collaborate. He also assembled a maquette for another photo collection, this one all pictures of Greenwich Village, in a format similar to that of *Weegee's People*. In March 1968, he summoned the energy to give his lecture at the School of Visual Arts, where he was presented with an increasingly rare level of

In the last summer of Weegee's life, the photographer Syeus Mottel met him in Washington Square, then took him to dinner at Bernstein-on-Essex-Street, a kosher Chinese restaurant. Weegee reciprocated by taking him to a nudie movie that night.

respect, as part of "a continuing series of illustrated lectures on photography by the most important and influential people in the world."

A few months later, on a warm day in Washington Square, the young photographer and theater director Syeus Mottel spotted Weegee sitting alone on a bench. When Mottel asked him if he had advice for a budding photojournalist, he answered, not without bitterness, "Yeah. Sharp elbows." Mottel's pretty young girlfriend was with him, and he quietly asked her to chat up Weegee while Mottel made some portraits from a distance with a telephoto lens. She charmed Weegee enough that he accepted an invitation to dinner, proposing that they go to Bernstein-on-Essex-Street, a kosher Chinese restaurant. He was frail: Mottel was parked three blocks from Washington Square and noticed how slowly Weegee made the walk to the car, and that his trousers hung slack from his suspenders. They drove to Bernstein, where the owner spotted Weegee and treated him, Mottel remembered, "like he was the king." After dinner, Weegee extended an invitation to the couple to join him at the Village Cinema, on "free passes earned by reputation—for a badly made nudie film."

A young photographer named Bill Jay visited him in mid-1968, and he found it a sobering experience. Jay was beginning a four-decade project in which he documented hundreds of photographers in their own environments, and when he arrived to visit Weegee at the house on West Forty-Seventh Street, he was dismayed by what he saw. Weegee was disconsolate, his arms thin, his room cluttered with beat-up photographic gear and piles of pictures. "A forgotten old man with only his life's work for company" is what Jay later recalled seeing. "Take all my prints," Weegee told him glumly. "No one knows I'm still alive." It was an eerie re-enactment of the Stieglitz scene, but this time with Weegee as the man sitting on the bed, half-forgotten, in despair.

That last June, Weegee did summon the energy to put up a show, but it was far from MoMA, or the Gallery of Modern Art, or any of the start-up galleries that were beginning to appear in the old factory buildings south of Houston Street. The best venue he could wangle was a dumpy sandwich shop on West Third Street in Greenwich Village called Subs. A small display ad in the *Village Voice* sold it hard, touting a show BANNED BY THE GALLERY OF MODERN ART. The sign in the shop read WEEGEE IS HERE! But instead of standing in a museum auditorium, he was at a café table, next to five of the Forty Famous Pictures and a dozen of his best distortions, all mounted on a single crowded panel. It looked homemade, a bit like his first show at the Photo League, but smaller in every way.

Yet he gave it the old college try, running the movies and delivering his slide lectures from Friday through Sunday. Mellon Tytell, a young Village artist who'd recently met and befriended Weegee, recalled a few years later that the audience was "crude and uninformed." Didn't matter: "Weegee was all there for them. For three nights he performed, parading his pictures, documenting them with anecdotes with a gusto reminiscent of W. C. Fields. Despite the raunchiness of the circumstances, the Cokes and ham heroes, Weegee gave himself passionately to his audience, always provoking a response." Tytell found, in what could have been a humiliation, a small triumph. "He was ending his career in a cheap, dingy eating place, but he was concerned both with his work and the way in which it affected his audience. I took it as a supreme testimony to his dedication as an artist."

He had one or two sales left in him, but the phone was not often ringing. In August 1968, *New York* magazine, just five months into its lifespan, bought and ran a set of four caricatures of New York City's mayor, and they were so ideally suited that the editors affixed the headline "The Distortion of John Lindsay" to the story itself. In October, *See*, a small-ish men's magazine, ran a set of caricatures related to the forthcoming presidential election. "I take pictures with my third eye," Weegee told the editors, "the inner eye that sees what lies beneath the surface of the subject. What some call a pictorial distortion may, in truth, be the reality. And what we call reality may be a distortion of the truth." That last sentence, a concise justification of the last half of his career, were his final words in print.

Wilcox, like Syeus Mottel, had seen Weegee's step slowing down significantly in these months. Bill Jay, on his visit with Weegee, had noticed something else: that his speech was often incoherent. Weegee's handwriting, which had always been a loose scrawl, began to crisscross itself, making less and less sense. Late that fall he went into Park West Hospital, a private medical facility on West Seventy-Sixth Street that, ironically enough, had once been a place known for treating celebrities but was now itself headed into financial distress. It turned out that the weight loss and the speech problems were not just manifestations of age and diabetes but symptoms of a brain tumor. Weegee declined quickly, and the day after Christmas 1968 he was gone. He was sixty-nine years old and had outlived six of the nine newspapers that had bought his daily work. Of the survivors, the *Daily News* didn't run an obituary, but the *Post* did, and Weegee, for the first time in many years, managed to claim a sixth of a page in the *New York Times*.*

Wilma Wilcox took it hard. "She loved him very deeply," recalls her niece, Ellen Newberg, "and she had a horrible year." (Her mentor, Theodor Reik, died some months after Weegee did.) Weegee's family did not demand a Jewish burial, and she had his remains cremated. Wilcox herself ended up in the hospital for a long stretch around this time, owing to a terrible infection in her ankle, and when she held Weegee's memorial service, her leg in a cast, she could barely get there. When Newberg

---

* The *Times* obituary refers to him as "Arthur H. Fellig," using a spurious middle initial that first started to appear around this time and continues to follow Weegee around today. There is no trace of a middle name in Weegee's official paperwork, from birth record to bankbooks to Social Security card, and he never appears to have used it himself.

visited the following June, six months after Weegee's death, Wilcox was only then getting back on her feet.

She came home afterward to thousands of prints and an inchoate sense of their worth not as salable goods but as an artist's body of work. "A pure, simple idea," her friend Ira Richer recalls. "Disarming. And when he died, she was a friend to his legacy." Newberg remembers that when she visited Wilcox, Weegee's prints were literally ankle-deep in one large room. Wilcox continued her work of sorting and organizing that immense pile, and a year or so later, a tiny, intense woman came knocking.

Diane Arbus was the most galvanizing person in photography in the late sixties, at the forefront of a generation that valued photos with punch on the surface and emotional complexities and subtleties within. She, like Weegee, gravitated toward people at the edge of society. She was a far subtler printer than he, and her photos are often more composed and settled—after all, she wasn't jostling with five other newsmen behind a police wagon, trying to get the right angle. But she, too, loved to photograph nudists, circus acts, urban weirdos, always craving their outsiderness. Now she had been brought in by the Museum of Modern Art's John Szarkowski to help assemble a show devoted to press photography, sponsored by the *Daily News*. She wanted to go through every picture Wilma had.

Arbus spent three eight-hour days at Wilcox's brownstone, sorting and looking and absorbing. "The best thing this past week was the discovery of ALL Weegee's work," she wrote her ex-husband, Allan, around the end of October 1970. Wilcox, she said, "is a social worker, cultivated, midwestern, sterling, thoroughly his opposite ... We went through about 8000 prints of which I chose 383, some for the news show, some for a Weegee show which seems inevitable to me. He was SO good when he was good. Extraordinary!" (Arbus did add, "when he was bad he was pretty terrible." Still, she appreciated some of the distortions and even the girlie photos.) "Such wild dynamics make everybody [else] look like an academician. People pushing, shoving, screaming, bits of extraneous events thrust into the main one," a description that sounds a lot like "Their First Murder." Wilcox later said that Arbus's enthusiasm—she had told Wilma she was amazed by the scope of Weegee's work—"gave me a sense of confidence that my own feeling was accurate: That here was the work of a man who was much more than a newspaper photographer or a recorder of murders."

Was he an artist or an artisan? By the standards applied in his time, probably the latter, with pretensions to the former. But by our measure, there's no question. In the fifty years since Weegee's death, the sources of great art have opened up, allowing it to come from everywhere. Things that were completely disposable, such as comic books, are now understood to be not only commercial product but capable of conveying great emotion and sophistication. *Action Comics* No. 1 does not look like a van Gogh, but it acts on twenty-first-century viewers the way a van Gogh does, with evocative visual and textual power. The same is true of space-alien movies, of hip-hop DJ remixes, of Andy Warhol's party Polaroids. Things that seemed slight when they were made do not always turn out that way in the long run, when thinking people who sweat the details are the ones making them. Weegee was one of those people, and he did just that.

Judith Malina, who knew him well and saw him regularly during his Greenwich Village phase, was undoubtedly an artist and undoubtedly an activist. Asked whether Weegee was either of those things, she paused to think for a minute before answering. "He is, for most of us, that phenomenon of the artist and the anti-artist," she said. "And there are just a few people like that—I know a couple of them. And they're a very special kind of people.

"He was an activist who didn't want to be related to the rhetoric of activism," she continued, warming to the subject. "He hated the rhetoric—when I said, 'Look, you're not a revolutionary, and I'm a revolutionary!' he'd say, 'I don't know what you're talking about.' But he knew perfectly well what I was saying. It was a rejection of the rhetoric. He was very stuck on his image of being a man of the people, and he *was* a man of the people. He was very close to revolutionary ideals, and he could show it to us, but he didn't like us to talk about it." What made him an artist? "He wanted to see the soul of the person. He wanted to see the essence of the person." She paused, and smiled. "And he *certainly* wanted to see the tits of the person."

The exhibition Arbus worked on opened in January 1973, and it gained extra attention because she'd taken her own life during its preparation. Although there were dozens of photographs in the show, quite a few of their makers had already slipped into anonymity. Weegee had not and was beginning to become the avatar for them all, a role that he continues to occupy. One of his pictures in which we see another news photographer at work—we get to watch a professional watcher this time—became the cover of the exhibition catalogue.

Not quite five years later, in the fall of 1977, came the International Center of Photography's first Weegee retrospective, and an accompanying book put together by Louis Stettner. Around the same time, Da Capo, a reprint house, reissued most of Weegee's own books in inexpensive soft-cover editions. A small group that included Stettner, Wilcox, and Sid Kaplan soon entered into a deal to make a portfolio of fine-art prints from Weegee's negatives, and although the business part of that deal disintegrated, the photographs themselves got still more attention. The young group of artists loosely known later on as the Pictures Generation, coming of age in this era, were surely looking at them. These men and women not only embraced the gray area between true and factual, where Weegee often worked; they sometimes made art that was specifically about it, and incorporated their own faces and bodies into the image. It is not a huge leap from Weegee's posing-as-a-criminal *Life* story to Cindy Sherman's *Untitled Film Stills*, or from some of his put-together distortions to Laurie Simmons's *Walking Gun*.

Wilcox continued to work as a Quaker missionary, traveling to Kenyan villages and the West Bank to teach and support local cultures, and she took many (quite good) pictures of her own. On the side, she continued to lend Weegee's prints for exhibition, sell some of the mountains of duplicates to collectors, and generally coax Weegee back into public view wherever she could. In 1989, she and Da Capo published *The Village*, the book for which Weegee had assembled a mock-up in his last years, and it is an underrated, superb document. She was a generous gatekeeper, and she is the silent hero of Weegee's story. Had she not been there in his last years, it is entirely likely that the detritus of his life, including the enormous number of pictures he'd retained, would have gone into a Dumpster. At her death in 1993, it all went, by prior arrangement, to the International Center of Photography, which today holds it in about five hundred big gray archival boxes kept cool and dry. It is far and away the biggest single collection the center has: roughly nineteen thousand prints and six thousand negatives, plus reels of film, manu-scripts, tear sheets, and ephemera. That last category includes a pile of press badges (for the circus, the New York World's Fair, the Met-ropolitan Opera), one well-used Speed Graphic camera, and a battered fedora.

For a while, ICP had one other artifact. As the collection was trans-ferred over from Wilcox's brownstone and catalogued after her death, a small cardboard box surfaced. It had WEEGEE written on the lid. Miles Barth, then ICP's chief curator, thought it might contain a camera lens and opened it to discover something quite different. Wilma had never dispersed Weegee's ashes, and there he was, the man himself. A couple of members of ICP's staff grew uneasy about having his remains on the premises, and after some discussion they decided it was time for him to go. In 1998, just shy of thirty years after his death, Weegee finally left his beloved New York City for good, scattered at sea. No pictures were taken.

NOTES

The principal source for this book was the Weegee collection bequeathed by Wilma Wilcox to the International Center of Photography, now stored at Mana Contemporary, an arts center in Jersey City, New Jersey. I looked at most of Weegee's work for New York City newspapers on microfilm at the New York Public Library's Stephen A. Schwarzman Building on Forty-Second Street. I also drew heavily on the digital archives of the *New York Times*, the *Herald Tribune*, and many other papers on the ProQuest Historical Newspapers service; and Tom Tryniski's eccentric, peerless New York State newspaper-digitizing site, fultonhistory.com.

Weegee by Weegee (Ziff-Davis, 1961; republished in 2013 by Devault-Graves, with new annotations, under the title *Weegee: The Autobiography*) is a valuable, entertaining, hugely problematic source. It contains the only extensive record of Weegee's early life, and includes a number of anecdotes about his adulthood that are exaggerated or, in a couple of cases, fabricated. What is striking, however, is not its fakery but its fairly high level of accuracy: many of its fanciful-seeming stories turn out, when checked, to be built on (at least mostly) solid ground. Like Weegee's photographs, it is usually truthful if occasionally less than factual. I have tried to be simultaneously skeptical and generous about its contents, verifying many stories through alternative sources, accepting a few on faith, treating others as questionable, and dismissing some outright.

At ICP, the multiple manuscript drafts and query sheets relating to the production of *Weegee by Weegee* are inconsistently labeled. Some have two different sets of page numbers; others are missing pages. Many are crumpled, smudged, or torn. As a result, I found it impossible to attach meaningful pagination to these documents, and they are cited in the following notes simply as "*WBW* MS" and "*WBW* N&Q." Future scholars seeking individual quotations: Please forgive me. You will at least be entertained as you work your way through every page.

Two dozen or so early photographs mentioned here appeared uncredited in the New York papers, and I have been able, through somewhat unusual means, to attribute them to Weegee for the first time in eight decades. In March 1937, he photographed his apartment on Centre Market Place, including the tear sheets he had tacked to the wall. After enlarging the apartment photos, I was able to find most of the clippings through a very long, often interesting crawl through the New York dailies of the mid- to late 1930s. (I proceeded from the belief, which I think is sound, that Weegee didn't post anyone else's work on his wall.) That slow process also brought to light many previously unknown photos bearing Fellig credits. Microfilm, I can say with authority, is both invaluable and exhausting.

Unless otherwise indicated, most images by or of Weegee mentioned in the text refer to photographs in ICP's archive. They may be searched by title and keyword at icp.org, and I encourage the reader to do so.

ABBREVIATIONS

BHS	Interview on *The Ben Hecht Show*. Broadcast on WABC-TV, October 2, 1958.
FPTH	*Famous Photographers Tell How*. Spoken-word LP. Candid Recordings, 1958.
ICP	International Center of Photography, New York, NY.
LJN	Interview with Long John Nebel. Broadcast on WOR Radio, April 1964. W. Eugene Smith Archive Loft Recordings. Center for Creative Photography, University of Arizona. Reel 774, CDs 1–5.
MMM	Interview on *Mary Margaret McBride*. Broadcast on WEAF (AM 660), July 11, 1945. Motion Picture, Broadcasting and Recorded Sound Division, Recorded Sound Research Center of the Library of Congress, Washington, D.C.
NC	Weegee. *Naked City*. Essential Books, 1945.
NH	Weegee. *Naked Hollywood*. Pellegrini & Cudahy, 1953. Unpaginated; divided into four acts.
WBW	*Weegee by Weegee*. Ziff-Davis, 1961.
WBW MS	Manuscript drafts for *Weegee by Weegee*. ICP collection.
WBW N&Q	A loose group of documents, some headed "Notes and Questions," containing editor's queries on manuscript for *Weegee by Weegee* and Weegee's responses. ICP collection.
WP	Weegee. *Weegee's People*. Essential Books, 1946. Unpaginated.
WW	Barth, Miles. *Weegee's World*. Bulfinch/Little, Brown, 1997.
WWMM	Wilma Wilcox interview with Murray Martin for the Side Gallery, Newcastle upon Tyne, United Kingdom, February 1983.

INTRODUCTION

Note: Details of Weegee's life that appear in the introduction briefly and then are expanded upon in the body of the book will be cited in later chapters.

xiii **"In 1925":** Weegee, with biographical note appended by Peter Martin, "Weegee's Wonderful Women," *Glamour Photography*, Summer 1955, pp. 16–37.

xiv **"I wanted to go out and make a lot of money":** *WBW* MS.

xiv **Judith Malina remembered:** Author interview, July 2014.

xiv **"He rather likes to pass himself off":** John P. Lewis, "Rave Notice," *PM*, July 18, 1945.

xv **a big anthology:** Philip Van Doren Stern ed., text by Herbert Asbury, *The Breathless Moment* (New York: Alfred A. Knopf, 1935).

xv **We'll never know:** Luc Sante, in William Hannigan, *New York Noir: Crime Photos from the Daily News Archive* (New York: Rizzoli, 1999), p. 9. Also, Diane Keaton, *Local News: Tabloid Pictures from the Los Angeles Herald Express 1936–1961* (New York: Lookout/D.A.P., 1999).

xvi **in all the retellings:** Some version of this story appears in virtually every interview Weegee ever gave. *WW*, pp. 15–17, nicely summarizes the variations described here.

xvi **Charles Liotta, a photoengraver:** Morris Schwartz recollections, undated, probably 1996, ICP collection. Also, author interview with Mary Ann Liotta, July 2017.

xvi **Fellig worked in the darkrooms of the *New York Times*:** *WW*, p. 15; and correspondence between Morris Schwartz and Miles Barth, November 24 and December 4, 1996, ICP collection.

xvi **Cancellare, the photographer:** J. Y. Smith, "Frank Cancellare, Ex-UPI Photographer, Dies," *Washington Post*, July 16, 1985.

xvi   **"Like practically everything he ever owned":** Marc J. Parsons, "Weegee's Wedding," *Minicam Photography*, June 1947, pp. 40–44, 136–37.

xvii   **"a primitive":** Bruce Downes, in "Weegee—A Tribute," *WBW*, p. 3.

xviii   **"We tell ourselves stories":** Joan Didion, *The White Album* (New York: Simon and Schuster, 1979), p. 11.

CHAPTER 1

3   **the town of Zolochev:** For general background on Galicia, see Pinkas Hakehillot Polin, *Encyclopedia of Jewish Communities in Poland, Volume II*, ed. Danuta Dabrowska et al. (Jerusalem: Yad Vashem, 1980). Translated by Shlomo Sneh with the assistance of Francine Shapiro for https://www.jewishgen.org/. Also, the International Jewish Cemetery Project, http://www.iajgsjewishcemeteryproject.org/.

3   **poorest part of the empire:** Richard C. Frucht, *Eastern Europe: An Introduction to the People, Lands, and Culture, Volume 1* (Santa Barbara, CA: ABC-CLIO, 2005), pp. 52–53.

3   **telephone and telegraph service:** Gesher Galicia: The Bridge to Galicia, map, at https://maps.geshergalicia.org/galicia/austro-hungary-telegraph-telephone-1912/.

3   **roughly ten thousand residents:** Entry on JewishGen communities database, at https://www.jewishgen.org/Communities/community.php?usbgn=-1060974.

4   **three classes of Jews . . . "half-civilized":** Józef Szujski, cited by Larry Wolff, in *The Idea of Galicia: History and Fantasy in Habsburg Political Culture* (Stanford, CA: Stanford University Press, 2010), p. 264.

4   **Berisch and Rivka Fellig were:** Marriage record at http://agadd.home.net.pl/metrykalia /300/sygn.%201945/pages/PL_1_300_1945_0128.htm.

4   **had his own business:** *WW*, p. 12.

4   **Naftali Herz Imber:** Eddy Portnoy, "Weegee and the Two-Bit Nobodies," essay in *Weegee: Murder Is My Business*, ed. Brian Wallis (New York: Delmonico/Prestel, 2013), pp. 51–61. Also, Britannica.com entry at https://www.britannica.com/biography /Naphtali-Herz-Imber.

4   **born on June 12:** Birth record at http://agadd.home.net.pl/metrykalia/300/sygn.%20 2232/pages/PL_1_300_2232_0129.htm.

5   **political shift:** *WW*, p. 13. Also, additional information at http://www.jewishvirtual library.org/galicia-ukraine.

5   **vicious three-day pogrom:** Entry in *The Yivo Encyclopedia of Jews in Eastern Europe*, at http://www.yivoencyclopedia.org/article.aspx/Lviv.

5   **three million people emigrated:** *The Yivo Encyclopedia of Jews in Eastern Europe*, as well as *The American Jewish Year Book 1920–1921*, available at http://www.hillel.org/.

5   **Berisch went first:** Travel manifest, accessed through ancestry.com.

5   **twenty-two hundred other people:** SS *Pretoria* entry, "The Ships List," at http://www .theshipslist.com/ships/descriptions/ShipsP-Q.shtml.

5   **Abraham Zwerling:** Travel manifest.

6   **Seventeenth Ward:** *Annual Report of the Dept. of Health of the City of New York* (New York: Martin B. Brown Company, 1906), p. 371.

6   **a quarter as many residents:** Ritchie S. King and Graham Roberts, "Manhattan's Population Density, Past and Present," *New York Times*, March 1, 2012.

6   **Rivka was getting help:** Portnoy, "Weegee and the Two-Bit Nobodies," p. 53.

6   **"one [American] building that was outstanding":** MMM.

7   **only one extended story:** *WBW*, p. 8.

7   **"throwaways":** *WBW* N&Q.

7   **the children were headed to America:** Travel manifest.

7   **roughly thirty-five dollars per passenger:** Drew Keeling, "Transport Capacity Management and Transatlantic Migration, 1900–1914," *Research in Economic History* 25 (2008): 225–83. Cited at https://www.business-of-migration.com/.

7   **separate bathing areas:** Frederic J. Haskin, *The Immigrant: An Asset and a Liability* (Grand Rapids, MI: Fleming H. Revell, 1913), chap. 8. Transcribed at http://www .gjenvick.com/Steerage/1913-TheSteeragePassenger.html#ixzz4szhd56ci.

7   **seasick:** *WBW* N&Q.

8   **trachoma:** *WBW*, p. 9. Also, John Maxtone-Graham, *The Only Way to Cross* (New York: Macmillan, 1972), p. 160.

8   **banana:** *WBW*, p. 9.

8   **"I'm glad one thing":** MMM.

8   **52 Pitt Street:** U.S. Census, 1910, accessed through ancestry.com.

9   **notoriously dirty, infested with rats and bugs:** Sanford Sternlicht, *The Tenement Saga* (Madison: University of Wisconsin Press, 2004), p. 26.

9   **implicated the next year in a racket:** "Bad Egg Traffic Widespread Here," *New York Times*, December 2, 1910, p. 5.

9   **cited by the city's:** *Report of the Tenement House Department of the City of New York, Volume 2, July 1, 1903–December 1, 1905* (New York: Martin B. Brown Press, n.d.).

9   **Arthur was still angry:** Unpublished book proposal by Ted Schwarz, ICP collection.

9   **Father and son never really got along again:** Unpublished book proposal by Ted Schwarz, based on interview with Wilma Wilcox, held at ICP.

9   **"You don't look back on this life":** *WBW* MS.

9   **a *mikvah* . . . nine synagogues:** 1911 Bromley atlas in New York Public Library collection. Also, "The Synagogues of New York City," Museum of Family History Education and Research Center website, at www.museumoffamilyhistory.com/erc-syn-manhattan.htm.

9   **greenhorns:** *WBW*, p. 10, plus author conversation with Helen Georges, ca. 1992.

10   **sell dishes:** *WBW*, p. 12.

10   **Bernard was arrested:** "Girl Tracks and Traps Man Accused of Theft; Little Jennie Green Acts as Sleuth While on Her Way to School," *Brooklyn Daily Eagle*, March 16, 1910, p. 22.

10   **knocked down from burglary to vagrancy:** Ibid., plus Brooklyn Magistrate Court docket for March 16, 1910, New York City Municipal Archives.

10   **Cherry Street:** 1915 New York census records, accessed through ancestry.com.

11   **Jackson Street:** 1918 draft cards and 1920 census records, accessed through ancestry.com.

11   **wouldn't work on the Sabbath:** *WBW*, p. 12.

11   **bar mitzvah lessons:** Author interview with Philip Felig, May 2016.

11   **milliner:** Draft card, 1918, accessed through ancestry.com.

11   ***shammes:*** Portnoy, "Weegee and the Two-Bit Nobodies," p. 59.

11   **"I was the black sheep":** *WBW* N&Q.

11   **"the five of us":** *WBW*, p. 9.

11   **"five brothers and sisters":** *WBW* N&Q.

11   **"no closeness" . . . a divide:** Author interview with Liz Cooke, May 2014.

12   **going back to Felig:** Author interview with Philip Felig, May 2016.

12   **"A picture is like a blintz":** *WBW*, p. 82.

12   **daily paper . . . penny candy . . . the seventh grade:** Ibid., pp. 11–17.

12   **dropped out:** Melissa F. Weiner, *Power, Protest, and the Public Schools: Jewish and African American Struggles in New York City* (New Brunswick, NJ: Rutgers University Press, 2010), p. 27.

12   **street photographer:** *WBW*, p. 14.

CHAPTER 2

13   **Vest Pocket Kodak:** Advertisement in *Popular Mechanics*, May 1914, p. 104.

14   **"My first portrait":** *WBW*, opposite p. 1.

14   **"Right then":** "Modest and Assuming," *Newsweek*, July 23, 1945, pp. 74, 76. (Note: The unnamed *Newsweek* writer uses "dem," "dese," and other such spellings to mock Weegee's accent. I have decolloquialized the spelling here.)

15   **L. Lascelle:** Advertisement in *The World Almanac and Encyclopedia*, 1915 ed. (New York: Press Publishing Co., 1914), p. 883.

15   **"Horatio Alger was a phoney":** Ibid., p. 11.

15   **"the SCHMO Alger's exploits":** *WBW* N&Q.

15   **a state inspector:** *Fifteenth Annual Report of the Factory Inspector of the State of New York, for Year Ending November 30, 1900* (New York: James B. Lyon, State Printer, 1901), p. 314.

15   **Arthur wasn't old enough:** *WBW*, p. 15.

15   **product shots for catalogues:** Ibid., p. 14.

15   **They photographed dull events:** Francis J. Oppenheimer, "Father Knickerbocker's Theatre," *The Theatre*, May 1912, pp. 166, 168.

15   **"we used to take these black suits":** LJN.

15   **His first appearance:** New York census of 1915, accessed through ancestry.com.

16   **burned-out factories:** *WBW*, p. 15.

16   **"They didn't have enlargements":** "Modest and Assuming," *Newsweek*.

16   **"I would put a tube in my mouth":** *WBW*, p. 15. Also, "How to Make a Flash Lamp," *Popular Mechanics*, April 1909, p. 389.

16   **lasted two years . . . Fellig stormed out:** *WBW*, p. 16.

17   **"I was restless . . . My mother caught me":** *WBW* N&Q. A shorter published version of this story is in *WBW*, p. 20.

17   **"We called it kidnapping":** "Visiting Photographer Beats Drums for Film," *Los Angeles Times*, April 23, 1948.

17   **He named the pony Hypo:** *WBW*, pp. 17–19. Additional details ibid. Also, WWMM.

17   **toy automobile:** "Visiting Photographer Beats Drums for Film." Also, *WBW*, pp. 18–19.

18   **"contrastiest paper I could get":** *WBW*, p. 18. Also, *WW*, p. 15.

18   **"impossible to find work":** *WBW*, p. 20.

18   **get to the classifieds first . . . "Usually at about eight o'clock":** *WBW* MS.

18   **Loose-Wiles . . . "hole-puncher":** *WBW* N&Q. Shorter version in *WBW*, p. 23.

18   **bused dishes:** *WBW*, p. 20.

18   **"better sleeping accommodations . . . clean 'em up yourself":** *WBW*, p. 20. Also, "Modest and Assuming," p. 76.

18   **"too officious":** *WBW* MS. Similarly, Bob Lichello, "'The Famous Weegee' Wants a Woman from Mars Because . . . LADIES, YOU'RE NOT HUMAN!" *National Enquirer*, August 4–10, 1957, pp. 5, 12–13.

19   **a day here and a few hours there:** *WBW*, p. 23.

19   **The World War I draft . . . Seaman Studio:** Draft card, 1918, accessed through ancestry.com. Also, *WBW*, pp. 24–25.

19   **In Britain, the Seaman family:** Brett Payne, "Derbyshire Photographers' Profiles: Alfred Seaman & Sons," at http://freepages.genealogy.rootsweb.ancestry.com/~brett/photos/aseaman.html.

19   **a whorehouse visit:** *WBW*, p. 24.

19   **"The studios I haunted":** *WBW* N&Q.

19   **played the violin . . . bootlegger:** *WBW*, p. 27. Additional details, including "I used my camera case," in *WBW* N&Q.

20   **dropped by the violin room:** James W. Dean, "About New York," *Palm Beach Post*, November 19, 1924.

20   *Carpathia:* "A Group of *Titanic* Survivors," *New York Times*, April 19, 1912.

21   **In 1919:** John Chapman, *Tell It to Sweeney: An Informal History of the New York Daily News* (New York: Doubleday, 1961), chap. 1.

21   **At its peak:** Jonathan Mahler, "The Daily News Still Awaits a Savior," *New York Times*, May 17, 2015.

21   **started up the competing New York *Daily Mirror* . . . *Evening Graphic*:** V. Penelope

Pelizzon and Nancy M. West, *Tabloid, Inc.* (Columbus: Ohio State University Press, 2010), p. 9. (Note: In this otherwise excellent book, the founding date of Hearst's *Daily Mirror* is incorrectly given as 1922.)

22   a "daily freak": "The Press: Orgy," *Time*, February 27, 1927, pp. 31–32.

22   Hall-Mills case: Mara Bovsun, "A 90-Year Mystery: Who Killed the Pastor and the Choir Singer?" New York *Daily News*, September 16, 2012, http://www.nydailynews.com/news/justice-story/90-year-mystery-killed-pastor-choir-singer-article-1.1160659.

22   "Peaches" . . . "Daddy": Michael M. Greenburg, *Peaches and Daddy: A Story of the Roaring 20s, the Birth of Tabloid Media, and the Courtship that Captured the Hearts and Imaginations of the American Public* (New York: Overlook Press, 2008).

22   Ruth Snyder: Chapman, *Tell It to Sweeney*, pp. 99, 101; and *Daily News*, January 13, 1928.

CHAPTER 3

24   darkrooms of the *New York Times*: WW, p. 15; and undated Morris Schwartz recollections.

24   ninth floor: Correspondence with David W. Dunlap.

24   "Squeegee Boy": WW, p. 15.

24   New York *World*: "Modest and Assuming," p. 76.

24   Keystone: WBW MS.

24   around 1924: WW, p. 16.

24   Dorman . . . Pancho Villa: Anita Brenner, *The Wind that Swept Mexico: The History of the Mexican Revolution of 1910–1942* (Austin: University of Texas Press, 1943), pp. 296–97.

24   He ran Acme: Gray Strider, "The Inside Workings of a National News Photo Service," *Popular Photography*, July 1937, pp. 17–18, 80–81.

25   homing pigeons: Author interviews with Ida Wyman, February–April 2017. The pigeons were mentioned regularly in photo captions as well.

25   Harold Blumenfeld: Strider, "The Inside Workings," p. 17.

25   Peru and Romania: Ibid.

25   teased him about it: WW, p. 16. Also, Parsons, "Weegee's Wedding," p. 136.

25   he had no idea how this contraption . . . "humble and likeable": Unpublished Blumenfeld notes for program at ICP, October 16, 1977.

25   "Mr. Squeegee": WW, p. 16.

26   "scratchings and squealings": Harold Blumenfeld, "Weegee Alias Arthur Fellig," *Photographic Business & Product News*, February 1969, pp. 22–24, 43.

26   a thousand prints a day: Unpublished Blumenfeld notes.

26   double- and triple-exposure gags: Blumenfeld, "Weegee Alias Arthur Fellig," p. 23.

26   soft touch: Ibid., p. 24.

26   "educated dice": WBW, p. 29.

26   bring girls up: Ibid., p. 30.

26   Coburg: U.S. Census, 1930, accessed through ancestry.com.

26   padlocked his room: LJN.

26   living in the Acme darkroom: WBW, p. 30.

26   Bryant Park . . . sole of his shoe: MMM.

26   photoengravers: WBW, p. 30.

26   Charles Liotta: Undated Morris Schwartz recollections. Also, author interview with Mary Ann Liotta, July 2017.

27   At Acme, beating . . . "my crowning achievement": MMM. Also, WBW, pp. 33–35.

27   Wirephoto: "AT&T Archives: Pictures by Wire," AT&T Tech Channel, at http://techchannel.att.com/play-video.cfm/2011/8/26/AT&T-Archives-Pictures-by-Wire.

27   "Whoever got to the telephone company": LJN.

28   *Shenandoah*: LJN. Also, WBW, p. 31.

28 *New York World-Telegram: WBW*, p. 33–34.
28 **first-edition deadline:** Joe Strupp, "Afternoon Delights," *Editor & Publisher*, October 1, 2005.
29 **five dollars per photo:** Ibid., p. 41.
29 **"scared stiff . . . I know you're afraid":** *FPTH*.
29 **columnist named James W. Dean:** "James W. Dean, 47, Ex-Newspaperman," *Brooklyn Eagle*, August 15, 1941.
29 **printed a jokey little anecdote:** James W. Dean, "About New York," *Elmira Star-Gazette*, June 15, 1925.
29 **suddenly selling radios:** James W. Dean, "Sidelights of New York," *Saratogian*, October 1, 1925.
29 **enormous press undertaking:** LJN.
30 **rig up a darkroom on an airplane:** MMM.
30 **Michael Sacina:** Daniel Blau, ed. *Extra! Weegee* (Munich: Hirmer, 2017), pp. 319, 335; and Robert Talley, "The Men Who Went Thru Hell with Sergt. York," *Jamestown Evening Journal*, November 11, 1929.
30 **Miss Colored America:** Blau, *Extra! Weegee*, pp. 192, 331; and "Women Jail Fake Beauty Contest Promoter," *New York Age*, September 19, 1931. Also, untitled item in *Brooklyn Daily Eagle*, August 8, 1931, p. 9; and "Negro Pageant for New York," in *The Billboard*, March 28, 1931, p. 139.
31 **ICA Trix:** *WBW*, p. 34.
31 **Speed Graphic:** graflex.org.
32 **"the cops will assume that you belong":** *NC*, p. 240.
32 **"his love":** Ibid., p. 10.
32 **he'd cheat on it:** Catalogues for B&J Press Cameras, 1941 and 1945.
32 **In early 1929:** Herbert Corey, "Weegee and Widow Philosopher Find Life on Speak-Easy Tour," *Minneapolis Star*, January 5, 1929. Also, Sloane Gordon, "Herbert Corey, the Anecdote Man," *Pearson's Magazine*, April 1915, pp. 441–47.
33 **Some papers called the column "About New York's Days and Nights"; others, "Manhattan Days and Nights":** It appeared as the former in the *Hamilton Daily News* (Hamilton, OH), January 9, 1929, and as the latter in the *Oakland Tribune*, January 10, 1929.
33 **an actual event:** Author conversation with Ryan Adams of Daniel Blau Gallery.
35 **Except that few of them:** Michael R. Peres, ed., *The Focal Encyclopedia of Photography*, 4th ed. (Waltham, MA: Focal Press, 2007), pp. 754–55. Also, http://image.eastmanhouse.org/files/GEH_1955_04_07.pdf.
35 **More than thirty years later:** *WBW*, p. 28.

CHAPTER 4

36 **By the early thirties:** Burton B. Turkus and Sid Feder, *Murder Inc.: The Story of the Syndicate* (New York: Farrar, Straus and Young, 1951; reprint Da Capo, 1992). Also, Carl Sifakis, *The Mafia Encyclopedia, Third Edition* (New York: Facts on File, 2005).
36 **"garage in Brooklyn":** *BHS*.
36 **"I sent back word":** *WBW*, p. 79.
37 **"official photographer":** "Murder Is My Business," manuscript by Weegee, ICP archives, reproduced in Wallis, ed., *Weegee: Murder Is My Business*, pp. 9–11.
37 **"When there isn't much doing . . . great hopes":** MMM.
37 **nearly a quarter . . . hardboiled lingo:** Pelizzon and West, *Tabloid Inc.*, p. 63.
37 **Jake Lingle:** Ibid., pp. 57–84.
37 **"shooting acquaintance" . . . "awful dope":** *BHS*.
38 **In June 1931:** Case file No. 187298, New York City Municipal Archives.
38 **"asked me for an aspirin":** *BHS*. Also, *WBW*, p. 59.

38   **appeared in the next day's *Post*:** "Bronx Beer Runner in Toils," *New York Post*, June 18, 1931.

38   **"From then on . . . we were friends":** Interview transcript, Box 7, Mike Wallace Papers, 1956–1963, Bentley Historical Library, University of Michigan (hereafter "Wallace transcript"). Abbreviated version published as Mike Wallace, "Is Murder a Dying Art?" *New York Post*, March 4, 1958.

38   **Vincent Coll:** "Coll Killing Laid to Chicago Gang," *New York Evening Post*, February 8, 1932.

39   **George Washington Bridge:** LJN.

39   **Watson . . . four-generation family:** Judith Keller, "An Elusive Fame: The Photographs of Weegee," in *In Focus: Photographs from the J. Paul Getty Museum* (Los Angeles, CA: Getty Publications, 2005). Also, posts at http://www.a-r-t.com/watson/ and www.delmarwatsonphotos.com; author interview with Judith Keller, June 2015; and e-mail correspondence with Antoinette Watson.

39   **wanted to go by bus:** Unpublished Blumenfeld notes.

40   **first night in town:** WWMM.

40   **"My job was to stay in the darkroom":** MMM.

42   **nudist colony:** WBW, pp. 77–80. Background in Brian Hoffman, *Naked: A Cultural History of American Nudism* (New York: New York University Press, 2015). Also, "Modest and Assuming," p. 76.

42   **2561 Broadway . . . raid:** Hoffman, *Naked*, p. 33. Also, "3 Held in Nudist Raid," *New York Times*, April 14, 1934.

42   **"routine and planned stories" . . . "resented him":** Unpublished Blumenfeld notes.

43   **"a successful day would be one white girl and one black girl":** WBW MS.

43   **"Reporters worked an eight-hour day":** Author interview with Nicholas Pileggi, May 2015.

43   **it had receded somewhat:** Pelizzon and West, *Tabloid Inc.*, pp. 112–13.

43   **"Success with his night-prowling":** Unpublished Blumenfeld notes.

43   **"two straight whiskeys":** Ralph Steiner, "Weegee Lives for His Work and Thinks Before Shooting," *PM*, March 9, 1941.

43   **"I took my little camera":** MMM.

44   **Moran's:** WBW, p. 65.

44   **Headquarters Tavern . . . "the hole":** "Police Tavern Robbed," *New York Times*, April 18, 1941.

44   **pork chops:** Author e-mail with Nicholas Pileggi, May 2015. (He says they were great.)

44   **Herold:** "Pistol That Shot Redwood Was Sold to a Police Chief," *New York Times*, February 23, 1937.

44   **until recently been a poolroom:** "Held for Theft Near Police Centre," *New York Times*, March 11, 1930.

44   **Lava:** "Think of It! Some Vets Let the Postman Ring Thrice," *Brooklyn Daily Eagle*, June 15, 1936.

44   **No. 2 had Isaac Davidoff:** "Cops' Tailor, 'Cleaned' of Coat, Is All Steamed Up; Probe Pressed," *Brooklyn Eagle*, November 30, 1940; "Dave the Tailor Dies: Isaac Davidoff, 84, Worked on Police Uniforms 40 Years," *New York Times*, April 5, 1954.

44   **John Jovino:** George H. Corey, Hannah Fried, and Russell Maloney, "Locusts and Billies," *New Yorker*, July 25, 1936, p. 9.

45   **leased by newspapers:** Joseph Mackey, "Weegee Fellig," *Who*, September 1941, p. 11.

45   **Around the start of 1935:** Various magazine stories from the era place his move-in date in 1934 or 1935, and in the WBW manuscript, Weegee says, "I stayed at Acme until 1935." There is a glancing reference in WBW to developing negatives at "my hotel," which suggests that he took a furnished room in the neighborhood before renting the Centre Market Place apartment.

45   **half room on the stair landing:** Author interview with Anthony Imperato, January 2017.

45   **"my studio":** *WBW*, p. 74.

45   **seventeen dollars a month:** *WBW*, p. 42. Also, "Weegee," *Time*, July 23, 1945.

45   **On the bookshelf:** "Modest and Assuming," p. 76.

45   **NYPD had begun using radio:** Edwin Teale, "Riding the Night Patrol with the Radio Police," *Popular Science Monthly*, March 1933, pp. 13–15, 103, 104. Also, Harry Blesy, "Chronology of Police Radio," post at rfpd.tripod.com/id18.html; and *Rules and Regulations and Manual of Procedure of Police Department of the City of New York, Revised to December 16, 1940*, New York City Civil Service Commission, 1937.

46   **would ring with every single alarm:** "Speaking of Pictures . . . A New York Free-Lance Photographs the News," *Life*, April 12, 1937, pp. 8–11.

46   **twenty cigars:** Steiner, "Weegee Lives for His Work."

46   **Most people thought he slept in his clothes:** Mackey, "Weegee Fellig," p. 11.

46   **installed no telephone:** *WBW*, pp. 63, 94.

46   **cadge rides . . . "broomstick" . . . Model A Ford:** Ibid., pp. 41–42.

46   **Louis D'Amico Jr.:** In the published edition of *WBW*, Weegee's driver and whorehouse companion is called "Tony" and lives on the same block. In one manuscript draft of the book, however, he is named Louie, the son of a family living upstairs. The 1940 census lists the D'Amico family, with a twenty-two-year-old son named Louis, at 5 Centre Market Place. His name and address were almost surely obscured to anonymize the brothel activities.

46   **"sex-mad letter carrier":** *WBW* MS.

46   **West Seventies . . . May . . . "holes cut in the wall":** *WBW*, pp. 41–44 . Weegee does not note the location, beyond "Amsterdam Avenue in the sexy seventies," but Polly Adler biographer Debby Applegate notes that West Seventy-Second Street was a locus of brothel activity.

46   **"No wet decks for me":** *WBW* MS.

47   ***World-Telegram* . . . entire news bureau:** Thomas Kunkel, *Man in Profile: Joseph Mitchell of* The New Yorker (New York: Random House, 2015), pp. 79–82.

47   **Schulman, an ace:** Sammy Schulman and Robert Considine, ed., *"Where's Sammy?": The Story of an Ace News Photographer* (New York: Random House, 1943), pp. 92–104.

47   **"Most fires happen":** Steiner, "Weegee Lives for His Work."

47   **"still loved each other":** *WBW* MS.

47   **In January 1936:** "'Clubs' Only Picks, Dud Alarm Shows," *Brooklyn Daily Eagle*, January 27, 1936.

CHAPTER 5

49   **"Others wouldn't":** Unpublished Blumenfeld notes.

50   ***Daily News* had become:** Ad in *New York World-Telegram*, February 5, 1937.

50   **Winchell:** Neal Gabler, *Winchell: Gossip, Power, and the Culture of Celebrity* (New York: Alfred A. Knopf, 1994), passim.

51   **carrier-pigeon team:** *WBW*, p. 39.

51   **Jimmy Breslin put it:** Gregg Stebben, *The Little Red Book of New York Wisdom* (New York; Skyhorse, 2011), unpaginated.

51   **New York *Sun* was a stuffy:** "The *Sun* Is Sold," *Life*, January 16, 1950, pp. 39–40, 42. Also, E. B. White, introduction to Don Marquis, *the lives and times of archy and mehitabel* (New York: Doubleday, 1950), pp. xvii–xxiv.

52   **"The *Post* called the *Sun* 'a yellow dog'":** Walter Winchell, *Winchell Exclusive* (Upper Saddle River, NJ: Prentice-Hall, 1975), p. 43.

52   **250,000:** Ad in *New York Post*, October 1, 1936.

52   **had no night photographer:** Rosa Reilly, "Free-Lance Cameraman," *Popular Photography*, December 1937, pp. 21–23, 76–79.

52   "The city editors are glad to see": Ibid.

53   "the Weegee service": LJN.

53   He continued to shoot: Reilly, "Free-Lance Cameraman," p. 76.

53   As the sun came up: *WBW*, pp. 37–40. Also, Reilly, "Free-Lance Cameraman," p. 76.

53   two for five dollars: *WBW*, p. 47.

53   "I would casually mention . . . in fierce competition": Ibid., pp. 40–41.

53   "I take off my shoes": Steiner, "Weegee Lives for His Work."

53   loose working agreement: Reilly, "Free-Lance Cameraman," p. 76.

53   *Jewish Daily Forward*: *WBW*, p. 41.

53   *Daily Worker*: User I2010, "Finding Weegee," post on the Back Table: Archives and Special Collections at New York University, June 2, 2011, at https://wp.nyu.edu /specialcollections/2011/06/13/credit-weegee-the-daily-worker-photographer/.

53   "One good murder a night": *WBW*, p. 42.

53   he sold comparatively little: *WBW*, pp. 46–47.

54   "dry shooting": LJN.

54   It ran in the *Daily News*: Wilma Wilcox's bequest to ICP, inherited from Weegee, includes many copies of newspaper pages, printed from microfilm, on which photographs have been marked and annotated. A number of these are not represented by actual prints in the collection. The general belief is that Wilcox perhaps knew that these other photos (for example, the image mentioned here, of Centre Market Place) were Weegee's as well. I have treated them as "likely Weegee" rather than "confirmed Weegee."

54   involved Dutch Schultz again: LJN, and (in a curiously redacted version, without Schultz's name) *WBW*, p. 68. Lots of entertaining background, including the rusty bullets, in Paul Sann, *Kill the Dutchman!* (New Rochelle, NY: Arlington House, 1971).

55   West Forty-Seventh and East Fifty-First: Mackey, "Weegee Fellig," p. 11.

55   "Most of your job": Reilly, "Free-Lance Cameraman," p. 22.

55   "If they wanted a quiet little snooze": Weegee, "Murder Is My Business" manuscript, reproduced in Wallis, ed., *Weegee: Murder Is My Business*.

55   "He snaps Moriarity's baby": Reilly, "Free-Lance Cameraman," p. 22.

55   fire truck covered in icicles: *New York World-Telegram*, February 19, 1936.

55   water-main break: "Broken Main Ties Up Queens Traffic," *New York Post*, and untitled clipping in the *New York Sun*, February 28, 1936; "Streets in Queens Flooded by Broken Water Main," *New York Times*, February 29, 1936.

56   picketing elevator operators: "Elevator Strike Spreads to Wall St. and Park Ave.," *New York Post*, March 2, 1936; "Women Pickets on the Upper West Side," *New York Sun*, March 2, 1936.

56   pictures of city workers: "Rice Has Large Force to Guard Health," *New York Times*, March 3, 1936; and "Strikers on Job as City Health Inspectors—Sale of Heaters Booms," *New York World-Telegram*, March 3, 1936.

56   "They called me their underworld contact . . . I had done my job": LJN.

56   Acme's early-morning editor: Letter from E. Stuart Fergusson to Miles Barth, October 23, 1995, ICP collection.

56   holdup gang's young female lookout . . . the final: "Keeps Gangland Code," *New York Journal*, May 18, 1936.

57   amateur who happened to be on the scene: *New York Mirror*, June 30, 1936; also "Talk of the Town: Notes and Comment," *New Yorker*, July 25, 1936, pp. 9–10.

57   nearly broke . . . back to his darkroom job: *WBW*, p. 47.

57   the temperature: "Temperatures Yesterday: Max. 78," *New York Times*, front page, August 2, 1936.

57   Edgar MacKnight: *WBW*, pp. 48–50; and extensive coverage in all nine New York dailies, notably the *Post*, August 1 and 2, 1936.

58   "a gentlemen's agreement": WBW, p. 49.

59 **"Me and Leo Katcher didn't know about the agreement":** Lichello, "'The Famous Weegee' Wants a Woman from Mars . . . ," pp. 5, 12–13.

61 **Katcher earned:** "Leo Katcher, Reporter and Writer, Dies at 79," *New York Times*, March 2, 1991.

61 **William Hessler:** "Gang Stabs B'klyn Man 48 Times," *New York Post*, August 5, 1936; "Stabbed, Tied, Left in Trunk by Vice Gang," *New York World-Telegram*, August 5, 1936.

62 **"Editors demand people in pictures":** "Speaking of Pictures . . . A New York Free-Lance Photographs the News," p. 8.

62 **painting it out with stippled:** Ibid.

63 **Dominick Didato:** Wallis, ed., *Weegee: Murder Is My Business*. Also, "It's Bad Luck to Chisel in on Lucky," *New York Post*, August 7, 1936; and "Victim of Vice Gang Fury," *New York Evening Journal*, August 7, 1936.

64 **It was the fifth murder of the month:** Hannigan, *New York Noir*, pp. 67, 154–55.

64 **"I gave them all my love and care":** BHS.

64 **The *Daily News* ran the gory one:** Hannigan, *New York Noir*, pp. 67, 154–55.

65 **"I made the stiff look real cozy":** WBW, p. 45.

65 **Twice in the next two weeks:** "Rescue Squads at Work in Telescoped Third Av. 'El' Cars," *New York World-Telegram*, August 14, 1936; and "Fire in Home Opens Their Eyes," *New York World-Telegram*, August 21, 1936.

CHAPTER 6

66 **On August 8:** "Burglar Suspect Shot to Death as He Climbs Cemetery Fence," *New York Post*, August 8, 1936.

66 **a section of the old Fulton Fish Market:** "Landmark Collapses in Shadow of the Skyscrapers," *New York Post*, August 11, 1936; "Section of Fulton Market Pier Falls into East River," *New York Sun*, August 11, 1936.

66 **tenement fire:** "Fire in Home Opens Their Eyes."

66 **At around 4:00 a.m.:** "Where Cop's Car Sent Men to Death," *New York Post*, August 21, 1936; "Where Policeman's Auto Catapulted Truckman to Death," *New York Herald Tribune*, August 22, 1936.

67 **"The unpardonable crime":** LJN.

67 **ten-foot focus . . . prefigured lens aperture:** NC, p. 239.

67 **"make the camera human":** WBW N&Q.

68 **"With concentration":** NC, p. 239.

68 **anguished wife:** "Speaking of Pictures . . . A New York Free-Lance Photographs the News," p. 9. Also, "Victim, Widow and Cafe in Village Brawl," *New York Post*, September 21, 1936.

68 **shoot-out on the Upper West Side:** "G-Men Trap Kidnapper in Wild Siege," *New York Post*, December 15, 1936.

68 **girls in pinafores, saved from a shipwreck:** "Rescue Becomes Lesson for Sisters," *New York World-Telegram*, September 10, 1936.

68 **Times Square on Election Night:** "There Was a Sound of Revelry by Night—And How!" *New York Post*, November 4, 1936.

68 **fifty-ton whale:** LJN. Also, "Police to Sink Moby Dick," *Brooklyn Daily Eagle*, November 14, 1936.

70 **Seamen's Church Institute:** "Eviction of a Striking Seaman (Broke) from the Church Institute." *New York World-Telegram*, November 28, 1936. Also, "No Dough—No Sleep," *Daily News*, November 28, 1936.

70 **as far away as Iowa:** "Eviction of a Striking Seaman," *Algona Upper Des Moines*, December 8, 1936.

70 **preparing to launch:** Robert L. Elson, *Time Inc.: The Intimate History of a Publishing Enterprise, 1923–1941* (New York: Atheneum, 1968), pp. 269–331.

71   **"go up to *Life* magazine":** Gretchen Berg, "Weegee," *Photography*, Summer 1976, pp. 1–4, 24, 26.

71   **power failure at Newark Airport:** "When It Was Oil Lamp and Candlelight Time in Newark," *New York Post*, December 29, 1936.

71   **another good fire photo:** "Direct Firemen at Big Blaze in Williamsburg," *New York Sun*, December 23, 1936.

71   **Anna Sheehan:** "It Was Our First Quarrel," *New York Post*, January 2, 1937.

71   **hit-and-run:** "Driver, Here Are the Pain and Sorrow and Fright Which You Have Caused," *New York World-Telegram*, January 9, 1937. Also, "Picture Record of Grief and Agony Rises to Haunt Fleeing Motorist," *Xenia Daily Gazette*, March 18, 1937, and Reilly, "Free-Lance Cameraman," p. 76.

72   **Barneys:** "Portrait of a Holdup Man," *New York Post*, January 7, 1937.

73   **bathtub murder:** "Speaking of Pictures . . . A New York Free-Lance Photographs the News," p. 9.

73   **As did the arrest of a pretty, tough young woman:** "Woman in Black Is Captured Attempting Her Fourth Holdup," *New York Sun*, February 15, 1937.

73   **alias Norma Parker, alias Jean Williams:** Case file, Complaint No. 211734, New York City Municipal Archives.

73   **spinning a yarn:** *WBW*, pp. 61–63.

73   **counterfeiting bust:** "Fortune in Fake Cash Seized," *Daily Mirror*, February 9, 1937.

73   **Murder Inc. rubout:** "Murder in a High-Powered Car," *New York Post*, January 30, 1937.

73   **ICE WAGON:** LJN.

74   **Luc Sante:** Hannigan, *New York Noir*, p. 10.

74   **He had learned to "slant pictures":** Mackey, "Weegee Fellig," p. 11.

75   **"We'll assume":** Steiner, "Weegee Lives for His Work."

75   **in the *Herald Tribune* and the *Post*:** "Eighth Freak Crash in 8 Years on Williamsburg Bridge," *New York Herald Tribune*, January 16, 1937. Also, "Driver—the Eighth—Dies in Freak Crash," *New York Post*, January 15, 1937.

75   **a subway . . . derailed:** Reilly, "Free-Lance Cameraman," pp. 76–77; and "Rescue Squads at Work."

76   **"I helped to make the 'Little Flower' famous":** *WBW* MS.

76   **a band of jewel thieves:** *FPTH*; LJN; *WBW*, p. 69. Also, "Fortune in Jewels and Cash in Stolen Gem Drama," *New York Post*, January 25, 1937.

76   **"Especially on a Sunday":** LJN.

77   **"Editors don't like it":** *FPTH*.

77   **celebrity criminals:** BHS.

78   **"The only ones that tried":** Arthur "Weegee" Fellig, with introduction by Louis Stettner, ed., *Weegee* (New York: Alfred A. Knopf, 1977), p. 11.

78   **pack of cigarettes:** Mackey, "Weegee Fellig," p. 11.

CHAPTER 7

This chapter was reconstructed from news items and photo credits in all nine New York dailies from April 19 through 24, 1937: the morning *Times*, *Herald Tribune*, *American*, *Daily News*, and *Daily Mirror* and the afternoon *Post*, *Sun*, *World-Telegram*, and *Journal*. Additional details come from Reilly, "Free-Lance Cameraman"; and BHS.

CHAPTER 8

84   **its editors had proceeded:** Elson, *Time Inc.: The Intimate History*, p. 305.

84   **night-in-the-life-of-police-headquarters:** "Speaking of Pictures . . . A New York Free-Lance Photographs the News," p. 8, and Wallis, ed., *Weegee: Murder Is My Business*, p. 26.

84 **tight scripts:** Dora Jane Hamblin, *That Was the Life* (New York: W. W. Norton, 1977), pp. 68–73.

85 **"catfish":** Pelizzon and West, *Tabloid Inc.*, p. 149.

86 **Minsky's:** "The Police Go to Burlesque Show . . . to Stand Guard," New York *Sun*, May 3, 1937.

86 **a good car-crash picture:** *WBW*, p. 47.

86 **tenement collapse:** "Tenement Tragedy Is Senate Object Lesson," *Life*, August 23, 1937, p. 24. Also, "Pictured Record of Havoc Wrought by Torrential Storm," *New York Post*, August 12, 1937.

87 **busiest and most lucrative night:** Reilly, "Free-Lance Cameraman," pp. 77–78.

88 **settled for a picture:** "Arrested," *Daily Mirror*, February 17, 1937.

88 **muttered his name:** The full (and compellingly strange) transcript appears in Sann, *Kill the Dutchman!*, pp. 60–68.

88 **"a symphony in brown":** "Schultz's Buddy Nabbed by Police," *New York Post*, February 17, 1937.

89 **taking a little nap:** *WBW*, p. 45.

90 **Omero Catan and George Horn:** "Rivals Wait 30 Hours to Be First Through Tunnel," *Life*, January 3, 1938, p. 14.

90 **two other guys:** Undated newspaper clipping seen on Weegee's apartment wall; variant photo in Acme files, September 30, 1936.

90 **similarly posed:** "Hitch-Hikes from Chicago to Attend the World Series," New York *Sun*, October 7, 1937.

90 **a brace of young women:** "When Dime Store Girls Sit Down at Woolworth's on West Fourteenth," *New York Post*, March 18, 1937.

91 **The mailbox photo:** LJN. Also, "Wrapping Paper," *PM*, December 20, 1940.

91 **"His friends all said":** WWMM.

93 **In another interview:** Earl Wilson, "Weegee," *Saturday Evening Post*, May 22, 1943, pp. 37–39.

94 **A fedora moved:** Kay Reese and Mimi Leipzig, "Interviews with ASMP Founder: Herb Giles," 1993, at https://www.asmp.org/resources/about/history/interview-founders/herb-giles/.

94 **"Every newspaper has staff photographers":** Reilly, "Free-Lance Cameraman," p. 22.

94 **"You work with them all the time":** LJN.

94 **COCKROACH CAFÉ . . . "Predictions!":** Mackey, "Weegee Fellig," p. 11.

94 **"He didn't have any good rebuttals":** Author interviews with Ida Wyman, February–March 2017.

94 **"modest and assuming":** "Modest and Assuming," p.74.

94 **saw a rival try to exact revenge:** Stettner, *Weegee*, p. 5.

95 **walked away for a moment:** Stettner says this incident occurred in June 1938, but the Westminster Kennel Club Dog Show happened in February of that year. He either has the date wrong or he's mixed the dog show up with another event.

95 **"They were famous":** WWMM.

95 **had zippers sewn:** Wilson, "Weegee," p. 37.

CHAPTER 9

97 **"The ex-darkroom man":** Fellig, *Weegee*, p. 12.

97 **"During the night":** LJN.

97 **"The easiest kind of a job":** FPTH.

98 **"a very large living":** Ibid.

98 **three times the average American:** "100 Years of U.S. Consumer Spending: Data for the Nation, New York City, and Boston." BLS Report 991, Bureau of Labor Statistics, 2006, chap. 3: 1934–36.

98   **his father died:** Death certificate 18432, September 23, 1938, New York City Municipal Archives.

98   **his mother lived with:** U.S. Census, 1940, accessed through ancestry.com.

98   **"used up five cars":** LJN; also, Weegee, "Murder Is My Business" manuscript; similarly, *WBW*, p. 76.

98   **1938 Chevrolet:** *WBW*, pp. 51–52. Also, *Chevrolet 1938 Specifications*, Chevrolet—Central Office Engineering Department, available from gmheritagecenter.com.

98   **"Riding around with me":** *WBW*, p. 55.

98   **he was fleeced:** Ibid., p. 58.

98   **"fire shoes" . . . "murder shoes":** Wilson, "Weegee," p. 37; also Steiner, "Weegee Lives for His Work."

99   **carry a bunch of disguises:** *WBW*, p. 52. Also, LJN.

99   **interior was littered:** George Gilbert, "Reminiscences of Weegee," unpublished short memoir, ca. 1978, ICP collection, p. 2.

99   **darkroom in its trunk:** Author conversation with Christopher George, May 2013.

100   **Winchell . . . permit for a police radio:** Gabler, *Winchell*, pp. 219–21. Also, *WBW*, p. 51. No records survive confirming that Weegee was the first and only freelance photographer with a radio, but his permit number was 15, suggesting that only a few individuals had preceded him.

100   **twenty-five dollars per year . . . eighty bucks:** Mackey, "Weegee Fellig," p. 11.

100   **"I made application":** *WBW* N&Q.

100   **"I knew the boys":** Wallace transcript, p. 2.

100   ~~seventy-five-cent investment: LJN.~~

101   **named Barney Stein:** "Barney Stein; Photographer, 84," *New York Times*, July 2, 1993. Although this story notes that he joined the *Post* staff in 1939, his credits (probably freelance) began to appear frequently a year or so earlier.

101   **Irving Haberman:** *WBW* MS. Also, biography at ihimages.com.

101   **fight with the *Post*:** Steiner, "Weegee Lives for His Work." Although the editor is not named, *WBW*, p. 38, says that Weegee's night work often called for him to "make a selling pitch with Paul Sann," the *Post*'s night city editor around this time.

101   **Stettner later said:** Recorded remarks by Stettner at International Center of Photography, October 16, 1977, ICP collection.

102   **stopped using the *Post*'s darkroom:** Mackey, "Weegee Fellig," p. 11.

102   **yearling steer:** "Don Jose Brennan Throws Ferdinand Jr.," *New York Post*, December 6, 1938.

102   **Robert Joyce:** "Dodger Fan Kills Man, Shoots Pal for Barroom Wisecracks," *New York Post*, July 13, 1938. Also, "William Diamond Rites on Monday," *Brooklyn Daily Eagle*, July 16, 1938.

103   **"Editors told me":** "So You Want to Be a Free-Lance!," *Good Photography*, no. 7, 1941, p. 10.

103   **"The dopey editors":** *FPTH*.

104   **"I don't know their names . . . but I did hear someone call him 'Pincus.'":** NC, p. 71.

104   **tenement house on Bartlett Street:** "Mother and Son Die in B'klyn Fire," *New York Post*, December 14, 1939; "Firemen Make Rescues at Fatal Blaze," *New York Sun*, December 14, 1939.

104   **Many months later:** "Guilty in 2 Fire Deaths; Brooklyn Landlord Failed to Install Retarding Devices," *New York Times*, May 27, 1941.

104   **got the great one:** "As 2 Kin Died," *Daily Mirror*, December 15, 1939. Also, *WBW*, pp. 66–67.

104   **"Boss, this is a roast":** *FPTH*.

105   **Weegee expressed pride:** MMM. Also, "Prevent This," *The People's Voice*, October 7, 1944.

105   and also cynicism: *WBW*, p. 67.
106   cake box: Lichello, "'The Famous Weegee' Wants a Woman from Mars," pp. 5, 12–13.
106   David "the Beetle" Beadle: Brian Wallis, ed., *Weegee: Murder Is My Business*, pp. 76–79.
107   probably from the *Daily News*: A photo in the next morning's paper shows a similar scene.
107   He had asked a cop: Wallace transcript, pp. 8–9.
107   "my favorite murder": A picture of Weegee lecturing shows the image on a poster, labeled thus.
107   Around dusk: "Street Scene in New York," *New York Post*, November 17, 1939. "Murder in New York," *Life*, November 27, 1939, p. 27. Additional details in Wallis, ed., *Weegee: Murder Is My Business*, pp. 72–75; and *WBW*, p. 66.
107   at 12 Prince: U.S. Census, 1940, accessed through ancestry.com.
107   "take a nice little ride": FPTH.
109   police evidence photographer: Wallis, ed., *Weegee: Murder Is My Business*, p. 72.
109   burst of flash powder: FPTH. In a variant of this story in *WBW*, p. 66, he says he used three flashbulbs instead of flash powder.
110   For years afterward, he joked: NC, p. 78. Also, recorded Q&A with Weegee conducted by Peter Sellers, ca. 1964, ICP collection (hereafter "Sellers-Weegee Q&A").
110   paying its standard rate: In the course of the Sellers-Weegee Q&A, Weegee inadvertently slips up and admits that he got a per-page rate rather than a per-bullet rate.
110   won him a national award: Contest results reprinted in *Louisville Courier-Journal* Sunday magazine, March 10, 1940.
110   twenty-five-dollar . . . "*your medal*": Mackey, "Weegee Fellig," p. 11.
110   He doesn't remember much: Author interview with Vito Cosenza, March 2015.

CHAPTER 10

111   "I keep to myself": NC, p. 11.
111   he never joined: Author interview with New York Press Photographers Association historian Marc A. Hermann, June 2016.
111   Photo League: Anne Wilkes Tucker, *This Was the Photo League* (New York: Stephen Daiter Gallery, 2001). Mason Klein and Catherine Evans, *The Radical Camera: New York's Photo League, 1936–1951* (New York: Jewish Museum/Columbus Museum of Art/Yale University Press, 2011).
112   Morris Engel and Ruth Orkin, met: E-mail correspondence with Mary Engel.
112   "just liked being there": Author interview with Arthur Leipzig, August 2014.
112   "$3.50 in 1939, plus an extra $1.50": *Photo Notes*, February 1938–Spring 1950, anthologized in facsimile in Nathan Lyons, ed., *Photo Notes* (New York: Visual Studies Workshop, 1977).
113   Weegee attended the Crazy Camera Ball: John Adam Knight, "Photography," *New York Post*, June 20, 1941.
113   entered a photo in the Photo Hunt and placed second: Ibid. Also, *Photo Notes*, June 1941. Photo identified by note on back of print in ICP archive.
113   Walter Rosenblum once noted: Tucker, *This Was the Photo League*, p. 12.
113   "He'd often walk into the darkroom": Author interview with Arthur Leipzig, August 2014.
113   "he was after me": Author interview with Erika Stone, June 2015.
113   Wilma Wilcox: WWMM.
113   Hartland Township: U.S. Census, 1900, accessed through ancestry.com.
113   Columbia University's New York School of Social Work: E-mail correspondence with Columbia's Office of the University Registrar.
113   a block from the Photo League's clubhouse: Columbia School of Social Work historical timeline, https://socialwork.columbia.edu/about/historical-timeline/.

114   **and then hold forth . . . "the delight of the small audience":** Gilbert, "Reminiscences of Weegee," pp. 1–2.

114   **an attraction between them formed:** WWMM.

114   **pork barrel:** Undated excerpt from testimony by Wilma Wilcox, in fax from attorney Andrew L. Deutsch with cover letter of December 7, 1993, ICP collection.

114   **Greenwich Village apartment:** "An Interview with Wilma Wilcox," accompanying release of *The Village,* 1989, ICP collection.

114   **"pots and pans":** Author interview with Ira Richer, June 2015. Also, Keller, "An Elusive Fame," p. 99.

114   **"a good-looking wife":** Reilly, "Free-Lance Cameraman," p. 78.

115   **"Messages?":** Peter Martin, "Arthur (Weegee) Fellig (1899–1968)," essay in catalogue for San Francisco Museum of Modern Art exhibition, 1984, p. 9.

115   **Ralph McAllister Ingersoll:** Paul Milkman, *PM: A New Deal in Journalism* (New Brunswick, NJ: Rutgers University Press, 1997).

116   **"most intelligent million":** Wolcott Gibbs, "A Very Active Type Man," *New Yorker,* May 2, 1942, pp. 21–30, and May 9, 1942, pp. 21–30.

116   **"written in words and pictures":** Ralph Ingersoll, memorandum, May 14, 1940, Ralph Ingersoll Papers, Howard Gotlieb Archival Research Center at Boston University.

116   **"over half *PM*'s space":** Ibid.

116   **"make customers reach for a nickel":** Ibid.

117   **"They'd climb":** Gibbs, "A Very Active Type Man," part II, p. 22.

117   **retainer of seventy-five dollars per week:** *WBW,* p. 86.

117   **Ben Hecht . . . also got seventy-five dollars:** Letter from Ingersoll to Hecht, December 19, 1940, private collection.

118   **had an effect on public opinion:** Claire Bond Potter, *War on Crime: Bandits, G-Men, and the Politics of Mass Culture* (New Brunswick, NJ: Rutgers University Press, 1998), passim.

118   **9.7 killings per thousand . . . 6.2:** "Homicides in 1940 Lowest in 25 Years," *New York Times,* October 1, 1942.

118   **Chicago . . . half:** "Chicago Homicide Rates per 100,000 Residents, 1870–2000," at www.encyclopedia.chicagohistory.org/pages/2156.html.

118   ***Life* ran a big story:** "Murder Inc.: Justice Overtakes the Largest and Most Cruel Gang of Killers in U.S. History," *Life,* September 30, 1940, pp. 86–96.

118   **legendary Margaret Bourke-White:** Milkman, *PM: A New Deal in Journalism,* p. 46. Also Loren Ghiglione, *CBS's Don Hollenbeck* (New York: Columbia University Press, 2008), p. 44; and Berg, "Weegee," p. 4.

118   **Engel, who was . . . Leipzig, who was even younger:** Ibid.

119   **"had a sense of timing":** Author interview with Arthur Leipzig, August 2014.

119   **Fisher thought even less:** Alfred Gescheidt, "Remembering Weegee: From the Recollections of Alfred Gescheidt," *ASMP News* (newsletter of American Society of Media Photographers, New York), (July/August 1997): 1, 6.

119   **Ingersoll overheard him:** NC, p. 241.

119   **"I can't spell":** LJN.

119   **Dashiell Hammett:** Gibbs, "A Very Active Type Man," part II, p. 21.

119   **"At first I was scared":** NC, p. 241.

120   **began screaming and hooting:** Matthew Gurewitsch, "Weegee's Day at the Beach," *Smithsonian,* June 2009, pp. 8–11.

121   **resold the crowd photo:** "Heat Wave," *New York Times,* July 28, 1940.

121   **circulation department accidentally lost:** Christopher B. Daly, "When the 99% Had a Paper," *Columbia Journalism Review* (January/February 2012): http://archives.cjr.org /essay/when_the_99_had_a_paper.php.

121 **swimsuit-clad cuties:** Untitled item, *PM*, June 23, 1940.

122 **bombing at the world's fair:** "Murder at the World's Fair" and "Police Question 150 Subjects in Bombing at World's Fair," *PM*, July 5, 1940.

122 **lightning strike:** "Lightning, Rain, Trouble," *PM*, July 12, 1940.

122 **Joseph Elsberry McWilliams:** Robert Lewis Taylor, "The Kampf of Joe McWilliams," *New Yorker*, August 24, 1940, p. 34.

122 **Winchell called him "Joe McNazi":** Gil Troy, "When America Rejected Its Home-grown 'Joe McNazi,'" *Daily Beast*, September 4, 2016.

122 **what readers saw in the paper the next day:** "McWilliams, Fascist Candidate, Faces His Future Undiscouraged," *PM*, July 8, 1940.

122 **striking number of car crashes:** "Chief Danger Point on Henry Hudson Parkway Is at 72d. St. Entrance." *PM*, July 21, 1940.

123 **Weegee once delivered a similar story:** LJN.

124 **"This work" . . . "my memorial":** *WBW*, pp. 67–68.

125 **Except his chronicle . . . more fanciful:** Author interview and correspondence with Jim Kolea, November 2016 and August 2017.

CHAPTER 11

127 **close call:** "Gas Blasts Rock Park Central," New York *Sun*, May 10, 1940.

127 **ran an action shot:** "Down to Safety," *New York Journal-American*, July 20, 1940.

127 **lobbed a story:** "Obtained Fire Rescue Photos," *Editor & Publisher*, August 3, 1940, p. 16.

127 **at least one such picture before:** "Rescued at 53d Street Fire," New York *Sun*, August 31, 1938.

128 **Weegee in his undershorts:** "Weegee the Wag," *PM*, July 28, 1940.

128 **litter of kittens:** "Five Kittens and Two Puppies Form One Happy Family," New York *Sun*, July 18, 1940. Also, "So It's Raining Cats and Dogs," *PM*, July 18, 1940.

128 **"mental masturbating":** *WBW*, p. 28.

128 **tenement house burned down:** "Cold Weather Brings Work for City Firement," *PM*, December 18, 1940.

129 **Macy's Thanksgiving Day Parade:** "Macy's Santa Claus Comes to Life in W. 106th St," *PM*, November 21, 1940.

130 **a car ended up in the river:** "End of a Fast Auto Ride," *PM*, July 29, 1940.

130 **a burning house:** "You Can't Put Me Out of My Own House . . . Even If It's On Fire," *PM*, October 10, 1940.

130 **moonshining operation:** "Alky Raid," *PM*, October 11, 1940.

130 **barge rammed and half sunk:** "British Traffic in East River," *PM*, October 18, 1940.

130 **a horrible domestic dispute:** "Woman Set Afire . . . Husband Seized," *PM*, December 5, 1940.

130 **a scattering of teeth:** Mackey, "Weegee Fellig," p. 11.

130 **FBI's attempt to deglamorize criminal behavior:** Potter, *War on Crime*.

130 **MAIL EARLY:** "Wrapping Paper," *PM*, December 20, 1940.

130 **opening night at the Metropolitan Opera:** "The Opera Opened Last Night," *PM*, December 3, 1940.

131 **one more great story:** "Ermine-Wrapped Patron Caught in Gambling Den," *PM*, December 23, 1940.

132 **"Picture of the Week":** "Gambling Lady Scuttles Anonymously from New York 'Joint' Following Police Raid," *Life*, January 6, 1941, pp. 20–21.

132 **Christmas Eve:** "Weegee Covers Christmas in New York," *PM*, December 26, 1940.

132 **When the *Times*'s John J. Gordon:** "*Times* Reporter Retires After 34 Years at Police Headquarters," *PM*, January 13, 1941.

133   **4 Centre Market Place:** "Press Building Opened," *New York Times*, September 29, 1940.

133   **phone books:** Cedric Larson, "New York City Police Department Launches New Public Relation Policy," *Journal of Criminal Law and Criminology* 41, no. 3 (1950–1951): 364.

133   **"They could easily have been cops":** Author interview with Nicholas Pileggi, May 2015.

133   **a print . . . hung on the wall:** Jeanne Toomey, *Assignment Homicide: Behind the Headlines* (Santa Fe, NM: Sunstone Press, 1998), p. 7.

133   **shoot-out on Fifth Avenue:** John Faber, *Great News Photos and the Stories Behind Them* (New York: Dover Press, 1978). Also, Wallis, ed., *Weegee: Murder Is My Business*, pp. 80–85; Christopher George, "Mad Dogs," group of posts at weegeeweegeeweegee .net/tag/mad-dogs; and panel discussion by Brian Wallis, Paul Milkman, and Jason Hill at Steven Kasher Gallery, New York, February 6, 2016.

134   **Weegee got his own crack:** "Gunman Doesn't Want His Picture Taken," *PM*, January 16, 1941.

135   **got the chair:** "Funeral Held for Espositos," *New York Times*, March 17, 1942.

CHAPTER 12

136   **A chef who was stabbed:** "Rocco Finds His Pal Stabbed," *PM*, July 31, 1941.

136   **revisited Steeplechase Pier:** "Weegee Revisits Coney Island . . . ," *PM*, January 20, 1941.

136   **went to Washington:** "A N.Y. Police Reporter's Impressions of Washington," *PM*, March 2, 1941.

137   **one of those increasingly rare gangland rubouts:** "Death in the Evening: The Underworld Catches Up with One of Its Own," *PM*, April 18, 1941.

137   **a car wreck on Second Avenue:** "New York Street Scene: Second Avenue at 5 a.m.," *PM*, July 2, 1941.

137   **squirrel gathering nuts:** "Hoarding for Winter," *PM*, October 6, 1941.

137   **"my drunk picture":** *FPTH.*

137   **a murder victim on the street:** "This Is a New York Sidewalk Audience . . ." *PM*, February 7, 1941.

138   **"When I became a free lance":** Letter to Edward Steichen, n.d. (probably 1948), Department of Photography Exhibition Files, 399.6, Museum of Modern Art Archives, New York.

138   **that one ran in the *Daily News*:** *Daily News*, June 27, 1940.

138   **Another strikingly similar picture:** "Fire Escape Offers a Cool Escape from East Side's Heat," *New York Evening Journal*, July 9, 1936.

138   **ran in *PM*:** "The Hot Weather Last Night . . ." *PM*, May 23, 1941.

140   **Louis Liotta:** Joyce Wadler, "Candid Cameraman," *People*, December 11, 1989.

141   **"Later . . . people seeing those pictures":** *WBW*, p. 95.

142   **"high life" and "low life":** Thomas Kunkel, *Genius in Disguise: Harold Ross of* The New Yorker (New York: Random House, 1998), p. 322.

142   **In 1934, a man named Sammy Fuchs:** "Sammy's Bowery Follies," *Life*, December 4, 1944, pp. 57–60. Also, Robert D. McFadden, "The Bowery Follies Folds in a Last Vaudevillean Fling," *New York Times*, September 28, 1970.

143   **WBYN:** Photographs of Sammy's show a banner over the stage advertising the show.

143   **a small-time murder:** "Brooklyn School Children See Gambler Murdered in Street," *PM*, October 9, 1941.

144   **The words probably came from Don Hollenbeck:** Ghiglione, *CBS's Don Hollenbeck*, pp. 43–45.

CHAPTER 13

146 **first of many lectures:** "Club Activities," New York *Sun*, July 25, 1941.
146 **One talk that he gave at the City College:** Norman C. Lipton, "'Weegee' Top Free-Lance Tells How He Does It!" *Photography Handbook* 10, 1942, pp. 8–13, 134–35.
147 **"more scared than when guns are blazing":** "Art Notes," *Daily Worker*, August 20, 1941.
147 **publicize the exhibit:** John Adam Knight, "Photography," *New York Post*, August 25, 1941. Also, "Weegee Has a Salon," *PM*, August 27, 1941.
147 **The show opened on August 13:** *Photo Notes*, September 1941.
148 **dead on a tenement rooftop:** "Murder on the Roof," *PM*, August 14, 1941.
148 **The power of the show:** Installation views of the exhibition are held in ICP's archive.
148 **a picture that he later admitted setting up:** Earl Wilson, "A New York Camera Sees Odd Things," *New York Post*, April 11, 1942.
148 **Jerry Austin:** "O'Dwyer Tackles 'Midget Vice Ring,'" *Brooklyn Eagle*, April 17, 1940.
148 **On the morning of August 17:** "Three Women Trampled to Death in Excursion-Ship Stampede," *PM*, August 18, 1941.
149 **Italians stayed on their side:** *American Guide Series: New York City Guide* (New York: Works Progress Administration/Random House, 1939), p. 119. Also, Paul Meskil, *The Luparelli Tapes: The True Story of the Mafia Hitman Who Contracted to Kill Both Joey Gallo and His Own Wife* (Chicago: Playboy Press, 1976), p. 18.
149 **"New York at night":** "Murder Is My Business," *Photo Notes*, September 1941.
150 **Even the *Times* put a little item:** "Notes of Camera World," *New York Times*, September 14, 1941.
150 **guestbook:** ICP collection.
150 **he'd placed an item:** John Adam Knight, "Photography," *New York Post*, December 31, 1941.
151 **newer stamp reading:** Research by Christopher George, compiled in posts at weegeeweegeeweegee.net/category/stamps/.
151 **the *Esquire* spin-off *Coronet*:** Weegee, "I Cover the Newsfront," *Coronet*, March 1942.
151 **in a magazine called *Good Photography*:** Weegee, "So You Want to Be a Free-lance!" p. 10.
152 **while covering a fire in 1941:** "Police Report: Weegee Covers an Arrest and a Fire," *PM*, February 17, 1941.
153 **Ingersoll . . . had seen . . . flooded store:** Gibbs, "A Very Active Type Man," part II, p. 23.
153 **visit to the Eden Musée:** "Weegee Revisits Coney Island . . ." Also, "Spring Clicks with the 150,000 at Coney . . . Weegee Just Clicks," *PM*, March 24, 1941.

CHAPTER 14

156 **opera hats:** "No Handstands at Met Opening," *PM*, November 25, 1941.
156 **a grim little local scene:** "Gunmen," *PM*, December 7, 1941.
157 **His first *PM* photograph after Pearl Harbor:** "New York Has Its First Air-Raid Alarms, but the Enemy Fails to Make Appearance," *PM*, December 10, 1941.
157 **parking ticket:** "For Eddie Grosso . . . ," *PM*, January 6, 1942.
157 **Joe McWilliams look foolish:** "Stooge for Bund Leader Guards our Waterfront," *PM*, March 3, 1942.
157 **showed a banner:** "Eight Stars," *PM*, February 17, 1942.
157 **Irma Twiss Epstein:** "Here Is Nurse Accused of Killing Baby," *PM*, February 9, 1942.
157 **fight about the war:** "Sailors," *PM*, February 20, 1942.
157 **men over forty-five:** "As New York Men, 45 to 64, Signed Up," *PM*, April 26, 1942.
157 **photographed a collision:** "Jeep and Patrolwagon," *PM*, July 21, 1942.

157 **litter-of-puppies photos:** "Up at the Dixie Rose A.C.," *PM*, August 2, 1942.
157 **group of Lower East Side kids:** "Young East Siders Hang Jap in Effigy to Advertise Their Scrap Hunt," *PM*, October 11, 1942.
158 **a six-year-old named Joseph Luparelli:** "Small Fry on Lower East Side Honor Big Brothers in the Services," *PM*, October 18, 1942.
158 **One of the most notorious mob figures:** Meskil, *The Luparelli Tapes*, pp. 16–23. Also, 1940 U.S. Census, accessed through ancestry.com.
158 **cheering in the streets:** "Little Italy Celebrates and Gives Thanks . . ." *PM*, September 9, 1943.
158 **X-level:** "Weegee, Free-Lance News Photographer . . ." *PM*, May 31, 1943.
158 **C-level . . . placards:** His window sticker and the sign are both visible in photographs of the car.
158 **war rally:** "Times Sq. Last Night," *PM*, April 21, 1942.
158 **blackout drill:** "What It Was Like in Last Night's Midtown Blackout," *PM*, May 1, 1942.
159 **mid-1930s:** Andy Finney, "History of Infrared Photography," unpublished manuscript, 2010, citing Kodak Museum, Harrow catalogue, 1947, p. 90, Folder 8, Box 111, Kodak Historical Collection, University of Rochester River Campus Libraries.
159 **first used it:** "What It Was Like in Last Night's Midtown Blackout."
159 **anti-halation layer:** Peres, *The Focal Encyclopedia of Photography*, 4th ed., p. 559.
159 **"Made with invisible light":** *NC*, p. 180.
160 **a single young woman:** Ibid.; and WWMM.
161 **one of the two sets of pictures:** "Before, After Accident," *PM*, December 28, 1942. Also, *NC*, p. 206.
162 **flashguns gold-plated:** John Adam Knight, "Photography," *New York Post*, October 12, 1942.
162 **Emmett Kelly, made it into *PM*:** "Weeping Willy and Smiling Kelly," *PM*, May 7, 1943.
162 **"the minute they see the camera":** "Weegee, as Clown, Covers Circus from the Inside . . . These Are Pictures He Took of the Crowd," *PM*, July 9, 1943.
165 **The Duke of Windsor:** "The Windsors Meet Weegee," *PM*, May 16, 1943. Also, details in "Weegee's Circus," *U.S. Camera*, August 1943, pp. 18–21, 60.
165 **had known all along:** MMM.
165 **the image then won first prize:** "From the Editor," *PM*, July 13, 1943.
166 **Beaumont Newhall:** Entry in online Dictionary of Art Historians, https://dictionary ofarthistorians.org/newhallb.htm.
166 **artistic possibilities of television:** Nancy Newhall, "Television and the Arts," *Parnassus* 12, no. 1 (1940): 37–38.
166 **exhibit . . . called *Action Photography*:** Press releases and installation views, MoMA "Exhibitions and Events" page, at https://www.moma.org/calendar/exhibitions/2314 ?locale=en.
166 **Harold Edgerton:** "Ultraspeed Flash Lamp," *Popular Science*, February 1941, pp. 208–10.
166 **fifty-nine pounds:** "Ultraspeed Flash Lamp," p. 210.
166 **The *Times* ran a rather stuffy:** "Display of Photos Opens Here Today," *New York Times*, August 18, 1943.
167 **The *Herald Tribune* was grumpier:** Herbert Kubly, "Action Photo Exhibit Reveals How Birds Fly, Athletes Move," *New York Herald Tribune*, August 29, 1943.
167 **as far as Seattle:** Henry Art Gallery records, at http://64.13.250.214/exhibitions/past /227/1943.
167 **A few months later:** "Death in Brooklyn," *U.S. Camera*, February 1944, pp. 18–19.
168 **telling a friend at the Photo League:** *Photo Notes*, June 1943.

CHAPTER 15

171   **a thousand murders . . . "I don't waste my genius":** Wilson, "Weegee," p. 37; *WBW*, p. 75.

171   **"When there was nothing major":** Author interview, January 2017.

172   **the Brooklyn prosecutor Burton Turkus:** Turkus and Feder, *Murder Inc.*

172   **"the famous New York news photographer":** A. J. Ezickson, "Press Flashes," *Popular Photography*, July 1944, p. 80.

172   **Wilcox recalled . . . "provoked":** "An Interview with Wilma Wilcox," accompanying release of *The Village*, 1989, ICP collection.

172   **Another of his hot-weather pictures:** "Cooling Off on the East Side," *PM*, June 14, 1943. Similarly, "They Got in to Cool Off," *PM*, June 28, 1943.

172   **A whiskey shortage got him:** "Whisky Shortage," *Life*, December 13, 1943, p. 38.

172   **"The Critic":** The general narrative of this evening has been reconstructed from *NC*, pp. 124–37; author interview with Mary Ann Liotta, July 2017; "The Metropolitan Opens," *Life*, December 6, 1943, pp. 38–39; the evening's coverage in the *New York Times*, *Brooklyn Eagle*, and *New York Herald Tribune*, November 23, 1943; "Mrs. George Washington Kavanaugh and the Ancient Art of Social Climbing," a profile at http://mrmhadams.typepad.com/blog; and Christopher George's comprehensive post, *Fans in a Flashbulb* (blog), at fansinaflashbulb.wordpress.com/2014/11/22/well-done-71-years-ago-today/.

173   **In 1942, he'd happened upon:** "Weegee Brings Back a 'Different' Picture of Opera's Opening Night," *PM*, November 29, 1942.

173   **Sam Vandivert later said:** Track 2, CD 3, Reel 154, W. Eugene Smith Archive Loft Recordings.

173   **"same old smell of camphor":** "The Metropolitan Opens," p. 39.

174   **"Tiffany's front window":** "Mrs. Kavanaugh's Luck," *Life*, December 2, 1946, p. 46.

174   **twenty carats each:** "The Reported," *PM*, November 28, 1943.

174   **"I didn't know Society":** *WBW* MS.

174   **waiting since 4:30 a.m.:** Howard Taubman, "Opera First Night Tribute to Russia," *New York Times*, November 23, 1943.

174   **porte cochere:** Author's e-mail exchange with the Metropolitan Opera's Peter Clark. He confirmed the location with former Met house manager Alfred Hubay, whose first night as an usher was that very evening, November 22, 1943.

174   **find out for himself:** *WBW* MS.

174   **"go back to your corpses . . . *fuck that nonsense*":** Unpublished letter to John Faber, April 13, 1960, private collection (hereafter "Unpublished letter to Faber").

175   **pronounced "DEE-shees":** Charles Earle Funk, *What's the Name, Please?* (New York: Funk and Wagnalls, 1936), p. 44.

175   **semi-memoir:** Elizabeth Wharton Drexel, *Turn of the World* (1912; reissue, New York: Lippincott, 1937).

175   **Hermann Goering had snapped it up:** "Miffed by No. 2 Nazi," *New York Journal-American*, December 16, 1940.

176   **"keep up morale":** "The Reported." Also, *NC*, p. 125.

176   **"could almost smell the smugness":** *NC*, 124.

176   **until he was in the darkroom:** Weegee, "A Shot in the Dark," *Parade*, March 16, 1958, p. 2.

176   **"This is an unposed shot":** Bruce Downes, ed., *1960 Photography Annual* (Chicago: Ziff-Davis, 1959), p. 230.

176   **"that was really honest":** *WBW* MS.

176   **They didn't want it:** *WW*, p. 26; also WWMM.

177   **described to an aquaintance as "dopey":** Unpublished letter to Faber.

177 **Grace Doherty:** "Opera Critic," *Daily News*, November 22, 1943.

177 **a horse named Silver:** Taubman, "Opera First Night Tribute to Russia."

178 *Art in Progress:* Exhibition files, https://www.moma.org/calendar/exhibitions/3385.

178 **the paper tacitly acknowledged:** "A Weegee Gets Attention at Museum of Modern Art," *PM*, June 2, 1944.

179 **"With this picture":** Weegee, "This Is My Best . . ." *Art Photography*, August 1953, pp. 32–35.

179 *Life* **magazine photographed her at home:** "*Life* Goes to Opening Night at the Opera with Mrs. George Washington Kavanaugh," *Life*, December 18, 1944, p. 90.

179 **lost a five-thousand-dollar bracelet:** "Mrs. Kavanaugh's Luck."

179 **"too divine":** Weegee, "A Shot in the Dark."

179 **"an *enormous* amount of family lore":** Author interview with Alexandra Warner, June 2014.

179 **Even more extraordinary:** Matthew Gurewitsch, "A Night at the Opera," *Smithsonian*, November 2005, pp. 18–20. Also, "Notes and Comment," *New Yorker*, February 12, 1990, p. 29.

180 **she buried her baron husband:** "Lord Decies Dies in England at 77," *New York Times*, February 2, 1944.

180 **she herself died the following June:** "Lady Decies, Widow of Irish Peer, Dies," *New York Times*, June 14, 1944.

180 **"He felt that this picture":** WWMM.

180 **moment presented itself:** *NC*, p. 92.

180 **"She wanted to trade pictures . . . my friends are kinda critical":** *WBW* MS.

CHAPTER 16

181 **Wilma Wilcox was back in his life:** WWMM.

181 **re-enrolled:** Author e-mail correspondence with Columbia University provost's office.

181 **"It was based around the relationship":** WWMM.

182 *Look* **that summer:** "Who Should Wear the Pants?" *Look*, August 8, 1943.

182 **the Di Maggios:** "105 Cops Searching House to House for Missing Child on Lower East Side," *PM*, July 6, 1943.

182 **when he got home safe:** "Jimmy Di Maggio, 3, Missing 8 Days, Is Found in Automat," *PM*, July 12, 1943.

182 **antic young women:** "Considering the Fact . . . ," *PM*, August 29, 1943.

182 **pensive faces:** "The News About Mussolini Comes to Broadway and 42d St," *PM*, August 1, 1943.

182 **extremely unsober response:** "Little Italy Celebrates and Gives Thanks . . . ," *PM*, September 9, 1943.

182 **enforced only in fits and starts . . . "three-piece rule":** William N. Eskridge Jr., "Privacy Jurisprudence and the Apartheid of the Closet, 1946–1961," *Florida State University Law Review* Rev. 703 (Summer 1997): 723.

183 **Another cross-dressing portrait:** Malcolm Logan, "Meet Myrtle from Myrtle Av.," *New York Post*, November 26, 1943.

184 **The first story broke:** Coverage in all New York dailies, August 2 and 3, 1943.

185 **Walter White:** "Negro Leader Confers with Police Commanders," *PM*, August 2, 1943.

185 **Dan Keleher:** "Demonstrations Follow Shooting of Negro Soldier . . . ," *PM*, August 2, 1943.

185 **A few weeks later:** "Police Called to Give Negroes 'Freedom from Fear,'" *PM*, November 18, 1943.

185 **Her skin appears fair:** Author interview with Monique Trinkleback, February 2017.

187 **On the night of December 18:** Many references incorrectly date this photo to 1937,

and many others misplace it in a similar-looking building at the Brooklyn end of the bridge. The correct information can be found in Philomena Mariani and Christopher George, *The Weegee Guide to New York* (New York: International Center of Photography/DelMonico Books, Prestel Publishing, 2014), p. 17.

187   **three flashbulbs:** Herb C. McLaughlin, "Fire," *Minicam Photography*, March 1947, pp. 17–25, 139–41.

187   **the *San Francisco Chronicle*:** Original *Chronicle* print in author's collection.

187   **Wilcox once remarked:** WWMM.

187   **"Get punch into your pictures":** NC, p. 241.

187   **That's how the editors:** Weegee, "Punch in Pictures," *U.S. Camera*, March 1943, pp. 15–18.

189   **later interviews reveal:** Wallace transcript, p. 9, and LJN.

189   **started a radio show:** Earl Wilson, "Saloon Editor on the Air—Don't Miss Him If You Can," *New York Post*, September 8, 1943.

189   **classes at the Photo League:** "'Weegee' Offers Course in Photo-Journalism," *Popular Photography*, September 1943, p. 76.

189   **Look tear sheet:** "This Is Erotic Ecstasy . . ." *Look*, December 12, 1944, pp. 32–34. Weegee's annotation from ICP collection. More about these photos appears in NC, pp. 112–15.

190   **had pulled the genre:** Beaumont Newhall, *The History of Photography from 1839 to the Present Day*, 2nd ed. (New York: Museum of Modern Art, 1964), chap. 8.

190   **At this stage of his life:** "Weegee Meets a Great Man," *PM*, May 7, 1944. Also, NC, pp. 233–35.

190   **wrote Nancy Newhall:** Letter to Beaumont Newhall, April 22, 1944, Box 157, Beaumont and Nancy Newhall Papers, 1843–1993, Getty Research Institute, Los Angeles, CA.

191   **had a small show up:** John Adam Knight, "Acting Makes Photos Better," *New York Post*, July 13, 1944.

191   **"a regular Weegee-type fire":** "Out of Focus: Short Short Camera Stories," *Popular Photography*, February 1944, p. 16.

191   **the early morning of July 5, 1944:** "Weegee Knew Something Was Brewing—And It Was!" *PM*, July 6, 1944. Also, NC, p. 207.

191   **Two beat cops had given him a lift:** Weegee, "Weegee Goes Psychic," *Popular Photography*, February 1945, p. 81.

191   **Shavey Lee . . . "Why waste the film on us?":** MMM.

192   **an office in the corner building:** C. Brooks, "The Typond-Lee Agency, 40 Mott St.," post at *Asian American History in NYC* (blog), https://blogs.baruch.cuny.edu/asian americanhistorynyc/?p=239

192   **pavement above it buckled:** "Gas Blasts Chinatown When Pavement Sags," *Brooklyn Eagle*, July 5, 1944.

CHAPTER 17

194   **"Grandma Moses . . . primitive way":** WBW MS.

194   **gave a talk:** WBW, p. 81, plus manuscript page marked "Introduction—2," ICP collection.

194   **Herb Giles:** Reese and Leipzig, "Interviews with ASMP Founder: Herb Giles." Also, Nancy Newhall, letter to Beaumont Newhall, April 11, 1944, Box 157, Beaumont and Nancy Newhall Papers, 1843–1993, Getty Resarch Institute, Los Angeles, CA.

194   **Paul Strand:** Paul Strand, "Weegee Gives Journalism a Shot of Creative Photography," *PM*, July 22, 1945.

195   **"Things got quiet":** Manuscript for *Naked City*, page marked "No. 1 Copy," ICP collection.

195   warm, enthusiastic introduction: *NC*, pp. 6–7.

196   "At auto accidents": Ibid., p. 241.

196   "time for gadgets": Ibid., p. 240.

196   "get all the information you can": Ibid., pp. 239–40.

196   a tough one to sell: *WBW*, pp. 81–82.

196   By 1943, Random House was producing: Many such titles can be found, an example being Isak Dinesen's *Winter's Tales* (New York: Random House, 1942).

196   Book-of-the-Month Club: John K. Hutchens, "For Better or Worse, the Book Clubs," *New York Times*, March 31, 1946.

196   *New Yorker . . .* considered dropping back to biweekly publication: Kunkel, *Genius in Disguise*, p. 355.

197   ladies' room: *WBW*, p. 82.

197   Charles Pearce: Joseph Mitchell, *Up in the Old Hotel* (New York: Pantheon, 1992), p. 681. Also, Kunkel, *Man in Profile*, p. 223.

197   Mitchell, after hanging around: David Streitfeld, "The New Yorker's Joseph Mitchell, Past Pluperfect," *Washington Post*, August 6, 1992.

197   neither in Mitchell's files nor *The New Yorker*'s archives: Author e-mail correspondence with Thomas Kunkel, Mitchell's biographer.

197   censorship tangle: "'U.S Camera' Banned in Boston," *Publishers Weekly*, no. 140, 1941, p. 2223.

197   Frank Henry: *WBW*, pp. 82–83.

197   handled Duell, Sloan's Essential Books imprint: Letter from Frank C. Henry to Mark Hellinger, May 13, 1947, private collection.

197    $1,625: Royalty statement, May 1, 1946, ICP collection.

197   press release: "Book Notes," *New York Herald Tribune*, November 29, 1944.

197   June 11: Carolyn Coggins, "What Goes on Backstage in the Literary Pageant," *Atlanta Constitution*, June 3, 1945.

197   July 18: "Books—Authors," *New York Times*, June 27, 1945.

197   "postponed continually": Coggins, "What Goes on Backstage."

198   "really a job . . . a holy crusade": *WBW* MS.

198   newspaper truck drivers' union: "Newspaper Sales Tied Up by Strike," *New York Times*, July 1, 1945.

198   Every paper but *PM*: Arthur Leipzig, "Strike at the Daily News," in *Growing Up in New York* (Boston: Imago Mundi/David R. Godine, 1995).

198   *Mary Margaret McBride*: Susan Ware, *It's One O'Clock and Here Is Mary Margaret McBride* (New York: New York University Press, 2005).

198   the show had been prerecorded: *WBW*, p. 84.

199   *Crime Club*: "Radio Highlights for Today," *New York Post*, July 23, 1945.

199   *Crime Quiz*: "Radio Highlights for Today," *New York Times*, August 4, 1945.

199   *Margaret Arlen Show . . .* WQXR: *WBW*, p. 84; and MMM.

199   the drivers' union and the papers settled: "News Strike Ends Under WLB Terms; Old Pact in Effect," *New York Times*, July 18, 1945.

200   *Time* trotted out: "Weegee," *Time*.

200   *Newsweek* went for near mockery: "Modest and Assuming."

200   The *Herald Tribune*'s: Richard Crandell, "A City Caught Unaware," *New York Herald Tribune*, August 26, 1945.

200   The Chicago *Tribune*'s critic: Will Davidson, "A Photo Reporter Covering New York," *Chicago Tribune*, July 29, 1945.

200   in the *Hartford Courant*: "Manhattan en Deshabille," *Hartford Courant Magazine*, July 29, 1945.

200   a brief, chipper tease in the *Los Angeles Times*: Lucille Leimert, "Confidentially: Book Review," *Los Angeles Times*, July 27, 1945.

200 **enthusiasm in the *San Francisco Chronicle*:** Joseph Henry Jackson, "Bookman's Note-book," *San Francisco Chronicle*, July 13, 1945.

200 **Toronto *Globe and Mail*:** "New York Photos," *Globe and Mail*, December 29, 1945.

200 ***Washington Post*:** "The Post's Books of the Week," *Washington Post*, July 29, 1945.

200 **Independent Jewish Press Service:** William B. Saphire, "Best Seller Weegee—The East Side Photog," *Jewish Advocate*, August 16, 1945.

200 **Newspaper Enterprise Association:** "Are You a Good Judge of Faces?" *Middlesboro* [KY] *Daily News*, August 14, 1945.

201 **The great Harlem Renaissance poet:** Langston Hughes, "Christmas Books," *Chicago Defender*, December 8, 1945.

201 **that of the *New York Times*:** Russell Maloney, "Portraits of a City," *New York Times*, July 22, 1945.

201 **backhanded compliment:** John Adam Knight, "Photography," *New York Post*, July 19, 1945.

202 ***PM* sent Arthur Leipzig:** Tom O'Connor, "Weegee's Coming-Out Party," *PM*, July 19, 1945.

203 **a short review the previous day:** Lewis, "Rave Notice."

203 **Paul Strand:** Paul Strand, "Weegee Gives Journalism a Shot of Creative Photography." *PM*, July 22, 1945.

204 **Philippe Halsman:** "Shy, Sensitive Weegee," *Popular Photography*, September 1945, p. 39. Also, Philippe Halsman, ed., and Yvonne Halsman, *Portraits* (New York: Abrams, 1983), p. 78 and unpaginated appendix.

204 **"Listen . . . life is beauty":** Mary Ellen Slate, "The Magazines," *Popular Photography*, October, 1945, p. 58.

204 **single light source:** Halsman, *Portraits*, appendix.

204 **"that's only done in the movies":** NC, p. 240.

204 **The Chaucer Head:** Weegee photographed the window.

204 **The Vendome Book Shop:** "Book Notes," *New York Herald Tribune*, August 22, 1945.

204 **Scribner's:** *WBW*, p. 85.

204 **Macy's:** Ibid.

205 **fourteen thousand copies:** Royalty statement, May 1, 1945, ICP collection.

205 **sold about twenty-five thousand copies:** Letter in Box 379, Farrar, Straus and Giroux, Inc. Records, Manuscripts and Archives Division, New York Public Library.

205 **two-sentence letter:** Alfred Stieglitz to Weegee, September 11, 1945, ICP collection.

205 **fleeting part of a second . . . "truly a great photographer":** FPTH.

205 **Pier 90:** Alvin Rosenfeld, "74 Million $$ Wait 1 GI; 14856 Home," *New York Post*, October 9, 1945.

CHAPTER 18

206 ***Seventeen*:** Telegram from Behri Pratt, September 11, 1945, ICP collection.

206 ***Coronet*:** Telegram from Garvis Johnson, September 12, 1945, ICP collection.

206 **and for a new spin-off:** Telegram from Margaret Hockaday Bischoff, August 14, 1945, ICP collection.

206 **sailors in town:** Kerry William Purcell, *Weegee* (London: Phaidon, 2004), plate 54 and facing page.

206 **when a water-main break:** "Water Break Stops 'El,'" *New York Post*, June 21, 1945.

206 **A few of his observers:** "The Nature of Human Behavior: Morbid Curiosity," *Look*, August 7, 1945, pp. 28–31.

206 **stern pop psychology essays:** Ibid. Also, "The Nature of Human Behavior: Grief," *Look*, October 2, 1945, p. 29; and "The Nature of Human Behavior: Hysteria," *Look*, November 27, 1945, pp. 70–71.

206 *Seventeen* . . . **was willing to pay:** Telegram from Behri Pratt, September 11, 1945, ICP collection.

206 PLEASE CALL OR COME IN: Telegram from *Vogue* magazine, October 3 (probably 1945), ICP collection.

207 **Liberman . . . the previous year:** Vince Aletti, "Alexander Liberman: A Definitively Modern Man," *New Yorker*, November 5, 2013, https://www.newyorker.com/books/page-turner/alexander-liberman-a-definitively-modern-man.

207 **dark suits:** Deirdre Carmody, "Alexander Liberman, Conde Nast's Driving Creative Force, Is Dead at 87," *New York Times*, November 20, 1999.

207 **two stories a week at seventy-five dollars:** *WBW* MS.

207 **Weegee had . . . already sold one photograph to *Vogue*:** "In New York, Victory V's . . . ," *Vogue*, September 1, 1945, pp. 116–17.

207 **"There was my picture":** *WBW* MS. Similarly, *WBW*, p. 93.

207 **"I had them wave their arms":** Ibid.

208 **up in Connecticut:** "Fun Times Working at Condé Nast in Greenwich!," February 14, 2016, at https://greenwichfreepress.com/around-town/fun-times-working-at-conde-nast-in-greenwich-58902/.

208 **letter from Allene Talmey:** Letter from Talmey "to whom it may concern," December 3, 1945, ICP collection. For evidence of her fearsomeness, see Mary Cantwell, *Manhattan When I Was Young* (New York: Houghton Mifflin, 1995), pp. 88–89.

208 **Alicia Markova:** *WBW*, p. 90. Also *WP*, chap. 8, and "New York . . . Around the Town," *Vogue*, December 1, 1945, pp. 141–47.

208 **bought himself a tuxedo:** *WBW*, pp. 87–89. Also, Earl Wilson, "The Good Wilson Tour . . . ," *New York Post*, October 24, 1945.

208 **ease among three worlds:** *WBW* MS. Similar point in *WBW* N&Q.

208 **by the end of 1944:** A story in *Editor & Publisher*, December 30, 1944, lists *PM*'s photographers, omitting Weegee.

208 *PM itself was beginning to run out of gas:* Milkman, *PM: A New Deal in Journalism*, chaps. 7 and 8.

208 **"We're hypothyroid":** Memo by John P. Lewis, March 5, 1946, Ingersoll Papers, Howard Gotlieb Archival Research Center at Boston University, box 70.

208 **finally breaking even:** Quoted in *Editor & Publisher*, October 20, 1945.

209 **In his 1946 diary:** Ingersoll Papers, Howard Gotlieb Archival Research Center at Boston University, Box 70.

209 **"Between the high . . . wide":** Daly, "When the 99% Had a Paper."

209 **signed a copy of *Naked City*:** Inscribed copy in private collection.

209 **"Post Photo by Weegee":** A typical example is "Garment District Stages Own Unofficial V-J Day," *New York Post*, August 10, 1945.

209 **"I now had women":** *WBW* MS. Similarly, *WBW*, p. 93.

209 **Halsman . . . ran into him:** Halsman, *Portraits*, appendix.

209 **"a girl with a healthy body and a sick mind":** Ibid. Also *BHS*.

209 **Cities Service:** *WP*, chap. 10. Also, *WBW*, pp. 94–95.

210 **ran them in its corporate magazine:** Telegram from Merle Thorpe, November 27, 1945, ICP collection.

210 **He showed up in a Graflex ad:** *Popular Photography*, January 1945, p. 63.

210 **Burke & James:** 1945 catalogue, author's collection.

210 **Diamond Gadg-it Bag:** Ad appears in, among other places, *Popular Photography*, June 1948, p. 13.

210 **back at the Museum of Modern Art:** Cecelia Ager, "Stuart Davis," *Vogue*, January 15, 1946, p. 81.

211 **story after story:** *WBW*, pp. 89–91.

212 **five new photos:** The first four are cited above; the fifth, a portrait of the columnist

Joseph Alsop, appears in Allene Talmey, "Vogue's Spotlight," *Vogue*, May 1, 1947, pp. 142–43, 187–88.

212   **all the way to Washington:** "Their Names Are Famous, But Their Faces . . . ?" *Vogue*, March 15, 1946, pp. 166–67, 214.

212   **He later told an interviewer that he quit *Vogue* after two years:** Berg, "Weegee," p. 4.

212   **lit up warmly:** Author interview with Philip Felig, May 2016.

212   **briefly been in the hospital:** "Weegee in Hospital," *PM*, April 15, 1946.

212   **on the night of May 20:** *WBW* MS.

212   **"An airplane had crashed into a skyscraper . . . I said NO, I did not go":** *WBW* MS. A cut-down version of this story appears in the published version of *WBW*, p. 126, relocated from the period just after the publication of *Naked City* to January 1954. That is almost surely an editing error; Weegee had sold his car and given away his police radio years before, and there was no such plane crash that year.

213   **junker with rusted-out fenders:** Toomey, *Assignment Homicide*, p. 7. Photographs from the mid-1940s also show the wear and tear on the car.

213   **At a luncheon:** Clip Boutell, "Authors Are Like People," *New York Post*, May 23, 1946.

213   **"I took the radio and smashed it":** Manuscript for *Weegee's People*, p. 1, ICP collection.

CHAPTER 19

214   **took some time to loaf:** *WP*, introduction.

214   **signed a book contract:** Mary Ellen Slate, "The Magazines," *Popular Photography*, June 1946, p. 126.

214   **teach a class in Chicago:** Morris Harkness, "Summer Seminar Planned," New York *Sun*, June 27, 1946.

214   **a talk in July at the Photo League:** Morris Harkness, "Weegee at Photo League," New York *Sun*, July 11, 1946.

214   **Manhattan Camera Club:** Morris Harkness, "Among the Clubs," New York *Sun*, September 19, 1946.

214   **Brooklyn Camera Club:** Advertisement, *New York Post*, August 15, 1946.

214   **two attendees walked out:** Mary Ellen Slate, "The Magazines," *Popular Photography*, June 1946, p. 16.

214   **invited *Life* along:** "Weegee Shows How to Photograph a Corpse," *Life*, August 12, 1946, pp. 8–10.

215   **a lecture he gave a year or so earlier:** It was at the Gamut Arts Club in Greenwich Village.

216   **"Full-Flavor Blended":** Ad slogan can be seen (among many other places) in *Life*, September 20, 1943, p. 88.

216   **a day in September 1942:** "Little Italy Smacks Lips over Truck Smash," *Brooklyn Eagle*, September 9, 1942.

216   **"Greenwich Village isn't what it used to be":** Ross Wetzsteon, *Republic of Dreams: Greenwich Village: The American Bohemia, 1910–1960* (New York: Simon & Schuster, 2002), pp. ix–xv.

217   **picking up messages and mail at Julius':** *WP*, introduction and chap. 9. Also, conversation with Julius' present-day bartenders, who will happily chat about Weegee if asked.

217   **Bunk Johnson:** Biographical information at http://www.redhotjazz.com/bunk.html and https://en.wikipedia.org/wiki/Bunk_Johnson.

217   ***Glezele tei:*** Thanks to my colleague Jesse Green for the explanation.

218   **Scheduled first for August:** Boutell, "Authors Are Like People."

218   **teed up with excerpts:** Weegee, "Weegee's People," *Minicam Photography*, March 1947, pp. 60–63; Weegee, "New York Off Guard," *Look*, July 23, 1946, pp. 48–51.

218   **Boston Book Fair:** "People Who Read and Write," *New York Times*, November 3, 1946.

219 **the Photo League's darkroom manager:** *Photo Notes*, August 1946, p. 1.

219 **"beer-and-pretzel party":** Ibid., p. 2.

219 **Jean Polacheck:** Author e-mail exchange with her granddaughter Angeliska Polacheck.

219 **Beaumont Newhall himself:** Beaumont Newhall, "Camera with a Zest for Life," *Saturday Review of Literature*, December 28, 1946, p. 15.

219 **"on the whole better":** Richard F. Crandell, "Camera Eye," *New York Herald Tribune*, December 8, 1946.

219 **"Weegee's happy now":** "A Happier New York," *St. Paul Pioneer Press*, undated clipping, ICP collection.

219 **The African American *Amsterdam News*:** Constance Curtis, "About Books and Authors," *New York Amsterdam News*, November 16, 1946.

219 **Bruce Downes:** Bruce Downes, "Weegee's People," Popular Photography, December 1946, pp. 86–87, 170, 172, 174.

219 **Langston Hughes:** "Famous People Give Personal Reading Lists," *New York Amsterdam News*, December 21, 1946.

220 **Graflex photo contest:** Morris Harkness, "Winners in Second Annual Graflex Contest," *New York Sun*, December 2, 1946.

220 **Swain Scalf:** "Winning Photo," *Chicago Daily Tribune*, November 25, 1946.

220 **The book party:** "Weegee's Party," *U.S. Camera*, February 1947, p. 29.

220 **November 11:** Advertisment in *PM*, November 10, 1946.

220 **worn down to the second button:** "Weegee's Wonderful Women," *Glamour Photography*, p. 36.

220 **moving-picture film . . . filmed by WCBS:** "Weegee's Party," *U.S. Camera*, p. 29.

220 **film from his book launch:** *Weegee's Cocktail Party*, 1950, ICP collection.

220 **stripped his apartment:** Parsons, "Weegee's Wedding," p. 41.

220 **"next venture":** "Weegee's People," *PM*, November 10, 1946.

221 **Dowling's:** Advertisement, *New York Post*, November 21, 1946.

221 **out of town:** Parsons, "Weegee's Wedding," p. 40.

221 **display ads:** One may be seen in the *New York Post*, December 9, 1946.

221 **Atwood:** Parson, "Weegee's Wedding," p. 40.

221 **Twelve weeks later:** Certificate of Marriage Registration, No. M5956, February 25, 1947, and Marriage Certificate, February 28, 1947, City of New York.

CHAPTER 20

222 **farmer's daughter:** New Hampshire Births and Christenings Index, 1714–1904, and U.S. Passport Applications, 1795–1925, accessed through ancestry.com.

222 **was forty-six, and for twenty-two of those years:** Town of Reading [MA] Certificate of Marriage, July 15, 1924.

222 **town house on Marlborough Street:** R. L. Polk, *Polk's Boston City Directory, 1945 Edition* (Boston: R. L. Polk, 1945), p. 82.

222 **Edward had died:** Death certificate No. 8104, September 18, 1946, Registry Division of the City of Boston.

222 **by February . . . Hotel Breslin:** Certificate of Marriage Registration, No. M5956.

222 **She joked that:** Jay Nelson Tuck, "Weegee Takes a Bride and Photog Pals Shoot the Works," *New York Post*, February 28, 1947.

222 **clipped ten years off:** Marriage Certificate, February 28, 1947.

222 **from then on:** Certificate of Death No. 89-179633, State of California Department of Public Health.

223 **Lee Sievan:** Her photographs of the ceremony are in the collection of the New York Public Library, and her husband, Maurice, witnessed the Felligs' marriage certificate. The other photographers and reporters mentioned here are either credited or named in

the *Post* (Tuck, "Weegee Takes a Bride") and *Minicam* (Parsons, "Weegee's Wedding") stories.

223 **"Weegee, of course, directed the photographers":** Robert Fuhring, "The Magazines," *Popular Photography*, July 1947, pp. 138, 140.

223 **It was perhaps thirty steps:** The China Lane was at 20 Mott Street; the explosion, in front of 38 and 40 Mott. I paced it off.

224 **"I gotta cut my movie":** Parsons, "Weegee's Wedding," p. 42.

224 **thirty minutes of raw film:** Fuhring, "The Magazines," p. 138.

225 **"He plans to spend a year":** Mary Ellen Slate, "The Magazines," *Popular Photography*, January 1947, p. 16.

225 **"We give up the dump":** Parsons, "Weegee's Wedding," p. 42.

225 **Hotel Elmwood:** Tuck, "Weegee Takes a Bride."

225 **two hundred dollars:** Parsons, "Weegee's Wedding," p. 43.

225 **West Forty-Sixth Street:** Correspondence from 1947 and 1948, ICP collection.

225 **The lease for the room on Centre Market Place:** Conway, *The Origins of Television News in America*, pp. 137–38.

225 **"Cost me plenty":** Parsons, "Weegee's Wedding," p. 42.

225 *Racketbusters Roundtable:* Thanks to collector David Goldin, proprietor of the Radio-GOLDINdex, for digitizing the premiere episode from a disc in his collection.

226 **Harry Feeney:** *New York Post* radio listings, August 7 and September 18, 1947.

226 **coined the term** *Murder Incorporated:* Turkus and Feder, *Murder Inc.*, pp. 20–21.

226 **young photographer named John Morrin:** John Morrin, unpublished short memoir, ICP collection; and Gilbert, "Reminiscences of Weegee," pp. 3–4.

226 **Around the beginning of 1947:** Jacquelyn Judge, "Puck with a Camera," *'47: The Magazine of the Year*, pp. 152–57.

228 **Kertész had also distorted photographs:** See André Kertész, *Distortions* (New York: Alfred A. Knopf, 1976). Also, introduction to catalogue *de-Formations*, exhibition at Bruce Silverstein Gallery, February 26–April 18, 2015.

228 **heavily manipulated pictures:** See, for example, the work of William Mortensen, at http://www.whmortensen.com/.

228 **Coney Island crowd photo:** Author interview with Sid Kaplan, January 2017.

228 **Steichen . . . stepped in:** "Edward Steichen Appointed Head of Photography Dept.," press release, July 15, 1947, Museum of Modern Art, https://www.moma.org/research-and-learning/research-resources/press_archives/1940s/1947/2?high_contrast=false.

228 *Family of Man:* Exhibition records at https://www.moma.org/calendar/exhibitions/2429.

229 **" 'You're really creating' ":** *WBW* MS.

229 **"Steichen says it's a new era":** "Visiting Photographer Beats Drums for Film."

229 **make a fortune:** "People in Photography: Weegee at Work," *People Today*, August 13, 1952, pp. 37–39.

229 **Mark Hellinger had been:** Jim Bishop, *The Mark Hellinger Story* (New York: Appleton-Century-Crofts, 1952).

229 **was going to be titled** *Homicide:* The narrative about the title change, and about the purchase of the title from Weegee, is drawn from the *Naked City* material in the Mark Hellinger Collection at the University of Southern California's Cinematic Arts Library.

230 **Malvin Wald . . . handed a copy:** Bishop, *The Mark Hellinger Story*, p. 330.

230 **Hellinger paid $3,500, a portion of which went to Duell, Sloan:** Letter from Mark Hellinger to Frank Henry, May 13, 1947, private collection.

230 **put Weegee on the film's payroll at $100 per week:** Bishop, *The Mark Hellinger Story*, pp. 330–31.

230 **Altogether, he got $2,100:** Financial tally for 1947, ICP collection.
230 **Dassin and Hellinger wanted:** James Sanders, *Celluloid Skyline* (New York: Alfred A. Knopf, 2002), pp. 327–32. Also, Inez Whiteley Foster, "Shooting Manhattan," *Christian Science Monitor*, September 11, 1948.
231 **juggler:** Bishop, *The Mark Hellinger Story*, p. 336. ICP has Weegee's photograph of the juggler, Bill Brown.
231 **nudging Hellinger to put him in the movie:** LJN.
231 **got *Harper's Bazaar* to run a page:** "Filmed in New York," *Harper's Bazaar*, February 1948, p. 253.
231 **probably by Lee Sievan:** Sievan's photos, like Weegee's, are at ICP.
231 **including a guest spot:** NBC radio index entry, Recorded Sound Reference Center of the Library of Congress, Washington, D.C.
232 **Jimmy Cagney:** John McCabe, *Cagney* (New York: Alfred A. Knopf, 1997).
232 **reviewed the final cut . . . then died:** Bishop, *The Mark Hellinger Story*, pp. 357–67.
232 **an hour's worth:** "Visiting Photographer Beats Drums for Film" says 1,700 feet of film.
232 **shot some of it on the same locations:** Leonard Lyons, "The Lyons Den," *New York Post*, January 21, 1948.
232 **Eastman Kodak lab:** Ibid. Expanded version of story, LJN. Also, two letters from Eastman Kodak (November 26 and December 11, 1947), quoted in undated American Society of Magazine Photographers release titled "Weegee Report," Folder 18, Box 51, Amos Vogel Papers, 1896–2001, Columbia University Libraries Archival Collections (hereafter "Amos Vogel Papers").
232 **had also elected not to return:** Letter from Eastman Kodak Film Processing Service to Weegee, February 26, 1948, ICP collection.
232 **Amos Vogel:** Interview with Kenneth Anger in Scott MacDonald, *A Critical Cinema 5: Interviews with Independent Filmmakers* (Berkeley: University of California Press, 2006), p. 41.
233 **bag of reels . . . only film he ever edited:** Amos Vogel lecture, ca. 2004, recalled by Christopher George, who attended.
233 **exclusive deal:** Letter from Amos Vogel to Weegee, November 13, 1947, Folder 8, Box 93, Amos Vogel Papers.
233 **MoMA held a screening:** Lyons, "The Lyons Den."
233 **a short run at the New School:** John Adam Knight, "Photography," *New York Post*, March 11, 1948.
233 **reacted even more sourly:** Ibid.
233 **"I'm not guessing what the verdict will be":** Barnett Bildersee, "Mr. Weegee Shoots the Works," *PM*, March 14, 1948.
233 **"O boy, me for California":** "Visiting Photographer Beats Drums for Film."

CHAPTER 21
234 **They exited the train:** Weegee, "Weegee Goes Hollywood," *Popular Photography*, March 1949, pp. 51–55, 160.
234 **disdain:** Ibid.
234 **"Land of the Zombies":** George Baker, "The Photo Spotlight," *Los Angeles Times*, December 4, 1949. (Here he says "Land of Zombies," but the "the" appears in subsequent uses, including the title of a chapter in *WBW*.)
235 **6606 St. Francis Terrace:** Correspondence and photo stamps, ICP collection.
235 **a dual row:** Photograph in Los Angeles Public Library collection, http://jpg3.lapl.org/pics42/00070648.jpg, and contemporary maps.
235 **installed a telephone . . . "You can't be cute":** *WBW* MS.
235 **eccentricity of dress:** Weegee, "Weegee Goes Hollywood."
235 **Gene Kelly:** *WBW*, p. 100. Also, Berg, "Weegee," p. 4.

235   run in the screening room at Universal-International: Thornton Delehanty, "Wee-
      gee Looking for New Fame, Now Wants to Go Before Camera," *New York Herald Tri-
      bune*, May 9, 1948.

235   two more public viewings: "Visiting Photographer Beats Drums for Film."

235   new score: Letter to Amos Vogel, undated (probably April 1948), Folder 8, Box 93,
      Amos Vogel Papers.

235   There were also some cuts: Untitled item, *PM*, March 21, 1948.

235   agreed to appear: Correspondence with Amos Vogel, April through July 1948, Folder
      8, Box 93, Amos Vogel Papers.

236   He finally admitted it: Delehanty, "Weegee Looking for New Fame . . ."

236   Ingo Preminger: Application form, October 26, 1948. SAG-AFTRA archives. Phone
      conversation with archivist Valerie Yaros. Also, author interview with Jim Preminger,
      July 2016.

236   *Every Girl Should Be Married . . . practied his delivery:* "Hollywood . . . Land of the
      Zombie," undated manuscript (two drafts) by Weegee, ICP collection.

236   for which Weegee was paid $250: Weegee, "Weegee Goes Hollywood." (He actually
      says "$250 a day," and this was a one-day job.)

236   a week beforehand: *WBW* MS.

237   *Anna Lucasta:* Walter Winchell, "Gossip of the Nation," *Philadelphia Inquirer*, Sep-
      tember 6, 1948.

237   he'd spoken too soon: Berg, "Weegee," p. 4.

237   got his Screen Actors Guild card: SAG-AFTRA archives. Phone conversation with
      archivist Valerie Yaros.

237   eight days of work: Production notes, *The Set-Up*, RKO Radio Pictures Studio Rec-
      ords (Collection PASC 3), UCLA Library Special Collections, Charles E. Young
      Research Library, University of California, Los Angeles.

237   "I couldn't change my shirt": Arthur (Weegee) Fellig, "Big Town Weegee Goes Hol-
      lywood," *Los Angeles Mirror*, November 26, 1950.

238   Bachrach . . . got a set of those: Ibid.

238   he called *Land of Zombies:* Baker, "The Photo Spotlight."

238   *San Francisco:* "Inventor of the Elastic Lens Is Here to Show It Off," *San Francisco
      Chronicle*, April 30, 1950.

238   "the subconscious camera": Ibid.

238   carrying case: A publicity photo with Red Skelton, likely released by M-G-M in con-
      nection with the film *The Yellow Cab Man*, shows Weegee with the camera case. ICP
      collection.

238   dropped by . . . Margaret . . . seemed cheery at first: Ida Wyman, with Melanie
      Herzog, *Chords of Memory: Photos* (privately printed, 2014), pp. 13–22.

239   "Dear Vilma": Letter to Wilma Wilcox, December 14, 1948, ICP collection.

239   his mother died: Beckie Fellig died March 18, 1949, New York City Death Index,
      1949–1965, accessed through ancestry.com.

240   Fraymart Gallery: "Photos Depict Facets of Life," *Los Angeles Times*, July 24, 1949.

240   Paul Kantor Gallery: Suzanne Muchnic, "Paul Kantor, 83; L.A. Dealer Showed
      Many Emerging Artists," *Los Angeles Times*, December 31, 2002.

240   screened: "Art Events," *Los Angeles Times*, July 31, 1949.

240   signed a contract . . . $4,500 . . . an extra $250: Contract, October 1, 1949, and
      associated correspondence, ICP collection.

240   spoke about it later: In a United Press wire service story by Harman Nichols, "Shutter
      Sharpie Is Doing All Right in Hollywood Job," published in (among other places) the
      North Tonawanda Evening News of September 27, 1950, Weegee claimed "$5,000 a
      month" for use of his trick lenses. Lucy Key Miller, in her *Chicago Tribune* column of
      September 22, 1950, has him saying "$5,000 a minute."

240 the Elastic Lens: Weegee, "Weegee's Elastic Lens," *Popular Photography*, August 1952, pp. 77–80. Also, Irving Desfor, "Camera Club News," AP story carried in *Prescott Evening Courier*, July 15, 1952. (In this one, the rental fee is five thousand dollars for five days.)

241 distorted pictures of L.A.'s City Hall: "If Things Look Out of Shape at City Hall— Blame the 'Elastic Lens'!" *Los Angeles Herald-Examiner*, May 24, 1950.

241 similar set of photos of NBC headquarters: "Looks Like 'Weegee' Used a 'Squeegee'— But He Didn't," *Hollywood Citizen-News*, May 25, 1950.

241 confided to a friend: Author interview with a subject requesting anonymity.

241 fell hard for a stunt girl: "Weegee's Wonderful Women," p. 36. Also, Martin, "Arthur (Weegee) Fellig (1899–1968)," p. 14.

242 Cheeta the chimp: Mildly expurgated version, *WBW*, p. 102. Full version in Berg, "Weegee," p. 4.

242 it was around 1950: This date is difficult to pin down. Weegee's mail continued to come to St. Francis Terrace through 1950, but photographs from 1948 show his North Hudson Avenue address stamp. (They may have been stamped later.) It is plausible that the North Hudson address was a studio, and that he used both addresses for a time as his marriage gradually came apart.

242 Margaret bought a business: Sales documents, Los Angeles County records, book 31375, p. 131.

242 do not appear to have formally divorced: In ICP's file of correspondence regarding the publication of Louis Stettner's edition of Fellig's *Weegee* (Knopf, 1977), there are several exchanges of letters about the prospect of a claim on royalties from "Mrs. Arthur Fellig."

242 pawnshop receipt: *NH*, act 3. The date has been retouched out of the published version of the photo but can be seen on ICP's print.

245 The first of those gigs started in early 1950: The narrative about the *Sleeping City* tour is reconstructed mostly from the account in *WBW*, his newspaper appearances in each city, and the budget records, correspondence, and memoranda in the Universal Studios Archive, Cinematic Arts Library, University of Southern California.

245 photo-contest tie-in: Advertisement in *New York Post*, September 14, 1950.

246 Through the week of September 11: Telegram from Phil Gerard to David Lipton and Al Horwits, Universal Studios Archive, dated September 11, 1950. The available microfilmed copies of the *Post* from that week are taken from a local edition, specific to the Bronx, that did not carry these photographs.

246 charmingly unstructured local TV program called *Johnny Olson's Rumpus Room*: One kinescope of the show (not the episode in which Weegee appeared) is known to exist, in the Johnny and Penny Olson Papers in the Wisconsin Historical Society Archives. Thanks to Amy Sloper for viewing the film and describing it to me.

246 Schlitz beer and . . . Muntz: *WBW*, 108.

246 "left the film": Ibid., p. 105.

246 A *Globe* columnist interviewed him: Ted Ashby, "Weegee Knows a Wonderful Place to Eat but Won't Tell," *Daily Boston Globe*, September 20, 1950.

247 an unsuccessful attempt: *WBW*, p. 107.

247 the *Chicago Herald-American* ran a full page: "While Chicago Sleeps," *Chicago Herald-American*, September 22, 1950.

247 The *Tribune* interviewed him: Lucy Key Miller, "Front Views and Profiles: Ouija Board Magic," *Chicago Tribune*, September 22, 1950. Also, Charles Babcock, "Among the Authors," *Chicago Tribune*, October 1, 1950.

247 Four papers in Washington: Telegram from Charles Simonelli to David Lipton, Al Horwits, and Archie Herzoff, September 22, 1950, Universal Studios archive. As is true of the *New York Post* stories mentioned above, most of these stories seem to have

run (if indeed they did run) in early or partial editions that were not preserved. Two that have survived are "'Weegee' Stays Awake to Find 'Psychic Shots,'" *Washington Post*, September 25, 1950, and "End of the Chase," *Washington Evening Star*, September 25, 1950.

247 **In Cleveland:** "Night in the City," *Cleveland Press*, September 27, 1950.
247 **The *Minneapolis Star* went for those:** "Weegee Pictures Minneapolis After Midnight," *Minneapolis Star*, October 11, 1950.
247 **Its rival the *Tribune*:** "Guess What," *Minneapolis Sunday Tribune*, November 26, 1950.
247 **In nearby St. Paul:** Simonelli telegram, September 22, 1950, Universal Studios archive.
247 **The *Milwaukee Sentinel*:** Weegee, "While Milwaukee Sleeps," *Milwaukee Sentinel*, September 25, 1950.
247 **St. Louis Star-Times:** Simonelli telegram, September 22, 1950, Universal Studios archive.
247 **"Spirits of St. Louis":** *WBW*, p. 111.
247 **the *Atlanta Constitution*:** "N.Y. Crime Photographer Turns Camera on Atlanta," *Atlanta Constitution*, October 26, 1950.
247 **Denver turned out to be:** "While Denver Sleeps," *Rocky Mountain News*, October 14, 1950. Also, Weegee, "But the Jail Sleeps On," undated clipping, *Rocky Mountain News*, ca. October 1950.
247 **Larimer Street:** Denver telephone directory, 1950. Thanks to James Rogers of the Denver Public Library for address and context.
248 **Dorothy Oswald:** Model release, October 15, 1950, ICP collection.
248 **New Orleans:** "'Weegee' Has Trouble Here with a 'Sleeping City,'" *New Orleans Item*, October 4, 1950. Also, *WBW*, pp. 111–13.
249 **Cup Cake:** *WBW*, p. 113, and photo from ICP collection.
249 **Amy Warrens:** *WBW* MS.
249 **claiming that he'd stayed one step ahead:** *WBW*, p. 110.

CHAPTER 22

250 **was contracted . . . Weegee's consultancy:** Ibid. Also *WBW*, p. 101; and Berg, "Weegee," p. 24.
250 **"The Los Angeles drunk tank":** Ezra Goodman, "On the Bum in Hollywood," *Daily News*, March 19, 1951.
250 **get his burlesque dancer friend Amy Warrens:** *WBW* MS.
252 **"I was pretty sick of Hollywood":** *WBW*, p. 116.
252 **a small apartment at 250 West Forty-Seventh Street:** Correspondence, ICP collection. Visible in *The Naked Eye*, dir. Louis Stoumen (1957). Also, Lichello, "'The Famous Weegee' Wants a Woman from Mars . . . ," p. 5.
252 **Columbia Lecture Bureau:** CLB brochure, Folder 8, Box 93, Amos Vogel Papers. Also, *WBW*, p. 124.
252 **"too risqué":** *WBW* MS.
252 **nine hundred people:** *WBW*, p. 125.
252 **shared a shower:** Ibid.
252 **five hundred dollars per night:** CLB brochure, Amos Vogel Papers.
253 **"no foreign news at all":** Chapman, *Tell It to Sweeney*, p. 277.
253 **"blintzes crisis":** *WBW*, p. 38.
253 **PM, after being sold:** Milkman, *PM: A New Deal in Journalism*, pp. 208–10.
253 **the *Sun* had died:** "The Sun Is Sold," *Life*, January 16, 1950, p. 39.
253 **white-brick apartment houses:** Prominent among the early "whitebricks" is Manhattan House, 200 East Sixty-Sixth Street, discussed in Elliot Willensky and Norval

White, *The AIA Guide to New York City*, 3rd ed. (New York: Harcourt Brace Jovanovich, 1988), p. 394.

253 **Third Avenue el:** Lawrence Stelter, *By the El: Third Avenue and Its El at Midcentury* (New York: H&M Productions, 1995), p. 116.

253 **the Lower East Side began to experience:** Jane Jacobs, *The Death and Life of Great American Cities* (New York: Random House, 1961), notably p. 48.

253 **Greenwich Village:** Wetzsteon, *Republic of Dreams*, preface.

254 **Espresso fed poetry:** Local lore has it that Caffe Reggio, on MacDougal Street, introduced cappuccino to the United States when it opened in 1927, and it continues to serve both. The "four corners" coffeehouses at the intersection of Bleecker and MacDougal Streets, all now defunct, were active into the 1990s.

254 **Dan Merrin, who edited lots of them:** Author interview, January 2017.

254 **Martin Goodman, publisher of Mutual Magazine:** "Field Guide to Wild American Pulp Artists," https://www.pulpartists.com/Goodman.html.

254 **which would have been prosecutable:** Gay Talese, *Thy Neighbor's Wife* (New York: Doubleday, 1980), chaps. 2–5.

254 **Bob Harrison:** Henry E. Scott, *Shocking True Story: The Rise and Fall of* Confidential, *"America's Most Scandalous Scandal Magazine"* (New York: Random House, 2005), pp. 15–16. Also, Tom Wolfe, "Purveyor of the Public Life," in *The Kandy-Kolored Tangerine-Flake Streamline Baby* (New York: Farrar, Straus and Giroux, 1965), pp. 180–203.

254 **enthusiastic about Weegee's distortion pictures:** *WBW*, pp. 96–97.

255 **"two snappers":** *WBW* MS.

255 **"a little lost creature":** Martin, "Arthur (Weegee) Fellig (1899–1968)," p. 14.

255 **"There were many of those sweet young things":** Ibid.

255 **Judith Malina:** Author interview, July 2014.

256 **a low-pitched men's magazine:** "After Sundown," *Night and Day*, October 1952, pp. 27–29.

256 **A year later:** Vincent Tajiri, "Weegee, U.S.A," *Art Photography*, April 1954, pp. 4–9.

256 **Another magazine:** Harry Bardon (as told to), "How We Licked the Teen-Age Sin Clubs," *Tab*, February 1955, pp. 52–57.

257 *Night and Day,* **over several issues:** "The Dramatics of Nighttime," *Night and Day*, January 1953, pp. 11–13; and "Conspicuous Distortion," *Night and Day*, January 1953, pp. 27–29; "The Big Stare," *Night and Day*, January 1954, pp. 27–29; untitled feature about Basin Street nightclub, *Night and Day*, January 1954, pp. 39–41; "This Is Hollywood," *Night and Day*, April 1954, pp. 11–13; "And Beyond," *Night and Day*, January 1954, p. 15.

257 **Dan Merrin, the editor:** Author interview, January 2017.

257 **five sets of photos by Weegee in Eye:** March, July, September, October, and November 1953 issues.

257 **One, in Stag:** Weegee, "I'll Be There—For a Murder!" *Stag*, September 1953, pp. 21–27.

257 **When an editor at Brief:** *WBW* MS, and published edition, pp. 117–18. Also, "Movies Are Better than Ever," *Brief*, October 1953, pp. 11–17.

258 **Art Students League:** *WBW*, p. 118.

258 **friends of Weegee's:** Author interview with Joan Gropper, October 2017.

258 **general distaste he had for wedding photography:** LJN.

258 **Erika Stone:** Author interview, June 2015. Also, Photo-Representatives press release, "Introducing Our Photographers and Our Stock," ca. 1953, ICP collection.

259 **met a graphic designer:** Author interviews with Joan Harris and Anton Mikofsky, May and July 2017, and Mel Harris's introduction to *NH*.

259 **known to call people:** Letter from Stanley Colbert to Miles Barth, October 8, 1995, ICP collection (hereafter "Colbert letter to Barth").

259   **grew somewhat frustrated:** Ibid.
261   **the Weegee Nippletickler:** *WBW* MS.
261   **Miles Orvell:** Keller, "An Elusive Fame," p. 99.
261   **Stanley Colbert sent it:** The narrative about the publication of *Naked Hollywood* has been reconstructed from the records of Farrar, Straus and Giroux, which absorbed Pellegrini & Cudahy in April 1953. Farrar, Straus and Giroux, Manuscripts and Archives Division, New York Public Library. Also, Boris Kachka, *Hothouse* (New York: Simon and Schuster, 2013), pp. 64–65.
261   **inscribed a copy to him:** Colbert letter to Barth.
261   **a small paperback:** Weegee, as told to Mel Harris, *Weegee's Secrets of Shooting with Photoflash* (New York: Designers 3, 1953).
261   **Francine:** Author interviews with Joan Harris and Anton Mikofsky, May and July 2017.
261   **Bobby Seebacher:** Author interview with J. Robert Seebacher, May 2016. Also, his wife, Joanne, appeared on PBS's *Antiques Roadshow*, Episode 1903 (recorded August 9, 2014), and had the family's prints and a signed copy of *Weegee's Secrets* appraised.
262   **flatly dismissive:** John Adam Knight, "Photography," *New York Post*, March 19, 1953.
263   **one of the first issues of *Playboy*:** "Nudes by Weegee," *Playboy*, May 1954, p. 15.

CHAPTER 23

265   **The Concord Camera Circle:** General sources for this section include Jim Linderman, *Camera Club Girls* (New York: Dull Tool Dim Bulb Books/Blurb Books, 2009); and an additional post by Linderman titled "Weegee, Bettie Page, and the FBI: The Last (?) Unpublished Photographs and What Did the FBI Know About Bettie Page," at http://dulltooldimbulb.blogspot.com/2011/06/weegee-bettie-page-and-fbi-last.html.
265   **picked up a camera back in the thirties . . . YMCA:** *American Photography*, February 1951, p. 112.
265   **studio on Forty-Seventh Street:** Linderman, in "Weegee, Bettie Page, and the FBI," says he was at 218 West Forty-Seventh Street.
265   **a weekend business:** This and the following section about Bettie Page and the arrests in South Salem come largely from Richard Foster, *The Real Bettie Page* (New York: Carol Publishing, 1998), pp. 42–46; and the documentary *Bettie Page Reveals All* (2012), dir. Mark Mori.
265   **caches of their pictures:** Author interview with Eric Kroll, April 2017.
266   **box lunch from a local Chinese restaurant:** This and multiple other details of the day come from two stories appearing in the *New York Age*: "Fines Nude Models and Y Club Head," August 2, 1952, and "Nude Pic Shooting Above Board but Cass Pays $5," August 23, 1952.
266   **Sometimes he'd have sixty people:** Photograph, Jonny Wilson collection.
266   **"Guest artist: Weegee":** Advertisements in the *New York Post*, September 6, 1956, and subsequently.
267   **The models were charged:** "Art Poses in Woods Bring $5 Fines to 27," *New York Times*, July 29, 1952. Also, "Photographers Fined," *New York Times*, August 10, 1952.
267   **Weegee got out of there with a five-dollar fine:** Special thanks to Mark Mori for sharing the Village of South Salem records from the arrests. According to the town clerk, the originals were discarded shortly after he obtained his copies.
268   **Jonny Wilson:** Author interview, May 2016.
268   **Grand Central Palace:** Program from the National Photographic Show, February 12–16, 1953, private collection.
268   **tossing them:** Photographs from the day are in ICP's collection.
268   **prop gilded throne:** Author interview with Sid Kaplan, January 2017.

268   **"Whoever pays me the most":** Letter and recollections from Alfred Gescheidt to Miles Barth, April 1, 1996.

268   **Sid Kaplan met Weegee:** Author interview, January 2017.

269   **At some point around 1955:** Weegee told this story in detail many times; one good account is in Berg, "Weegee," p. 26.

269   **point of view of the flashgun:** Weegee, "Distortions," in *Salon Photography* (Greenwich, CT: Fawcett Publications, 1954), pp. 4–11.

269   **backstage on Ed Sullivan's show:** John Wolbarst, "Weegee Goes to 35mm," *Modern Photography*, October 1954, pp. 100–101.

270   **a little bit concocted:** Negatives from La Rosa shoot in author's collection.

270   **he had already started using more modern equipment:** Author e-mail exchange with Christopher George, September 2017.

270   **likely been given one by his friend Al Levin:** Author interview with Joan Gropper, October 2017.

270   **Donald Dery:** Author interview, ca. 2013.

271   **Maxwell Bodenheim:** LJN. Christopher George, the Weegee expert at the International Center of Photography, is skeptical about the attribution of the postmortem pictures to Weegee. He notes circumstantial details like the size of the prints and the stamps on the back, neither of which is seen elsewhere in his archive, plus the fact that Weegee was out of the spot-news business by 1954.

271   **ran into Helen Gee:** Helen Gee, *Limelight* (University of New Mexico Press, 1997), pp. 235–37.

272   **in the magazine *Night and Day*:** "Weegee Visits the Village," *Night and Day*, June 1955, pp. 11–15.

273   ***Candid* and *Tab* and *Stag*:** Respectively, the issues of May 1954, February 1955, and January 1955.

273   ***Cars*:** "Weegee Looks at Cars," *Cars*, June 1953, pp. 12–15.

273   **In 1955, he began a new method:** "Stretch Caricatures," *Vogue*, July 1955, pp. 74–75. Also "People Are Talking About . . . ," *Vogue*, August 1955, pp. 76–77.

CHAPTER 24

275   **He made more of them:** "How Your TV Heroes Look to Weegee's Magic Camera," *Look*, May 1956.

275   **award from the Art Directors Club:** Letter from Allen F. Hurlburt to Weegee, July 3, 1957, and award certificate, ICP collection.

275   **Another *Look* assignment:** "Weegee Spoofs the New Spring Hats," *Look*, April 16, 1957, pp. 88–91.

275   **Even *TV Guide*:** "Point of View: Weegee Takes a Look at the Stars of Some of the Season's New Shows," *TV Guide*, February 23–March 1, 1957, pp. 28–29.

275   **Authenticolor:** "Weegee's Caricatures," *Popular Photography*, September 1956, pp. 44–45, 77, 80.

275   **A jazz bandleader:** Hugo Montenegro and His Orchestra, *Ellington Fantasy*, Vik/RCA, 1958.

275   **A smaller magazine:** "Comic Camera," *Pageant*, January 1956, pp. 12–15.

275   **sold Mel Harris his half of the rights:** Author interview with Joan Harris, May 2017.

275   **Amos Vogel bought *Weegee's New York*:** Amos Vogel Papers, Folder 8, Box 93.

275   **started pitching himself to advertising agencies:** WBW, pp. 118–23.

275   **an ad that Designers 3 produced:** Award certificate, ICP collection and catalogue, AIGA archive. Thanks to AIGA's Heather Strelecki for research assistance.

276   **National Electrical Contractors Association:** Ad appearing in *Buildings*, April and October, 1958.

276   **University Loudspeakers:** Undated copy, ICP collection.

276   **He also later claimed:** *WBW*, pp. 118–23.

276   **Over the course of a few nights in 1954 and 1955:** The dates for these photographs come from an extremely well-informed guess made by Ricky Riccardi, Louis Armstrong's archivist. Armstrong played four engagements at Basin Street in those years: August 10–September 5, 1954, April 16–27, 1955, May 5–20, 1955, and June 25–July 8, 1955. Some of the pictures appeared in print in September 1954 ("Wanted: An Adjective to Fit Satchmo," *Night & Day*, September 1954, pp. 28–29), putting them at the beginning of that summer's run. But others are likely to have been made on May 15, 1955, because Gary Crosby (who appears in some of the backstage shots) appeared with Armstrong on Ed Sullivan's CBS show that evening. Sullivan ends the segment by saying, "Now, get on back to Basin Street!"

276   **odd habit of EMPHASIZING several KEY WORDS:** Many bits of Armstrong's writing appear in Terry Teachout's *Pops: A Life of Louis Armstrong* (New York: Houghton Mifflin Harcourt, 2009).

277   **a lively and clever assignment:** "Weegee's Caricatures." Also, *WBW*, p. 129.

277   **Halsman . . . showed off some recent work:** "Weegee's Caricatures."

278   **he even helped get one off the ground:** *Photographers Showplace*, nos. 1 through 4, July 1956 through November 1957. Also, *WBW*, p. 134.

278   **Michael St. John:** *Photographers Showplace*. Also, Ken Quattro, "The Gospel According to Archer St. John," *Alter Ego* 77 (November 6, 2012): 3–15. Additional information, e-mail correspondence with Ken Quattro.

279   **Arguably the best demonstration of Cinerama:** Most of this section comes from *The Story of Louis de Rochemont's* Windjammer (New York: Random House, 1958). Also, "Windjammer Filmed in New Process," *Christian Science Monitor*, April 1, 1958; details of the system are from http://in70mm.com/cinemiracle/index.htm; and e-mail correspondence with David Strohmaier.

280   **kind murmuring:** Archer Winsten, "*Windjammer* at Intimate Roxy," *New York Post*, April 10, 1956.

280   **Around 1957, he was diagnosed with diabetes:** Barth, in *Weegee's World*, says it was 1957; Sid Kaplan, in interviews, recalls that it was around then; Louis Stettner in *Weegee* says it was 1953. Many of the dates Stettner places on photographs in his book are a couple of years off, and I have elected to go with Barth's.

280   **"the white pills":** Letter from Weegee to Wilma Wilcox, January 27, 1959, ICP collection.

281   **Wilma later said that they lived together continually:** Letter from Wilma Wilcox to Ken Greengrass, February 20, 1985, ICP collection.

281   **he drifted in with her:** Author interview with Sid Kaplan, January 2017.

281   **on City Island:** Author interview with Ellis Barnhart, February 2017.

281   **Cherry Street:** New York City telephone directory, 1958.

281   **he'd mail her in care of . . . her office in Midtown:** Various late 1950s correspondence, ICP collection.

282   **In 1958, he gave up the Forty-Seventh Street studio:** Suzanne Johnston, "As I Remember Weegee," *The Photo Review* 22: 1 (Winter 1999), pp. 8–14

282   **Lou Stoumen:** Thanks to the Lou Stoumen archive at the Museum of Photographic Arts, San Diego, for supplying digital copies of the shooting script and the film itself.

282   **Appearing on the interview show *Night Beat*:** Episode list, http://ctva.biz/US/TalkShow/NightBeat.htm. Also, *WBW*, p. 136.

282   **He even made an appearance:** TV listings, *Long Island Star-Journal*, March 27, 1957. (In *WBW*, p. 136, Weegee refers to an appearance on "the Jack Paar Show," but Paar did not take over the show till that July; he either made two visits or was referring to *Tonight* generally.)

283   **When Steichen included Weegee:** Press release and checklist, at https://www.moma
      .org/calendar/exhibitions/2439.

283   **For a magazine called *Slick*:** "Which Shape Do You Like?" *Slick*, May 1957, pp. 40–43.
      The model is not credited in the story, but the photographer Peter Gowland was also
      there that day, and his pictures show (and identify) Nurmi with Weegee. Confirmed in
      phone conversation with Mary Lee Gowland.

283   **He also did a number of stories:** "Death in the Streets," *Hi, The Tall Magazine for
      Men*, May 1957, pp. 31–33. "Weegee's Greenwich Village," *Ho! The Long Magazine for
      Men*, September 1957, pp. 14–17. "Assignment: Sleep," *Ho!*, November 1957,
      pp. 16–21. "Weegee's Weirdos," *Ho!*, January 1958, pp. 16–21.

283   **he and his distortions:** "'The Famous Weegee' Wants a Woman from Mars."

284   **A much friendlier Weegee:** Les Barry, "Weegee Covers the Circus," *Popular Photogra-
      phy*, April 1958, pp. 126–27.

285   **Dick Randall was:** See *The Wild Wild World of Dick Randall* (Mondo Macabro USA),
      dir. Pete Tombs, at https://www.youtube.com/watch?v=LxFhScV_u3s. Also, author
      interview with Corliss Randall.

285   **dashing about and fretting:** *WBW* N&Q.

285   *Holiday in Brussels:* Author interviews with Corliss Randall and Lorraine Lasker,
      June 2017. Also, A. H. Weiler, "View from a Local Vantage Point," *New York Times*,
      July 27, 1958; "Film on Brussels Fair Opens Here in August," *New York Post*, July 31,
      1958; and *WBW*, pp. 131–32.

285   **Chaplinesque tramp:** Leonard Lyons, "The Lyons Den," *New York Post*, July 31, 1958.
      Also, *WBW*, p. 132.

285   **it made it onto NBC:** TV listings for June 22, 1958, *Tarrytown Daily News*, July 21,
      1958.

285   **"The World's Fair is wonderful . . . access was mostly free . . . the secret formulas":**
      Two undated 1958 letters to Wilma Wilcox, ICP collection.

286   **Elsa Dorfman:** Author interview, August 2017.

286   **made a habit of going by the Israeli pavilion:** "More Weegeeisms," p. 3, undated man-
      uscript in ICP collection.

286   **accidentally found himself on a hard-news story:** "Victim Leads Hit-Run Race After
      Driver," *New York Post*, August 12, 1958.

286   **Just a few weeks later:** Letters to Wilma Wilcox, October 16, 21, 24, and 28, 1958,
      ICP collection. Also, letter to Wilcox, October 14, 1958, private collection; and author
      interview with Paul Mason.

286   **a Grimm Brothers adaptation called *The Magic Fountain*:** *WBW*, pp. 140–42, refers
      to this film as an adaptation of the fairy tale "The Elves and the Shoemaker," which
      does not really describe *The Magic Fountain*. The writer Daniel Kothenschulte (see
      notes for chapter 25) has offered that Weegee might have worked on the 1956 German
      film *Die Heinzelmännchen*. That seems unlikely; in addition to the fact that *Die
      Heinzelmännchen* was released two years before what Weegee explicitly calls "my first
      trip to Germany," a viewing of that film reveals none of the trick shots to which he
      refers. *The Magic Fountain* does contain a few moments that he describes, as well his a
      cameo appearance. I suspect that the "Elves and the Shoemaker" encapsulation is sim-
      ply a mistake, not least because he attributes that story to Hans Christian Andersen
      rather than the Grimms.

287   **the great Duke Ellington:** Letter to Wilma Wilcox, November 15, 1958, ICP collection.

287   **At least once she got fed up:** Letter to Wilma Wilcox, October 24, 1958, ICP collection.

288   **A postcard followed:** Letter to Wilma Wilcox, October 25, 1958, private collection.

288   **successful television series:** It's not clear whether Weegee had any relationship with
      the show at all, but, if he did, it was not extensive. The archives of its producer, Herbert

Leonard, contain some discussion of the rights with Mark Hellinger's widow but none with Weegee. Nor did he retain contracts or check stubs; he also barely mentions the series in interviews or his books, although the film comes up often. See the Herbert Leonard Papers, UCLA Library Special Collections, Charles E. Young Research Library, University of California, Los Angeles.

288   **documentary about himself:** Letter to Wilma Wilcox, November 15, 1958, ICP collection.

288   **Havana:** Letter to Wilma Wilcox, January 27, 1959, ICP collection. Also, "Weegee's a Wizard," *Miami Herald*, January 7, 1959.

288   **Sherwood Schwartz:** Letter to Wilma Wilcox, June 9, 1959.

288   *Naked Paris:* WBW, p. 139. Also, undated letter to Wilma Wilcox, ca. 1958, ICP collection.

288   **John Huston:** Letter from Ernest Anderson to Gladys Hill, March 1, 1960, Folder 874, Box 92, John Huston Papers, Margaret Herrick Library, Academy of Motion Picture Arts and Sciences, Beverly Hills, CA.

288   **"dickering":** Letter to Wilma Wilcox, October 13, 1961, ICP collection.

288   **had to send Wilma:** Letters to Wilma Wilcox, April 29 and May 2, 1960, ICP collection.

288   **Art Buchwald:** Art Buchwald, "Weegee's Looking for New Angles," *New York Herald Tribune*, January 24, 1960.

289   *Weegee's Creative Camera:* Weegee with Roy Ald, *Weegee's Creative Camera* (Garden City, New York: Hanover House, 1959).

289   **short instructional movie:** *Wee Gee's Camera Magic*, United World/Castle Films, 1960.

289   **a slit down the corner:** Author interview with Sid Kaplan, January 2017.

289   **Las Vegas:** WBW, p. 137. Also, letter to Wilma Wilcox, March 31, 1959, ICP collection.

290   **off to Los Angeles:** Letters to Wilma Wilcox, May 7; June 9, 16, 21, and 22; and August 4, 1959; ICP collection.

290   **reactivating his lapsed California driver's license . . . North Hollywood:** Letter to Wilma Wilcox, June 22, 1959, and address books, ICP collection.

290   **Mapleton Hotel:** Letters to Wilma Wilcox, April 10, 13, and 14, 1960, ICP collection.

290   **smuggled an enlarger:** WBW, p. 148. (Weegee stayed at the Mapleton on and off for several years, and it's not clear on which visit this incident happened.)

290   **allowing him to sell a few caricatures to the *Daily Mirror*:** "Weegees: Look What They've Done to the Duke," [in the *Sunday Mirror*, then called the *Sunday Pictorial*], February 14, 1960; "They're Weegees!" *Daily Mirror*, March 11, 1960; "Weegee's Gee-Gees!" *Daily Mirror*, April 25, 1960.

290   **a couple to the *Sunday Graphic*:** "Weegee the Famous Puts Picasso in Focus," *Sunday Graphic*, September 18, 1960.

290   **some to the *Times*:** "Reflective Photography," London *Times*, October 11, 1960.

290   **a few across the Channel:** "L'Amour de la Vie," *Paris-Match*, February 13, 1960.

290   **tailored extra-generously:** WWMM.

290   **a columnist for a very short-lived newspaper called the *New York Item*:** Leo Glassman, "World's Top Photog to Write Column for *New York Item*," *New York Item*, June 1, 1961. Surviving copies of the column, which was titled "Foto Finish," appear in the issues from June 1, 15, and 22, and July 13, 1961, ICP collection.

291   **losing his virginity:** WBW, p. 19.

291   **whorehouses:** Ibid., pp. 24, 31–33, 42–44.

291   **picking up girls:** Ibid., pp. 56–58.

291   **bedding young bohemian women:** Ibid., p. 125.

291   **"a small top and a big bottom":** Ibid., p. 139.

291   **denigrates dilettante photographers:** Ibid., p. 150.

291   **inferiority complex:** Ibid., p. 55.

291   **misstates the number of brothers and sisters he has:** Ibid., p. 9.

291   **An essay by Bruce Downes:** Ibid., pp. 1–6.

292   **"Most important":** Letter to Wilma Wilcox, October 14, 1961, ICP collection.

CHAPTER 25

293   **"$50,000 was put up":** *WBW*, p. 133.

293   **have attached a name:** Bill Warren, *Keep Watching the Skies: American Science Fiction Movies of the 1950s: The 21st Century Edition* (Jefferson, NC: McFarland and Company, 2010), p. 104.

293   **did most of her shooting:** *WBW*, p. 133.

294   **wearing nothing but his Hasselblad:** An extraordinary photo attests to this.

294   **remembers Ralph Toporoff:** Author interview, May 2016.

294   **Weegee himself sketched out a scenario:** Manuscript in ICP collection.

296   **"Here's how it all started":** Ibid.

297   **fell off and was injured:** Letter to Wilma Wilcox, December 27, 1962, ICP collection.

297   **sold Price his hat and coat:** Author interview with Toporoff, May 2016.

298   **He'd worked as a press photographer:** Philippe Mather, *Stanley Kubrick at Look Magazine* (Chicago: Intellect/University of Chicago Press, 2013), pp. 15–20. Also, Vincent Lobrutto, *Stanley Kubrick: A Biography* (New York: Dutton, 1997), p. 12.

298   **a few with infrared film:** Erica Fahr Campbell, "Lightbox: From Photography to Film: Stanley Kubrick Enters the Ring," Time.com, November 1, 2012, at http://time.com /3792976/from-photography-to-film-stanley-kubrick-enters-the-ring/.

298   **"I knew him around":** Sellers-Weegee Q&A.

298   **Kubrick had been attentive:** Mather, *Stanley Kubrick at Look Magazine*, p. 16. Also, George Case, *Calling Dr. Strangelove: The Anatomy and Influence of the Kubrick Masterpiece* (Jefferson, NC: McFarland and Company, 2014), p. 96.

298   **"Stanley says to me":** Sellers-Weegee Q&A.

298   **there's a £750 fee:** Daniel Kothenschulte, "Caked or Distorted: What Was Photographer Weegee Doing on the Set of Dr. Strangelove?" essay in *Kinematograph 20: Stanley Kubrick* (Deutschesfilmmuseum, 2014), pp. 96–101.

298   **staying at the Mapleton again . . . luxury car:** Letter to Wilma Wilcox, February 16, 1963, ICP collection.

300   **scene went into the vaults:** Kothenschulte, "Caked or Distorted," pp. 96–101.

300   **on Steve Allen's TV show:** Sellers on *The Steve Allen Show*, undated clip, ca. 1964, at https://www.youtube.com/watch?v=0yWn_8SUWtg. Also, John O'Brian, *Strangelove's Weegee*, exhibition catalogue (Vancouver: Presentation House Gallery, 2013).

CHAPTER 26

302   **"Very discouraging":** Letter to Wilma Wilcox, September 10, 1963, ICP collection.

302   **a second how-to book:** Weegee, with Gerry Speck, *Weegee's Creative Photography* (London: Ward Lock & Co., 1964).

302   ***Sunday Telegraph:*** "Stars of the Greatest Show on Earth: The Co-Optimists of 1964," *Sunday Telegraph*, December 29, 1963.

302   ***South Wales Echo:*** "Art—or Gimmick?" *South Wales Echo*, November 11, 1963.

302   **Edinburgh *Evening News and Dispatch:*** "It's Just Crazy!" *Evening News and Dispatch*, November 21, 1963.

302   **a few newspapers and magazines on the Continent:** "Weege Trekd de Wereld Het Masker Af," *Elseviers Weekblad*, September 23, 1961; "Weegee," *Point de Vue: Images du Monde*, November 23, 1962, pp. 18–19; and various other magazine clippings in ICP collection.

302   **The USSR in the early sixties . . . Fanny James and her nephew, Rafael Hyams:** Marshall I. Goldman, *Détente and Dollars: Doing Business with the Soviets* (New York: Basic Books, 1975), p. 140. Additionally, "Alfred's Camera Page: Technical and Optical Equipment (Ltd.)," at http://cameras.alfredklomp.com/toe/. Thanks to Sjaak Boone, who unearthed the incorporation papers of TOE.

303   **met up with Fanny James:** Letters to Wilma Wilcox, September 10 and 15, 1963, ICP collection.

303   **The Coventry *Express*:** "Speedy Godiva!" *Coventry Express*, September 20, 1963.

303   **trip to Moscow:** Letters to Wilma Wilcox, October 15, 19, and 22, 1963, ICP collection.

303   **He invited Wilma:** Letter to Wilma Wilcox, March 10, 1963, private collection.

303   **less oppressive than Paris:** LJN.

303   **Hong Kong follow-up . . . back in London:** Letter to Wilma Wilcox, October 22, 1963, ICP collection.

304   **His agency, Photo-Representatives, had gone out of business:** Author interview with Erika Stone, June 2015.

304   **so much housing being built:** *BHS*. Also, *WBW*, p. 135.

304   **"lousy":** *FPTH*. Also, Fellig, *Weegee*, p. 3.

304   **cold-water flat:** *WBW*, p. 72.

304   **"was all right until NYU came in":** Lichello, "'The Famous Weegee' Wants a Woman from Mars."

304   **Wilma Wilcox . . . Salvation Army . . . pension:** Author interview with Salvation Army archivist Susan Mitchem. (Sid Kaplan recalls visiting Weegee, and possibly Wilma, at a ground-floor apartment across the street from this house before they moved in, so it is possible that they shared an earlier place.)

304   **Theodor Reik's clinic:** Author interview with Ellen Newberg, ca. summer 2015.

304   **enough of a down payment to buy:** Undated, untitled statement by Wilma Wilcox, beginning "I purchased my home . . . ," ICP collection.

304   **sorting and indexing:** Letter from Wilma Wilcox to Ken Greengrass, February 20, 1985, ICP collection.

305   **"Forty Famous Pictures:"** WWMM.

305   **Each weekend that summer:** Ibid.

305   **On a script:** "Fair Treatment," undated script, ICP collection.

305   **distributed nationally via United Press International:** "It's a Mad World's Fair!" Photo set, UPI, May 24, 1965.

305   **greeting cards:** Published by 4 Seasons Cards, ICP collection.

305   **tried to get Allan David:** Letter to Allan David, April 3, 1966.

305   **Tokyo:** LJN.

305   **created a plan:** Undated document, "Le Procede Optique Weegee/Phototechnics Inc.: A proposal for the organization of a new company interested in the development of unique and original photographic technqiues and processes with broad commercial organization," ICP collection.

305   **Ruth Buzzi:** Letter from Ruth Buzzi to Weegee, May 9, 1966, and author's instant-message interview, 2016.

308   **approached a friend at the *Post*:** WWMM.

308   **briefly attempted to re-create his very first success:** Author interview with Miles Barth.

308   **at the Bridge Theater:** Press release for December 5–7 and January 16–17 screenings, no year (probably 1965 and 1966), ICP collection. Also, program, Ben Morea and Aldo Tambellini Papers; TAM 530; Series 1, Folder 8, Box 1; Tamiment Library/Robert F. Wagner Labor Archives, New York University.

308   **Film-Makers' Cinematheque:** Harvey Fondiller, "Weegee's Living Screen," *Popular Photography*, September 1966, p. 44.

308   **swirly color slides:** Ibid. The color photos appear in an unattributed, undated clipping in ICP's collection.

309   **Color Box:** Berg, "Weegee," p. 26.

309   **at the end of February 1967:** An original handbill for "Caterpillar Changes," reproduced in the online catalogue of Recordmecca, a memorabilia dealer, puts the date of Weegee and Warhol's film screenings on either February 18 or February 25.

309   **"mystik luv films":** Joe Milutis, *Ether* (Minneapolis: University of Minnesota Press, 2006), p. 124.

309   **Warhol was an admirer:** Andy Warhol, ed. Pat Hackett, *The Andy Warhol Diaries* (New York: Warner Books, 1989), entries for June 20, 1981; April 15, 1984; and December 22, 1986.

309   **"Warhol snubbed him":** Author interview with Ira Richer, June 2015.

310   **The screening . . . at the Gallery of Modern Art:** Handbills and press releases, ICP collection. Also Jacob Deschin, "Looking Back 30 Years," *New York Times*, April 9, 1967.

311   **The next day did not:** Mort Young, "Weegee's Lens Show Is Kissed Off," *World Journal Tribune*, April 13, 1967.

311   **that Sunday at the Bleecker Street Cinema:** Handbill and press release, ICP collection.

311   **When the photographer Alfred Gescheidt ran into him:** Gescheidt, "Remembering Weegee."

312   **good humor seemed to be drying up:** Fellig, *Weegee*, p. 18.

312   **"My real name is Arthur Fellig":** Berg, "Weegee," p. 2.

312   **his friend George Gilbert bumped into him:** Gilbert, "Reminiscences of Weegee," p. 4.

312   **more and more time in the darkroom:** Fellig, *Weegee*, p. 18.

312   **an enormous bowl:** Author interview with Sid Kaplan, 2017.

312   **As Weegee got frailer:** Ibid.

312   **He planned another book:** Unpublished Blumenfeld notes.

312   **School of Visual Arts:** Handbill, ICP collection.

313   **A few months later:** John Strausbaugh, "Crime Was Weegee's Oyster," *New York Times*, June 20, 2008. Also, accompanying video on nytimes.com, and undated recollections of the day by Mottel, ICP collection.

314   **Bill Jay:** Jay customarily annotated his prints with three or four sentences of backstory; this note comes from one in the collection of Columbia College Chicago.

314   **That last June:** Advertisement in *Village Voice*, June 20, 1968.

314   **Mellon Tytell:** Unpublished recollections by Mary Ellen (Mellon) Gregori-Tytell, ICP collection.

314   **In August 1968:** Jimmy Breslin, "The Distortion of John Lindsay," *New York*, August 26, 1968, pp. 15–16.

315   **In October, See, a smallish men's magazine:** "Presenting: The Candidates," *See*, October 1968, pp. 25–31.

315   **slowing down:** WWMM.

315   **often incoherent:** Another of Jay's annotated prints notes this. Author's collection.

315   **Weegee's handwriting:** Notepad, ICP collection. It can be dated to the final months of Weegee's life, because it includes the address and phone number of Walter Bernard at *New York* magazine, who began work there on July 1, 1968.

315   **Park West Hospital:** "Weegee the Photographer Dies; Chronicled Life in 'Naked City,'" *New York Times*, December 27, 1968.

315   **had once been . . . headed into financial distress:** Carter B. Horsley, "Small, Failing Hospitals Are Valuable Sites for Developers," *New York Times*, January 7, 1979. Also, "Two Hospitals File for Bankruptcy," *New York Times*, May 14, 1976.

315   **symptoms of a brain tumor:** WWMM. Also, "Weegee the Photographer Dies . . ." There is very little detail to be had about Weegee's final illness. His doctor, Lester

Rothman, died in 1998, and his practice's records have since been destroyed. According to a post investigating the death of guitarist Eddie Lang at Park West (http://bixography.com/langmedicalreport.html), a lawyer named S. Weinman reported that all the institution's records were destroyed in a Brooklyn warehouse fire after the bankruptcy.

315 **Post:** "Crime Photographer Weegee Dies," *New York Post*, December 27, 1968.

315 **Wilma Wilcox took it hard:** Author interviews with Ellen Newberg, ca. summer 2015, and Sid Kaplan, January 2017.

315 **Theodor Reik:** Alden Whitman, "Dr. Theodor Reik, Freud Protege, Is Dead at 81," *New York Times*, January 1, 1970.

316 **Diane Arbus:** Arthur Lubow, *Diane Arbus: Portrait of a Photographer* (New York: Ecco, 2016), pp. 500–503. In addition, Patricia Bosworth's fine *Diane Arbus: A Biography* (New York: W. W. Norton, 1984; reissued 2005), p. 238, makes the tantalizing assertion that, around 1965, Arbus had "gone with him [Weegee] on assignment in his battered Chevrolet, which was equipped with police radio and makeshift darkroom in the trunk," shooting in the fashion that made him famous. This seems unlikely, as he was (apart from the aforementioned brief attempt to return to the spot-news business) long past his police-radio days, and the Chevrolet was twenty years gone. In the Bosworth Papers at the Howard Gotlieb Archival Research Center at Boston University, a letter from the curator John Coplans, who knew Weegee well, states with some vehemence that Bosworth is incorrect.

316 **a show devoted to press photography:** John Szarkowski, ed., *From the Picture Press* (New York: Museum of Modern Art, 1973).

316 **"The best thing this past week":** Letter to Allan Arbus and Mariclare Costello, ca. late October 1970, excerpted in *Diane Arbus: Revelations* (New York: Random House, 2003), p. 212.

316 **"gave me a sense of confidence":** WWMM.

317 **Malina, who knew him well:** Author interview, June 2014.

317 **The exhibition Arbus worked on:** Szarkowski, *From the Picture Press.*

318 **the International Center of Photography's first Weegee retrospective:** *Weegee the Famous*, September 16–November 6, 1977.

318 **Stettner, Wilcox, and Sid Kaplan:** Author interview with Sid Kaplan. Also, letter from Louis Stettner to Wilma Wilcox, July 29, 1986, and related legal documents, ICP collection.

318 **work as a Quaker missionary . . . Kenyan villages . . . West Bank:** Wilma Wilcox photographs documenting trips, author's collection. Also, Wilma M. Wilcox, *Quaker Volunteer: An Experience in Palestine* (Richmond, IN: Friends United Press, 1977).

319 **one other artifact:** "Photo Op: Remains of the Day," *New York Times*, October 22, 1995. Also, ICP memoranda and dispersal paperwork (April 19, 1994, through July 2, 1998), and author's e-mail correspondence with Ellen Handy and Christopher George.

ACKNOWLEDGMENTS

Michael Signorelli waited a very long time for this book to show up at Henry Holt and made it all hang together when it finally did. He is (to misquote Oliver Wendell Holmes on the subject of FDR) a first-rate editor with a first-rate temperament. Fellow authors: sign with him.

Kristine Dahl made me rewrite the proposal three times, then sold it in three days. I could not have asked for a better deal maker and publishing-industry navigator, and if you ever have the chance to have her negotiate anything on your behalf, take it. Fellow authors: sign with her.

The team at Henry Holt is of course responsible for taking a pile of typescript and turning it into a book. Thanks to Stephen Rubin, Maggie Richards, and Gillian Blake, for running Holt the way you'd want it to be run; Meryl Levavi and Karen Horton for creating a finely made, read-able, covetable object; Christopher O'Connell and Jenna Dolan, for sweat-ing the small stuff on all those words; Serena Jones, for ninth-inning relief pitching; and Marian Brown and Ruby Rose Lee for their respective roles in the delivery room.

Thanks also to surrogate eyes and hands in the libraries of four cit-ies: Elizabeth Garber-Paul in New York, Katie Charles and Angelina Del Balzo in Los Angeles, Olivia Nuzzi in Washington, and Edward Patrick Huycke in Chicago.

And for interviews, help, background, and advice: Jolanta and Tom Alberty, Debby Applegate, Don Baida, Quindi Berger, Ellis Bernhart, Daniel Blau, Sjaak Boone, Ruth Buzzi, Peter Clark, Ned Comstock, Liz Cooke, Vito Cosenza, Kelsey Desiderio, Maggie Downing, David W.

Dunlap, Mary Engel, Philip Felig, Joanna Grossman, Joan Harris, Marc A. Hermann, Jason Hill, Sid Kaplan, Jim Kolea, Eric Kroll, Michael Kusek, Evelyn Lahaie, Barry Lane, Lorraine Lasker, James Lileks, Arthur Lubow, Rachel Maddow and Susan Mikula, Judith Malina, Paul Mason, Philippe Mather, Dan Merrin, Paul Milkman, Susan Mitchem, Susan Morgan, Mark Mori, Matthew Mottel, Jim Muller, Ellen Newberg, James Avery Penney, Jean Pigozzi, Nicholas Pileggi, Claire Potter, Jim Preminger, Bret Primack, Corliss Randall, Ricky Riccardi, Ira Richer, Peter Roberts, Naomi and Nina Rosenblum, James Eli Shiffer, Amy Sloper, Deborah Solomon, Carole David Stone, Erika Stone, Heather Strelecki, David Strohmaier, Terry Teachout, Ralph Toporoff, Monique Trinkleback, Loring Vogel, Joyce Wadler, Melinda Wallington, Antoinette Watson, Jonny Wilson, Ida Wyman, Valerie Yaros, and George Zimbel.

And for much more: Ellen and Alex, again, for allowing a long-dead fourth person to join our household for several years. Connie, Peter, and Paul Bonanos, without whom I would not be. Frank and Fran McDermott, for the bottomless supply of babysitting and meatballs. Adam Moss, Ann Clarke, and Jared Hohlt, for applying the Elastic Lens to the definition of "vacation." Taffy Brodesser-Akner, Melissa Dahl, Justin Davidson, Wendy Goodman, Jesse Green, Joe Hagan, Madison Malone Kircher, Carolyn Murnick, and Chris Smith for early reading, advice, and periodically talking me in off the authorial ledge. Many, many other colleagues at New York, for listening ad infinitum. Frankie Thomas, for transcribing. (Highly recommended, by the way.) Too many librarians to name, for finding everything. (They should all be better paid.) Brian Wallis, for his early blessing and later conversation. Erin Barnett, Claartje Van Dijk, and the extremely tolerant team at the International Center of Photography, for turning themselves inside out to accommodate my limited research schedule.

Two more people deserve special thanks. One of them is a woman I never met. After Weegee's death, Wilma Wilcox believed in his importance as an artist before most other people did. She kept his photographs dry (mostly; there was one flood) and safe, sorted and catalogued them, and continually made them available to exhibitors and collectors, for comparatively little material gain. She is, like so many of the under-appreciated female partners of male artists, largely responsible for his continued reputation.

The other is a member of ICP's curatorial staff, and he deserves (as the old newspapermen say) a little extra ink here. Christopher George is the world's uncontested expert on Weegee. He has devoted a large portion of his career to looking at Weegee's pictures and understanding them: where they were made, how they were made, where they ran, what they say. (I once saw him glance at a print and say "probably 1945." *How do you know?* "The paper.") Chris shared material from his own eBay trawling and spent extensive time with me as I went through Weegee's photographs and papers at ICP; he answered more e-mails than I can count; and he read a draft of this book's manuscript and offered both fine-grained corrections and suggestions and some personal enthusiasm. Weegee, having found such a devoted posthumous caretaker to pick up where Wilma Wilcox left off, is a lucky man. Having had access to Chris's capacious memory and enthusiasm for his subject, I am almost as lucky.

Speaking of luck: the first morning I walked from the train station in Jersey City to ICP's archive to begin going through Weegee's photographs of corpses and car crashes, I myself was hit by a car. It knocked me into the air, and I landed hard on the pavement. The only thing that kept me from hitting my head on the asphalt was a big old Polaroid camera I was carrying on a shoulder strap, because I fell on it. Not even Weegee himself could have concocted a better metaphor. This one's true.

INDEX

Page numbers in *italics* refer to illustrations.

Abbott, Berenice, 112, 178, 214
Acme Newspictures, xiv, xvi, 24–44, 47, 51,
    53, 71, 84, 100, 105, 140, 151, 171,
    222, 305, 312
    Weegee and, 24–43, 49, 56, 57, 60, 81,
    83, 86, 94, 98, 120, 182, 200, 208, 209
Action Photography (exhibition), 166–68,
    171, 178
Adams, Ansel, 167, 178
Addams, Charles, 91
advertising, 14, 15, 275
    photos, 210–11, *211*, 275–76
African Americans, 30–31, 66, 82, 83, 112,
    148–49, 184–86, 219
    photos, *31*, 184–86, *186*, *248*
Ahearn, Frankie, 88, *89*
Ald, Roy, 278, 289
Allen, Steve, 282, 285, 300
Alsberg, Cora, 149
Ameko factory fire. *See* "Simply Add Boiling
    Water"
American, 49–50, 51
American Place, An, 111, 190, 191
American Society of Magazine
    Photographers, 233, 235
"An American Tragedy: No Autograph," *263*
Amsterdam News, 219
animal photos, 94–95, 128–29, 136, 140,
    157, 216, 241
Arbus, Diane, 316–18
Armstrong, Jimmy, 162

Armstrong, Louis, 217, 276–77, *277*
Art in Progress (exhibition), 178–79
Art Photography, 255, 256
Associated Press, xiv, 38, 43, 53, 54, 60, 84,
    98, 101, 102, 117
Atlanta, 247
Austin, Jerry, 148
Austria-Hungary, 3–4, 6, 7
Authenticolor, 275
Avery, Frances, 173

"Balcony Seats at a Murder," 107, 109, *109*,
    110, 133
B. Altman & Co., 133–35
Bandy, Robert, 184
Barrett, Roy, 163
Barry, Les, 284
Barth, Miles, 308, 319
Bartlett Street tenement fire, 104–5, *105. See
    also* "I Cried When I Took This Picture"
Basin Street, 276–77, *277*
Bayonne, New Jersey, 57–61
Bayonne Evening News, 59
BBC, 301, 303
Beadle, David "the Beetle," 106–8, *108*
beauty pageants, 30–31, *31*
Beer, Anita, 258
Berkley Books, 262
Berlin, Irving, 141
Berliner Illustrirte Zeitung, 70
Birskowsky, Frank, 161–62

Bleecker Street Cinema, 311
Bloom, Claire, 271
Blumenfeld, Harold, 25–26, 39–43, 49, 312
Bodenheim, Maxwell, 271
Bogart, Humphrey, 204, 229
bohemian culture, 253–55
bootlegging, 20, 29, 36
Boston, 218, 246
Boston Globe, 246
Bourke-White, Margaret, 91, 118, 282
Boutell, Clip, 213
Bow, Billy, 30
Bowery, 18, 95, 132, 142–43, 149, 161, 191, 195, 220, 242
boxing, 29
Brandt, Bert, 222
Breathless Moment, The (anthology), xv
Breslin, Jimmy, 51
Bridge Theater, 308
Brief, 254, 257, 258
Broadway, 50, 52
"Broadway gun-girl," 73, 74. *See also* Gutowski, Nellie
Brooklyn, 8, 10, 21, 25, 36, 61–63, 68–69, 87, 101, 104–5, 112, 143–45, 172, 239
Brooklyn Bridge, 66, 187, 188
Brooklyn Camera Club, 214
Brooklyn Dodgers, 102, 103
Brooklyn Eagle, 47
Broun, Heywood, 52
Browning, Edward "Daddy," 22
Brunette, Harry, 68
Brussels, 285–86, 306
Buchwald, Art, 288–89
Burke & James, 32, 210
burning-in, 228
Buzzi, Ruth, 305–7

Café Royal, 217–18, *218*
Cagney, Jimmy, 232
Caldwell, Erskine, 197
Calvacca, Anthony, 223
cameras, 13–16, 31–32, 67, 98, *99*
    Brownie, 57
    Nikon, 270
    Polaroid, 270–71
    Speed Graphic, 31–32, 43, 54, 57, 76, 78, 95, 151, 162, 163, 179, 191, 210, 219, 268–70, 282, 288, 298, 319
    35-millimeter, 134, 270
    view, 13–14, 17
Candid, 254, 273

Capone, Al, 36, 37, 247
caricatures, 273, *273*, 274–77, 283, 302, 315
Carr, Cass, 265–68
carrier pigeons, 51
cars, 46, 242
    Chevrolet coupe, 98–99, *99*, 100, 107, 119, 158, 173, 213, 225, 295
    crash photos, 53–57, 64–67, 71–75, 82–88, 93, 102, 122–24, 130, 137, 147, 157, 161–62, 172, 271, 307
Cars, 273
Cartier-Bresson, Henri, 134
Catan, Omero, 90
CBS, 220, 225, 245, 276, 286
celebrity photos, 21, 77–78, 81, 130, 143, 165, 239–40, 271–79, 302
Central Park, 137, 200
Centre Market Place studio, 45–56, 69, *69*, 133, 151, 213, 220, 225
Chalmers, Arthur, 87–88
Chaucer Head Book Shop, 204
Chicago, 15, 22, 25, 36, 47, 80, 118, 214–15, 247
Chicago Herald-Tribune, 247
Chicago Tribune, 22, 200, 220, 262
child photos, 66, 75, 107–10, 138–45, 157–58, 207, 228, 261
Chinatown, 158, 191–92, 223, 312
Cigar Institute, 165
Cinema 16, 232–33, 235
Cinerama, 279–80
circus photos, 162–63, *164*, 165, 284
Cities Service, 209–10, 275
Cleveland, 25, 247
close-ups, 64
clown photos, 162–63, *164*, 165
Colbert, Stanley, 259, 261
Coleman, Robert, 163
Coll, Vincent "Mad Dog," 38–39, 134
Color Box, 309
Columbia Lecture Bureau, 252
communism, 53, 112, 236
Concord Camera Circle, 265–68
Condé Nast, 207, 208
Coney Island, 119–26, 153, 185
    photos, 119–25, *125*, 126, 153–54, *154*, 155, 157, 160, 172, 173, 228, 232, 245, 311
Confidential, 254
Connolly, Vincent, 198–99
Conte, Richard, 245
Cooke, Liz, 11, 12

Corey, Herbert, 32–33
Coronet, 151, 206
corporate photos, 209–10
Cosenza family, 107, 109, *109*, 110
Coventry *Express*, 303
covered faces, 77
Crandell, Richard, 200
credits, photo, 65, 69, 71, 76, 78, 81, 95, 117, 120–21, 168
  newspaper rules, 101
  rubber stamps, 100–101, 151, 168, 189, 209, 311
Crime Club, 199
Crime Photographer, 245
crime photos, 21, 36–41, 57–68, 72–79–83, 102, 106–10, 118, 130–35, 142–45, 154, 172, 271
  end of, 212–13
Crime Quiz, 199
"The Critic," 172–77, *177*, 178–80, 183, 199, 203, 220, 228, 240, 261, 305
cross-dresser photos, 182–84, *184*
Cuba, 288
Cummings, E. E., 197
Curtis, Tony, 240, 244

Da Capo, 318
Daily Mirror (London), 290
Dalí, Salvador, 226–27, *227*, 228
D'Amico, Louis, Jr., 46–47
Dassin, Jules, 230–32, *233*
dates, falsified on photos, 126
David, Allan, 305
Davidoff, Isaac, 95
Davis, Sammy, Jr., 278, *279*
Davis, Stuart, 210–11, 226
Dean, James, 29, 271
Decies, Lady. *See* Drexel, Elizabeth Wharton
de Dienes, Andre, 257
de Gaulle, Charles, 302
DeMille, Cecil B., 259–60
Dempsey, Jack, 29
Denove, Joseph, 81–82
Denver, 247–48, 250
Depression, 30, 37, 43, 49, 98, 130, 217, 252
de Rochemont, Louis, 279–80, 285
Dery, Donald, 270
Desert Inn, 289
Designers 3, 259, 261, 275
Detroit, 221
Dewey, Thomas, 38

Diamond, Jack "Legs," 78
Diamond Gadg-it Bag, 210, *211*
Didato, Dominick, 63–65, *65*, 66
Di Maggio kidnapping, 182
distortion photos, 226–27, *227*, 228–29, 232, 238–41, 251, 254–63, *263*, *264*, 269–73, *273*, *274*, 279–84, *284*, 290, 292, 302, 305, 307, 312, 315, 316
Divine, Father, 81–83, 95, 118
dodging, 228
Doherty, Grace, 177
Dorfman, Elsa, 286
Dorman, Robert, 24–25, 28, 57
Dowling's, 221
Downes, Bruce, 219, 233, 278, 291–92, 296
Drexel, Elizabeth Wharton, 175–77, *177*, 178–80, 199, 203
Dr. Strangelove (movie), 298–99, *299*, 300–302
dry shooting, 54, 68
Duckett & Adler, 15–16, 34, 43, 109
Duell, Sloan and Pearce, 197, 198, 205, 214, 221, 230

Eastman, George, 13
Eden Musée, 153–54, *154*, 155
Edgerton, Harold, 166
Editor & Publisher, 110, 127
Eisenstaedt, Alfred, 277–78, 282
Elastic Lens, 240–41, 247, 251, 269, 273, 279, 280, 296, 303
electric chair, 22–23, 135, 172
Elisofon, Eliot, 277
Elizabeth Street, 63–65, *65*, 91, 157, 216
Elkins, Manny, 53
Ellington, Duke, 287
Ellis Island, xiii, 5, 7–8, 11, 234
Ellison, Ralph, *Invisible Man*, 227
Empire State Building, 134, 212–13
Engel, Morris, 112, 118
Engels, Walter, 177
Epstein, Irma Twiss, 157
Eskell, Bertram Cecil, 173
Esposito, Anthony "Mad Dog," 133–35, *135*
Esposito, William, 133–35
Essential Books, 197
European Picture Service, 134
Evans, Walker, 185
Every Girl Should Be Married (movie), 236, *237*
excursion-boat photos, 148–49
Expo 58 (Brussels world's fair), 285–86, *306*
Eye, 254, 257

Fagin, Ruth, 271
Falkenburg, Jinx, 231
fascism, 116, 122–23, 157
FBI, 118, 130
Feeney, Harry, 36, 226
Feinstein, Irving "Puggy," 118
Felig, Elias, 4, 230
Fellig, Arthur. *See* Weegee
Fellig, Bernard, 4–12, 17, 98, 195
Fellig, Feibish, 5
Fellig, Jacob, 11
Fellig, Margaret Atwood, 221–24, 234, 291
    marriage to Weegee, 221–24, 224, 238,
      241–42, 246, 252, 290
Fellig, Rachel, 11
Fellig, Rebecca, 4–12, 15, 17, 98, 195, 219, 239
Fellig, Yetta, 11
female criminal photos, 57–61, 73–79, 83
Fergusson, E. Stuart, 56
Field, Marshall, III, 115
Fifth Avenue, 133–34
film, 32, 51, 53, 61, 98, 134, 220
    infrared, 158–62, 175–76, 245, 257–58,
      298
    Polaroid, 270–71, 292
    roll, 284
Film-Makers' Cinematheque, 308, 309
fire escape photos, 138, *139*, 140–41, 153,
    173, 228
fire photos, 46–47, 53, 56, 64–68, 71, 75,
    81, 88, 95, 102–7, 127–30, 147–48,
    153, 187–88, 216, 307
Fisher, Alan, 101, 118, 119, 121, 131
flash, 16, 34–35, 78, 95, 155
    bulbs, 35, 45, 61, 66, 67, 93, 98, 110,
      127–28, 159, 165, 166, 175, 187, 261,
      269–70
    infrared, 158–62, 175–76, 245, 257–58,
      298
    powder, 16, 34, 35, 109
flophouses, 18, 95, 142, 216
Flynn, Errol, 240
Footlight Varieties (movie), 241
Fortune, 115
Forty Famous Pictures, 63, 305, 314
`47: The Magazine of the Year, 227
France, 70, 130, 175, 288, 294–97
Frank, Robert, 271
Fraymart Gallery, 240
Fuchs, Sammy, 142–43
Fulbright, J. William, 212
Fulton Fish Market, 85, 196

Gabor, Zsa Zsa, 260
Gallery of Modern Art, 310–11
Gallo, Joseph "Crazy Joe," 158
gambling, 36, 131–32
gangster photos, 36–39, 54, 57, 61–65, 73,
    78, 82–89, 106, 118, 130, 137, 142,
    156, 158, 172, 215, 307
Gee, Helen, 271–73
George Washington Bridge, 39
Germany, 7, 9, 70, 102, 111, 122, 130, 180,
    270, 286–88
Gescheidt, Alfred, 311–12
Gibbs, Wolcott, 116–17, 153
Gilbert, George, 114, 312
Giles, Herb, 194–95
Gill, Donald, 183
girlie magazines, 254–58, 273, 278
girlie photos, 30–31, 56, 254–56, 261–67,
    278–79, 283, 316
Glamour Photography, 255
glass plates, 32, 53
Gleason, Jackie, 274
Glendening, William, 67, 75
Goldstein, Martin "Buggsy," 78, 82, 118
Good Photography, 151
Gordon, John J., 132–33
Gordon, Morris, 223
Gordon, Waxey, 102
Gould, Joe, 197, 220, 260
Graflex, 31, 210, 220
Graham, Martha, 166
Grand Central Terminal, 18
Grant, Cary, 236
Grauman's Chinese Theatre, 243
Gray, Henry Judd, 22, 154
Great Britain, 6, 19, 290, 297–302
Greco, Angelo, 107, *108*, 109–10
Green, Harry, 81–82
Greenwich Village, 68, 114, 207, 216–18,
    222, 239, 243, 253–55, 271–72, 283,
    304, 308–14, 318
Grossman, Sid, 111–12
Gutowski, Nellie (aka Norma Parker), 73,
    74, 88

Haas, Max Peter, 134
Haberman, Irving, 101, 104, 118, 121, 136
Hall-Mills case, 22
Halsman, Philippe, 204, 209, 277, 278
Hammett, Dashiell, 119
Harlem, 30, 81–82, 102, 149, 183–84, 195,
    201, 216

Harlem Document, 149
Harper, Helen, 83
Harper's Bazaar, 206, 231
Harris, Mel, 259, *260*, 261–64, 275
Harrison, Bob, 254–55
Hartford, Huntington, 311
Hartford Courant, 200
Hauptmann, Bruno Richard, 47, 134
Headquarters Press Building (the Shack),
    133, 157
Headquarters Tavern, 44, 133
Hearst, William Randolph, 21, 49
Hearst newspapers, 21, 43, 49–51, 81, 120
Hecht, Ben, 80, 117, 235
Heenan, Frances "Peaches," 22
Hefner, Hugh, 262–63
Hellinger, Mark, 229–33, 235
Hell's Kitchen, 21, 106, 118, 304
Henry, Frank, 197
Henry, O., 200, 201, 227
Henry Hudson Parkway, 122–23
Herrick, George, 131
Hess, Ervin, 54
Hessler, William, 61–63
Hessler trunk-murder photo, 61–63, *63*, 85,
    118
Hi, 283
Hi! Jinx, 231
Hicks, Wilson, 84
high-low life, 142–43, 151, 172–80, 196,
    197, 217, 242–44
Hindenburg, xv, 166
Hine, Lewis, 112
hit-and-run photos, 71–72, 75, 161–62
Hitler, Adolf, 122, 130, 158
Ho!, 283
Holiday in Brussels (movie), 285–86, 293,
    306
Hollenbeck, Don, 144
Hollywood, 37–40, 229–52, 259–64
Hollywood *Citizen-News*, 241
Hollywood Ten, 236
homosexuality, 182–84, 217
Hoover, J. Edgar, 68
Hopper, Hedda, 260
Horn, George, 90
Horwits, Al, 245
hot weather photos, 119–26, 128, 138–41,
    160, 172
Howard, Tom, 22–23
Howdy Revue, 182
Hughes, Langston, 201, 219–20

human-interest photos, 128–30, 171–80,
    212
Huston, John, 288, 293
Hyams, Rafael, 302, 303
Hypo the pony, 17–18, 308

ICA Trix, 31
"I Cried When I Took This Picture," 105,
    105, 148, 166, 167, 240
Idiot Box, The (film), 307, 310
Imber, Naftali Herz, 4, 5
immigration, 5–12, 21, 112, 141, 157, 158,
    234
Imp-Probable Mr. Weegee, The (movie),
    295–97, 297
Independent Jewish Press Service, 200
infrared photography, 158–61, 175–76, 245,
    257–58, 298
Ingersoll, Ralph McAllister, 115–17, 119,
    121, 131, 153, 208
internal caption photos, 90–92, 106–8,
    180, 187–88, 248
International Center for Photography, xviii,
    318–19
  Weegee retrospective (1977), 318
International News Service, xiv, 47, 50, 53
Ireland, 6, 21
Italy, 6, 9, 158, 182

James, Fanny, 302, 303
Jay, Bill, 314, 315
jazz clubs, 217, 276–77, 280
Jerry, Edward, 222
Jessel, George, 285
jewel thieves, 76–79
Jewish Daily Forward, 53
Jews, 3–12, 52, 112, 116, 121, 122, 149, 182,
    184, 207, 211, 217–18, 286, 315
Johnny Olson's Rumpus Room, 246
Johnson, Agnes Olson, 76–79, 88
Johnson, Bunk, 217
Jorgensen, Christine, 278
Journey into Light (movie), 250–51, *251*
Jovino, John, 44, 45, 133
Joyce, Robert, 102–3, *103*
Judd, Winnie Ruth, 39–40
Judge, Jacquelyn, 227

kaleidoscope effects, 269–74, 279–81, 286,
    289, 292, 305, 312
Kaplan, Sid, 172, 268–69, 280, 318
Karsh, Yousuf, 277, 278

Katcher, Leo, 58, 59, 61
Kavanaugh, Mrs. George Washington, 174–77, *177*, 178–80, 199, 203, 220
Keleher, Dan, 185
Kelly, Emmett, 162
Kelly, Gene, 235
Kennedy, John F., 302
Keppler, Victor, 277, 278
Kertész, André, 228
Khrushchev, Nikita, 302
Knight, John Adam, 150, 201–2, 233, 262
Knopf, Alfred A., xv
Kodak, 13, 159, 166, 191, 232, 233
Kolea, James and Katherine, 126
Krim, Herbert, 150
Kubrick, Stanley, 298–301
Kuhn, Fritz, 102, 148
Kusama, Yayoi, 309

labor strikes, 56, 70, 112, 198, 199
L.A. Camera Exchange, 243
La Cava, Joseph "Little Joe," 106
Lafayette Street, 71–72, 75
La Guardia, Fiorello, 75–76, *77*, 162, 185, 198
Land of Zombies (movie), 238
Lane, Kingdon, 308
Lang, Fritz, 250
Lange, Dorothea, 186
Lansky, Meyer, 36
La Popular, 247–48
La Rosa, Julius, 269, 270
Lasker, Sigmund, 285, 286
Las Vegas, 289–90
Laszlo, Alador, 148
Lee, Shavey, 191–92
Leipzig, Arthur, 112, 118, 202
Levin, Al and Joan, *161*, 258, 270
Levinstein, Leon, 271
Levitt, Helen, 134, 178
Lewis, John, xiv, 203, 208
libel suits, 43
Liberace, *273*, 274, 278
Liberman, Alexander, 206–7, 211–12, 274
Lichello, Bob, 283
Liebling, A. J., 52
Life, 70–71, 84–87, 112, 115–18, 204, 254, 257, 277, 318
    Weegee and, 70–71, 84–86, *86*, 87, 95–97, 110, 132, 148, 172, 177–78, 214–15
Limelight, 271, 272
Lincoln Tunnel, 90

Lindbergh, Charles, 47, 122
Lingle, Jake, 37
Liotta, Charles, xvi, 26
Liotta, Louis, 140, 173, 175
Little Caesar (film), 37
Little Italy, 106, 112, 137, 149, 157, 158, 172, 182
London, 290, 297–303
Look, 116, 168, 182, 189, 206, 218, 254, 275, 298
Los Angeles, 25, 39–42, 230, 232, 234–52, 259–64, 290
    1932 Olympics, 39–41, *41*, 42
Los Angeles Examiner, xv, 241
Los Angeles strip clubs, *244*
Los Angeles Times, 200
Lower East Side, xiii, 6–14, 17, 21, 36, 112, 121, 132, 138–41, 149, 157–58, 172, 231, 236, 249, 253, 254, 281, 286, 304
Luce, Henry, 70, 115
Luciano, Charles "Lucky," 36, 64
Luparelli, Joseph, 158
Lyon, George, 116
Lyons, Leonard, 52
Lythcott, Alphonse, 185
Lythcott, Bernice, 185–86, *186*
Lythcott, Leonard, 185–86, *186*

M (movie), 250
Macfadden, Bernarr, 21, 42
Mackay, Ellin, 141
Mackey, Joseph, 146
MacKnight, Edgar, 57–61
MacKnight, Gladys, 57–60, *60*, 61, 78, 283
MacKnight, Helen, 57–61
Macy's, 204
    Thanksgiving Day Parade, 129, *129*, 130
Madison Avenue, 102
Madison Square Garden, 94, 95, 143, 163–65, 284
magazine business of 1950s, 254–57
Magic Fountain, The (movie), 287
Magoon, Seymour, 82
mailbox photo, 91–92, *92*, 93
Malina, Judith, xiv, 255–56, 317
Maloney, Russell, 201
Mancuso, Peter, 144–45
mannequin photos, 151–52, *152*, 153, 214–15, *243*, 291, 294, 296
Mansfield, Jayne, 277, 278
Margaret Arlen Show, 199
Markova, Alicia, 208, 212

Marks, Lawrence, 87–88
Martin, Peter, xiii, 115, 255
Mary Margaret McBride, 198–99, 246
Mason, Paul, 287
McBride, Mary Margaret, 198–99, 246
McCarthyism, 262
McCleery, William, 117, 120, 176, 195
McCrary, Tex, 231
McWilliams, Joseph Elsberry, 122–23, *123*, 148, 157, 203
Merrin, Dan, 254, 257
messenger photos, 41, *41*
Metro Photo Shop, 191
Metropolitan Opera, 130–31, 156, 172–80, 195
MGM, 240
Michie, Charles, 122
Milwaukee, 247, *248*
Milwaukee Sentinel, 247
Minicam Photography, 134, 218
Minneapolis, 247
Mirror (Los Angeles), 238
Miss Colored America pageant, 30–31, *31*
Mitchell, Joseph, 52, 142, 197, 197n
    McSorley's Wonderful Saloon, 197
Model, Lisette, 178
Modern Photography, 262, 270
Monroe, Marilyn, 257, 260, *273*, 274
Morgan, Barbara, 166
Morrin, John, 226, 265
Motion Picture Association of America, 229, 230
Mottel, Syeus, 313, 315
Mott Street, 191–93, 199, 223
movie audience photos, 160–61, *161*, 257–58
movies, 14, 18, 37, 40, 220–21, 279
    Weegee's career in, 220–25, 229–37, 237, 238–52, 279–81, 285–89, 293–301, 307–11
    see also specific movies
Mulberry Street, 106
Mullen, Lawrence, 73
Murder Incorporated, 36–39, 73, 82–83, 118, 142, 172, 225–26, 257
Murder Is My Business (exhibition), 147–50, 194
murder photos, 36–41, 53–68, 73–74, 80–81, 87–88, 91–93, 97, 102, 106–10, 117–18, 130–37, 142–56, 167, 171–72, 204, 206, 214–15, 257, 271, 307
Murdoch, Rupert, 52

Museum of Modern Art, 111, 166–67, 178, 194, 201, 210, 226–29, 257, 311, 316–18
    Action Photography, 166–68, 171, 178
    Art in Progress, 178–79
    Seventy Photographers Look at New York, 283
Mussolini, Benito, 122, 158, 182
Mutual Broadcasting System, 225
Mutual Magazine Corporation, 254, 257
My Bare Lady (movie), 294, *295*
"Myrtle from Myrtle Avenue," 183

NAACP, 184–85
Naked City (book), 195–205, 208, 209, 218–20, 261, 298
    book party, 202–3, *203*
    reviews, 199–205
    sales, 204–5, 214
Naked City, The (movie), 229–32, 235, 236, 245, 288
Naked Eye, The (movie), 282, 285
Naked Hollywood (book), 259–60, *260*, 261–63, *263*, 264, 268, 275, 305, 307
Nathan, Simon, 220
National Crime Syndicate, 36
National Enquirer, 283, *284*
Nazism, 102, 116, 122, 130
NBC, 241, 246, 285
Nebel, Long John, 91–93
neon, 241
Newark, 54, 71
Newark Evening News, 54
Newberg, Ellen, 315, 316
New Deal, 52, 116
Newhall, Beaumont, 166–67, 190, 214, 219, 228
    Photography 1839–1937, 166
Newhall, Nancy, 166–67, 178, 190–91
New Orleans, 217, 249, 250, 254, 257
New School, 233
Newspaper Enterprise Association, 200
newspapers, xiv–xv, 18, 49–53, 167
    afternoon, 28–29, 50–51
    credit rules, 101
    evening, 50–51
    left-leaning, 116–26
    morning, 49–51, 53
    1920s photography, 20–35
    1930s photography, 36–110
    1940s photography, 111–249
    1950s changes in, 252–53
    of 1960s, 307

spot news in, xv, 20, 49, 51, 62, 70, 107–8, 127, 136, 216, 307
tabloid, 21–23, 50, 57, 116, 118, 130
see also specific publications
Newsweek, 200
New York City, 6–12, 15, 21, 36, 195, 230
of 1950s, 252–55
of 1960s, 304
see also specific streets, buildings, and neighborhoods
New York *Daily Mirror*, 21, 22, 37, 43, 45, 50, 53, 57, 60, 71, 73, 88, 101, 104, 116, 132, 183, 229, 307
New York *Daily News*, xv, 21, 31, 37, 50, 53, 54, 58, 71, 87, 101, 116, 118, 125, 131, 132, 177, 229, 250, 253, 316
Weegee and, 21–23, 64, 70, 78, 81, 107, 138, 154, 171, 315
New Yorker, The, 44, 52, 91, 116, 142, 150, 196, 197, 201
New York Evening Graphic, 21–22, 42, 43, 142, 254
New York Evening Journal, 51, 81–82, 138
New York Herald Tribune, 21, 29, 39, 49, 53, 66–67, 75, 83, 87, 116, 132, 167, 200, 219, 289, 307
New York Item, 290
New York Journal-American, 46, 52, 56, 64, 72, 127, 163, 307
New York magazine, 314–15
New York Police Department (NYPD), 44–48, 55, 69, 73, 74, 84–86, 100, 102, 131–35, 172, 184, 229
headquarters, 44–48, 55, 133, 157
photos, 67, 74, 84–88, 91–93, 102–8, 132–35, 156, 192, 216
radio, 45–46, 95, 100, 151, 212, 213, 225
New York Post, 20, 38, 45, 85, 88, 140, 147, 183, 189, 223, 262, 265, 286, 308
Weegee and, 52–68, 72, 75, 79, 81, 101–2, 104, 110, 123, 150, 201, 202, 209, 246, 315
New York Press Photographers Association, 111
New York State Censorship Board, 235
New York *Sun*, 51, 101, 253, 307
Weegee and, 51–56, 66, 71, 81, 104, 120, 128
New York Times, xvi, 20, 21, 24, 25, 49, 53, 55, 56, 58, 132–33, 150, 166, 174, 177, 199, 205, 252
Weegee and, 121, 125, 201, 315

New York *World*, 18, 20, 24
New York World-Telegram, 28, 45, 47, 51–56, 60, 62, 65, 101, 118, 226, 253, 307
Weegee and, 60, 62, 65–72, 76, 81
Night and Day, 256–57, 272
Night Beat, 282
Nikon, 270
nudist colonies, 42, 56, 293–95
Nurmi, Maila, 283
Nussenbaum, Julia, 80–81, 118

observer photos, 107–10, 137–38, 144–45, 152, 160, 172–80, 212, 239, 266–67
O'Connor, Tom, 202
Odd Fellows Lodge, 148–49
O'Hara, John, 197
Olympic Games
of 1932, 39–41, *41*, 42
of 1936, 57
opera photos, 130–31, 156, 160, 172–80, 199, 216, 228
Orkin, Ruth, 112
Orvell, Miles, 261
Ouija board, xvi, 26, 47, 199

Paar, Jack, 241, 283
Page, Bettie, 266–67, *267*
Pageant, 275
Paris, 175, 288, 294–97
Paris-Match, 290
Parker, Dorothy, 235
Parker, Norma. *See* Gutowski, Nellie
Parks, Gordon, 277
Parsons, Louella, 260
Parsons, Marc, 222
participatory journalism, 164
Patterson, Joseph Medill, 21
Pearce, Charles, 197
Pearl Harbor, 156, 157
Peerless stores, 245
Pegler, Westbrook, 52
Pellegrini & Cudahy, 261, 262
Peniel Mission, 242–43
Pennsylvania Station, 18, 26
Pepper, Sally, 150
Peter the Hermit, 243–44, 260
Petrillo, Sammy, 285, 293
Photo Arts, 233
Photographers Showplace, 278–79, 289
photography, 13–18, 112
commercial studios, 15–23
darkroom procedures, xvi, 14, 18, 24–28,

photography (cont'd)
41–42, 53, 99–100, 113, 120, 227–29, 275, 289
history of, 13–14, 166
infrared, 158–62, 175–76, 245, 257–58, 298
night, 26, 35, 47, 50, 67, 97
technology, 14–16, 35, 45, 53, 67–68, 134, 158–59, 166, 270
tintypes, 13–15, 17
see also cameras; film; flash; specific photographers, techniques, and themes
Photo Hunt, 113
Photo League, 111–15, 125, 134, 138, 141, 146, 168, 173, 189, 201, 214, 219, 258, 314
Murder Is My Business, 147–50, 194
Photo Notes, 149
Photo-Representatives, 258, 304
Piazza, Ben, 237
Picasso, Pablo, Guernica, 167
pictorialism movement, 228
Pictures Generation, 318
Pileggi, Nicholas, 43, 133
Playboy, 254, 262, 263, 279
Plimpton, George, 163–64
PM, xiv, 115–26, 150, 185, 195, 197, 198, 216, 220, 223, 233, 261, 311
decline of, 208–9, 233, 253
Weegee and, 115–35, 136–45, 156–59, 162–65, 171–80, 182, 185, 190, 192, 202–3, 208–9, 233
Polacheck, Jean, 219
Poland, 3, 8, 9, 130
Polaroid pictures, 270–71, 292
politics, 51, 68, 76, 122–23
Polo Grounds, 90
Pomerantz, Arty, 286
Popular Photography, 25, 95, 114, 172, 191, 204, 219, 223, 225, 234, 277, 284, 291
posed photos, 59, 62, 85, 90–94, 138–41, 148, 175–80, 195, 228
Powell, Marty, 88, 89
Pradier, Irma Louise, 87
Preminger, Ingo, 236
Preminger, Otto, 236
Pressman, Barney, 72
Preston, George, 81
Price, Sherman, 294–97
Prince Street, 107–10
Prohibition, 36, 84, 102, 117, 130
prostitution, 36, 46, 132

"psychic" pictures, 191–93, 214
Pulitzer, Joseph, 20

Queens, 18, 55, 73, 102, 121

racial discrimination, 30, 184–86
Racies, Lawrence, 225
Racketbusters Roundtable, 225–26
radio, 45, 143, 156, 189, 198–99
police, 45–46, 95, 100, 151, 212, 213, 225
Weegee on, 198–99, 225–26, 231, 245–447
Randall, Dick, 285, 293, 294, 296
Random House, 196
"Realism in Photography" (lecture), 194–95
Redwing, Robert, 78
Reilly, Rosa, 95
Reles, Abe "Kid Twist," 172
Rembrandt lighting, 106
repackaged photos, 256–57
repetition, 153
Reston, James, 252
retouching, 62, 63
Richer, Ira, 309–10
Riis, Jacob, How the Other Half Lives, 141
Ringling Bros. Circus, 162–63, 164, 165
RKO Radio Pictures, 237, 238, 241
Roberts, Terry, 88
Robinson, Edward G., 37
Rohauer, Raymond, 311
Roosevelt, Eleanor, 141–42
Roosevelt, Franklin D., 50, 68, 154
Rosenblum, Walter, 112, 113
Ross, Harold, 142
Ross, Lillian, Picture, 261, 262
Ross, Mischa, 80–81
Runyon, Damon, 143
Russia, 6, 9, 218, 302–3
Ruth, Babe, xv
Ryan, Patricia, 189

St. John Publications, 278
St. Louis, 247, 305
St. Regis, 208, 211
Salles, Sidney "Shimmy," 142
Sammy's Bowery Follies, 142–43, 173, 200, 202–3, 203, 216, 220, 222, 244, 282
Sandano, Lewis, 91–93, 130
San Francisco (movie), 238
San Francisco Chronicle, 187, 200
Sann, Paul, 101
San Remo bar, 255–56, 271, 272

Sante, Luc, 74
Sashalite, 35
Saturday Evening Post, The, 168, 181, 189
Saturday Review, 219
Savage, Owen, 70
Scalf, Swain, 220
Schiff, Dorothy, 52
Schlanger, Charles, 66–67
School of Visual Arts, 312–13
Schulman, Sammy, 47
Schultz, Dutch, 37–38, 54, 56, 61, 64, 76, 78, 88, 99
Schwartz, Sherwood, 288, 290
Scoop!, 227
Screen Actors Guild, 237
Scribner's, 204
Scripps-Howard newspapers, 24, 25, 52
Seaman Studio, 19, 23
Seamen's Church Institute, 70, 75
See, 315
Sellers, Peter, 298–301
Set-Up, The (movie), 237
Seventeen, 206
Shangri-La (movie), 293–94
Shannon, Leonard, 238
Sheehan, Anna, 71
Sheridan, Ann, 259–60
Sherman, Cindy, *Untitled Film Stills*, 318
Sherwin, Mark, 209
showgirl photos, *244*, 260–61
Siegel, Benjamin (Bugsy), 36
Sievan, Lee, 220, 223, 231
Simmons, Laurie, *Walking Gun*, 318
Simms, Blanche, 102
Simonelli, Charles, 245, 249
"Simply Add Boiling Water," 187, *188*
Sinatra, Frank, 189, 204, 220, 239, 282
Siskind, Aaron, 112
six-foot shot, 67–68
Skelton, Red, 240
Sky Farm, 42
slapstick, 48
sleeper photos, 89–90, 138–41, 153, 160, 173, 216, 219, 245, 247
Sleeping City, The (movie), 245–49
Sleeping City tour, 245–40, 256, 257, 275, 305
Slick, 283
Smith, W. Eugene, 112
Snyder, Ruth, 22–23, 154–55
Society photos, 130–31, 141, 142, 174–80
speakeasies, 33–34

Speed Graphic, 31–32, 43, 54, 57, 76, 78, 95, 151, 162, 163, 179, 191, 210, 219, 268–70, 282, 288, 298, 319
sports photos, 29–30, 39–42
Spot Bar and Grill photo, 107, *108*
spot-news photography, xv, 20, 49, 51, 62, 70, 107, 108, 127, 136, 216, 307
squeegee boys, xvi, 24, 25
Stag, 254, 257, 273
Staten Island, 86
Stegner, Wallace, 197
Steichen, Edward, 138, 228–29, 283
Steiger, Rod, 261
Stein, Barney, 101
Steiner, Ralph, 112, 131
Stern, J. David, 52
Stettner, Louis, 94–97, 101, 105, 150, 194, 263, 280, 312, 318
Stieglitz, Alfred, 111, 166, 167, 178, 190–92, *192*, 228
    Weegee and, 190–92, 196, 205, 312, 314
Stone, Erika, 258, 304
Stone, I. F., 123
Stork Club, 143
Stoumen, Lou, 282, 285, 286
Strand, Paul, 194–95, 203–4
strobe, 166
Stuyvesant Casino, 217
subconscious camera, 238, 308
Subs (restaurant), 314
subway, 21, 27, 75–76, 253, 304
Sullivan, Ed, 22, 269–70, 276
Sunday Telegraph (London), 302
Sussman Volk delicatessen, 211
Swift, Anna, 131–32
Szarkowski, John, 316

Tab, 256, 273
tabloids, 21–23, 50, 57, 116, 118, 130, 245
"Talent Scout," 263
Talmey, Allene, 208
Tapedino, Frank, 71–72, *72*, 161
Tarzan's Peril (movie), 241–42
Taylor, Don, 236
Teletype, 40, 43, 46, 55, 76, 85, 100
television, 166, 220, 241, 269–70, 276, 279, 288
    Weegee on, 246, 282–83
tenements, 6–12, 64, 66, 104–10, 112, 128, 138–41, 253
    collapse, 86–87
    fires, 64, 66, 104–5, 128

ten-foot shot, 64, 67–68, 109
"Their First Murder," 143–44, *144*, 145,
    146, 166, 167, 305, 316
35-millimeter camera, 134, 270
Time, 22, 70, 200
Time Inc., 70–71, 110, 115
Times Square, 24, 68, 80, 158, 182, 234,
    252, 280, 282
tintypes, 13–15, 17
Titanic, 20
Tonight, 241, 282–83
Toporoff, Ralph, 294, 296–97
Toronto *Globe and Mail*, 200
Torres, Henrietta and Ada, 104–5, *105*, 167
trade shows, 268
train wreck photos, 75–76
trick lens. *See* distortion photos
Tuck, Jay Nelson, 223
Tugboat Ethel, 143, 173
Tunney, Gene, 29
Turkus, Burton, 172, 225
Tursen, Maxine, 102
TV Guide, 275
20th Century-Fox, 230
typewriter, 99, *99*, 151
Tytell, Mellon, 314

Ukraine, 3, 4–7
United Press, 24, 28
United Press International, 24, 305
U.S. Camera, 167, 187, 197, 220
Universal-International Pictures, 230, 235,
    245–49

Vaccaro, Tony, 275
Valentine, Lewis, 87, 134, 185
Vandivert, Sam, 173
Van Gelder, Robert, *Smash Picture!*, 57
Velvet Underground, 309
Vendome Book Shop, 204
Vest Pocket Kodak, 13
Vice Squad (movie), 252
Vierkötter, Paul, 35
Village, The (book), 318
Village Voice, 309, 314
V-J Day, 206, 207, 212
Vogel, Amos, 232–33, 235, 259, 275
voyeurism, 46–47, 160, 179
Vogue, 206–7, 210–12
    Weegee and, 206–7, 210–12, 226, 227,
    274
Vu, 70

Wald, Malvin, 230
Waldorf-Astoria, 142, 208
Ward, Lock & Company, 302
Warhol, Andy, 309, 317
    Weegee and, 309–10, *310*
Warner, Alexandra, 174, 179
Warner, Charles, 179–80
Warner Bros., 229–30
war pictures, 156–59, 172
Warrens, Amy, 249, 250
wartime restrictions, 158–59, 172, 196, 217
Washington, D.C., 136–37, 184, 212, 247,
    293–94
Washington Heights, 185–86
Washington Post, 200
Washington Square, 216, 219, 308, 313
water-main breaks, 191–93, 206, 223
Watson, George, 39–40
wax museum photos, 153–54, *154*, 155
Weegee, xiii–xviii, *31*, *41*, *63*, *69*, *86*, *99*, *164*,
    203, *211*, *215*, *224*, *237*, *243*, *251*, *260*,
    281, *284*, *295*, *297*, *299*, *306*, *310*, *313*
    birth, 4–5
    childhood, 4–15, 308
    commercial breakthrough, 57–65
    death and legacy, 315–19
    early photo jobs, 15–43
    education, xvii, 9–10, 12
    fame, 151, 168, 206–9, 215, 255, 312
    health problems, 212, 280, 312–15
    Jewishness, 4, 9–12, 121, 182, 184, 207,
    286, 315
    lectures, 146–47, 150–51, 194–95, 214–15,
    218, 252, 268–69, 303, 308, 312–13
    magazine work, 206–13, 254–58, 273–79
    movie career, 220–25, 229–37, 237,
    238–52, 279–81, 285–89, 293–301,
    307–11
    1930s photography, 36–110
    1940s photography, 111–249
    persona, xiii–xviii, 14, 26, 33, 42, 47–38,
    94–96, 126, 146–47, 151, 162, 206,
    249, 266, 268, 296, 312
    physical appearance, 14, 31, 40, 46, 85,
    95, 131, 182, 220, 235
    press on, xvii, 94, 95, 149–51, 166–67,
    187–89, 198–205, 219–21, 233, 262
    relationships with other photographers,
    60, 94–96, 101, 132–33, 190–92, 205,
    228–29, 277
    shift from crime to slice-of-life subjects,
    130–45

women and, 23, 46, 56, 113–15, 181–82,
    190, 209, 219–24, 238–39, 241–42,
    249, 255–56, 266–68, 281–84, 291
working methods, xvi, xvii, 14, 18,
    24–42, 47, 53–83, 87–107, 113,
    119–26, 134, 140–45, 153, 158–65,
    172–80, 187–89, 196, 207–12,
    226–32, 240–41, 256, 261, 268–75,
    289, 305, 312, 315
    see also specific photographs, books, movies,
    and themes
Weegee by Weegee (book), 290–92
Wee Gee's Camera Magic (movie), 289
Weegeescope, 269
Weegee's Creative Camera (book), 289–90
Weegee's Creative Photography (book), 302
"Weegee Shows How to Photograph a
    Corpse," 214–25, 215
Weegee's New York (movie), 232–40, 262,
    275, 280, 288, 310, 311
Weegee's People (book), 214–21, 254, 312
Weegee's Secrets of Shooting with Photoflash,
    261–62, 268
"Weegee's Women," 279
Weegee the Famous, xiii, xv, 14, 24, 26, 33,
    151, 168, 189, 206, 209–10, 249, 266,
    268, 296, 311, 312
Weisberger, John, 82
Westinghouse, 261, 262, 268
Weston, Edward, 178, 282
We the People, 246
White, Walter, 185
Wide World Photos, 24, 53, 84
Wightman, Donald, 57–60, 60, 61

Wilcox, Wilma, xviii, 113–15, 160–61, 172,
    173, 180, 318–19
    Weegee and, 113–15, 181–82, 187, 219,
    223, 239, 246, 281–82, 287–91,
    304–5, 310, 315–19
Williamsburg Bridge, 66, 75, 230
Wilson, Earl, 143, 181, 189
Wilson, Jonny, 268
Winchell, Walter, 22, 43, 50, 52, 100, 120,
    122, 133, 143, 236
Windjammer (movie), 279–81, 281, 285
Windsor, Duke and Duchess of, 165
Wirephoto, 27–28
Wise, Robert, 237
Wishman, Doris, 293
Wolbarst, John, 269, 270
Woolworth's, 90, 133
World Journal Tribune, 307
world's fair
    (1939), 121, 122
    (1958), 285–86, 306
    (1964), 305
World War I, 3, 5, 19, 20, 30, 32
World War II, 156–59, 172, 176, 179–82,
    196, 206, 207
Wyman, Ida, 94, 238

Yankee Stadium, 90
Yellow Cab Man, The (movie), 240–41,
    280
Yiddish Rialto, 217–18, 218

Zenit camera, 303
Zwerling, Abraham, 5, 6

ABOUT THE AUTHOR

Christopher Bonanos is the city editor of *New York* magazine and is the author of *Instant: The Story of Polaroid*. He lives in New York City with his wife and son.

7/18

This is Weegee